FAITH IN WAR

SPEKTRUM: Publications of the German Studies Association

Series editor: David M. Luebke, University of Oregon

Published under the auspices of the German Studies Association, *Spektrum* offers current perspectives on culture, society, and political life in the German-speaking lands of central Europe—Austria, Switzerland, and the Federal Republic—from the late Middle Ages to the present day. Its titles and themes reflect the composition of the GSA and the work of its members within and across the disciplines to which they belong—literary criticism, history, cultural studies, political science, and anthropology.

Recent volumes:

Volume 31
Faith in War: Religion and the Military in Germany, 1500–1650
Nikolas M. Funke

Volume 30
Religious Plurality at Princely Courts: Dynasty, Politics, and Confession in Central Europe, ca. 1555–1860
Edited by Benjamin Marschke, Daniel Riches, Alexander Schunka, and Sara Smart

Volume 29
Healing and Harm: Essays in Honor of Mary Lindemann
Edited by Erica Heinsen-Roach, Stephen A. Lazer, Benjamin Marschke, Jared Poley, and Daniel Riches

Volume 28
Former Neighbors, Future Allies? German Studies and Ethnography in Dialogue
Edited by A. Dana Weber

Volume 27
The Origins of German Self-Cultivation: Bildung and the Future of the Humanities
Edited by Jennifer Ham, Ulrich Kinzel, and David Tse-Chien Pan

Volume 26
Invested Narratives: German Responses to Economic Crisis
Edited by Jill E. Twark

Volume 25
Football Nation: The Playing Fields of German Culture, History, and Society
Edited by Rebeccah Dawson, Bastian Heinsohn, Oliver Knabe, and Alan McDougall

Volume 24
What Remains: Responses to the Legacy of Christa Wolf
Edited by Gerald A. Fetz and Patricia Herminghouse

Volume 23
Minority Discourses in Germany since 1990
Edited by Ela Gezen, Priscilla Layne, and Jonathan Skolnik

Volume 22
Beyond Posthumanism: The German Humanist Tradition and the Future of the Humanities
Alexander Mathäs

Volume 21
Feelings Materialized: Emotions, Bodies, and Things in Germany, 1500–1950
Edited by Derek Hillard, Heikki Lempa, and Russell Spinney

Volume 20
Names and Naming in Early Modern Germany
Edited by Marjorie Elizabeth Plummer and Joel F. Harrington

For a full volume listing, please see the series page on our website:
http://berghahnbooks.com/series/spektrum

Faith in War

Religion and the Military in Germany, 1500–1650

NIKOLAS M. FUNKE

First published in 2024 by
Berghahn Books
www.berghahnbooks.com

© 2024 Nikolas M. Funke

All rights reserved. Except for the quotation of short passages
for the purposes of criticism and review, no part of this book
may be reproduced in any form or by any means, electronic or
mechanical, including photocopying, recording, or any information
storage and retrieval system now known or to be invented,
without written permission of the publisher.

Library of Congress Cataloging-in-Publication Data

A C.I.P. cataloging record is available from the Library of Congress
Library of Congress Cataloging in Publication Control Number: 2024013486

British Library Cataloguing in Publication Data

A catalogue record for this book is available from the British Library

ISBN 978-1-80539-617-8 hardback
ISBN 978-1-80539-618-5 epub
ISBN 978-1-80539-619-2 web pdf

https://doi.org/10.3167/ 9781805396178

~: CONTENTS :~

Acknowledgments	viii
Introduction	1
Chapter 1. "A New Order of Soulless Men"? Reassessing a Stereotype	16
Chapter 2. Making Christian Armies: Military Religious Structures and the Challenge of Religious Pluralism	42
Chapter 3. Religion, Morality, and Military Everyday Life	74
Chapter 4. Confession: Conflict, Indifference, Coexistence	113
Chapter 5. Dying, Death and Burial in the Military	164
Epilogue	192
Bibliography	198
Index	227

∾ ACKNOWLEDGMENTS ∾

This book has been shape-shifting for many years now and over the course of its gestation it has been helped along by the support of many individuals and institutions.

Naomi Tadmor proved an exceptional supervisor of my doctoral research, whose assiduousness, criticism, and encouragement allowed me to complete the dissertation from which this book has grown.

Paul Betts and Lyndal Roper were supremely genial examiners, whose comments and suggestions improved this book greatly. Both Paul and Lyndal were immensely supportive in the earlier stages of my postdoc years. Lyndal also very kindly invited me to take part in her postgraduate get-togethers at a time when I was in dire need of contact with other early modernists.

The History Department at the University of Sussex awarded me a bursary without which the project would have been financially unviable. The *Stipendium* from the Dr. Günther Findel Stiftung allowed me to carry out research at the Herzog August Bibliothek in Wolfenbüttel for six months, which gave me vital access to primary and secondary materials. The German Historical Institute Washington DC and the BMW Centre of German History, Georgetown University, gave me the chance to present my research at an advanced stage during the seventeenth Transatlantic Doctoral Seminar in 2011. The input, criticism, and encouragement from the convenors, mentors, and fellow doctoral students helped me greatly.

Michael Kaiser took the time in the very early stages of this project to set me straight about some fundamentals. Jan Willem Huntebrinker very generously made his doctoral thesis available to a stranger and invited me to participate in a workshop in Frankfurt, where I made some very important contacts, it would later turn out. The *Stipendiaten* and other researchers I met in Wolfenbüttel helped me formulate and refine questions early on. Helmut Klingelhöfer, Hessisches Staatsarchiv Marburg, and Klaas-Dieter Voß, Johannes a Lasco Bibliothek Emden, helped me obtain scans from a distance. Anja Grothe, Craig Koslofsky, Maren Lorenz, Heike Preuß, and Ralf Pröve took the time to answer questions and discuss ideas.

The University of Sussex provided me with a wonderfully vibrant and stimulating academic environment. Especially Paul Betts, Ruth Charnock, Cesare Cuttica, Roger Johnson, Ben Jones, Claire Langhamer, Eugene Michail, Kevin

Acknowledgments ~ vii

Reynolds, Lucy Robinson, Becca Searle, and Elke Weesjes(-Sabella) became friends. Those Brighton years were happy ones: thank you.

At the University of St Andrews, I was made to feel very welcome by Bridget Heal, Steve Murdoch, Andrew Pettegree, and Guy Rowlands and their students Jan-Luigi Alessandrini, Flavia Bruni, John Condren, Jan Hillgärtner, Marc Jaffré, Nina Lamal, and Róisín Watson. It was a fun year up there!

At the next stop, the University of Birmingham, the early modern cohort were wonderful colleagues: Richard Cust, Elaine Fulton, Tara Hamling, Simone Laqua-O'Donnell, Jonathan Willis, Marga Small, whose sudden death remains entirely bewildering and deeply painful, and Kate Smith, the ideal person to explore the new environment with. The Arts Building Fourth Floor Crew were great company, not just at the pub: Jonathan Boff, Matthew Francis, Chris Moores, Dan Whittingham, Klaus Richter, and Manu Sehgal. Thanks also to Chris Callow, Nick Crowson, Matthew Hilton, Corey Ross, Gavin Schaffer, and Simon Yarrow.

Ulrike Ludwig offered me a job at the University of Münster and I am incredibly grateful for the many opportunities, the support, and the encouragement she has granted me over the years. Barbara Groß, Kerstin Dembsky, André Krischer, Kevin Lenk, Benjamin Seebröker, and Michael Sikora (who remains sceptical of my arguments) make Münster a very happy work environment. Simon Müller, SHK *extraordinaire*, thank you for all your hard work.

Andreea Badea, Bruno Boute, Martin Christ, Birgit Emich, Tom Hamilton, Julia Hahmann, Kat Hill, Iryna Klymenko, Laura Kounine, Jan Machielsen, Herjeet Marway, Hannah Murphy, Mike Snape, Hillard von Thiessen, Alex Walsham, Andy Wood, and Yuliya Yurchenko have all shaped my thinking in conversations and discussions at one time or another, and there are many seminar and conference audiences whose feedback helped me greatly.

Courtney J. Campbell, Elaine Fulton, Jamie Paige, and William Purkiss read chapters, suggested improvements, and caught mistakes.

David M. Luebke invited me to submit my manuscript to this series and I would like to thank him, the Spektrum Editorial Board, and the editorial team at Berghahn Books for their support. I am grateful to Readers 1, 2, and 3 for their encouragement and criticism, which I hope to have answered sufficiently.

Inestimable gratitude is finally due to my family, Anne and Werner Funke and my sister Jana. You have helped and encouraged me all my life. Courtney J. Campbell, thank you for all your love and support and for collaborating with me on Fritzi, the loveliest Würstchen of them all.

Introduction

Thomas von Lobecke went insane one night in 1558. He was a *Landsknecht*, a German infantry soldier, and had led a typical soldier's life committed to "gorging, boozing, fornication and contempt for God" when he broke into a Catholic church in Flanders and vandalized it.[1] He stripped naked, forced open chests and boxes, dressed himself in liturgical vestments, and paced through the church singing. When the local clerics found him in the morning, they noticed that all the communion wafers had disappeared from the tabernacle and asked the mad soldier what had happened to them. Lobecke replied that he had eaten them all in an effort to make up for the twenty-odd years in which he had not received the sacrament.

Whether this scene really took place is secondary to its meaning. In the popular imaginary of the sixteenth and seventeenth centuries, the story and its protagonist would have appeared neither surprising nor accidental. Lobecke fit a stereotype that associated soldiers with behaviors antithetical to the Christian life: whoring, boozing, gambling, cursing, blasphemy, luxurious dress, and, obviously, fighting and killing. While the notion that God punishes arch-sinners by smiting them with insanity may no longer seem intuitive to many twenty-first-century readers, the stereotype of the amoral, irreligious early modern mercenary has survived rather intact. Many historians writing today will probably still consider the Lobecke story an obviously stylized but essentially accurate illustration of early modern military immorality.

This book takes a more skeptical stance on the stereotype and a more positive view of soldiers' religious sensibilities. At the root of my argument lies the conviction that the stereotype of the irreligious soldier is frankly implausible. Why would hundreds of thousands of men reject wholesale the culture in which they had been raised just because they chose a particular profession? It would indeed be sensational if Europe's religious wars had been fought by anti-Christians, but this book can only offer a more modest claim: by and large, the following chapters suggest, soldiers were ordinary Christians whose views of the divine and the holy differed little or not at all from those of their civil-

2 ❦ *Faith in War*

ian contemporaries. They prayed, they followed the Christian life as well as circumstances permitted, they got married and baptized (and all too often buried) their children. Many also drank, whored, gambled, blasphemed, brawled, raped, killed, and dabbled in magic. All things considered, they appear to have been rather average early modern Christians.

The main focus of this book lies on the German-speaking lands of the Holy Roman Empire in the sixteenth and early seventeenth centuries, a period of profound military as well as religious change. The military sphere had begun to undergo dramatic transformations in the fifteenth century and continued on this trajectory in the following centuries. This "military revolution," whose causes, interpretation, chronology, and impact have exercised historians for several decades, stood in a dynamic relationship with the wider sociopolitical transformations in Europe.[2] Medieval warfare had centrally relied on the knightly heavy cavalry, composed predominantly of noble fighters, while commoners had mostly played an auxiliary role on the battlefield. It was not just the introduction of firearms but especially a groundbreaking fifteenth-century innovation in infantry tactics that had triggered a fundamental change in the size and social composition of European armies. Swiss infantry commanders developed a way to maneuver huge blocks of pikemen across the battlefield and turned a previously predominantly defensive formation into an effective offensive one. The Swiss *Reisläufer* were the first masters of this new form of fighting, but soon their northern neighbors copied them. The German infantry troops who employed these tactics became known as *Landsknechte*. Compared to the knightly cavalry, equipping these troops was cheap and training was relatively swift, but the pike formation needed hundreds of men in order to be effective. The spread of a new type of fortification, commonly referred to as the *trace italienne*, also contributed to the heightened demand for manpower, as armies now needed large contingents of workers, miners, and sappers as well as soldiers in order to engage effectively in sieges. The army train, composed of soldiers' wives, their children, victualers, craftsmen, and other people who made a living in the military economy, often outnumbered the fighting men. Combined, these changes caused an at least tenfold inflation of army size that continued throughout the early modern period.[3]

Warfare and the maintenance of troops were also becoming more permanent. Medieval campaigns tended to be seasonal affairs, lasting from spring until the autumn, but from the fifteenth century onward, states began to establish growing numbers of standing forces. After the formation of the Spanish *tercios* in the Italian Wars, the French Wars of Religion and the Dutch Revolt became the first major conflicts in which the old pattern of seasonal assembly and disbanding was broken and regiments were maintained over years, sometimes decades.[4] The Thirty Years War, finally, saw the greatest numbers of men permanently under arms that Europe had hitherto known. Soldiering had become a full-time profession and by extension an identity for commoners. As we will see in greater detail in the first chapter, this massification of the military caused great anxiety among contemporaries: commoners choosing to join the armies were not only thought to cause social strife by deserting their civilian profession, they also rebelled against God's social order, in which the military was the designated habitat of the nobility.

Beyond the military sphere, the religious landscape of Europe underwent rapid and fundamental change during our period of study. From its unlikely origins in the rather provincial German town of Wittenberg, the Reformation and its effects fragmented Latin Christianity and altered the sociocultural framework with breathtaking alacrity in the decades after 1517.[5] The heretical movement that became known as Lutheranism attracted followers from all walks of life, many of whom, guided by their independent interpretation of Scripture or inspiration from the Holy Spirit, took Luther's early message in wildly divergent directions. The first half of the sixteenth century witnessed the emergence of a dizzying array of new religious ideas, each laying claim to being the only interpretation of the faith that merited the label "Christian."[6] Over the course of the sixteenth century, the three major confessions of Catholicism, Lutheranism, and Calvinism gained a theological profile alongside a fourth category of miscellaneous religious movements that the labels "radical" or "Anabaptist" struggle to contain.

It is important to underline the international character of warfare in the period and the implications for the topic of this book. In war, Christians from all over Europe, from Portugal to Russia and Lapland to Sicily, encountered one another and their interpretations of the faith. Recent studies have revised the previously monolithic view of the three main confessions and show that both the Catholic–Protestant binary and the confessional labels "Catholic," "Lutheran," and "Calvinist" obscure great inter- and intra-confessional differences.[7] Religious practice and attitudes varied considerably from place to place, making it sometimes very difficult for Christians to recognize coreligionists from elsewhere. Even more confusingly, hybrid forms of worship emerged in many locales and across Europe a multiplicity of local religious "flavors" developed that often defy neat categorization.[8] The religious landscape was therefore constantly morphing well into the eighteenth century and the phenotype of Christianity practiced in a given community could not necessarily be assigned to a confessional camp with certainty. While to church leaders the definition and implementation of uniform doctrine was of utmost importance, communities and individuals were shaping and diversifying the religious options available to them, sometimes boldly, sometimes tentatively, in some cases consciously, in others obliviously. The consequences this had for the often multiethnic, multiconfessional armies of the period are obvious: Christians with often widely divergent religious beliefs and practices had to fight alongside and against one another. The ques-

4 ❧ *Faith in War*

tion of religious coexistence, toleration of difference, and its limits in the armies during Europe's "wars of religion" is therefore a pressing one and is the subject of Chapter 4. As a whole, this book illuminates how early modern military authorities as well as the people who lived in the armies coped with the challenge of confessional diversity, a topic that has thus far received little attention from military historians. We know a lot about increasingly sophisticated logistics, financial systems, the emergence of the fiscal military state, and the evolution of military strategy on the battlefield; what we will examine in the following chapters is how the military sphere managed the problem of religious pluralism.

The pluralization of Christian creeds and the emergence of confessional cultures were also reflected in the types of conflicts that erupted.[9] In the Holy Roman Empire, the Peasants' War (1524–25), the Anabaptist "Kingdom" of Münster (1534–35), the Schmalkaldic War (1546–47), and the Cologne (or *Truchsessische*) War (1583–88) all displayed a strong religious element. In many ways, confessional strife culminated in the Thirty Years War (1618–48), which drew in all major European powers at different stages.

The term "religious war" has been criticized as being too diffuse.[10] Franz Brendle and Anton Schindling have suggested the term "confessional war" (*Konfessionskrieg*) as a better characterization of the conflicts within Western Christendom, as genuine "religious wars" were only officially waged against the Ottomans.[11] Whether or not a war was fought over religion was by no means an unambiguous matter. Brendle and Schindling have stressed the importance of differentiating between the experience and interpretation of conflicts at four different levels: those of (1) the policymakers; (2) the groups and individuals actively and passively affected by the events; (3) the authors and readers of propaganda; and (4) the level of memory. The fact that the same conflict could be interpreted differently at each of these levels brings the issue into sharp relief: while imperial propaganda, for example, was consciously trying to dissimulate wars against Protestant princes as secular policing measures against rebels and breakers of the imperial peace, confessional propaganda focused almost exclusively on the religious dimensions of these conflicts and framed them unambiguously in binary terms of confessional opposition. For the larger population, too, confessional and religious motives and interpretations were believable and often dominant, and popular memory also recalls the Reformation period as one marked by religious strife.[12] We consequently have to ask where the military stood in all this. Did soldiers interpret their actions and experiences in the framework of confessional politics, and did they gain motivation through this interpretation of events as has been suggested?[13] Were they "mercenaries" in the pejorative sense, who only fought for pay? Or did they develop a mode of interpretation that was particular to their professional perspective?

In trying to answer these questions, we are treading new ground. Thus far, soldiers have featured in social and cultural studies of the Reformation era mainly as amorphous agents of the state, while military historians, with few exceptions, have studied the social history of the military from many different angles apart from the religious one. Writing about the religiosity of soldiers is not straightforward, not least because source materials that could illuminate military life from the inside are scarce and uneven before the later seventeenth century. The problem becomes even more pronounced when the inquiry concerns military religious practice or beliefs because contemporaries did not find these topics noteworthy enough to write about them and many aspects of religious life in the armies were not typically regulated or recorded. Another fundamental obstacle for historians interested in peaceful or non-agonal behaviors is that these are rarely documented. There is no occasion to produce records when people are getting along. We are thus forced to trawl through sometimes only tangentially related materials in the hope of catching glimpses of what interests us. From the perspective of modern and many early modern historians, the evidence presented here may sometimes seem impressionistic, and this is a limitation that should be acknowledged. I have, however, profited greatly from cultural histories of medieval warfare.[14] The medieval evidence often seems comparable to that which I was confronted with, and the methodologies of medievalist historians taught me to collate material from disparate sources. I have assembled the evidence I could find and striven to support my interpretations with comparisons to the civilian context, and hope, not surprisingly, that the result will be convincing.

In examining military religious life, we also must overcome a great deal of contemporary and historical prejudice. Echoing sensationalist or anxious early modern characterizations of soldiers, historians have emphasized the "unchristian" behaviors of the soldiery and tend to conclude that early modern armies were predominantly composed of amoral undesirables. Maybe because of the almost uniformly negative judgments of their contemporaries (which we will analyze in depth in Chapter 1) this stereotype has gone widely unchallenged and few historians have troubled themselves with the examination of the religious convictions of early modern soldiers. From the nineteenth century onward, the perceived lack of ideological and patriotic' attachment rendered the mercenary anathema to the nationalist fervor of the age. Gustav Freytag's lurid descriptions of the Thirty Years War's horrors shocked and titillated his readers and influenced both the popular imaginary and academic assumptions about soldiers for generations.[15] In the twentieth century, nationalists, socialists, and national socialists struggled with the ideological noncommitment of the *Landsknecht*. For socialists, the soldier was a class traitor who enforced princely despotism and preyed on the peasant. On the other side of the political spectrum, the unpatriotic, mutinous *Landsknecht* was antithetical to the national(-socialist) ideal and early modern German warfare was declared "entirely degenerate."[16] After 1945, military history became an academic "urchin"

6 ~: *Faith in War*

(*Schmuddelkind*) in Germany that few social or cultural historians were comfortable approaching.[17] While Anglo-American and French scholars wrote a "new" military history from the 1960s onward, their German colleagues only began to explore these questions with a three-decade delay. Since the 1990s, the social and cultural historiography of the early modern military has grown rapidly and has provided many valuable insights. The religious history of the military remains conspicuously unexamined, as—Michael Kaiser and Stefan Kroll's 2004 edited collection aside—there has been hardly any research into the spiritual dimension of soldiering in the German context before the end of the seventeenth century.[18]

This lack of serious interest has not prevented dismissive or negative but essentially unresearched comments repeating the putative truism of the irreligious soldier.[19] While it may be recognized, for example, that "the ethos of soldiering encouraged an *affected* disregard of established norms of religious behavior," this affectation swiftly morphs into an actual spiritual deficiency, amounting at most to a "mechanistic, death-bed type of piety."[20] Ultimately, soldiers are thought to have been "remarkable for the lack of any religious sensibility at all," which would indeed be remarkable were it not for the assumption that "the army milieu as a whole tended to be dechristianizing."[21] How army life could have achieved the cultural feat of "deprogramming" early modern soldiers is hard to fathom. The problem with such statements, apart from portraying soldiers as religiously abnormal, is that they imply the existence of a yardstick against which faith can be measured. Certainly, despite the doctrinal differences between the confessions, there remained a shared ideal of Christian comportment. But theologians and moralist writers were also painfully aware that few Christians actually met their exacting standards.

Questions regarding the influence of religious and confessional norms on the military sphere are posed throughout this book. The confessionalization paradigm has shaped especially German historiographical debate since the 1980s and questions surrounding the processes, the dynamics, and even the existence of confessionalization and the closely associated subject of "social discipline" shape historians' assumptions about early modern culture.[22] In essence, the confessionalization thesis argued that the statements of belief (*confessio* in Latin) that the three main churches formulated simultaneously demarcated them from one another and provided the internal programs of spiritual and social reform. The churches pursued these reform agendas in cooperation with the states, which, in turn, used ecclesiastical structures to exert political control into every parish. Heinz Schilling and Wolfgang Reinhard, the originators of the confessionalization thesis, took a strongly statist view and envisioned these changes as top-down processes, but this characterization of a "confessional coercion-state" (*konfessioneller Zwangsstaat*) soon elicited criticism.[23] Microhistorical and historical anthropological studies have seriously challenged many aspects of the confessionalization paradigm and have shown that religious pluralization and the development of confessional profiles was multilayered, non-teleological, unpredictable, contradictory, and chronologically messy. When it occurred, it was a process characterized by negotiation, pragmatism, and compromise with locally specific dynamics, rather than straightforward implementations of clearly defined reform programs from above.[24] It remains to be seen to what degree we can detect confessionalizing processes in the military of the period. It may seem intuitive to expect strong confessionalizing tendencies in such a hierarchical setting, but we have to bear in mind that the structures we have come to associate with the military were themselves evolving rapidly in the sixteenth and seventeenth centuries and, as we will see in the second chapter, the fact that the armies of the period were confessional composites proved a powerful obstacle to confessionalizing agendas that warlords may have harbored.

We also have to ask how the men and women who found themselves in the multiconfessional setting of the armies handled the challenge of religious diversity in their daily lives. Confessional coexistence has attracted scholarly attention only comparatively recently but there now exists a sufficient number of studies that illuminate the dynamics and contingencies of life in multiconfessional communities.[25] In most post-Reformation towns and villages, two or more confessions coexisted in a peaceful manner. Most people more or less decidedly identified with a confession in the later sixteenth century, but this did not mean that they were uncritical of their own creed or automatically hostile toward members of another. Bob Scribner described ordinary people's "tolerance of practical rationality" and C. Scott Dixon has discussed the "practical philosophy of tolerance," the latitudinarian "beliefs and attitudes of the people in the cities, towns and villages who actually experienced religious diversity at first hand."[26] Willem Frijhoff has introduced the very useful concept of *omgangsoecumene*, often translated into English as "the ecumenicity of everyday life" but maybe more accurately rendered as "the ecumenicity of social intercourse" or "acquaintance."[27] *Omgangsoecumene* highlights the fact that social contact often blurred confessional distinctions or emphasized other categories and norms of social life that were simply more relevant to the situation and the type of interaction.

Communities in general were centered around ideals of neighborliness and forbearance and dependent on reconciliation of their members, and oftentimes this moral system simply overrode matters of religion.[28] Many communities adopted an indifferent attitude toward religious allegiance and fanatics who threatened to whip up trouble between the members of bi- or multiconfessional communities were often met with unified, pan-confessional opposition.[29] So, while authorities could be pursuing policies of confessional purity, the populace often took a much more accommodating or indifferent stance. In

8 ❧ *Faith in War*

the absence of interference from above, Protestants and Catholics often lived peacefully together in the same communities, the same neighborhoods, streets, and houses. Confessional tension did increase in the decades around 1600 but the Thirty Years War led to a "growing dislike of religious fanaticism,"[30] and while Protestant and Catholic communities drifted apart and tended to segregate in the later seventeenth and eighteenth centuries, these tended to be gradual and nonconfrontational processes.

This is not to imply that the coexistence of the different denominations was without problems. Confessional conflict did erupt, but these tended to be isolated and painful occasions that served as reminders of the importance of negotiating difference peacefully.[31] Ultimately, it is important to emphasize that communities did not have to break apart over religious matters and that peaceful coexistence, toleration, cooperation, and indifference were as much part of post-Reformation society and culture as were conflicts; whether confessional conflict arose depended on the individual circumstances, on the willingness of communities to compromise, and not least on individuals.

What sets this book apart from the existing studies of confessional coexistence is that it does not examine a local or regional system of confessional coexistence but a professional one. In villages or towns, local tradition and custom, familial and neighborly relationships, parish and guild structures, and rehearsed strategies of accommodation could function as stabilizers that counterbalanced the disrupting influence of confessionalism. Armies, on the other hand, were transient and temporary communities, in which people from all over Europe encountered one another and had to negotiate their regional, linguistic, and confessional differences. The strategies of coexistence that military communities developed thus had to be accessible and accommodating to Christians from very diverse backgrounds, and they had to be transferrable, as individuals and groups moved in and out of regiments, changed sides, or were taken prisoner. Achieving a mode of coexistence was also arguably even more important in military life than it was in civilian contexts because in the armies, the struggle for survival was even more desperate. Horrific as they often were, battles were not the main cause of attrition. Military communities were constantly imperiled by hunger, disease, inclement weather, and often hostile civilian populations, and as the attempts of the authorities to provision or even pay troops typically failed, in-group cohesion was as vital as it was fragile. Deaccentuating confessional difference and cultivating strategies of coexistence were therefore of great importance.

Here, we are touching on an inherent tension in this study: we have to acknowledge that the military was a distinct socio-professional setting that functioned according to distinct imperatives, logics, and norms. On the other hand, the military was also a reflection of the society that produced it and while soldiers and their families consciously and deliberately entered a new social sphere when they joined the armies, they must have already possessed an ability to recognize and, if necessary, adapt to the demands of coexistence. The question, then, is not so much whether military life made people tolerant, which seems difficult to explain, but how the military context managed to mute and contain confessional antagonism.

The question of how confession and confessional thinking influenced life in the civilian and the military realms is a devious one because it suggests that there is a metric that could measure it. Older discussions surrounding confessionalization and social discipline tended to envision clerical and political elites as normative monopolists who laid out their vision of a pious polity in a variety of genres (creeds, church ordinances, moralist tracts, legal mandates, etc.) and handed these ideals down to the general populace, cast as passive recipients whose options were to conform or to deviate. This elitist concept has given way to a much more permeable and interactive view of religious change, but the underlying assumption that there existed a dominant set of religious and confessional norms that governed every aspect of life has remained widely unchallenged. This has led to a curious tension between what historians consider the normative framework of early modern culture and the conflicting behaviors we observe in the people who inhabited it.

To assume that soldiers were religiously atypical or that their circumstances somehow eroded Christian values presupposes a civilian reality in which these ideals were, in fact, realized. But this was not the case: early modern culture functioned according to different normative systems that governed different social settings. Normative imperatives often aligned but equally as often diverged, and they could even create contradictory behavioral expectations.

This is the central argument of Hillard von Thiessen's recently proposed analytical model of "normative rivalry" (*Normenkonkurrenz*).[32] The great advantage of Thiessen's model is that it considers religious norms as one among several normative systems that coexisted in early modern culture and that governed behaviors in different social contexts: there were religious norms, social norms, and norms that aimed at the common good, and these at times reinforced each other (Thiessen calls this "norm convergence") but often caused conflicting expectations on peoples' behaviors that led to normative rivalry. Even among the same social or professional group and in the same setting, contradictive norms could demand contradictory behaviors. A concrete example from the military sphere is the treatment of the female enemy population: military custom legitimized rape under certain circumstances but there also existed a quasi-chivalric norm to exempt women from military violence. Both behaviors could be sanctioned, and how soldiers acted toward women depended on setting, group dynamics, and not least the individual.

These normative contradictions were a fact of life and led to a constant state of indistinctness, which, according to Thiessen, defined early modernity as an

10   ❧ Faith in War

"Age of Ambiguity." People were usually able to accept this ambiguity and navigate it without necessarily realizing that they were favoring one set of norms over another in a given situation. Neither did they endure moral anguish by acting in ways that modern observers may consider inconsistent, contradictory, or hypocritical.[33] It was also accepted that different norms applied depending on the social role a person fulfilled in a given situation. By accepting that religious norms did not have an automatic primacy but had to compete with other normative systems in every aspect of life, from the family up to the level of international politics, we can free ourselves from the impulse to question why a given individual or groups compromised the demands of their faith in certain situations; they merely behaved in a manner suggested by other social or political norms.[34]

This normative ambiguity was by no means a harmonious state of affairs and the desire to establish an unequivocal normative system that could guide life in all matters was related to another characteristic of the period, namely the drive for purity.[35] That historians initially conceived of social disciplining and confessionalization as an elite attack on a backward and recalcitrant "popular culture" was influenced by the manner in which early modern theologians and moral writers of all confessions positioned themselves in opposition to a society that they considered fundamentally unchristian.[36] But their designs for an ideal society that completely surrendered to religious norms were explicitly not a reflection of how most people actually behaved and only a rather small segment of the intellectual elites ever attempted to realize this new moral utopia.[37]

Historians do well to remember this when they struggle with the temptation to criticize behaviors and beliefs in unduly contemporary, if not downright subjective terms. The idea that soldiers' "bad reputation" was "often well deserved" and that some new recruits "were probably fairly decent characters, although in an environment reputedly permeated with drink, gambling and violence they may not have stayed that way for long" is but one example that can illustrate this point.[38] Do gambling or drinking necessarily betray an indecent character? Is violence not a necessary virtue for a soldier? Do people who exhibit such behaviors "deserve" infamy? It seems important to reflect, briefly, on these questions because they are difficult to escape.

A feature of much social history, especially "history from below," is the tendency to find ancestors with whom we can empathize and maybe turn to for inspiration. Soldiers, in Peter Wilson's words, "occupied an ambiguous place in society as servants of the authorities who engaged in activities breaching the most basic Christian commandments."[39] This ambiguity is not only confined to the early modern period, it also affects the writer who approaches them today. Soldiers do not lend themselves easily to empathy, as their behaviors all too often appall. Peter Hagendorf, whose experiences figure repeatedly in this book, seems to have been a caring father and husband who mourned the deaths of eight children and that of his first wife Anna Stadlerin. But between marriages he also captured and maybe raped two young women.[40] Which of these aspects of Hagendorf's character should the historian emphasize? Neither, it seems, but the example shows the futility of trying to write about soldiers in the heroic mode or write them off wholesale as immoral.

A cultural-historical analysis of how soldiers interpreted and justified violence while maintaining their self-image as good Christians can shed some light on the nature, contingency, and elasticity of moral and religious norms in early modernity. This should not be mistaken for an apology, nor is it my intention to romanticize military life or soldiers when I analyze their attempts to limit violence in war or question the assumption that military violence was often confessionally motivated. Soldiers were still professionally and probably habitually violent; the point I am making is simply that confessional hatred seldom prompted the violence. Trying to understand the dynamics and contingencies of confessional conflict and confessional coexistence also aims at restoring a degree of agency to ordinary people in their navigation of the choppy religious waters of the Reformation period and the pitiful reality of war. Normative systems do not automatically determine actions but suggest patterns of behavior with an at times considerable scope for agency. Actors mostly behave in ways that have proven successful in the past, but at times they also act creatively or contravene expectations. They retain agency within historically and situationally contingent parameters, and the aim of this book is to examine the nature of these parameters in early modern military culture, the patterns of behavior we can observe, and the ways in which soldiers acted against this horizon of norms.

The following chapters move from the general sociocultural context to the peculiar professional one that shaped and regulated soldiers' daily lives before aspects of religious life in the armies are discussed. The first chapter problematizes and unpacks the stereotype of the irreligious soldier and introduces us to the sociocultural matrix within which we have to examine military religiosity. The vituperative allegations of military godlessness, as we will see, were leveled against soldiers rather uniformly in the period from 1500 to 1650 and changed little over time. While the stereotype has at times been recognized, historians have failed to contextualize it diachronically and synchronically, with the result that early modern soldiers appear exceptionally wicked. An exploration of similar allegations through time uncovers the long history of condemning soldiers as amoral or unchristian and suggests that the early modern vituperations did not necessarily reflect reality but the deep-seated Christian unease with men who make a living by killing. In a second step we will examine why this stereotype gained renewed purchase around 1500 and why soldiers at the time elicited such profound anxiety. Finally, the stereotype's influence on the lives of soldiers and their families must be considered.

12 ❦ *Faith in War*

The second chapter moves into the military sphere proper and analyzes the religious structures of the military and the character of institutionalized religion in the armies. The legal parameters were set out in the articles of war that were issued by the warlords and which each soldier pledged to follow. These martial law codes have survived in great numbers and allow us to trace how authorities sought to police religious practice among their troops. The chaplaincy of the period has received little scholarly attention, probably because field preachers were reputedly as impious as the men they tended to. As we will see, army chaplains were not inferior to civilian clergy; they were expected to meet the same criteria of comportment and fulfill the same pastoral duties. Devotional literature and prayer books for soldiers allow us to assess what religious values were conveyed to soldiers. The picture that emerges is one of undoubtedly "Christian" but not "confessional" values that military authorities sought to foster.

The third chapter examines the role religion played in soldiers' lives and the ways in which they deviated from certain religious norms. Autobiographical accounts form the main source base here and it becomes evident that military diarists were not, in fact, "godless" but "Christians" in every meaningful way. The examination of three transgressive behaviors that were commonly tied to soldiers (blasphemy, magic, and illicit or violent sex) rethinks the way in which "deviance" has been treated in the military. Interpreting these transgressions from the vantage of the soldiers themselves and comparing them to the way in which civilians actually behaved, rather than how moralists thought they should behave, the picture that emerges is far less extraordinary. All these "deviant" behaviors were widespread among the early modern laity; soldiers could merely indulge in them more freely than their civilian contemporaries.

The fourth chapter examines the occurrence of military religious violence in the generally tolerant context of army life. I argue that coexistence was characteristic of military everyday life, and that religious violence was atypical. The rare moments in which genuine religious violence occurred show that military religious violence followed much the same logic as civilian confessional conflict did. In their acts of religious violence, soldiers not only displayed hatred but betrayed a keen understanding of doctrinal difference and very accurately targeted those elements of worship and theology that separated their own from their victims' faith. Mostly, however, soldiers did not struggle with religious diversity and toleration, or, probably more often, indifference, was an integral fact of military life. Soldiers tended to ignore matters of confession and dealt with one another as Christians, not as sectarians. A survey of military attitudes toward the enemy shows that, generally speaking, confessional difference did not exacerbate violence between enemies and that a restrained and honorable conduct of war was, again, binding for all Christian soldiers. The picture of coexistence and violence that emerges is therefore rather surprising: Europe's "religious wars" were fought by armies composed of Christians of all denominations who mostly managed to contain confessional strife both in their own units and across enemy lines.

The last chapter examines military attitudes toward dying, death, and burial. Disease, hunger, and cold—rather than battle—killed soldiers and their families with relentless constancy, so that death was even more frequent an occurrence in the armies than in civilian communities. Unlike their sedentary contemporaries, however, people living in the military context had to face death in often chaotic circumstances that made adherence to the precepts of the *ars moriendi*, the art of dying well, difficult or impossible. Whether in battle or in the camp, soldiers and their families often died without clerical guidance, did not receive rites, and, if they were buried at all, ended up in mass graves in which friends and enemies were interred, irrespective of confession. The pragmatism that characterized soldiers' lives is thus encapsulated in military attitudes toward death and burial practices as well.

A Note on the Terminology

The term "soldier" will be used more frequently than "mercenary" in this book for practical as well as semantic reasons. German historians especially tend to differentiate between "mercenary" (*Söldner*) and "soldier" (*Soldat*),[41] but this distinction carries ideological overtones that seem unhelpful to me. Most of the men we will encounter in this book were mercenaries in the sense that they did not necessarily fight for their rightful ruler or their native country and they received pay for their services. Both German words, *Söldner* and *Soldat*, and their cognates in other European languages have the same etymological root, Latin *sol[i]dus*, which means either the late Roman coin or simply "pay." "Mercenary" is derived from Latin *mercennarius*, meaning "paid" or "hired," or "hired worker," while the root *merces* translates as "pay" or "wage." "Mercenary" and "soldier" thus both originally denoted men who rendered military service in exchange for pay. In the period of study, the differentiation between "mercenaries" and "soldiers" is always difficult and never objective and so it appears best to favor the more neutral word. A commonly used German term in the period of study was simply "Knecht," which will also be rendered as "soldier" as its modern English translation "servant" does not have military connotations and its English cognate "knight" denotes a socially more elevated, mounted warrior. *Landsknecht* (plural: *Landsknechte*) refers to German infantry soldiers until ca. 1600, when it widely fell from usage and "Knecht(e)" or "Soldat(en)" became standard.

The second issue concerns the terms "Christian," "religion"/"religious," and "confession(al)." As we will see, throughout the "confessional age" a vital com-

14 ❧ *Faith in War*

mon ground of doctrinally unmarked Christian values and norms remained
that could be cultivated to allow the functioning of a multiconfessional professional group such as the military. I will therefore use "Christian" or "religious"
when referring to such shared concepts, positions, or values with which Christians of all confessions could identify. Care should be taken not to confuse the
"religious" with the "confessional." If we consider "confession(al)" to refer to ar-
ticulated and distinctly Catholic, Lutheran, or Reformed outlooks, "religious"
might describe a less partisan, more universally "Christian" piety or worldview.
These distinctions will become clearer in the course of this study, but at this
point it may suffice to caution against conflating "Christian"/"religious" and
"confessional" as they denote different approaches to faith.

Notes

1. Kirchhof, *Wendunmuth*, vol. 1, 130–31.
2. Roberts, "The Military Revolution." For a relatively recent overview of the military revolution debate see Tallett's introduction to *European Warfare*.
3. Parker, *The Military Revolution*, 1–5; Tallett, *War and Society*, 9.
4. Gunn, "War and the Emergence of the State," 56.
5. On Wittenberg as the idiosyncratic point of origin for the Reformation, see Rublack, *Reformation Europe*, ch. 1; Roper, *Martin Luther*, ch. 4.
6. The emergence and usage of confessional labels during the German Reformation has recently been the subject of two enlightening studies: Witt, *Protestanten*; and Jörgensen, *Konfessionelle Selbst- und Fremdbezeichnungen*.
7. On the variety of Catholic practice across Europe see Nolde, "Andächtiges Staunen"; and
   from a pan-European perspective, Ó hAnnracháin, *Catholic Europe*. Diversity in the Lutheran context is examined by Kaufmann, *Konfession und Kultur*.
8. See for example Forster, *Catholic Germany*, 29; Plath, *Konfessionskampf*, 95, 96n, 100; or
   Spohnholz, "Multiconfessional Celebration of the Eucharist."
9. See most recently Maurer, *Konfessionskulturen*.
10. Brendle and Schindling, "Religionskriege," 19–22; Haug-Moritz, "Schmalkaldische Krieg,"
    94. See also Bremer, "Rhetorik und Semantik des Begriffs 'Religionshändel.'"
11. Brendle and Schindling, "Religionskriege," 19.
12. Ibid., 17.
13. Just two examples are Burkhardt, *Der Dreißigjährige Krieg*, 134; Trim, "Conflict, Religion
    and Ideology," 290.
14. Especially Kaeuper, *Chivalry and Violence* and *Holy Warriors*; Caferro, *John Hawkwood*; and
    Prietzel, *Kriegführung im Mittelalter*.
15. Freytag, *Bilder*, vol. 3.
16. Frauenholz, *Lazarus von Schwendi*, 20.
17. Pröve, "Vom Schmuddelkind zur anerkannten Subdisziplin?"
18. Kaiser and Kroll, *Militär und Religiosität*.
19. For example Redlich, *German Military Enterpriser*, vol. 2, 476; Fiedler, *Kriegswesen*, 90;
    Mellinkoff, *Outcasts*, vol. 1, 26; Swart, "From 'Landsknecht' to 'Soldier,'" 78–79; Barudio, *Der
    Teutsche Krieg*, 165.
20. Tallett, *War and Society*, 127–28. Emphasis added.

Introduction ∶~ 15

21. Ibid., 128.
22. For discussions of the "confessionalization" and "social discipline" paradigms see Loetz, *Mit Gott handeln*, 50–56; the contributions in Brockmann and Weiss, *Das Konfessionalisierungsparadigma*; and the discussion between Forster et al. in "Religious History beyond Confessionalization."
23. Reinhard, "Zwang zur Konfessionalisierung?"; Schilling, *Konfessionskonflikt und Staatsbildung*; and Schilling, "Konfessionalisierung im Reich."
24. Schmidt, *Dorf und Religion*; Schmidt, "Sozialdisziplinierung?" More restrained early criticism was voiced in Schulze's review of Schilling's *Konfessionskonflikt*. See also Robisheaux, *Rural Society*; and Plath, *Konfessionskampf*. Schilling himself later argued for a "pincer-movement" (*Zangenbewegung*) in "Disziplinierung oder 'Selbstregulierung'", 680.
25. A selection of monographs includes Grochowina, *Indifferenz und Dissens*; Luria, *Sacred Boundaries*; Volkland, *Konfession und Selbstverständnis*; Kaplan, *Divided By Faith*; Kaplan, *Reformation and the Practice of Toleration*; Dixon, Freist and Greengrass, *Living with Religious Diversity*; Spohnholz, *Tactics of Toleration*; Christman, *Pragmatic Toleration*; Kirchner, *Katholiken, Lutheraner und Reformierte in Aachen*; Luebke, *Hometown Religion*; and Scholz, *Strange Brethren*.
26. Scribner, "Preconditions of Tolerance and Intolerance," 38; Dixon, "Introduction," 9.
27. Frijhoff introduced this concept in 1979 ("La coexistence confessionnelle"). For a later reflection on the topic see his *Embodied Belief*, ch. 2.
28. Hsia, *Social Discipline*, 137.
29. Greyerz, *Religion und Kultur*, 181.
30. Forster, "Thirty Years' War," 167.
31. Luebke, *Hometown Religion*, 6.
32. Thiessen, *Das Zeitalter der Ambiguität*.
33. Ibid., 24.
34. Barbara Stollberg-Rilinger has observed the same tendency at the level of imperial politics in *Des Kaisers alte Kleider*, 85.
35. Burschel, *Die Erfindung der Reinheit*.
36. Hendrix, *Recultivating the Vineyard*; Thiessen, *Zeitalter der Ambiguität*, 41–43.
37. Ibid., 48.
38. Swart, "From 'Landsknecht' to 'Soldier,'" 78.
39. Wilson, *Europe's Tragedy*, 834.
40. Peters, *Peter Hagendorf*, 109–10.
41. For example Baumann, *Landsknechte*; Burschel, *Söldner*.

CHAPTER 1

"A New Order of Soulless Men"?
Reassessing a Stereotype

In a comical poem of 1558, the Nuremberg shoemaker and *Meistersinger* Hans Sachs described a devil's ill-fated attempt to catch a *Landsknecht* and take him to Hell.[1] Lucifer has been informed that a new "evil people" (*böses volck*) called the *Landsknechte* have come into existence in Germany and that these men are perpetually drunk, feast, gamble, swear, and brawl. Lucifer sends a demon called Beltzebock to a tavern to catch a specimen but the poor devil is so frightened by the soldiers' appearance and behavior that he flees in panic and returns to Hell empty-handed.[2] After listening to Beltzebock's report, Lucifer eventually realizes that the *Landsknechte* are too unruly and fierce to be permitted into Hell.[3]

One of Hans Wilhelm Kirchhof's fables takes this theme one step further.[4] After a great battle, many *Landsknecht* souls find themselves in the netherworld. In search of winter quarters, the souls make their way to Hell because of its famously warm climate. Their approach sends Hell's inhabitants into a state of panic, the gates are barricaded, and the demonic gatekeeper tells the *Landsknechte* that there is no place for them here; they should try Heaven. Grudgingly the soldiers take the road to Heaven where Saint Peter is rather surprised at their nerve to even try to get through the Golden Gate. When Peter slights them as blasphemers, he unwittingly starts a banter match that he is bound to lose. The leader of the *Landsknechte* reminds him loudly of his denial of Christ and—embarrassed and afraid that the other saints might hear—Peter appeases the soldiers by addressing them in typical *Landsknecht* manner as "dear brothers" and bids them to enter if they will shut up.

Both stories describe the same stereotypical military behaviors that were lamented by contemporary moralists, but here we find an element of admiration as well, as the *Landsknechte* render both demons and saints helpless in the face of this outrageous breed of human. The humor inherent in the idea that devils should be scandalized by human behavior presents the ability to distress a devil as a feat. In Kirchhof's fable, the *Landsknechte* entirely upend Christian

"A New Order of Soulless Men"? ❧ 17

concepts of divine and diabolical powers, and the fundamental fears regarding postmortem welfare or damnation find a release in the comical inversion of early modern notions of Heaven and Hell. Here, Hell seems like a pleasant place to spend eternity; the soldier souls go there because it is so nice and warm. They are not damned to Hell but demand entry and only trudge toward Heaven when they are barred from their first choice of a netherworldly abode. That the epitomes of depravity finally manage to shame Saint Peter into admitting them into Heaven is the ultimate inversion of traditional notions of postmortem judgment and sainthood. The *Landsknechte* quite sharply desacralize Peter and approach him on eye level as the man Simon who, after his denial of Christ, neither deserves the epithet *petros* nor the reverence of sanctity.

Examples like these show that the stereotypical characteristics of mercenary corruption could be a source of glee and admiration; they also attracted the ire and condemnation of moralists, who painted soldiers as the antithesis of Christian comportment. As we will see in detail, soldiers and especially commoners who voluntarily became *Landsknechte* were believed to enlist for all the wrong reasons. Anxious commentators alleged that laziness, greed, and the wish to sin unimpededly drove men into the armies, not obligation to a liege lord or the wish to defend a politically or religiously legitimate cause. For the most part, this stereotype has survived the centuries remarkably unchallenged and many historians continue to take these formulaic allegations at face value.[5]

The purpose of this chapter is twofold: it seeks to expose the notion of the "godless" soldier as a stereotype and, secondly, it offers explanations for why soldiers, especially those commoners who joined the army of their own volition, alarmed their contemporaries to such a high degree. In doing so, we will situate the military and its personnel in the wider sociocultural setting of the sixteenth and seventeenth centuries and take a civilian perspective, the perspective from which the most damning comments about soldiers were made. As the tenacious idea that early modern soldiers were irreligious deviants continues to fog our view, it is necessary to approach this stereotype in some detail: first, the stereotype and its formulaic nature has to be established; secondly, we will trace the historical roots of this stereotype right back to the earliest Christian texts to show that the condemnation of soldiers was by no means unique to early modernity; thirdly, we have to understand why these old anxieties were given renewed purchase around 1500. Finally, we have to ask what effect the stereotype had on soldiers and their families, to determine if this was merely a literary trope or a representation that tangibly influenced soldiers' social standing.

The *Landsknechte* were regarded as a distinctly new phenomenon and as such they attracted anxious scrutiny from a culture that was fundamentally suspicious of novelty and change. The appearance of the *Landsknecht* as a new warrior type also roughly coincided with the renewed concern with morals that characterized the late medieval and early modern periods, most commonly referred to in the historiography as "social discipline."[6] Questions and anxieties regarding social order and moral conduct wielded increasing influence and found their expressions in countless moralizing tracts as well as an ever-growing number of regulations issued by local and territorial elites in a bid to establish *gute Polizey*, a "good order."[7] We have to understand the allegations against soldiers in this wider cultural context of a changing moral(-izing) climate. J. R. Hale argued with good cause that the scrutiny with which soldiers were viewed in the sixteenth century "applied to no other occupation group in the century, whether courtier, cardinal or prince."[8] It should be added that no other character was so commonly associated with as many different categories of vice as the soldier either. Prostitutes were primarily sexual deviants, "sturdy beggars"—those who could work but would not—were sinful in their idleness. But soldiers, as we will see, allegedly offended against almost every moral value of Christian society. While this concentration of purported vice in a single social type was unique, it is important to stress that the sins soldiers were associated with—sexual licentiousness, boozing, gambling, idleness, blasphemy, and so forth—were thought to be endemic throughout society. In the sixteenth century, preoccupation with these vices led to the development of a whole genre of moralist literature known as *Teufelsbücher*, "devil books." In these tracts, specialist devils were presented as the causes of common social ills and authors warned of devils who instigated the superstitious veneration of saints, magic and blasphemy, oath swearing, dancing, martial problems, boozing, whoring, haughtiness, laziness, and so forth.[9] While the *Teufelsbücher* were a Lutheran genre, the moral concerns they expressed (with the exception of saint veneration, obviously) were shared by moralists of all Christian persuasions.

The stereotypical soldier as he will appear in this chapter embodied society at its most reprehensible, and we will encounter the formulaic allegation of "unchristian" behavior and "godlessness" over and over again. "Godlessness" in the early modern rhetorical context did not mean what we would consider "atheism" today. People who lived "godlessly" behaved *as if* there were no God to punish their sin, but this was not a cosmological statement about the existence or nonexistence of the divine. The charge of "godlessness" was inflationary in moralist literature and its vagueness lent it versatility: it allowed the author to stigmatize behaviors or people as "godless" without having to specify what exactly made them deserving of the epithet. "Godless" people could be heterodox, objectionable in their behavior or merely dangerously indifferent; the rhetorical objective of labeling someone or something as "godless" was to draw a line between the "Christian" accuser and his moral vision, and the damnable other.[10] The label "unchristian" was applied as generously and with the same intentions. Moralizing literature was characterized by alarmism and didactic hyperbole intended to highlight the chasm between the perceived social status quo and the envisioned ideal. Moralist authors considered only their own doctrine and vision for society deserving of the adjective "Christian" and the branding of deviants as "godless" and "unchristian" was an uncharitable but universal rhetorical reflex. Normative texts presented moral imperatives as absolutes and as there could be no *via media*, any aberration from that narrow path had to be "unchristian," "godless," "pagan," "heretical," "idolatrous," and so forth.[11] Given this rhetorical climate, allegations of soldierly "godlessness" should be considered a linguistic mode of marginalization that was typical of moral exhortations at the time. They should not be mistaken for descriptors of actual military unbelief, but seen as a common rhetorical strategy intended to steer an (often resistant) laity toward a moral standard that did not necessarily reflect popular notions of what was permissible and what was not.

The historical dimension of how stereotypes develop, function, and persist is rarely theorized, but insights into the nature of stereotyping derived from social psychology provide a valuable framework in which to think about stereotypes of the past.[12] Stereotypes as shared assumptions are socially, culturally, and historically contingent: they change over time to some degree but retain a central set of attributes and value judgments that is resistant to change. Jean-Claude Abric has proposed a way of understanding social representations that is helpful in analyzing stereotypes through time. Central to his model is the realization that stereotypes have a relatively stable core of attributes and a more changeable set of peripheral characteristics that anchor the stereotype in different social and historical settings.[13] This adaptable periphery allows stereotypes to embed themselves in changing cultural contexts while the assumptions at their core are preserved, which explains the troubling longevity of some stereotypes, for example those of the "lazy" poor or the "feeble and emotional" woman. As we will see shortly, the stereotype of the immoral soldier was at its core very old, but certain specifics and semantics changed over the centuries.

Establishing a Stereotype

Vilifications of soldiers, especially of the rank and file, are omnipresent in all kinds of early modern texts, from broadsheets and early newspapers to moral tracts and even military manuals. These diatribes rehearsed a catalogue of military vice that typically included laziness, gambling, luxuriousness, drunkenness, gluttony, brawling, looting, theft, robbery, sexual licentiousness, swearing, blasphemy, and general "godlessness." Chief among the denouncers of military depravity were theologians and moralist writers and condemnations of soldierly vice were voiced all over Europe. Erasmus of Rotterdam, for example, repeatedly wrote about soldiers in stark terms. Soldiers, in his estimations, may have been "idiots," but more devastatingly, Erasmus thought them "barbarians, . . . blackguards, murderers, and robbers."[14] A similar sentiment was expressed in

The Education of the Christian Prince (1516), written for the future emperor Charles V, in which armies were characterized as "a barbarian rabble, made up of all the worst scoundrels," a notion that led Erasmus to conclude that "there is no class of men more abject and indeed more damnable" than soldiers.[15] In the *Complaint of Peace* (1517), Peace declared that "godless soldiers" and "the criminal dregs of hired mercenaries" deserved "not the crucifix but crucifixion."[16]

With the onset of the Reformation, Protestant theologians became, in Ulinka Rublack's words, the "prime movers in public discourses about German values" and their discussions frequently identified soldiers as symptomatic of the deep depravity of Christendom.[17] In 1524, Johann Eberlin von Günzburg, a former Franciscan who had left his monastery in 1521 to become an early acolyte of Luther and Melanchthon's, identified the "useless, damaging and ruinous" wars of his time and especially the soldiers who fought them as the root cause of Germany's miseries.[18] Eberlin branded the *Landsknechte* a "new order of soulless men" who entered freely into a profession that endangered their souls, as army life accustomed men to "scolding, swearing, insults, cursing . . . whoring, adultery, defiling virgins, gluttony, boozing, . . . thieving, robbing, murdering."[19] "In short," he concluded, soldiers stood "bound completely in the power of the devil." Further to their personal corruption and foreseeable damnation, Eberlin regarded soldiers as a societal threat, as they abandoned their families, "their sweet fatherland and sworn service and required work."[20] Once corrupted, soldiers threatened to infect society with "their evil customs" and tempted others into "idleness, gambling, drinking, whoring, etc."[21] To Eberlin, soldiers not only endangered their own salvation, they became vectors of moral pollution that spread sin wherever they went.

Two years later, Martin Luther gave a somewhat more conciliatory and nuanced estimation of the military profession. He explained that, given the right motivation, the military profession could be a God-pleasing one.[22] Echoing medieval theologians of pious violence like Bernard of Clairvaux, who had maintained that a warrior killing an evildoer was not a "mankiller" (*homicidia*) but a "killer of evil" (*malicidia*), Luther likened the Christian soldier to a surgeon who amputates in order to save the patient.[23] Fighting for pay was not immoral either, as Luther considered soldiers' martial prowess to be God-given so that one could hire out his service "exactly as though his skill were an art or trade" and receive pay just like an artisan would.[24] While professional soldiering was thus not inherently unchristian in theory, in practice, Luther concurred with the moralist mainstream that "a great many soldiers belong to the devil."[25] The reasons he presented for this assessment were manifold: soldiers, he claimed, tried to suppress contemplation of God's judgment to prevent their conscience from interfering with their work. They also habitually blasphemed, and the professional warrior's suspected lust for war and refusal to ply a different trade until their lords called them to service was taken to indicate "laziness or roughness and wildness of spirit" and to be a clear sign that soldiers could not be "on good terms with God."[26] Luther did not limit his loathing to common professionals but also attacked the impoverished nobles and knights who destabilized society with their constant feuds: "The excrement of the eagle can boast that it comes from the eagle's body even though it stinks and is useless; and so these men can also be of the nobility."[27]

In a traditional manner, Luther tied the legitimacy of soldiering to the just cause of the war and conceded that the profession could at least theoretically be in accordance with the Christian life. His views were rather moderate in this instance, certainly owing to the fact that he was writing in response to a request for a theological opinion on the profession from the mercenary captain Assa von Cramm.[28] In his *Table Talk*, Luther exhibited clear revulsion for soldiers and, like Erasmus and Eberlin, considered them to be societal refuse unfit for any other profession and declared himself to be "the greatest enemy of the Landsknechte" who "would much rather live under the guardianship of Turks or Tartars than under theirs."[29] Luther was not as critical of war as Erasmus or Eberlin, but he shared their estimations regarding the immorality of the men who fought them.

The pacifist reformer Sebastian Franck's *War-Book of Peace* (1539) contained one of the strongest condemnations of war and the soldiery of the sixteenth century. To Franck, soldiers were "devils in human form" (*vermenschte teüffel*) and he repeatedly specified what made them so diabolical.[30] Soldiers were "idle arsonists, robbers, murderers, unchaste people, gamblers, drunks, blasphemers, shameful mercenaries . . . and all kinds of evil, executioner-like rapscallions."[31] Their sole occupation in times of peace was "to start all kinds of mischief in the towns, to burden land and people" and spend their time with "cards, dice, gambling, drinking, whoring, blaspheming and idleness" until given a chance to "practice their art of war," which consisted of "bloodshed, robbing, murder, burning, making widows and orphans."[32] Citing the polymath Heinrich Agrippa, Franck claimed that the word "warrior" (*krieger*) had degraded into a catch-all term for "merciless gnarls, tyrants, church robbers, thieves, murderers, adulterers, gypsies, fencers, whorers, gamblers, drunks, torturers, arsonists, witches, poison cooks, runaway knaves, daredevils, foolhardy people, . . . and the whole devil-rabble that is related to the guild of scoundrels."[33] In short, soldiers were antithetical to Christian morals.

In 1558, the Lutheran theologian Andreas Musculus updated Martin Luther's explanations regarding the God-pleasing conduct of war.[34] Musculus was less concerned with the social threat posed by military men than with their salvation. He was doubtful of it for four main reasons. Firstly, soldiers voluntarily endangered their lives by enlisting and, secondly, he alleged that "warriors [were] commonly evil, impudent, raw and bloodthirsty fellows."[35] Thirdly, he thought the "stabbing, strangling, murdering, robbing, taking, burning and harrying" of innocent people to be sinful, and, fourthly, soldiers' souls were tarnished by their "boozing, gorging, whoring, gambling, quarrelling [and] blaspheming" and would be judged accordingly by God. In times of war, "all evil knaves flock together in one heap and warriors are nothing else than a heap of raw, wild and impudent people with whom decency, honorability and piety have little room," making the army an "alluvium of all vices and godless behavior."[36] Soldiers were "sunk and drowned in all major vices and sins so that little blessedness [could] be hoped for in them" and their "clothes, gestures, words and deeds" made them behave "diabolically."[37]

Seventeenth-century writers perpetuated the stereotype. The anonymous evangelical field preacher who published a religious handbook for soldiers in 1620 did not condemn the soldiery summarily—his intention was to give Protestant soldiers a guideline toward salvation—but he also found space to rehearse the litany of soldier vice.[38] In his *Kriegs Belial*, a long tract first published in 1633, the Saxon theologian and ducal court preacher Arnold Mengering exceeded previous diatribes in polemical vigor when he presented soldiers as the children of the devil.[39] "Belial," Mengering elaborated, was the appropriate name for the military devil as it meant "the one without a yoke," fitting because the devil and his soldiery spawn rejected the "yoke of divine laws" (*jugo legis divinae*).[40] He imagined a soldier catechism that inverted the Decalogue, and a creed in which soldiers renounced every principle of Christian belief and even denied the existence of God, Christ, or an afterlife.[41] In many ways, *Kriegs Belial* appears as the culmination of military condemnation, as it presented the soldiery as a demonic sect, which had completely surrendered to the rule of the devil. Whereas previous authors described soldiers as men who had strayed from the norms of Christian society, Mengering characterized soldiers no longer as lapsed children of God but as the offspring of the devil Belial who was also their deity. In Mengering's tract, soldiers stood entirely outside of Christian society and its norms; they were the ultimate anti-Christian outsiders.

Such vilifications were not only voiced by theologians and moralists; we can also find them in the works of military authors whom one might expect to have been more charitable toward soldiers. Leonhardt Fronsperger, the most prolific sixteenth-century writer of German military manuals, protested the notion that *all* soldiers faced an eternity in Hell. Two pages on, however, he conceded that the current German way of warring was more "unchristian and sowish" than that of Jews and heathens and later declared most soldiers morally corrupt.[42] Martin Behm, who wrote a spiritual guide for professional soldiers at the end of the sixteenth century, also expressed his dim view of soldiers' piety. While many natural omens indicated the coming of the apocalypse, causing "the poor people to sit at home in worry and fear," soldiers showed no interest in amending their ways and continued to live more recklessly and wantonly than anyone else; even if the Devil himself ascended from Hell looking for troops, soldiers would flock to his employ as long as he paid well.[43] Only in the fourth part of his book did Behm introduce some nuance. He composed the "Articles of War for Christian Soldiers" and addressed the question of why people thought all soldiers to be "wild brothers and raw people" when there were "many godly, pious men" in the armies.[44] Behm saw three main reasons for this: slander from those against whom the legitimate authorities employed soldiers; a mania (*wahn*) of the masses who thought that someone could not kill in war unless they were "wicked and godless"; and thirdly, those evil soldiers who acted sinfully and gave the impression that the entire profession was composed of "wild bumblebees and mad folk."[45] Given the elevated status of many of the authors whose condemnations of soldierly godlessness we have surveyed so far, Behm's trivializing attribution of the stereotype to the delusions of the common people is surprising, especially since his book rehearsed the familiar catalogue of alleged soldier vice in an otherwise entirely unoriginal manner.

Johann Jacob von Wallhausen, captain of the Danzig militia, military advisor to several European potentates, and author of military manuals, also echoed the stereotype in 1615. Ideally, soldiers should have God in their hearts at all times, pray incessantly, and conduct themselves more piously than monks, as military life was incomparably more dangerous than life in a cloister. The reality as Wallhausen observed it inverted the norms of the Christian life with its "blaspheming, swearing, gorging, boozing, whoring, gambling, brawling, quarrelling, dancing, jumping, dissolute and frivolous talk, ribaldry, the defilement of God and women [and] vexation."[46] The military, once a "receptacle of all virtues," had become a "receptacle of nearly all vice," in which immoral behaviors were so abundant that even a heathen warrior of old would be scandalized.[47]

These examples show that the stereotype of the godless soldier was relatively uniform during the sixteenth and seventeenth centuries. In Abric's model of social representations, its core was composed of a stable, uniform set of immoral behaviors: whoring, greed, boozing, feasting, and gambling, different degrees of violence—both legitimized by their profession and illicit—and the immediately religious transgressions of blasphemy, defiance of the divine, and even allegiance with the Devil. The catalogue of vice that writers repeated in this formulaic manner was taken to prove a soldierly hostility toward Christian ethical norms and rendered the stereotypical soldier "godless."

It is precisely this formulaic fashion in which soldiers' vices were recounted, however, that is a strong indicator that we are not necessarily dealing with observations of reality but with a literary trope. The fact that the stereotype became connected especially with the *Landsknecht* around 1500 and characterized especially common soldiers for much of the period has been attributed to their singular amorality, but early modern writers simply reapplied an old literary trope to a new type of soldier.

Uncovering a Tradition

There are good reasons to think that the stereotype of the irreligious and amoral soldier indeed reflected a reality. The stereotype was fully formed around 1500, it appears to have appeared spontaneously and simultaneously with the establishment of the *Landsknecht* as a commonly depicted cultural type in printed media and art, and it associated a specific set of vices with this particular type of soldier. We are therefore given the impression that "a new order of soulless men" did indeed come into being in the last decades of the fifteenth century. But how can we account for this phenomenon and how could a stereotype have developed in such uniformity across western Europe? The answer presents itself when we widen our historical focus: Christian writers had condemned soldiers since the earliest times and the stereotype we have observed in the early modern period had, in fact, gradually formed over centuries.

The notion that soldiers tended to be dissolute and threatening characters can already be found in the earliest Christian texts. John the Baptist's admonition to the soldiers not to abuse their power and to be content with their pay reflects an association of soldiers with maltreatment and exploitation (Luke 3:14). Individual soldiers who violated this general rule stand out all the more starkly in the scriptures. Christ never condemned soldiers *explicitly* but his praise of the Gentile centurion of Capernaum for his unparalleled humility and faith (Matt. 8:5–13) derives its oxymoronic power from the fact that such faith could be found *even* among soldiers. Similarly, among the soldiers who tortured and mocked Christ, the leader of the crucifixion squad who realized Christ's divinity after he had played his part in the Passion (Matt. 27:54; Mark 15:39; Luke 23:47) was the singular exception.

Most early Christian writers took a pacifist line that propagated spiritual, not secular war. The language of the early churches frequently employed military terminology and imagery and created the ideal of the "soldier of Christ" (*miles Christi*).[48] Paul developed a decidedly bellicose register in his letters to the early congregations.[49] He rallied the Ephesians to "put on the whole armor of God" and wield "the sword of the spirit" in their battle against "the rulers of the darkness of this world, against spiritual wickedness in high places" (Eph. 6:10–18). In the first few centuries, such martial valor was thought only appropriate for *spiritual* soldiers of Christ, and most leaders of the early Church agreed that military service was incompatible with the faith. As the new religion spread throughout the Roman Empire, however, it also gained converts among soldiers who now had to negotiate conflicts between their military and spiritual duties.

The reaction of their fellow Christians was divided. Around the year 200, one Christian legionary refused to wear the laurel crown customary during victory sacrifices and was executed for his insubordination. To some Christians this martyrdom over a seeming triviality was embarrassing because it appeared to validate those pagans who took Christian pacifism and the refusal to partake in sacrifices as proof of the fundamentally antisocial nature of the Christ cult. Tertullian, however, praised the soldier martyr's steadfastness and condemned fair-weather Christians who compromised their faith rather than endanger themselves.[50] Tertullian went on to explain the spiritual dangers of the military profession and advised his readers not to join the legions in order to avoid dilemmas that threatened either their life or their salvation. Soldier converts should leave the legions as soon as they could, or in any case avoid actions not permitted to a Christian, which was nearly impossible. The early Church therefore already identified the fundamental conflict between the exigencies of soldiering and those of the Christian life that early modern writers still grappled with.

This tension produced several soldier martyrs like Maximilian of Tebessa. Executed in 295, Maximilian did not explicitly object to killing but to the military life in its entirety. When interrogated by proconsul Dion about why he did not want to serve in the army, Maximilian replied that his faith forbade sinning. To him "soldiering" (*militare*) was the same as "doing evil" (*malefacere*).[51] When asked what offences he thought soldiers guilty of, Maximilian retorted fairly cryptically, "you know what they do." In his protracted attempts to remove Maximilian's scruples, Dion mentioned the many Christians who served Rome, even in the imperial bodyguard. Evidently, few Christian soldiers thought their faith to be fundamentally at odds with their profession. Their numbers cannot be assessed with confidence, but the purge of Christian legionaries that escalated into the "great" Diocletian Persecution (302–3) suggests that their presence was widespread enough to cause anxiety, yet not too daunting to cripple the legions or cause a serious mutiny.[52] During the first two centuries of its existence Christianity thus already experienced the contradictions of theological pacifism, the few saintly conscientious objectors who embraced martyrdom over a sinful military life, and the contrasting reality of a growing number of legionaries who managed to reconcile soldiering with their Christian faith.

The Edict of Milan (313) prompted a radical change in the position on warfare in the Roman Church, and Christian "loyal indifference" toward the state gave way to an eagerness to take public responsibilities.[53] The doctrinal adjustments necessary for participation in secular affairs including military service were realized swiftly, and just one year after the edict, the synod of Arles threatened to excommunicate any believer who refused to serve in the army of a Christian emperor. But wielding worldly power posed a new problem: how could Christians justly fight secular wars? It took another century before Augustine of Hippo formulated the first viable Christian doctrine of just warfare that accommodated the demands of the spiritual as well as the political realm. His position on war was essentially a Christianized rendering of Greco-

26 ❧ *Faith in War*

Roman theories of the just war, which was legitimate for the purposes of defense, the recovery of lost goods and lands, and the punishment of enemy transgressions.[54] The Christian state could now defend wars as just, but the reality of wars, especially the men who fought them, remained a source of concern.

After the disintegration of the Western Roman Empire, the Christianization of the Germanic tribes and the consolidation of their kingdoms brought with it the increased problem of violence and warfare between Christians. The legions of the Roman Empire had been a predominantly peripheral phenomenon, employed in conquest or guarding the borders, whereas Germanic societies, in which generally speaking every free man was a warrior, were permeated with violence. Feudal society entailed a clearer division of social duties, determined predominantly by birth, in which waging violence was the privilege and duty of the nobility. At the same time, prestige and standing depended on honor, which in turn was most commonly gained and defended through violence. Feuds and other small-scale conflicts were a perpetual problem that proved impossible to eradicate for about a millennium. Low-ranking knights (*milites*), often landless and therefore dependent on the rewards of violence, were the greatest source of concern. The "Peace of God" and "Truce of God," promoted by the Church from the eleventh century onward to limit and guide violent conflict, were directed at the *milites* especially.[55] The Peace of God intended to exempt certain categories of noncombatants from military violence, while the Truce of God tried to limit the time available for fighting by prescribing periods of peace.

The language in which medieval critics disparaged the violent and otherwise immoral behavior of the knighthood begins to resemble early modern condemnations of soldierly vice more clearly. Crusading ideology was also partially driven by a desire to redirect the destructive potential of Christian warriors outward into the "God-pleasing" project of reconquering the Holy Land. Chroniclers recorded Urban II's appeal to the knighthood to go on crusade differently but agreed on the underlying sentiment. Fulcher of Chartres quoted Urban as saying: "Now will those who once were robbers become *Christi milites*; those who once fought brothers and relatives will justly fight barbarians; those who once were mercenaries for a few farthings will obtain eternal reward."[56] Baldric of Dol's pope was rather more outspoken: "you pervert [knighthood] in wickedness . . . you oppressors of orphans and widows, you murderers, you temple-defilers, you lawbreakers, who seek the rewards of rapacity from spilling Christian blood."[57]

Bernard de Clairvaux's *De laude novae militiae* (ca. 1130), the *apologia* for the Knights Templar, also criticized knightly misbehavior in a way that is strongly reminiscent of early modern condemnations. Punning on the near homophony of *militia* ("soldiery," "knighthood") and *malitia* ("knavery," "vice"), Bernard reserved the term *militia* for the Templars, while secular knights were summarily slighted as *malitia*.[58] Bernard criticized knightly pomp, flamboyancy, and effeminate fashions and commended the Templars for their commitment to "earn their bread," rejecting idle amusements like dice, chess, hunting, and falconry, and for avoiding the "vanities and deceitful follies" of "jesters, wizards, bards, bawdy minstrels and jousters."[59] Apart from their dissolute pastimes, worldly knights endangered their spiritual welfare when they fought and killed as a result of "flashes of irrational anger, hunger for empty glory or hankering after some earthly possessions"; they lacked right intention, one of the Augustinian requisites that made killing not sinful.[60] Bernard concluded that secular knights did not fight "for God but for the devil," as we have seen, another judgment echoed by early modern writers.[61] While Bernard's *De laude* is a particularly prominent example, warnings that a sudden death drenched in sin and its terrible consequences in the hereafter were a danger especially for young men were commonly offered, not only by clerics. Philip de Novara, for example, composed his *Les Quatre Âges de l'Homme* around 1265, toward the end of a busy life of war and politics in Outremer. He, too, warned that youths (by which he meant unmarried men up to the age of forty) were by their nature compelled to seek luxury, through their inexperience, arrogance, and stupidity likely to lose their lives in its pursuit, and due to their negligence in spiritual matters bound to face God in a less than promising condition.[62]

Compared to regular knights, men denounced as mercenaries attracted even stronger slurs such as "devastators" (*vastatores*), "arsonists" (*incendarii*), "robbers" (*raptores*), or "barbarians" (*barbarii*).[63] The distinction between "knights" and "mercenaries" was difficult to draw, especially for the lower and less affluent ranks, and often vanished altogether. Errantry, the quest for adventure and opportunities to prove one's bravery, was central to the chivalric code, as was *largesse*, the generous distribution of spoils among subordinate knights. An armed force gained cohesion through "a downward flow of largesse" from the warlord, which in turn secured "an upward flow of loyalty" among the *milites*.[64] In chivalric tales, such rewards usually came in the form of magnificent horses, weapons, or other goods, but in reality, cash payments became common in the thirteenth century.[65] Vassals were customarily obliged to serve their lord for forty days and expected recompense for time spent campaigning beyond this time. Consequently, it may have mattered ideologically whether a warlord bestowed a gift on a loyal knight or paid him for his service, but it is ultimately a moot point. Professional warriors were paid in one form or another and the difference between a "knight errant" and a "mercenary" was essentially a matter of perspective.

Popes repeatedly condemned the mercenary contractors (*condottieri*) and their troops who devastated the Italian peninsula from the thirteenth century onward. Pope Innocent III even called for a crusade against the marauding mercenary bands in France and Italy in 1215, and thereby placed mercenaries beyond the margins of Christian society.[66] Similarly, Urban V declared mercenaries "pagans, and people not redeemed by Christ's blood," and summarily excommunicated all European mercenaries and their employers in the bull *Clamat ad nos* (1366).[67] The bull had little effect, however, as warlords (including popes) had no choice but to hire mercenaries. The case of John Hawkwood, an immensely successful English *condottiere*, exemplifies the mixed messages the Church sent regarding the employment of mercenaries. His biographer William Caffero writes: "When Hawkwood fought for Milan against papal armies in 1371, the pope denounced him as a 'son of Belial.'" When Hawkwood joined the pope the next year and won several battles, he was hailed as "an athlete of God and a faithful Christian knight."[68] Demonizing the mercenary was thus not a genuinely religious statement but political rhetoric that invoked religious terms. The profession as such was problematic but its condemnation depended crucially on perspective and situation. When the papacy had the cash to hire mercenaries, it did; when they served a more solvent enemy, the Vatican reviled the profession. This contingency was readily recognizable and it seems that few paid attention to what Rome's position *du jour* happened to be. The Vatican used its religious powers and employed religious terminology to exert an influence on its secular affairs and set a precedent that would become the shared heritage of all confessions after the Reformation. Late medieval secular powers also condemned mercenaries in religious terms. In the mid-fifteenth century, Bohemian mercenaries were summarily accused of being Hussites to accentuate their depravity.[69] In this context, allegations of heresy also sought to tarnish the reputations of the Bohemians' employers. Duke Ludwig of Bavaria-Ingolstadt fell under the imperial ban in 1434 for hiring Bohemian contingents. During the Soest Feud (1444–49) the archbishop of Cologne's enemies branded him "the heretic" (*ketter*) for his reliance on Bohemian troops, and as late as 1504, Maximilian I could obtain crusading indulgences after his opponents had hired Bohemian mercenaries in the Landshut War of Succession.[70]

Rhetorical condemnations of soldiers were therefore established long before the *Landsknechte* emerged. Rooted in the earliest Christian texts, a negative trope developed that demonized objectionable military traits and led medieval writers to condemn warriors as "pagan," "unchristian," and "godless." Furthermore, it seems that the lower echelons of the military hierarchy elicited the greatest concerns. The stereotype and the rhetoric of the "unchristian" soldier were thus neither new nor specific to the early modern common infantryman when they were reapplied to the "new" type of soldier that emerged in the decades before 1500. This explains why condemnations of the *Landsknecht* were so thoroughly formulaic from the beginning. The stereotype did not arise spontaneously, nor was it necessarily reflective of reality. Early modern detractors merely transplanted a well-established rhetorical tradition onto the new type of warring commoners whose existence, as we will see in the following, was feared to threaten nothing less than the collapse of the Christian social order.

Rebels Against the Divine Social Order

As we have seen, the fiercest early modern denunciations were usually directed specifically at the lower ranks like the *Landsknecht* infantrymen. But what—apart from their martial prowess—made the rank and file so threatening? Fundamentally, these soldiers were perceived as uncontrollable and threatening to the social order. The divinely appointed social hierarchy envisioned a threefold division of society into those who prayed (clergy), those who ruled and fought (nobility), and those who toiled (commoners). To wage war and to control and wield violence was an aristocratic prerogative that was regulated, at least in theory, by the code of chivalry.[71] No comparable ideology was in place to control the rapidly growing numbers of soldiering commoners. In fact, the tenets of chivalry often *explicitly* did not apply to common infantry. The obligation of *clementia* ("clemency") to spare a surrendering enemy, for example, extended to mounted knights only; men-at-arms fighting on foot were not necessarily accorded such protections.[72] The presence of commoners in the military sphere as such was not new. Nicholas Wright has shown that only ten percent of the combatants in the Hundred Years War were formally knighted. The rest either thought their noble status self-evident, or claimed membership of the knighthood because they carried out the knightly work, irrespective of their birth.[73] Anxieties around these men grew in proportion to the growing massification of the armies in the late fifteenth century and the emergence of a potentially worrying mass of soldiers to whom the old martial customs generally did not apply.

Further compounding this problem was the notion that the knight's compliance with the chivalric code was his own responsibility and a matter of honor. As this ideology did not include commoners, however, *ius in bello* had to be updated to effectively control the changing character of warfare, a process that took several decades. As we will see in later chapters, soldiers had a very clear sense of what form and degree of violence was legitimate, but from an outside perspective, the new type of warrior initially appeared to operate in a legal gray zone at best. During this period, the mostly implicit military norms that governed violence within the military sphere were difficult to comprehend (or take seriously) for outsiders. In this context, we should note that the second half of the sixteenth century witnessed a marked increase in the publication of military manuals and literature on martial legal theory and praxis, which could indicate that they were responding to the pressing need for a legal handle on the changing realities of warfare.[74]

The initial problem of a widely unregulated military was compounded by the fact that soldiers eluded civil and ecclesiastical jurisdiction the moment they swore their oath on the articles of war and entered the autonomous legal realm of the regiment.[75] This legal separation of the civilian and military spheres could be a cause for concern. While proponents of social reform were busily—and often rather unsuccessfully—trying to implement new regimes of moral and religious discipline, for a long time the articles of war remained rather lax in this respect.[76] From the outside at least, the military therefore looked like a safe haven for those who wanted to lead a life of wantonness and dissolution, which further enhanced the view that it was the morally bankrupt who most eagerly sought out the military profession. In certain circumstances, military society could be presented as a well-regimented realm. Jan Willem Huntebrinker has shown that in contrast to the image of dissolution, an alternative mode of representing the military as a "good" order was propagated especially in military manuals.[77] He also points out, however, that portrayals of the hierarchical military order were intentionally designed to communicate a sense of legal containment of military power and therefore appear as a reaction to contemporary fears of an untamed soldiery.

While such representations, in addition to the supposedly moderating influence of noble officers and the quite rapidly evolving articles of war, might have alleviated the fears of untamed, godless common soldiers visiting violence upon defenseless civilians, there remained a fundamental problem, namely that commoners could never hope to be *de militari sanguine,* "of knightly blood."[78] Fighting in war was considered a natural monopoly but also a natural duty of the nobility for which they were thought to possess an innate competence. In other words, nobles were compelled to wage war by birth; it was not their choice. Commoners on the other hand had been put on Earth to support the warring caste with their labor; they were not supposed to become soldiers unless their sovereign called them to arms. For a commoner to want to fight, let alone have a penchant for violence, could be read as a sign of degeneracy.[79] Violence was regarded as pathological by some: Paracelsus, for instance, considered the warrior to be a choleric who was both internally, by his choleric temperament, and externally, by the influence of Mars, induced to be violent.[80] This was a common perception and it has been pointed out that around 1600 the choleric temperament was frequently represented as a soldier.[81] Against this background, the allegations of "innate depravity" the moralists leveled at soldiers begin to make sense to a modern reader: fundamentally, soldiers and other individuals who needlessly chose a life of violence could be considered to be of "poor stock."[82]

In the past, when commoners had been levied by their sovereigns, they had fought out of obligation and as subjects. The new soldiers were commoners who left their station in life of their own volition and therefore *chose* to violate the divinely instituted social order when they entered a realm that was not their designated habitat. Precisely the voluntariness with which commoners actively sought war instead of plying their civilian trade until they were called to serve had led Luther to the conclusion that they could not "be on good terms with God."[83] Those work-shy men who left their regular professions to become soldiers were accused of living off the peasants' labor in order to indulge in their

"A New Order of Soulless Men"? :~ 31

sinful boozing, gluttony, and idleness.[84] A commoner's resolution to become a *Landsknecht* could consequently already be regarded as sinful, but it was also feared to be a source of social instability. Leaving one's allotted station in life was feared to create gaps in the social brickwork, as by enlisting, the common soldier was no longer able to serve the purpose in society that God had allocated to him. This was Eberlin's point when he charged soldiers with deserting their families, country, and sworn service, and given that the size of armies positively exploded during the early modern period, such fears were not altogether unfounded.[85]

That soldiers entered their profession voluntarily also made them personally accountable for their deeds. The culpability for waging an unjust war had previously been solely that of the warlord; his followers, duty-bound to follow their liege, had been considered blameless.[86] A mercenary soldier, however, could no longer hide behind the prince: if he fought in an unjust war or behaved unjustly, he was personally accountable for this sin. Andreas Musculus addressed the problem in detail and claimed that commoners in the past had gone to war in the assuring knowledge that they were serving their rightful lord and thus God. The feudal levy had eliminated choice and the uncertainty regarding the justness of the cause that arose from it.[87] Musculus repeated Luther's arguments for why nobles should be soldiers and added that, as surplus Protestant noblemen could no longer be deposited in monasteries or be expected to work manually, wars were needed more than ever to keep these gentlemen occupied.[88] Turning his attention to commoners, he recommended that those who already were soldiers should stay in their profession and take great care to lead God-pleasing lives (as we have seen, this was a recommendation that Tertullian had already given to Christian neophytes thirteen centuries previously). Young men who had not yet learned an occupation and were entertaining the idea of becoming warriors could, strictly speaking, do so without imperiling their salvation. But Musculus warned of the immoral environment and suggested that they might find another occupation, as there were enough "evil knaves" (*böser buben*) to take their place in the armies.[89] Men who already had a profession should remain in it and only go to war to defend their home, their sovereign, or when soldiers were needed to fight the Ottomans. As these examples suggest, the fact that commoners were perceived to abandon their station in life in order to become soldiers caused trepidation and for a commoner to join the army could be interpreted as an act of rebellion against God's order.

Their dislocation and ambulant lifestyle meant that soldiers joined another marginalized social group, that of vagrants.[90] Robert Jütte defines vagrants as migrants who were "poor, unemployed, capable of earning a living, rootless and suspicious" and soldiers accounted for a significant portion of this section of society.[91] Anxieties surrounding vagrants and other mobile groups had multiple sources. They were considered masterless and thus uncontrolled and their constant mobility made them uncontrollable, as they eluded the social and legal mechanisms that regulated communal life. Sturdy beggars, those who could work but would not, were seen as morally reprehensible because they lived off the industriousness of others while they themselves were "useless to God and the world," as a late fifteenth-century chronicler remarked.[92] Finally, the association of the ambulant society of the road with criminality was often rather accurate. With regards to soldiers, Huntebrinker has clarified that contemporaries did distinguish between soldiers' necessary work-related wandering—to the muster or returning home—and the illegitimate loitering of the *Gartknechte*.[93] The *Gartknechte*, demobilized soldiers who tried to survive by begging and engaging in various degrees of criminal behavior, were staples in sixteenth and seventeenth-century mandates against vagrants and beggars. These veterans could endanger the safety of entire regions, especially if small bands amalgamated into larger *Garthaufen*, which could number several thousand unemployed, unpaid, and armed men and their families.[94] Ambrosius Pape, a Magdeburg pastor and writer of moralist literature, devoted a lengthy tract to the phenomenon of *garten*, in which he not only lamented the very real threat that the *Gartknechte* posed but, again, established a direct connection between the unemployed *Landsknechte* and the devil.[95]

But why did the ambulant lifestyle, which characterized the military profession, affect soldiers' moral and religious image? Early modern society did not perceive its constituents as "empirical-social" entities but in "normative-ethical" categories, so that lifestyle was taken to indicate a person's moral mindset.[96] As the household was considered the smallest unit of Christian society, those without a home and no stable existence could be considered antisocial and by extension even unchristian.[97] Sturdy beggars, aimless wanderers, and unemployed soldiers were all considered idlers: if they could roam, they could equally well support themselves by honest work. Peter Burschel has pointed out that early modern stigmatization of vagrants as "idlers" not only denied the dire destitution on the roads but also entirely ignored the fact that work became increasingly scarce as the sixteenth century progressed.[98] In the case of the soldiers, however, a rejection of manual labor was not just a matter of defamation but was defended by soldiers as a privilege of their special status as "free warriors."[99] *Landsknecht* songs often proudly contrasted the plight of the peasantry or other laborers with the work-free life of the soldier.[100] It appears, then, that the accusations of "idleness" were not groundless. At the same time, this aspect illustrates how civilian perspectives and military self-perception interpreted soldierly behavior in opposing ways: what soldiers claimed and defended as a proud warrior's privilege, moralist commentators branded as viciously decadent idleness.

What the examination of the stereotype, its long history, and its contextualization have shown so far is that what made soldiers "unchristian" and "godless" were actions and behaviors that may appear antisocial but not necessarily antireligious. While such a distinction is difficult to defend for the early modern cultural context in which the social and the religious were one, it is important to bear in mind that the stereotype did not encompass spiritual heterodoxy. Soldiers were accused of living in a "godless" manner suggestive of a dangerous indifference to God's laws, but in this they were not extraordinary: from a moralist's perspective, "godlessness" was a characteristic of the times.

The Stereotype and Its Social Effects

The stereotype applied to real people and we have to wonder to what degree social stigma affected men and their families when they left their homes to join the armies. Throughout the period of study, there was no shortage of men of all social backgrounds willing to join the armies, which suggests that the moralists' attempts to tarnish the profession were not entirely successful. The ability to derive hilarity from soldiers' outrageous behavior and their clear potential for fascination has been noted in relation to the humorous stories at the beginning of this chapter, and this points toward a greater cultural ambivalence toward soldiers than the survey of moralist vituperations suggests. *Landsknechte* occupied an ambiguous position in woodcuts from the early stages of the Reformation. They were frequently presented as the enemies of lecherous clerics and the pope and as champions of the Gospel, but also as the troops of the papal Antichrist.[101] The *Landsknecht* type in German imagery soon all but lost the potential to symbolize positive qualities, and while this rendered the *Landsknecht* an unlikely choice to represent pious fortitude, the stereotypical immoral mercenary did not cause uniform disgust.[102]

The degree to which the choice to become a soldier could impugn a man's reputation depended on his social background and his circumstances. For noblemen, military service remained a matter of course. Even high-ranking clerics like Salentin von Isenburg, archbishop of Cologne and prince-bishop of Paderborn, could take time off from their clerical duties to go to war without raising too many eyebrows.[103] But even noble soldiers were expected to show greater refinement than their stereotypical inferiors. Salentin's successor as archbishop of Cologne, Gebhard Truchsess von Waldburg, was thought to have been led into apostasy and rebellion by the soldiers whose indecent company he kept. The Cologne electoral councilor Gerhard von Kleinsorgen suggested as much in his account of the early years of the Cologne War (1583–88) when he rejected rumors that Gebhard's behavior was the result of a sincere conversion. Gebhard and his brother had spent the winter of 1582 with cavalry officers and soldiers and engaged in heavy drinking and dissolute living. Kleinsorgen found the situation summed up in Ecclesiastes 19:2: "Wine and women will make

34 ~: *Faith in War*

men of understanding to fall away," that is, to apostatize.[104] Soldiering therefore remained part of a normal aristocratic male life; the behaviors associated with common soldiers, however, were not necessarily exculpated by higher birth.

For commoners, poverty and desperation were legitimate reasons to join the armies. This also meant that poorer people were more likely to end up in the armies than sons of more affluent parents, not least because the families of the latter would often go to considerable lengths to prevent their relatives from taking this desperate step. The stigma of being related to a soldier was felt most keenly by the respectable urban elites and this potential for shame grew more acute as the sixteenth century progressed. Earlier in the century, joining the armies seemed like an honorable and profitable career move for the scions of non-aristocratic elite families like Sebastian Schertlin, whose father was a forest superintendent, councilor, and mayor of Burtenbach in Swabia. Schertlin joined the armies in 1519, aged twenty-two and equipped with an MA from the University of Tübingen, an education that would help him in his convoluted but highly successful military career and social ascent.[105] For Schertlin, becoming a soldier was the source of unabashed self-satisfaction and he was not shy to record his personal social advancement nor the money he made in detail.

This pride became more muted in later autobiographies penned by military men who had joined the armies as commoners. This may well be due to different personal temperaments, but it is also plausible that such a step carried greater social stigma as the sixteenth century progressed. Looking back on a successful life in the 1580s, Captain Georg Niege described his enlistment as a common soldier in his rhymed autobiography.[106] He tells a pitiful story of a studious young man who was forced into the army by poverty, overcame adversity, and built a remarkable career. Born in 1525, Niege earned a scholarship from his hometown of Allendorf in Hesse to study theology at the University of Marburg where he obtained his bachelor's degree in 1545. In the poem for that year, Niege describes that his circumstances became unbearable and that poverty drove him to enlist as a *Landsknecht*. Army life and the sinful behavior of the common soldiery shocked the former theology student, at least according to his autobiography, and Niege henceforth sought to better his station in life—and succeeded. He had a steep career in military and civilian administration, at several points commanded his own company of soldiers, fought all over the Holy Roman Empire, France, the Low Countries, and Scotland, and eventually became a respected judge and governmental official. His decision to join the army instead of continuing his studies had certainly paid off, but Niege told a lie: he was not destitute at all when he joined the army, as he could have extended his scholarship to a maximum of seven years.

Niege's decision to leave university coincided with the introduction of a new, stricter code of conduct for students, and the wish to escape the increasingly

"A New Order of Soulless Men"? ∾ 35

stuffy moral regime of the Marburg theology faculty may have played a role. The stipend he received was intentionally calculated to prevent the recipients from drinking too much, and perhaps Georg's student experience was not what he had hoped for.[107] But his sensibilities proved too delicate for the "heinous life" of the *Landsknechte*:

> I saw with anguish what wantonness occurred daily,
> with gorging, boozing, blaspheming, and swearing,
> so that I often hid in the hay and straw to escape it
> and left these fellows to their boasting and intimidations.
> In their merrymaking one soldier often injured another,
> wounded, crippled, and killed him.[108]

The first rung on the ladder back to respectability was to secure a position as a regimental scribe, a job that separated him from the rank and file, and his career took off from here. Especially given the ultimate profitability of his decision to join the army, one wonders why Niege invented poverty as a reason for his departure from the university. The most plausible explanation for old Niege's unease with his younger self's life choices was that the powerful stereotype of the "godless" soldier haunted him sufficiently to put a spin on his account of how he first joined the *Landsknechte*.

In many ways, Sebastian Schertlin's background and entry into the military realm was similar to Georg Niege's. But unlike Niege, who invented poverty to defend his enlistment, Schertlin had no compunction about his decisions whatsoever. A generation lay between Schertlin and Niege and it seems that the stigma grew in this time; what was maybe a bold but wise move for the older man shamed the younger.

Soldiering relatives could be embarrassing even to burgher families who did not quite live up to expectations of respectability in other respects. The family of the Cologne councilor Hermann Weinsberg, for instance, included several illegitimate relatives. Not only were these "bastard" children integrated into the Weinsberg clan, but their messy composition also amused the family. When Weinsberg's "natural or bastard" sister Gertrud had her own legitimate son baptized, their father joked that of his three recently born grandchildren, one was the illegitimate child of his legitimate son (this was Hermann's illegitimate daughter Anna), the second the legitimate child of his legitimate daughter, and the third the legitimate child of his illegitimate daughter.[109] The tragic fate of Weinsberg's nephew Johann Kuckelmann was no laughing matter, however. Johann's story appears typical in many ways, not just in terms of the events that led to his enlistment but also in the way he brought shame on his family. His uncle described him as a "wild fellow" who had ignored his family's financial advice and eventually hit rock bottom.[110] In 1567, he joined the Spanish army, but his luck quickly ran out: he was killed in Friesland when he tried to plun-

36 ❦ *Faith in War*

der a farm. The body was left unburied for several days. The entire affair—the young man's squandering, his desperate escape into the army, the circumstances of his death, the dishonorable treatment of his corpse, and his widow Tringin Wilderman's return to Cologne where she begged support from the family—caused considerable embarrassment and Weinsberg ended his entry with a plea that God may forgive Johann his sins.

For burgher families like the Weinsbergs, the decision of their relatives to join the armies was awkward; for others, it amounted to a social catastrophe. The reaction of Werner von Bert's relatives to his decision to become a soldier speaks of their disgust with the profession.[111] Werner, a younger son, had been sent away as an apprentice, but in late 1609, he ran away from his master and returned to his hometown of Wesel, apparently determined to join the army. His mother and friends of the family tried to dissuade him, but they eventually had to accept that Werner would be the first soldier in the family, as his uncle Heinrich von Weseken noted, not without adding the deflated plea "God convert him."[112] The von Berts tried to make the best out of a terrible situation. His brother bought him a fine horse worth 60 *reichsthaler*, thus making sure he would serve in the more prestigious cavalry, not the despised infantry, and secured him a position under a noble ensign.[113] If Werner had to be a soldier, he should at least serve among the social elite. Werner continued to tarnish his own and another family's reputations over the next two years that his regiment remained in the region. He bragged about an apparently invented affair with a burgher's daughter from nearby Borken, to which the unsuspecting "lover" and her parents responded by accusing Werner of being an "honor-thief" (*Ehrendieff*) before the town council.[114] These were serious allegations and the councilors showed leniency only because he was about to go to war and thus would remove himself from the community. His uncle's account shows that not just his immediate but the extended family considered Werner to damage their reputation: it had been a source of familial pride not to have a soldier for a relative.

Dissolute men like Johann Kuckelmann and Werner von Bert brought shame on their families because they conformed to the early modern soldier stereotype embarrassingly exactly. It was the recklessness or even willfulness with which they had maneuvered themselves into the disreputable position that was most disagreeable to their relatives. Werner's uncle Heinrich von Weseken showed considerable empathy with young men who were *forced* into soldiering by circumstance, like Hänßken Langenbergh, a boy from the neighborhood who had to enter military service after his father had bankrupted the family.[115] Contemporaries therefore did not summarily condemn the decision to join the armies but evaluated the circumstances. Poverty and destitution were acceptable reasons for commoners to take up soldiering and many men appear to have become soldiers for precisely these reasons. Less dramatically, one might add a general hope of social advancement to the list of reasons that seemed legitimate or at least acceptable. Overall, however, the social reputation of common soldiers worsened continuously until the mid-seventeenth century and in this sense, the steady reiterations of the catalogue of soldiers' vices, coupled with the very real and increasing devastation caused by warfare, affected soldiers' social standing negatively.

How this decline in reputation was reflected in the sociability between soldiers and civilians is less clear. Ann Tlusty has produced evidence from Augsburg that soldiers and craftsmen could be found drinking together in the sixteenth but not in the seventeenth century, and this may be related to gradually hardening boundaries within the society of orders.[116] In other places, however, early seventeenth-century authorities were alarmed because civilians and soldiers mingled *so much*, for example in Wesel, where especially young people found the dances and the untaxed alcohol of the Spanish occupiers very attractive indeed.[117] Overall, interactions between soldiers and civilians defy generalization. As we will see in greater detail in Chapter 3, there is evidence for a rather full spectrum of civilian attitudes toward soldiers, ranging from outright disgust to wariness to neutral interactions, friendship, and even love. The degree to which the stereotype of the godless soldier colored these encounters is often difficult to tell, but as we have seen, it was certainly potent enough to embarrass relatives of men who conformed to this stereotype too closely and it moved men to invent exculpating circumstances when their original motives for enlistment seemed too indelicate in an otherwise impressive autobiography.

Bob Scribner has described four different modes of classification of deviance that were operative in early modern German society: social dysfunctionality, economical dysfunctionality, vagrancy, and sociolegal anomalies.[118] Soldiers were extraordinary in the sense that they fit into *all* of these modes of classification. As we have seen, they were considered socially dysfunctional in a number of ways: they were perceived to upturn the divinely appointed social order, desert their station in life, and supposedly live in a godless manner. Soldiers were associated with economical dysfunctionality through their alleged love of luxury, their squandering of money on drink, prostitutes, and gambling, and their begging that arose from this wastefulness. They were professional vagrants. Finally, they were a legal anomaly as they belonged under regimental jurisdiction, beyond the reach of civil and ecclesiastical authority, a characteristic that will be explored in the next chapter. The soldier was therefore associated with the entire spectrum of deviance, and this unique concentration of transgressive behaviors in one sociocultural type goes some way to explaining why mercenary soldiers were presented as arch-sinners in normative sources. Regarding the "godlessness" of soldiers, we have seen that this allegation arose from social tensions and the transgression of moral ideals, but not necessarily, as far as the common list of vice is concerned, from genuine spiritual deviance. The epithets "godless," "unchristian," and so forth have been characterized as

38 ~: *Faith in War*

rhetorical devices to highlight the discrepancy between the envisioned ideal and the perceived reality of soldier life. There is consequently enough reasonable doubt as to the representativeness of the topos of the irreligious soldier and its application to real life. This opens up the possibility, indeed the necessity, to engage with religious attitudes in the military. The following chapters seek to provide some answers.

Notes

1. Sachs, "Der Teuffel lest kein Landsknecht mehr in die Helle faren."
2. Ibid., 58.
3. Ibid.
4. Kirchhof, *Wendunmuth* 13.
5. See Burschel, *Söldner*, 47.
6. Given the frequency with which these concepts have been discussed it seems unnecessary to provide a renewed overview in this context. For discussions of the "civilizing process" and "social discipline" paradigms see Breuer, "Probleme und Problemverlagerungen"; Hsia, *Social Discipline*; and more recently, with an extensive bibliography, Loetz, *Mit Gott handeln*, 50–56.
7. A helpful overview of the concept of *policey* in English is Isenmann, "The Notion of the Common Good." I would like to thank Jamie Page for pointing me toward this chapter.
8. Hale, "Explanations of War and Violence," 20.
9. A collection of twenty-four such tracts was compiled by the bookseller Sigmund Feyerabend and published as the *Theatrum Diabolorum*.
10. Piltz and Schwerhoff, "Religiöse Devianz," 32.
11. Auffarth, "Alle Tage Karneval?" 79–80.
12. For an insightful reflection on the beneficial integration of social psychological and historical studies, see Knights, "Historical Stereotypes and Histories of Stereotypes." I am following Knights's thoughts in this section.
13. A succinct outline of his model can be found in Abric, "Central System, Peripheral Core."
14. Erasmus, "Dulce bellum inexpertis," 415, 437.
15. Erasmus, "Education of a Prince," 282–83.
16. Erasmus, "A Complaint of Peace," 304, 309, 316.
17. Rublack, *Dressing Up*, 143.
18. Eberlin von Günzburg, *Mich wundert das kein gelt ihm land ist*. On Eberlin, see Peters, *Johann Eberlin von Günzburg*.
19. Eberlin, *Mich wundert das kein gelt ihm land ist*, Aii[v]-Aiii[R].
20. Ibid., Aiii[R].
21. Ibid.
22. Luther, "Whether Soldiers, Too, Can Be Saved," 96.
23. Kaeuper, *Chivalry and Violence*, 70.
24. Luther, "Whether Soldiers, Too, Can Be Saved," 131.
25. Ibid., 134.
26. Ibid.
27. Ibid., 101.
28. Luther's explication came just in time, as Cramm died from disease in 1528, see Spangenberg, *AdelsSpiegel*, vol. 2, 58[R]–60[R].

"A New Order of Soulless Men"? ❧ 39

29. Luther, *Tischreden*, vol. 4, 600 (#4987); vol. 2, 301 (#2039).
30. Franck, *Das Kriegbüchlin des frides*, xvii.
31. Ibid., xxxi[R].
32. Ibid., li[V].
33. Ibid., liiii[R]:
34. Musculus, *Beruff und stand*.
35. Ibid., Bi[V].
36. Ibid., Bi[R].
37. Ibid., Aiii[r].
38. Anon., *Auffrichtiger Teutscher Soldaten Regul*, 7, 11.
39. Mengering, *Perversa Ultimi Seculi Militia*, 431.
40. Ibid., 72.
41. Ibid., 660, 662-665.
42. Fronsperger, *Geistliche KriegßOrdnung*, III[R], XXI[R]–XXI[V].
43. Behm, *Kriegesman*, av[R]-av[V].
44. Ibid., 68[V].
45. Ibid., 69[R].
46. Wallhausen, *Kriegskunst zu Fuß*, 6.
47. Ibid., 7.
48. Cf. Harnack, *Militia Christi*, 47.
49. 1 Thess. 5:8; 2 Cor. 6:7; Rom. 6:13–14, 6:23, 13:12; see Harnack, *Militia Christi*, 12.
50. Tertullian, *Of the Crown*.
51. Anon., "Acta Maximiliani," 166–71.
52. Winkelmann, *Geschichte des frühen Christentums*, 27.
53. Demandt, *Geschichte der Spätantike*, 408.
54. Tyerman, *God's War*, 32.
55. See most recently Koziol, *The Peace of God*, as well as Contamine, *War in the Middle Ages*, 270-80, and Kaeuper, *Chivalry and Violence*, 73.
56. Quoted in Kaeuper, *Chivalry and Violence*, 75.
57. Ibid.
58. Bernard of Clairvaux, *In Praise of the New Knighthood*.
59. Ibid., 17, 37, 46–47.
60. Ibid., 38.
61. Ibid., 45.
62. Schulze-Busacker, "Philippe de Novare, les Quatre âges de l'homme," 115–17.
63. Burschel, *Söldner*, 45.
64. Kaeuper, *Chivalry and Violence*, 197.
65. Ibid., 225.
66. Baumann, *Landsknechte*, 14.
67. Caferro, *John Hawkwood*, 116, 127. Note that the pope mentioned the same devil that Mengering claimed had created the soldiery of the seventeenth century.
68. Ibid., 24.
69. Tresp, *Söldner aus Böhmen*, 98.
70. Ibid., 188-91.
71. On chivalric ideal and practice see Keen, *Chivalry*; Kaeuper, *Chivalry and Violence*.
72. Contamine, *War in the Middle Ages*, 257; Schmidtchen, "*Ius in bello*," 38. For descriptions of massacres of prisoners of war in the Middle Ages see McGlynn, *By Sword and Fire*. For the sixteenth and seventeenth centuries refer to Kroener, "Der Soldat als Ware."

40 ❦ Faith in War

73. Wright, *Knights and Peasants*, 9.
74. For example the many editions of Fronsperger's books or Count von Solms's "*Kriegsbuch.*"
75. Möller, *Das Regiment der Landsknechte*, 31–33; Huntebrinker, "Geordneter Sozialverband oder Gegenordnung?"
76. See Chapter 2.
77. Huntebrinker, "Geordneter Sozialverband oder Gegenordnung?" 184–87.
78. On the store set in noble officers see Contamine, *War in the Middle Ages*, 163. On the imagined genetic disposition of the nobility to fight and lead in war see Keen, *Chivalry*, 36; and Baumann, *Landsknechte*, 13.
79. Hale, "Explanations of War and Violence," 12.
80. Goldammer, "Der cholerische Kriegsmann," 95.
81. Huntebrinker, *Fromme Knechte*, 135–36.
82. Hale, "Explanations of War and Violence," 16.
83. Luther, "Whether Soldiers, Too, Can be Saved," 134.
84. Huntebrinker, *Fromme Knechte*, 119–57.
85. Eberlin, *Mich wundert das kein gelt ihm land ist*, Aiii[R].
86. Contamine, *War in the Middle Ages*, 264.
87. Musculus, *Beruff vnd stand*, Di[R]-Diii[R].
88. Ibid., Diii[V]; Luther, "Whether Soldiers, Too, Can be Saved," 127–28.
89. Musculus, *Beruff vnd stand*, Diiii[V].
90. On the migrant element of military life, see Asche, "Krieg, Militär und Migration"; Baumann, *Landsknechte*, 131–45.; Burschel, *Söldner*, 273–317; Huntebrinker, *Fromme Knechte*, 173–186.
91. Jütte, *Poverty and Deviance*, 147.
92. Cited in Jütte, *Abbild und soziale Wirklichkeit*, 46.
93. Huntebrinker, *Fromme Knechte*, 122-27
94. Burschel, *Söldner*, 293, 304–5.
95. Pape, *Bettel vnd Garteteuffel*.
96. Hippel, *Armut, Unterschichten, Randgruppen*, 4.
97. On the centrality of the family in early modern society see Münch, *Lebensformen*, 191–93.
98. Burschel, *Söldner*, 308–9.
99. See Baumann, *Landsknechte*, 121–22; Burschel, *Söldner*, 44, 137–140.
100. See e.g., Anon., "Von dem König aus Frankreich," 12.
101. Roper, "'The Common Man," 1, 4; Baumann, *Landsknechte*, 192–196.; Rogg, *Landsknechte und Reisläufer*, 182–194.; Burschel, *Söldner*, 30.
102. Rogg, *Landsknechte und Reisläufer*, 185.
103. Molitor, *Das Erzbistum Köln im Zeitalter der Glaubenskämpfe*, 200. A papal legate considered him "extravagant and peculiar" in 1576 while acknowledging his leading role among German Catholic princes and it is not clear that this comment was prompted by Salentin's frequent military exploits (ibid., 204).
104. Bruhns, *Tagebuch der Truchsessischen Wirren*, 36–37.
105. Schönhuth, *Leben und Thaten*.
106. Bei der Wieden, *Leben im 16. Jahrhundert*.
107. Ibid., 45–48.
108. Ibid., 50.
109. Weinsberg, *Das Buch Weinsberg, Liber Iuventutis*, fol. 194[R].
110. Ibid., fol. 530[V]–fol. 531[R.]
111. Bambauer and Kleinholz, *Geusen und Spanier*, 324.

112. Ibid.
113. I would like to thank Amanda Eiseman, formerly at the University of Illinois, for estimating the quality of the horse for me.
114. Ibid., 340.
115. Ibid., 390.
116. Tlusty, *Bacchus and Civic Order*, 151.
117. Kleinholz, *Protokolle des Presbyteriums*, 62.
118. Scribner, "Preconditions of Tolerance and Intolerance," 41.

CHAPTER 2

Making Christian Armies
*Military Religious Structures
and the Challenge of Religious Pluralism*

> Forming a moral conscience is an important matter for humans. But in war the formation of honor and of a defiant courage works much better. Priests should guide and instill conscience, commanders and officers [should instill] honor and courage.
>
> —Lazarus von Schwendi, "Kriegsdiskurs"

This pithy advice was included in the military manual that Lazarus von Schwendi, veteran soldier, diplomat, and councilor to three emperors, wrote in 1577 for the young archduke and future emperor Matthias. Schwendi, an irenic Catholic who never gave up hope that the schism would be resolved and counseled steadfast forbearance in the religious affairs of the Empire, nicely condensed the attitudes of military authorities toward the question of religion in the armies. Of course provisions for soldiers' spiritual welfare should be made, of course chaplains should be hired, and, of course, "unchristian" behaviors should be proscribed. But the primary concern of military authorities was to create operational armies, not godly ones. In order to achieve this, warlords had to take a different approach to the soldiers they employed than to the subjects they ruled. In the logic of the time, the latter *should* be convinced or coerced into confessional conformity, as it was the temporal ruler's responsibility before God to prevent his subjects from damning themselves through religious error and sin. The relationship between a warlord and his troops, on the other hand, was predominantly professional, and even though armies were de facto ambulant communities, they existed only temporarily and were often composed of other rulers' subjects. The religious dimension of the professional setting that military authorities constructed for their troops—for example through the legal codes they issued or the chaplains they hired—mattered nevertheless, as all armies were confessional composites and the containment of religious tensions was of great importance to prevent internal conflict.

For any aspiring sixteenth or seventeenth-century warlord, the task of assembling, maintaining, and governing armies could be daunting. Apart from the competition for the best troops between political actors, logistical demands that more often than not exceeded capacities, the chronic inability to raise sufficient funds, and the resultant bankruptcies experienced by even the wealthiest warring crowns, the troops themselves were deeply worrisome. Soldiers were notorious for their readiness to desert, go on strike, or mutiny if pay was outstanding, when living conditions were too bad, or if they felt that their employers were not honoring their end of the contract in other ways. We have also seen that soldiers were portrayed as downright diabolical, but be that as it may, princes depended on these men if they wanted to fight wars.

While these difficulties were rooted in the structures of premodern European warfare, religious fragmentation exacerbated them after 1517. Especially in the German lands, the Reformation made fast advances among all social strata, including soldiers of all ranks. The potential for conflict that this division created was quickly recognized by military authorities. The word "potential" must be stressed here, because military society generally managed to contain confessional conflict remarkably well. This chapter begins to answer the question of how this feat was achieved by examining how military authorities created a professional realm that accommodated Christians of all denominations.

Investigating the means by which authorities sought to facilitate confessional coexistence in this period may seem counterintuitive. Not only are we dealing with the period of religious war among Christians, but more generally we think of early modern authorities as being engaged in the enforcement of confessional homogeneity, not the cultivation of multiconfessional environments. The ambition, intensity, and success of confessionalization varied greatly both geographically and chronologically, but there remains the basic fact that civilian authorities endeavored to reform their subjects according to uniform doctrinal precepts. While confessionalizing programs aimed at the establishment of orthodoxy among the populace, it often came at the hefty cost of social division and strife. Confessionalization defined, built, and defended doctrinal borders and sought to homogenize populations through the eradication of dissent and the destruction of the irenic or indifferent modes of coexistence that emerged in many multiconfessional locales. In some instances, military force—either threatened or concrete—became a tool of religious coercion, but we know rather little about how confessionalization played out *within* the military. As we will see, isolated attempts at introducing decidedly confessional measures in the armies only occurred from the 1630s onward in the Holy Roman Empire and had very little (if any) effect. For most of the period, warlords had to

44 ❧ *Faith in War*

repress their confessionalizing inclinations in relation to the armies they employed. In order to wage war against enemies secular and religious, warlords had to make their armies tolerant social spaces.

While historians have examined the religious governance of the "standing" armies that were established across Europe from the later seventeenth century onward, the preceding period we are concerned with has received far less attention. Studies on the later seventeenth and eighteenth centuries have found that neither confessionalization nor social discipline played much of a role in military life.[1] Ralf Pröve has shown that by around 1700, toleration had become a central value of military law and that intolerance was denounced as unchristian in military society.[2] He also describes conflicts between confessionally minded secular and confessionally indifferent military authorities who defended toleration as a military custom, indicating a marked difference in military and civilian confessional attitudes around 1700.[3] It remains to be seen if this tolerant atmosphere developed in reaction to earlier confessional strife or whether the military had always remained free from confessional tensions throughout the Reformation period.

The primary tasks of this chapter are to provide an outline of the religious provisions that warlords made for their troops; to get a sense of the religious attitudes they sought to foster; and to determine the degree to which confessionalizing ambitions were reflected in their organization. Examining the ways in which military authorities regulated religious life is important for several reasons. At the most fundamental level, legal and organizational structures set the parameters within which religious life unfolded and thus shaped it. Legal codes in particular were intended to guide behaviors and therefore reflect the wishes, concerns, and ideals of the authorities that developed and implemented them. Finally, the professional environment in which people negotiated their confessional differences also had a profound influence on their ability to coexist and successfully manage conflict.

We will move from the general to the specific: First, religious attitudes manifested in the articles of war will be examined in order to understand the broader legal setting in which military religious life took its course. As the regiment was not just an autonomous legal realm in the abstract but an actual ambulant community, the role of the field preacher—the company's parish priest, as it were—matters greatly, as these men were in charge of spiritual life and often were the only clerics available to soldiers and their families. The organization and provision of adequately trained clergy was a major preoccupation of all churches in the period, and, as we will see, the attendant problems were even more pronounced in the military than they were in civilian parishes. Finally, we will turn to spiritual literature aimed at soldiers. Official prayer books that were issued by warlords to their soldiers only appeared in the 1630s, but they had informal precursors that are instructive when trying to gain a sense of the spiritual values authors wanted to communicate to soldiers.

Religious Regulations in Articles of War

Upon swearing their oath, soldiers entered military jurisdiction under the authority of the regimental colonel and his staff. They remained in this legal realm until they were dismissed, were captured, died, or the regiment as a whole was disbanded. Each regiment was an autonomous legal entity, a total institution with its own jurisdiction, executive personnel, and legal code, the so-called articles of war (*Artikelsbriefe*).[4] The articles were essentially lists of rights and duties on which soldiers swore an oath, and at least theoretically formed the basis on which disputes were decided and transgressions punished. The contents of the articles were based on custom and precedent and addressed the most frequent problems and offences encountered on campaign. These rules were read to the assembled men at the muster and their oath on the articles formally constituted the regiment. The regiment was therefore a sworn corporation with its own legal code and its own judicial structure autonomous from the civilian legal landscape. The fact that this corporation severed all ties with civilian legal authority set it apart from artisans' guilds or universities, for example, which exhibited similar traits (sworn constitution, corporate rules, and policing) but represented suborders *within* civil society; military regiments were legal realms beyond the reach of civilian authorities.[5]

Legal authority and jurisdiction lay with the colonel (*Obrist*), whose pivotal legal role brings one of the great differences between modern and premodern armies into sharp relief.[6] We tend to assume a strict military chain of command through which orders and regulations are implemented from the very top to the very bottom. The main obstacle to such a smooth command structure lay in the very nature of military enterprise: colonels were contractors who retained and, if necessary, defended a great deal of autonomous legal authority over their regiments. The articles of war consequently set out the legal parameters within which military society was *expected* to function, but it was the contracting colonels, their legal staff, and not least the jurors (*Schöffen*) who interpreted and enforced them in their regiments. The articles of war recognized this, as they oftentimes suggested a punishment for a given offence but explicitly deferred to the colonel's judgment. It is therefore important to bear in mind that despite what the articles of war stated, their implementation depended on the respective colonel and his staff and could vary wildly.

There were several routes through which a verdict could be reached. In many situations, especially in cases of desertion, unsanctioned plunder, or violence, officers and commanders simply ordered suspects to be punished without process. Hans Wilhelm Kirchhof denounced the "atrocious and tyrannical temper" of officers who hanged their men "like dogs" before giving a detailed description of how an orderly trial should be conducted.[7] The *Landsknecht* regiments of the sixteenth century had a special form of communal trial, the *Spießrecht* ("trial of the pikes"), in which the entire regiment took part and decided the verdict by majority vote.[8] This corporate trial was employed when the honor of the entire regiment had been sullied by a crime, but it is unclear how often this cumbersome process was actually put into practice. The most common form of jurisdiction was the *Schultheißengericht*, named after the *Schultheiß*, the presiding military judge.[9] The *Schultheiß* was assisted by his staff as well as up to twenty-four jurors (*Schöffen*), appointed from among the number of officers, NCOs, and the *Führer* (veterans elected by the common soldiers to give legal advice and to sit on juries). The defendant was represented by an advocate (*Fürsprech*) and the *Profos*, otherwise employed in policing the regiment, functioned as prosecutor.

Few men involved in military jurisdiction had a formal education in law; in fact there is good evidence that military society resented and resisted the influence of "learned" Roman law fiercely.[10] This tension between the introduction of a perceived "foreign" legal paradigm and the traditional legal norms and customs that Roman law was supplanting affected early modern society in general, but in the armies legal custom prevailed for longer. From the mid-sixteenth century onward, authors of military manuals advocated for trained jurists to establish superordinate military courts attached to the commander in chief's headquarters, but on the regimental level justice continued to be administered by veteran soldiers who were well-acquainted with military custom and precedent.[11] The articles are often the only concrete set of norms accessible to the historian, while custom, precedent, and other factors that influenced justice (the social and economic capital of the parties involved, the situation in which a certain behavior occurred, or the situation in which a verdict was handed down) remain ephemeral because they were not recorded. In conjunction with political and military expediency, this normative pluralism explains why the letter of the law as contained in the articles of war was handled very flexibly in the early modern period and more often than not left crimes that were not directly detrimental to the operational effectiveness of the regiment unsanctioned.

Legal codes such as the articles of war were in many ways descriptive of a legal ideal, not a reality. Like the *Policeyordnungen* in the civilian setting, the articles of war can be seen as declarations of authority and statements of intent that possessed considerable worth in themselves, irrespective of actual enforcement. Merely publishing them showed that the military authorities intended to further the common weal and maintain order and, in this sense, the military paralleled the civilian setting.[12] Even in the more stable context of the standing armies, military law and jurisdiction was predominantly tokenism that provided ex post alibis and excuses for transgressions committed by individual or groups of soldiers.[13] As communications of ideals and intent, however, the articles of war are valuable because they allow us insights into how military authorities adapted the military legal framework in reaction to the problem of religious pluralization.

The articles of war evolved rapidly during the sixteenth and early seventeenth centuries both in terms of scope and character. Around 1500, they tended to pithily outline the mutually agreed duties and obligations between soldiers and their employers. By the later sixteenth century, they had turned into detailed service regulations, but the religious stipulations underwent little change.[14] The field ordinances (*Feldordnungen*) from the second half of the fifteenth and the early sixteenth centuries already contained most of the religious and moral prohibitions that became staples of the later articles of war. They criminalized the plundering of churches, the maltreatment of clerics, blaspheming, gambling, and drunkenness, and sought to remove (unmarried) women (or "whores") from the army train.[15] The main formal difference between these earlier field ordinances and the articles of war was that the latter combined the regulations of the field ordinance with a short oath that the soldiers swore by God.[16]

Most articles of war limited the religious regulations to this bare minimum and warlords hardly ever issued more explicit confessional demands. The articles under which soldiers served the Anabaptist Kingdom of Münster from January 1535 are a singular exception.[17] Jan Bockelson (or Jan van Leiden), the "king" of Münster, reserved the term "Christian(s)" exclusively for Anabaptists, while anyone who had not received adult baptism was referred to as "heathen." Apart from the already unambiguous wording, the articles contained a number of orders that addressed potential conflict among the troops arising from matters of faith. Given the dire situation of the "New Jerusalem," van Leiden had to make concessions regarding the faith of those soldiers who were willing to serve him and could find a way into the besieged city. While the prophets had followed a "zero-tolerance" policy inside the city replete with forced mass-baptisms for about a year, van Leiden could not be picky in hiring defenders of his kingdom.[18] Adult baptism was waived as a precondition for service and men who had not yet "gained reason" and remained "heathen" could still enter the king's service as long as they refrained from arguing with or insulting the "Christians."[19] Another peculiar article forbade insulting the "heathen authorities" as these, too, were part of God's plan and thus deserving of a modicum of respect. The "Babylonian tyranny" (*babilonischenn tyranni*) of priests, however, was to be freely abused, as the clergy perverted God's word to uphold their control. False preachers or prophets among the troops were to be expelled or killed.[20] The Münster articles of war are noteworthy for their religious thoroughness but they are atypical for the very same reason: warlords generally could not afford to express confessional preferences in the articles of war they issued.

The typical absence of confessional demands or regulations in military law may seem remarkable at first sight, but it was in keeping with imperial policies regarding religion and war and the requirements of warfare in general. Although the period is commonly regarded as replete with confessional wars, it

48 ~: *Faith in War*

is important to realize that the Empire did not officially lead a single religious war in the sixteenth and seventeenth centuries other than the wars against the Ottomans.[21] In fact, it was vital that religious differences were downplayed as much as possible if the Empire was to function at all. The reign of Charles V and his brother Ferdinand, who dealt with the political day-to-day in Central Europe, set several precedents for imperial religious policy, including approaches toward religion in the armies.[22] The Empire depended on all its estates, Catholic and Protestant, for their contributions to military service. Unity in military affairs was as critical as it was difficult to achieve. The Empire faced powerful enemies, France to the west and the Ottomans to the east and south, two major powers that became allies in their wars against the Habsburgs. To these external enemies was added a growing internal threat in the form of the increasingly numerous and recalcitrant Protestant princes and cities that established the Schmalkaldic League (1530–31) as an alliance to protect Protestant interests.[23] When war with the German Protestants finally broke out, the Habsburgs were anxious to present the Schmalkaldic War (1546–47) as a war against breakers of the imperial peace, not against heretics.

Dissimulation of the true motives of the war was essential, albeit in an inversion of the still current tendency to suspect premodern politics of using religion as a pretext for secular gain-seeking: Charles and Ferdinand undeniably had religious motivations but they did their best to present their actions as a strictly secular necessity.[24] The *Achtbrief* declaring the imperial ban on the leaders of the League (20 July 1546), John of Saxony and Philip of Hesse, was printed and circulated throughout the Empire. It explicitly addressed officers and common soldiers. Charles and his advisors went to great lengths to present the Lutheran leaders as common rebels and breakers of the peace who were also guilty of *crimen laesae maiestatis*.[25] Not only did the emperor stress that his motivations were not religious, he accused the elector and landgrave themselves of using religion as a "cloak" (*Teckenmantel*) for their crimes.[26] In the ensuing propaganda war—it produced about 170 different texts in ca. three hundred editions[27]—the "rebels" in turn tried to expose the emperor's religious motives and his desire to exterminate Lutheranism.[28] The example of the Schmalkaldic War shows the importance of trying to paper over doctrinal division at the level of imperial politics.

On a smaller scale, avoiding confessional rifts among troops was imperative for every warlord. The highest priority was to assemble a force of adequate numbers of able men with good equipment; the soldiers' religious affiliation was a concern no warlord could realistically afford. The zeal a sovereign may have shown toward his subjects had to yield to the dictate of the mercenary market.[29] Warlords could try to influence the confessional composition of their armies by sending recruiters into specific regions. Philip II of Spain, for example, was keen on recruiting Catholics for the regiments he sent into the

Netherlands and this proclivity was well known among the recruiting officers. Christoph Sigmund Römer, who had been tasked with the recruitment of a new infantry regiment in early 1575, stressed that he had already filled all vacancies for officers with Catholics in a letter dated 20 March, a feat he evidently felt would please the king.[30] Catholic officers aside, confessional demands seem to have decreased with rank. Spanish recruiters did avoid certain regions and territories, for example the Austrian Habsburg lands, because King Philip suspected all Austrians of Protestantism and preferred soldiers from Germany. But the place of recruitment was not necessarily identical with the soldiers' place of origin and was a poor indicator of their confession. Soldiers were mobile by nature and men looking for employment traveled over long distances to southern Germany, where there was constant demand for recruits.[31] It would therefore be mistaken to assume that men recruited in a certain area shared the confessions of the local population, which, as we know, was often heterogeneous anyway.

Even Philip II's predilection for Catholic soldiers was bounded by pragmatic concerns and necessity, however. His patronage network in the Empire included several Lutheran nobles and the king and his ministers appear to have differentiated starkly between Lutheran heretics, who were deemed at least individually reliable, and Calvinist heretics, who were entirely beyond the pale.[32] There were several north German military enterprisers who negotiated exemptions from fighting Lutheran coreligionists, which their employers granted as long as they fought Calvinists.[33]

Similar observations can be made when we turn to the employment of Scottish troops by the Swedish crown. It is often assumed that their shared Protestantism provided a common cause, priming Scots to fight for the Swedes in the Baltic, Poland-Lithuania, and later in the Thirty Years War. But we should be cautious: in the Scottish Highlands, where many of the troops were levied for Swedish service, the Reformation had not been a success everywhere, not just because Gaelic-speaking Presbyterian clergy were difficult to come by but also because Catholicism simply remained compelling to many people.[34] While we therefore have good cause to question whether the Scots rank and file were uniformly Protestant, we have concrete evidence that many Scots Catholics made careers as officers in Swedish and Danish service, where they commanded regiments and entire army contingents.[35]

What do these observations regarding recruitment tell us? Fundamentally, and this should be spelled out, it was clearly *preferable* to warlords to hire troops who shared their confession. It was probably equally *preferable* for many soldiers, especially those who were levied abroad, if the "cause" for which they went to war aligned with their personal beliefs (we will return to the question of motivation in Chapter 4). For now, we can draw the preliminary and not exactly astounding conclusion that confessional congruence was desired but

50 ~: *Faith in War*

that confessional difference was no hindrance when it came to hiring troops or entering service. Even if enough men of the right creed were available, discharging soldiers of other confessions threatened to strengthen the enemy, as the soldiers could simply join their ranks. As a result, all armies of the sixteenth and seventeenth centuries were confessional composites, and especially in the Thirty Years War, when surrendering troops were habitually incorporated into the forces of their captors, armies tended to be religiously highly diverse.[36]

A warlord was therefore well advised to provide a legal framework that accommodated soldiers of all confessions and precluded religious tensions as far as possible. This meant that the articles of war codified universal Christian values but disregarded doctrinal specifics. As early as 1522, an imperial ordinance obliged chaplains to preach in a manner that did not invite national or confessional disputes.[37] His Catholic convictions may have inspired the articles Charles V issued for his 1541 Turkish campaign, as they still protected the saints from blasphemy, but they did not make confessionally specific demands on the soldiers' faith.[38] By this time, the conflicts that could arise from confessional tensions among the soldiery threatened to cause serious problems in the imperial armies. It was therefore decreed again at the imperial diet at Speyer in 1542 that preachers must not address contentious doctrinal matters.[39] In 1544, the new imperial articles took account of the nationally and confessionally heterogeneous makeup of the force that Charles was sending on another French campaign and incorporated a stipulation that stated explicitly that "no nation shall malign or affront another with words or gestures nor shall they get involved in disputations because of the faith."[40] The imperial war council apparently also feared that Protestant contingents could affirm their faith violently and added a clause forbidding soldiers to "undertake anything in any way that is against the old religion," thus protecting Catholicism without prejudicing against Protestants.[41]

Such explicit prohibitions against debating or preaching contentious confessional matters are not found in later articles of war, but the Empire as a whole entered a new phase when the Peace of Augsburg gave official recognition to Lutheranism in 1555. Charles's hopes that he could ultimately preserve the unity of the Church had been shattered and he abdicated. His successors, however, had to adapt to the reality of a bi-confessional empire composed of Catholic and Lutheran estates, while Calvinism rapidly gained converts in several regions as the century progressed. The imperial articles of war (*Reichsartikelbrief*) that Maximilian II instituted at the Diet of Speyer in 1570 sought to create a uniform legal military code for all troops operating within the Empire as well as regiments that were levied there for service abroad.[42] For over a century, they were used as the template for imperial and German Catholic articles of war and they were void of any signs of religious preference.[43] The second article addressed religious issues and prohibited soldiers from impious behavior such as blasphemy, and admonished them to pray for victory and attend sermons and services whenever possible.[44] The imperial war council therefore thought worship and preaching important for soldiers but implicitly left it to the respective colonel to implement worship and regulate observance in his regiment.

The *Reichsartikelbrief* introduced a novelty in the context of military law as it introduced a basic version of "church discipline" to the armies: soldiers were not only expected to attend religious services but to behave piously and pay attention as well.[45] In order to enforce this, the provost was given powers to arrest soldiers "found in wine cellars or taverns or other frivolous locations during service or sermon" and to punish them "according to the colonel's judgment." Secondly, the selling of alcohol was forbidden during services or sermons. While the alcohol ban indicates that some soldiers preferred spirits to the spiritual, promoting appropriate behavior and sustained attentiveness during services was chronically difficult among soldiers and civilians alike. In Marc Forster's estimation, among civilians such behavior "reflect[ed] not a popular rejection of the Mass but the unwillingness of some to treat the whole church service with the kind of reverence the clergy wanted" and we may assume the same for soldiers.[46]

In the late sixteenth century, the efforts to foster greater moral restraint among subjects that had exercised civilian authorities across the confessional spectrum for decades began to encroach on the military sphere in so far as rules governing moral conduct became more elaborate.[47] Maurice of Nassau's 1590 articles for the armies of the United Provinces became the model for Protestant military ordinances: Sweden developed them further after 1617 and the Danish articles of the 1620s as well as the English and Scottish ordinances of the 1640s were in turn based on the Swedish articles.[48] The 1625 Danish articles of war that Christian IV issued for his troops in Germany contained detailed stipulations regarding the punishment of religious transgressions.[49] The first paragraph began with the reminder that it was God who bestowed fortune on an army and ordered officers to always instruct the soldiery to pray for His favor, not to miss sermons, and to hear them happily and soberly.[50] Common soldiers found drunk at sermons should be put in shackles, while officers were to lose their commission the third time they attended a service intoxicated. The second article also aimed at keeping the service sober and reiterated the alcohol ban during the sermon unless an ill person needed fortification. The third and fourth articles dealt with two registers of blasphemy (we will return to those in the third chapter). The soldiers' oath, which occupied the final page of the 1625 articles, ended in the formula: "so help us God and his holy Gospel, through Jesus Christ, AMEN."[51]

The articles of war under which Gustavus II Adolphus led his troops into the Thirty Years War took the policing of religious conduct to an even higher level.[52] A cursory glance at the Swedish articles already shows that this legal

52 ~: *Faith in War*

code was a departure from the traditional form: regulations were detailed on twenty-eight pages, subdivided into twenty-four *tituli* and 112 articles. Three *tituli* addressed religious matters in nineteen articles. The first article introduced a prohibition of different kinds of idolatry (*Abgötterey*): false worshippers, idolaters, witches, and weapon enchanters were to be apprehended, put on trial, and expelled from the army should they offend again.[53] Blasphemy was dealt with at length in articles II–VI.[54] If a soldier showed irreverence or made a farce of the service or the sacraments, he was to be tried before the *consistorium ecclesiasticum*. This consistory was a novel institution under the presidency of a senior cleric who was assisted by the preachers of the respective regiments (*assessores ordinarij*).[55] *Titulus* II concerned services and sermons. While other articles of war usually envisioned one service per week, the Swedish articles ordered short services that consisted of prayers and hymn singing to be held twice a day.[56] Article VIII addressed the intriguing problem of chaplains who did not attend the service—errant pastors appear repeatedly in this particular code—and specified that absentee chaplains should pay half their month's pay into a fund for sick and wounded soldiers. Soldiers who skipped service were fined and faced twenty-four hours in the pillory on the third offence.[57] A preacher found drunk when he had to hold a service was to be reprimanded twice and removed from the army the third time.[58] Every Sunday and on feast days a full service with a sermon was to be held during which time no alcohol was to be sold (a standard rule by now), but neither were feasts or carousals allowed and transgressors faced a fine.[59]

The articles of war show that approaches toward the regulation of religious and moral conduct differed depending on the warlord who issued them, especially as the seventeenth century progressed. The drive toward a stricter religious—but not confessional!—regime is noticeable across the doctrinal spectrum from the second half of the sixteenth century onward.[60] The differences lie in the degrees to which confessional attributes featured in the regulations. Imperial and Catholic articles generally phrased religious rules in confessionally unmarked terms. Protestant princes showed a marginally greater readiness to include confessionally connoted terms and phrases, for example references to the sanctity of the Bible, but it must be emphasized that these codes never prejudiced against Catholics nor contained stipulations that could be interpreted as religiously divisive. The letter of martial law applied to all Christians, irrespective of confession.

It is impossible to reconstruct military legal reality in the period to any appreciable degree.[61] Outside of the urban setting, trials were mostly oral affairs that were rarely written down, a documentary problem that the temporary nature of the regiments only exacerbates because trial records—if they were kept in the first place—were probably discarded once the regiment was disbanded.[62] Jan Willem Huntebrinker has discovered the *Gerichtsbuch* of Wolfgang von

Mansfeld's regiment of 1625–26 in the Haupstaatsarchiv Dresden, but this is a singular find and none of the recorded cases had a religious dimension.[63] A relative wealth of court martial records appears rather abruptly in the later seventeenth century, but even so, Maren Lorenz's study of military–civilian relations between ca. 1650 and 1700 shows that religious transgressions were tried exceptionally rarely and only in conjunction with other, more serious crimes.[64] The absence of court martial records makes it impossible to determine if, how, and with what frequency offenses against the articles of war were punished. It is unlikely, however, that religious transgressions ranked highly on the average colonel's list of priorities. Unless they had offended seriously against their superiors, most officers enjoyed extensive protection from disciplinary action due to their often noble birth, their military indispensability, or both.[65] Common soldiers could be more expendable, but colonels also had a vested interest in keeping their troops contented as the threat of mutiny or desertion was constant.[66] In this sense, a legal practice that focused on the resolution of internal disputes and the prosecution of offences that threatened military effectiveness but that was otherwise permissive was a good way of strengthening the troops' loyalty toward their commander. Given that even gross acts of violence inflicted on the civilian population mostly went unpunished or that plundering frequently turned into a racket in which officers and common soldiers worked hand in hand, it seems unlikely that comparatively minor offences like absences from religious services or drunkenness among attendees were prosecuted with determination.[67]

While we have to assume that most religious transgressions went unpunished, there is scattered evidence from the Thirty Years War that on occasion some warlords entertained the idea of bringing about greater confessional homogeneity in their armies. Count Tilly, the commander of the Catholic League, intermittently received reprimands from Maximilian of Bavaria over the appointment of officers.[68] Tilly needed reliable and talented men and their confession was apparently unimportant to the commander nicknamed the "monk in armor" for his deep Catholic piety. The duke and his council, however, occasionally demanded the appointment of Catholic officers and the dismissal of those who were of the "adverse religion" (*widrigen religion*).[69] Tilly, it seems, filed these letters away and carried on undeterred. Military expediency and confessional idealism could thus be a source of disagreement between the commanders and their employers, but such thoughts of confessional homogenization almost exclusively concerned officers and were pursued half-heartedly, if at all.

A second example dates to the months following the assassination of Albrecht von Wallenstein (25 February 1634), when an evidently optimistic imperial war council attempted some confessional housekeeping. Circulated by letter, a list of orders concerning worship in the imperial army (dated 13 July 1634) suggests a bid at curtailing the legacy of Wallenstein's notorious confes-

54 ❦ *Faith in War*

sional indifference now that this overmighty subject was dead and his troops were under new command. Among other matters of religious organization, the order explicitly forbade "heretical" (*kezerisch*) worship. Tellingly, it also clarified how Protestant colonels should implement Catholic worship in their regiments: they were to order one of their Catholic officers to hire a Catholic field preacher.[70] The proscription of Protestant worship was exceptional in the military context and there is no evidence that it had an impact on religious practice in the imperial army. At least in 1643, the Lutheran Electoral-Saxon regiments in imperial service had explicit permission to maintain their own preachers and worship, albeit only in private houses or in the open field.[71] Though feeble, the order illustrates that the imperial war council had a clear sense of the multiconfessional composition of the emperor's troops as it not only took Protestant colonels in imperial service as a given but also assumed that there were Catholic officers serving under their command. By permitting the colonels to have one of their Catholic subordinates hire the chaplain, the council also offered a path in which the colonel did not personally have to make an appointment that would go against his conscience.

Such spasmodic and perfunctory attempts at confessionalization betray the unease that warlords could experience with the multiconfessional nature of their armies. It is also revealing, however, that these efforts always remained more or less unofficial and were not publicly proclaimed or enshrined in martial law. The *ratio belli* forced warlords to resign to the fact that confessional homogeneity was theoretically and maybe personally desirable but practically unattainable.

Religion in the Regiment—The Chaplaincy

In legal terms, then, military authorities created a work environment that accommodated Christians of all denominations. But these men and their families also had to be provided with spiritual care and the field preacher took the place of the parish priest. Writing about field preachers, again, is difficult because documentation pertaining to this office is exceedingly patchy. Despite occasional endeavors to formalize and centralize the chaplaincy, such efforts only bore fruit in the context of the standing armies that were established in the later seventeenth century. Until then, most military chaplains were either the court preachers of noble officers who joined their masters in the field, or they were hired specifically for the position, or they were Catholic regulars who were sent to serve as chaplains by their orders.

Although chaplains were supposed to be attached to every company, in practice a shortage of military pastoral staff was endemic. Kirchhof lamented the chronic lack of chaplains and the unavailability of spiritual care for the soldiers.[72] Count Tilly sent begging letters to Maximilian of Bavaria in June 1621, asking for at least one, ideally two Jesuits so that masses, sermons, and confessions could resume again and he and his men were no longer rendered "helpless" in spiritual matters.[73] Beginning in the sixteenth century, occasional efforts were made to counter the scarcity of preachers by centralizing their assignment. In the imperial army, the first vicar-general, charged with the religious care for the whole army, was appointed in 1534, but the office was filled only sporadically until the end of the Thirty Years War.[74] It seems that the imperial vicar-general and his chaplains (there were only six in 1639)[75] had a supplementary role in the provision of spiritual care and were simultaneously supposed to supervise and examine the existing regimental clergy.

In France and the Netherlands, the Jesuits were invited to undertake some concerted field missions in the later sixteenth century, which are interesting for their intentions, if not for their success in creating pious, uniformly Catholic armies.[76] The first mission accompanied the papal army that Pius V sent in support of the French crown at the outbreak of the Third War of Religion in 1569, another followed in 1591–92, and the Duke of Parma established a central chaplaincy for the Spanish army in Flanders in 1585 that continued its work into the 1630s.[77] The experiences in France and the Netherlands showed that the active support from commanding officers was vital for the functioning of the missions. It also became clear that the degree to which the missionaries' efforts to reform the soldiery produced results directly correlated with regular pay and the availability of provisions. During the aborted mission in the papal army in 1569, the soldiers initially eagerly took the opportunities for confession, preaching, mass, and catechesis offered by the Jesuits. As the support infrastructure broke down during the campaign, however, the missionaries' insistence on the harsh punishment of looters cost them sympathies among the officers, who evidently had a more forgiving appreciation of the hardship the soldiers endured. With the troops struggling to survive and the officers alienated by the fathers' lack of charity toward the soldiers' plight, the mission collapsed. As soon as the plague began to ravage the papal forces, the Jesuits were forced to abandon the reform of evil soldierly living, as they were ordered to set up a hospital and ensure pious soldierly dying.[78] In the Netherlands, the field mission set up under Farnese for the Spanish Army in the 1580s functioned comparably better, but the numbers of centrally organized chaplains were not exactly staggering either.[79] There were twenty-four Jesuit chaplains until 1600, when the army and the navy had to share the fathers and the loss of the Jesuits to the army was made up by a dozen Franciscans.

In the Holy Roman Empire, it took until 1643 for Ferdinand III to turn to the Society of Jesus for the establishment of a field chaplaincy. His confessor, Dr. Johann Ganns S. J., set up the field mission (*Feldmission*) with the dual purpose of missionizing the army and supervising the existing clergy. Putting the Jesuits in a position of authority over all chaplains, including regulars who catered to the troops, drew resistance from several religious orders, so a new arrangement was developed in which a Jesuit headed the field mission and a secular cleric assumed supervision over the field preachers as vicar-general.[80] The mission was endowed with an annual stipend of 3,000 *reichsthaler*, an initial sum of 3,000 guilders for horses, wagons, servants, books, and so-called field chapels, large tents in which mass could be celebrated.[81] How well the mission fared in the five years before the end of the Thirty Years War is unclear but the fact that it took the imperial army this long to establish a centralized system for the provision of spiritual care and quality control of its existing clergy suggests that these matters had low priority.

The Swedish articles of war for the army in Germany envisioned a comparable system in 1632 and clearly laid out the chaplaincy's duties and its organization in five articles under *Titulus* III.[82] The intention was to ensure that well-trained, well-behaved chaplains were attached to every regiment. Article XV stipulated that only formally ordained preachers were eligible for the position and stressed that the chaplains were to be assigned centrally to the regiments, not hired privately by the respective officers. The next article described the aforementioned *consistorium ecclesiasticum* under the presidency of the oldest court and field preacher. Article XVII returned to the apparent problem of officers employing their own chaplains. It reiterated the prohibition of hiring preachers privately and forbade officers to discharge chaplains assigned to them without the knowledge and consent of the *consistorium* and their colonel. Chaplains who proved "godless and reprobate" were to be tried before the *consistorium* and dismissed from service should the allegations prove true (Article XVIII). Finally, the consistory was given the power to prosecute wayward chaplains without them being reported by their officers in order to ensure that any offences were punished.[83] The purpose of having chaplains in the army was, after all, to set a good example to the common soldiery.

The Swedish model seems groundbreaking in its level of attention to long-lamented issues, namely the dire lack of chaplains and the poor training and wanting piety of those that were available. The case of Samuel Gerlach, who served as a chaplain in the Swedish army, however, indicates just how difficult it was to translate the high aims of the Swedish articles into reality: Gerlach's career violated the regulations at every turn. A graduate from the University of Tübingen in 1629, Gerlach worked as a private tutor for a patrician family until they could no longer afford his services. The family recommended him to a relative, Friedrich Ludwig Chanovsky von Langendorff, a colonel in the Swedish army, who hired Gerlach as his field preacher in 1631.[84] Gerlach found himself in an unhappy situation, because the colonel was often absent from the regiment and his new chaplain lacked in authority without him.[85] After the Sack of Augsburg in April 1632, Gerlach met Jacob Fabricius, Gustavus Adolphus's court preacher, who took him into the royal camp.[86] As we have seen, the Swedish articles of war forbade officers to hire their own field preachers. They also stated that only clerics who were formally ordained were eligible for that position and had to be assigned to the regiments by the consistory. None of this was observed in Gerlach's case: he was hired privately by Chanovsky, it is uncertain if he had been ordained at that point, and it seems that he got into contact with Fabricius (and through him maybe with the consistory) by accident. The chaplaincy in the Swedish contingents under Gustavus Adolphus's direct command was in no better shape than it was in the army under Field Marshal Horn to which Chanovsky's regiment belonged. Three out of four chaplaincies were vacant, and the Swedish Master of the Horse Albrecht von der Schulenburg was delighted to take Gerlach as his field preacher because the new arrival meant that he could send the inexperienced young man he was currently employing back to university.[87] Only in mid-July was Gerlach finally officially ordained as field preacher of the *Altgrün* regiment under the Calvinist colonel Adam von Pfuel, with whom he soon clashed over doctrinal matters.[88] Pfuel began to interfere with Gerlach's preaching, a presumption that greatly offended the Lutheran preacher, who considered his commander to be an insolent *parvenu*. After a few months, Gerlach secured the prestigious position as field preacher of Field Marshal Horn's cavalry bodyguard regiment (*Leibregiment*) and served there until his health began to deteriorate. Horn then made him the first and only Lutheran pastor of Dahenfeld near Neckarsulm, but Gerlach fled the town after the Swedish defeat at Nördlingen and had to become a field preacher again, this time in a cavalry regiment in Bernhard of Saxe-Weimar's army.[89] After Sweden and France became allies in 1635, Gerlach resigned from his position, according to his biographer Bernd Autenrieth apparently because he was not willing to serve the French crown.[90]

As Gerlach's case shows, the Swedish legal code was ambitious on paper but evidently failed in praxis. The Swedish system could not provide nearly enough field preachers, nor does the supervision it tried to impose seem to have functioned even remotely. Colonel Chanovsky ignored the articles of war when he privately hired Gerlach, and even in the royal army, under the auspices of the king, his court preacher Fabricius, and the field consistory, the informal hiring and swapping of chaplains seems to have continued. That the Lutheran Gerlach was assigned to the Calvinist Pfuel's regiment may indicate that the consistory was trying to prevent the colonel from hiring his own reformed preacher. Gerlach's doctrinal clashes with Pfuel (and his experiences in Chanovsky's regiment) show clearly how integral agreement between preacher and commander was. The conflict also reveals that individual officers took an interest in the pastoral care of their troops and tried to govern their clerical staff in this respect. In this sense, the private appointment of preachers certainly worked better than the centralized system, because the colonel could hire someone that suited him doctrinally.

58 ❧ *Faith in War*

It is difficult to tell what kind of guidance or training military chaplains received. Instructional literature directed at field preachers did not appear until the early eighteenth century, which is surprising, given that the provision of well-trained clergy lay at the heart of the reform programs of all churches from the sixteenth century onward. Johann Ludwig Hocker, whose manual appeared in 1710, knew of only one other such book that had been published while his own manuscript was awaiting print.[91] Hocker's tract is of particular interest to us because it was an adaptation of a military church ordinance that Daniel Rücker, court preacher to Bernhard of Saxe-Weimar and president of the field consistory in the duke's army, had drafted in 1643 but that had never been published.[92] Hardly any earlier guidance on the chaplain's office can be found. The articles of war generally do not deal with the field preachers, aside from the mid-sixteenth-century injunctions against sectarian preaching, but the frequent references to services and sermons imply that the presence of clerics was taken for granted. Military manuals addressed the chaplaincy only in passing. Leonhart Fronsperger, the most prolific German military author of the mid-sixteenth century, prefaced his brief outline of an infantry chaplain's duties with a damning assessment. While he advised every captain to strive to employ "a learned, Christian, able and honorable" chaplain, Fronsperger thought such men to be rare, as "the parishioners are commonly like the parson . . . the sheep like the shepherd, as lambs are rarely raised among wolves."[93] Fronsperger did not explain why he deemed the infantry chaplains so questionable, but the neutral way in which he wrote about their colleagues in the "noble" cavalry suggests that he suspected the infantry clerics of dissolution merely because they were willing to minister to the *Landsknechte*.[94] His low esteem of the infantry chaplaincy is also noticeable in his description of how the chaplain helped with the captain's shopping and ran errands in a way that made him resemble a servant with a spiritual side more than a serious cleric. Fronsperger's portrayal was not entirely fanciful, as there is evidence that chaplains could also be used as nannies. In Freiburg in 1641, a Jesuit named Michel not only tended to the garrison commander's baby but carried it around in public, which profoundly irritated the Cistercian Conrad Burger, who remarked on this impropriety repeatedly.[95]

Other military manuals were not as explicitly dismissive as Fronsperger's but treated the chaplaincy in a similarly cursory manner, if at all. With the salient exception of the chaplaincy, Count Solms's *Kriegsbuch* described every military office in detail. The preacher was only listed alongside minor staff with the comment that his duties were self-explanatory.[96] While the reference to the field preacher could hardly be pithier, it is revealing in so far as Solms apparently did not consider the duties of a military chaplain to be any different from those of other clerics. Hans Wilhelm Kirchhof did provide an outline of the chaplains' duties, namely "to preach God's Word in the field, comfort the sick, and administer the holy sacrament to them, also to baptize new-born children and to perform what else belongs to this office."[97] The specifically military content only concerns the peculiarities of holding a service in the open field, during which the pastor was to sing hymns that were "otherwise customary in churches."[98] These passages imply that the field preacher's duties were regarded as identical to those of a parish cleric and that he provided the usual pastoral care in an unusual, transitory environment. The condemnatory tone of Fronsperger's widely read book and the scarce attention chaplains are paid in military manuals of the time have prompted some historians to postulate that field preachers were of little importance in the military and that the "quality of chaplains tended to be low."[99] Inadequately trained and insufficiently pious clerics, both military and civilian, were a problem in the period, but this does not mean that only ecclesiastical refuse was employed in the military. It seems that field preachers were hardly dealt with in military literature not because the authors thought that they were unimportant but because it was considered superfluous to provide specific explanations when the duties of a chaplain were the same as those of a parish priest.

This impression is corroborated by the wording of the letters of reference for Johannes Northausen, who spent some time as a field preacher in a German regiment in the Netherlands in the late 1570s.[100] Northausen's former commanding officer, *Rittmeister* Friedrich von Wehren, described his chaplain's performance and gave an assessment of his character.[101] Northausen had "preached God's Word in the pure form," administered "the Christian and most venerable sacraments according to Christ's pure institute," and proven his good, Christian moral conduct.[102] Again, the description of a field preacher's duties seems identical with that of a regular cleric, but in Northausen's case, we can directly compare his military reference to a civilian one. After his stint in the army he became a pastor in Greussen, county Schwarzburg, where he ran into problems after about eighteen months and was dismissed from his position over doctrinal disputes.[103] His superiors accused him of "unbearably gross wrongdoing and impure doctrine" and removed him from his position without knowledge or consent of his parishioners.[104] Fearing that the unjust treatment and especially the lack of a reference would obstruct his future career, he asked the pastors in the neighboring parishes to attest to the purity of his doctrine and conduct. His colleagues obliged and wrote:

> Thus, we declare and attest that . . . he fulfilled his office faithfully and assiduously, handled his doctrine correctly and that he conducted himself modestly and irreproachably in his lifestyle, which is amply confirmed by his parishioners and everyone else.[105]

On the verso side, five of his colleagues gave brief individual statements. The Kirchheiligen pastor Martin Pottin, for example, attested to his "unadulterated doctrine and blameless lifestyle" (*doctrina non vulgari vitaq[ue] inculpata*), the

60 ❦ *Faith in War*

same criteria that *Rittmeister* Wehren had affirmed. Field preachers and parish clergy therefore had to meet the same standards, purity of doctrine and blameless moral conduct. In addition to this, regular theological training seems to have been sufficient preparation for an appointment in the military.

But while the required education and comportment of civilian and military clergy were identical, field preachers had to be much more physically robust than their colleagues in the parishes. Johann Ludwig Hocker's Lutheran manual for chaplains bears eloquent witness to the taxing nature of ministering in the field. Field preachers suffered the same hardships as the common soldiery and had to minister to the sick and dying amid disease and the suffocating stench of the field hospitals and the soldiers' quarters.[106] Hocker had personally seen seven or eight "handsome and strong" colleagues die from exhaustion and disease on a single campaign and advised prospective chaplains to consider their constitution thoroughly before agreeing to take the job.[107] Apart from being in particularly rude health, preachers also had to be vocally gifted because they had to preach in the field, not in the acoustically advantageous setting of a church building. Field preachers had to both be loud—their voices should carry at least twenty paces—and enunciate clearly, as there was little use in a preacher bellowing so loudly that "three regiments can hear him but even those standing next to him [cannot] understand" him.[108] Holding communion in the open field posed its own challenges. Hocker addressed some of the practical accidents a chaplain might encounter and gave advice on what to do when the wind blew the hosts off the communion plate or how to react when a communicant knocked over the chalice and drenched the hosts in communion wine.[109]

It cannot have been easy to find clerics willing to serve in the army under such circumstances, especially as chaplains were not remunerated well at all. Fronsperger suggested pay of twelve gulden for the chaplain in the provost-general's retinue, the same pay grade as the drummer or a blacksmith.[110] This was very good money compared to the eight gulden a regular colonel's chaplain earned.[111] Reinhard von Solms accorded the chaplain the second-lowest pay grade at double the pay of an ordinary soldier; in comparison, the executioner earned twice as much.[112] Quoting an imperial patent, Wilhelm Dillich's *Kriegß-buch* advised paying chaplains—*if* they were present—a generous 24 gulden, the same amount an ensign earned.[113] The often low pay, combined with the hardships of military life, suggest that becoming a field preacher was not an aspiration for many clerics. It has to be considered, however, that the chaplains often seem to have negotiated their appointments directly with the colonels or their staff, so their actual pay could have been higher than the military manuals suggest. When court preachers joined their masters on campaign, the pay suggestions in the military manuals did not apply either.

Apart from the squalid living conditions and poor pay, concerns about their good reputation may have precluded many clerics from joining the army. Leonhard Fronsperger's low esteem of field preachers' moral comportment has been noted and there is more evidence that a certain stigma surrounded clerics who were willing to cater to soldiers. Anxiety about his good reputation becomes apparent in the dedication of a sermon that Zacharias Theobald gave at Pilsen in 1618, where he catered to two infantry regiments under captain Wolff Friedrich Lamminger.[114] Theobald described how his decision to preach in the army had caused talk among friends and enemies alike and that doubts had been voiced over whether it was befitting for a pastor to join an army in the field.[115] He stressed that he had followed the vocation of Captain Lamminger and had therefore been officially appointed. He pointed to biblical examples to suggest that Joshua and Elijah had been "field preachers" as well and rejected insinuations of unbecoming adventurousness. Theobald insisted that it was the duty of a cleric who took his position seriously to preach and teach wherever he was needed and argued that soldiers required pastoral care like everyone else. He called upon Captain Lamminger and all the other officers to attest to his good conduct in order to counter imputations concerning his character and lifestyle. Theobald's fear that his current appointment might jeopardize his reputation is clearly evident, and efforts to preclude speculation regarding Johann Northausen's decision to become a field preacher are also noticeable in his military reference cited above. It stated clearly that Northausen had joined the regiment following a "formally issued appointment" (*uff ordentliche beschehne Volation*), a circumstance that Northausen himself was eager to stress, and that he had left the regiment, again, after having received a formal appointment elsewhere.[116] The suspicion in early modern society of vagrants and those who left their homes is the most likely explanation for these comments. They asserted that Northausen was an upright man of the cloth who lived and worked in well-ordered circumstances, not a dissolute vagrant hiding from a shady past in the demimonde of the army.

Encounters between civilian pastors and their military counterparts produced differing comments about field preachers' qualities. Christoph Thodaenus, a Lutheran pastor who was rescued from the carnage of the Sack of Magdeburg by a Spanish colonel, had a few inimical encounters with the Spaniard's Catholic chaplain.[117] If Thodaenus needed proof of Catholic clerical ineptitude, he found it over dinner: the padre spoke no Latin, the language he was supposed to use in his liturgy, and failed to say a prayer after dinner. Henceforth, Thodaenus only referred to the Spaniard as a "base beast" (*rudus pecus*), "the *sacrificulus*" (a pagan sacrificing priest), or sarcastically as "the holy Herr Pater."[118] These comments on the priest's ability were based on personal and confessional antipathy, however, not on his office. Thodaenus was not prejudiced against military clerics as such, as he wrote amiably about a Lutheran field preacher in Caspar von Potthausen's regiment, which stood in imperial service at the time.[119] In other situations, encounters between field preachers and parish clergy could be cordial, even across confessional boundaries. Samuel Gerlach, the Lutheran field preacher in Swedish services whose career we have surveyed above, was billeted with the Catholic priest in Öttingen and their relationship seems to have been thoroughly genial. When Gerlach's unit moved on, the priest wrote his motto "I pray and fast" with the addition "In pleasant memory" in Gerlach's friendship book (*Stammbuch*).[120] Jacob Möser, the Lutheran pastor and later superintendent of Staßfurt near Magdeburg, had numerous encounters with Catholic military clerics, many of whom were billeted in his house over the years, and included "loose fellows" and a "wicked dog" but also "a good man," and some very likeable Jesuits.[121]

These varied assessments, made by parish clerics after often uncomfortable and at times frightening encounters with strangers, are interesting in two respects. On the one hand, they show that the pastors did not judge the field preachers simply on the grounds of their office but seem to have commented on their individual bearing. On the other hand, they betray the perhaps surprising but evidently genuine estimation that clerics of other confessions could well be decent men. That there were unruly, unsavory, even "godless" field preachers should be of no surprise as the cross-confessional reform of the clergy—military *and* civilian—was still a work-in-progress in the period. There is little to suggest, however, that clerical dissolution was more widespread in the military than in the civilian parishes.

But how should chaplains deal with the fact that their flocks were bound to be confessionally diverse? Again, we find no detailed guidance, but there is scattered evidence that suggests how this problem was approached: the preachers had to cultivate the shared common ground of Christian belief that remained between the confessions. The injunctions against sectarian preaching in the articles of war already reflected this attitude; the chaplains were not supposed to act as confessional agitators but speak to all Christian soldiers. An instruction for Jodocus Sünnecken, the priest in charge of the imperial field hospital in 1635, directed him on how to deal with the Protestant soldiers in his care. Sünnecken should try to convert them to Catholicism, but if he failed, he was expected to turn to "other consoling spiritual teachings and exhortations" for the benefit of the soldiers' "poor souls."[122] Even the most Catholic emperor's war council evidently also considered a dying Protestant soldier to be deserving of spiritual consolation and recognized that a Catholic priest could provide this if he chose the right words. On the Lutheran side, Johann Ludwig Hocker stressed that a field preacher had to be able to open the minds and move the hearts of an admittedly difficult audience. Many soldiers had little religious education, so the preacher had to explain himself plainly, omit lengthy exegeses in favor of concrete spiritual guidance, and find a register appropriate to the audience, even if that relied on coarse language impermissible in a civilian context.[123] Other soldiers were very well versed in religious matters and keen on theological debates, especially when they did not share the preacher's confession, while yet others defended their atheist, syncretic, or confessionally indifferent positions with fervor and, it seems, intellectual skill.[124] Hocker advised preachers not to shy away from such debates and even preach against religious error, but to do so with humility, meekness, and empathy.[125]

Field preachers, Protestant and Catholic alike, were therefore to minister in the multiconfessional environment of the military with Christian forbearance, not confessional aggression. They were naturally expected to adhere to their doctrine and guide their flock according to its precepts, but they should also draw from the spiritual traditions that the confessions continued to share when soldiers of other creeds needed consolation.

Religious Literature

Religious literature aimed at soldiers appeared rather late and constitutes a small genre, but it also reflects the non-divisive—or at least not belligerent—Christianity that we have observed in the military legal framework and in the way the chaplaincy was expected to operate. Propagandistic tracts urging soldiers to fight for their respective confessional truth appeared whenever sectarian conflict was erupting in the Empire or abroad. Primarily written for agitation, these texts maybe induced some men to enlist, but they did not provide any spiritual guidance or consolation in their daily lives as soldiers.[126] As we have seen in the previous chapter, many authors who discussed the military profession had strong opinions on soldierly depravity, focused on vituperation rather than edification, and rarely offered practical spiritual advice to soldiers. Theologians like Luther and Musculus outlined an ideal of pious soldier life, but their learned opinions were of little direct use to soldiers in the field.[127]

Leonhart Fronsperger's works were widely read, so his *Spiritual War Ordinance* (*Geistliche KriegßOrdnung*, 1565) may have reached those military men who could afford his books, especially after the tract became a standard appendix to the numerous editions of his military handbooks.[128] Fronsperger compiled the *Geistliche KriegßOrdnung* from other theological texts without changing their arguments in the hope that soldiers would better themselves.[129] The result was essentially an adaptation of Luther's line of reasoning interspersed with references to humanist writers (especially Erasmus) and copious examples and cautionary tales drawn from the Bible and the classical authors. Although Fronsperger could not bring himself to entirely redact the lurid condemnations of the soldiery, the *Spiritual War Ordinance* was intended to provide Christian soldiers with answers to central questions regarding, for example, the justness of taking up the military profession or the appropriate behavior of a Christian soldier. Fronsperger's text is characteristic of military

64 ᔈ *Faith in War*

spiritual literature in so far as it did not take an obvious confessional side. The diligent reader would find the few references to Luther in the text, but as there were no anti-papist or belligerently Protestant comments, Fronsperger potentially provided counsel to Protestant and Catholic Christians alike. Although not all authors could entirely refrain from the occasional sectarian comment, an ecumenical tone and approach to spiritual guidance is typical of the genre until the end of the Thirty Years War. Works like Fronsperger's had a predominantly formative purpose, as they answered fundamental theological questions regarding the military profession, but contained no practical instructions for spiritual life in the field. Only later in the sixteenth century did authors begin to include prayers for key occasions in a soldier's life, for example when he prepared for battle, when a victory had been won, or when he faced death.[130]

The first Catholic soldier catechisms were produced by Jesuits for the French and Spanish armies. Emond Auger published his *Le pedagogue d'armes* in Paris in 1568 and in the following year, Antonio Possevino provided council in Italian in his successful *Il soldato christiano*. Thomas Sailly, who supervised the *missio castrense* in the Netherlands, reworked Possevino's catechism into rather different Spanish and French versions in 1588 and 1590, respectively, and later produced a Dutch liturgy for use in the army in 1595.[131] It is likely that some copies of these circulated in armies fighting in Germany, but their numbers were probably rather small. What is more, it seems that the Jesuits were eager to produce vernacular catechisms for use in France and the Netherlands, expressly so that literate soldiers could read them themselves, but neither they (nor anyone else) produced German translations. It appears that German Catholic soldiers could not draw on any catechisms or prayer books in their native language until after the Thirty Years War.

One of the earliest genuine prayer books for soldiers was published in 1616 by Stephan Puchner, who only identified himself as a citizen of Landsberg an der Warte.[132] Puchner's book marks a departure in religious literature aimed at military men in so far as it was meant as a practical religious aid and its stated purpose was the provision of spiritual comfort to soldiers who often had no access to a preacher in their time of need.[133] He hoped that soldiers would find edification and solace by reading his book, or, if they were illiterate, having others read it to them.[134] Puchner's forty-page book contained five brief but explicit anti-papal barbs, such as "enemies of the Gospel" or naming the pope along with the Turk as blasphemers; enough to position the author but certainly not more bellicose than the prayer books that were used in Lutheran parishes. It is important to note that the prayers specifically attacked the papacy, not Catholics in general, as it would be a mistake to think that German Catholics were particularly fond of the papacy in this period. Anti-papalism was deeply rooted in German Catholicism decades before the Reformation and anti-papal Lutheran hymns were sung with gusto in some Catholic parishes well into the seventeenth century, so the barbs against the Pope were probably not particularly offensive to many German Catholics.[135] Furthermore, rather than a confessionally explicit self-designation, the universalist term "Christian" was used as an adjective in the titles of the prayers and as a noun to denote the speaker and those for whom he prayed. Typical for literature of the confessional age, "Christian" was intended to describe the respective author's confession exclusively, but as every confession described itself as "Christian," the label could be inclusive unless it was further qualified. In Puchner's book, the lack of such additional specificity rendered most of the prayers—maybe inadvertently—ecumenical in tone so that they could conceivably be said by adherents of all confessions.

The first official military prayer books were, again, issued by the Swedish army. The first was a forty-page booklet written by the president of the field consistory Johannes Botvidi and published contemporaneously with the Swedish invasion of Germany in the summer of 1630.[136] It is noticeable that the majority of the prayers were neither very confrontational nor distinctly Protestant in tone or content. Prayers addressed the general affliction of Christendom and asked for the forgiveness of sins, the protection of the king and his army, and safety from evil and pestilence. Confessionally partisan attitudes are only explicit in one prayer that asked for the protection of all Protestants and to safeguard the purity of God's Word and the sacraments from the attacks of "heretics and wrong doctrine: especially against the papists."[137] The book also contained three prayers against the enemy; one appears to have been specifically written, while the other two were adaptations of King Asa's and Judas Maccabee's biblical prayers.[138] While confessional bias in the Old Testament prayers would be surprising indeed, it is noteworthy that Botvidi's own prayer did not contain any reference to contemporary confessional strife.

Two years later, a new, expanded prayer book was published, this time written by the royal chaplain Jacob Fabricius.[139] Fabricius's book specified in the title that the prayers it contained were to be used by Swedish field preachers. The prayers were intended to complement the Psalms and the "usual" litany, again cross-referencing civilian devotion as we observed above. The Swedish court preacher and, by extension, the Swedish crown thus envisaged field services adhering to regular church litany during which the prayers from Fabricius's book could be used. Again, explicitly martial prayers or passages are rarely found. The first sixty-one pages were dedicated to morning and evening prayers as well as four prayers that addressed the "general affliction of Christendom."[140] They contained supplications for guidance, correction and forgiveness, and protection of the speaker, the royal army, the royal family, other Christian sovereigns, widows and orphans, pregnant women, and young mothers.[141] The prayers invoked God to avert danger, hunger, pestilence, bad weather, and a bad death, and in one instance even asked God's mercy and forgiveness for the enemy.[142]

66 ❖ *Faith in War*

The general tenor of the updated Swedish military prayer book thus remained not distinctly military but contained supplications that are thinkable in many religious contexts. Only three prayers were directed against the enemy. The first one contained a confessional remark when it asked for protection against the enemies of the Gospel and "the Pope's atrocity and idolatry."[143] The other two battle prayers were confessionally more inclusive, maybe owing to the rapidly increasing confessional heterogeneity of the Swedish army at this point in time.[144] Most of the Swedish and Finnish soldiers died soon after the invasion of Germany and by the end of 1631 about two-thirds of the Swedish army were composed of Germans and Scots, so Lutherans, Calvinists, and growing numbers of Catholics would be hearing Fabricius's prayers.[145]

Although their existence yet again shows the aspirations on behalf of the Swedish king and his staff to provide the army with a comprehensive and standardized system of pastoral care, we cannot determine how the Swedish field chaplains used the prayer books. The prayers included in this and the other prayer books are not indicative of a putative "military" religion. Although individual prayers were included for occasions that were specific to the military context, very few communicate bellicosity. On the contrary, especially in view of the explicit reference to the regular church litany in the title of the 1632 version, they represent an attempt to preserve and foster fundamental Christian virtues such as charity and forbearance. These were *Christian* values, however, not decidedly *Protestant* ones, as apart from isolated and brief anti-papal barbs, they showed no partisan content. Unlike most civilian propaganda, which was steeped in the language and logic of confessional antagonism, military prayer books were not intended to agitate sectarian warriors but to provide Christian soldiers with spiritual care amid the chaos of war. The prayers, like the professional and legal setting in which they were spoken, accommodated adherents of all Christian creeds.

Conclusion

In terms of their organizational structure, then, the armies were tolerant spaces. The articles of war reflected the Reformation in so far as they became less confessionally specific, initially explicitly banned sectarian preaching, and carefully avoided stipulations that could be construed as carrying confessional bias. This was primarily due to military pragmatism, as the inclusive Christian phrasing precluded conflicts that confessionally charged clauses would have produced in the confessionally heterogeneous armies of the period. The carefulness with which warlords phrased their legal codes simultaneously tells us something important about soldiers: they clearly were not the religiously indifferent, "godless" mercenaries that they were commonly portrayed as. If warlords had to check their confessionalizing impulses in designing the legal and structural framework of their armies, soldiers must have carried personal confessional convictions that could be offended.

The contracting colonels who assembled, equipped, fed, and ultimately owned the regiments were interested in maintaining an efficient fighting force and often apparently adopted a cynical approach to discipline: as long as soldiers were obedient, loyal, and able to fight when they had to, and their behavior did not threaten the cohesion of the regiment, colonels had little interest in prosecuting offences against civilians or risking alienation by policing niceties such as attendance at religious services or blasphemy. As we will see in the following chapters, soldiers and their families also did not need coercion to follow the Christian life, as they generally did so voluntarily.

The clerics who catered to military communities have received a lot of attention in this chapter for two reasons: firstly, their role is imperfectly understood and secondly, they provided the religious link between the military authorities and the troops. The examination of their duties has shown that these were essentially identical with those of the parish clergy, such that field chaplains needed no further training when they took up a post in the military. This suggests a degree of normalcy that is a valuable counterweight to contemporaneous and historiographical suggestions that the military religious life was deficient in comparison to that in the parish. Regarding the perceived "quality" of military clerics, it is difficult to come to clear conclusions. The chaplains we have encountered in this chapter certainly do not suggest that they were more debauched than their civilian colleagues, some of whom could be downright scandalous characters, as visitation protocols proved throughout the period. While clerical dissolution and poor training were endemic across the confessional spectrum, the low pay, poor living conditions, and social stigma attached especially to infantry chaplains imply that many clerics joined the armies for want of better prospects. Catering to soldiers brought with it the need to tone down confessional fervor and it is again difficult to tell how much restraint this necessitated on behalf of the chaplains. Evidence from the civilian context shows that in many confessionally mixed locales, the local clerics and their parishioners developed modes of worship and of religious parish life that accommodated all members of the community.[146] Whether such sophisticated degrees of ecumenical religious life developed in the regiments with any frequency is unclear but, as we have seen, at least the sermons and prayers were expected to include Christians of all denominations and chaplains were also required to give solace to sick and dying soldiers who did not share their creed. If they had problems finding the right words, chaplains could draw on a small but growing genre of books containing predominantly ecumenically phrased prayers for the edification of all Christians.

68 ❧ *Faith in War*

From the articles of war to the chaplaincy and the prayer books, the military realm was consequently structured around universal Christian, not confessional, norms and values, and provided a professional setting that accommodated all Christians. This leads us to the question of toleration, which was not a positive value in the early modern mind but denoted resentful inaction in the face of the undesirable. This view of toleration seems to fit the attitudes of warlords described in this chapter. But how soldiers and their families moved in this tolerant professional setting, how they negotiated religious difference in their daily lives, and how their religious convictions and needs were affected by the realities of the military life are questions that will guide the remainder of this book.

Notes

1. Pröve, *Stehendes Heer*; Pröve, "Reichweiten und Grenzen der Konfessionalisierung"; Nowo-sadtko, "Die Schulbildung der Soldatenkinder," 293–94.
2. Pröve, "Reichweiten und Grenzen der Konfessionalisierung," 82–9.
3. Ibid., 83.
4. Bonin, *Grundzüge der Rechtsverfassung*; Beck, *Artikelsbriefe*; Möller, *Regiment*; Baumann, *Landsknechte*, 103–8; Burschel, *Söldner*, 129–45; Prinz, *Der Einfluss von Heeresverfassung und Soldatenbild*. Most recently, Huntebrinker has argued convincingly for the great influence that regimental legal autonomy had on the military as a social group: *Fromme Knechte*, 304–14.
5. See Huntebrinker, "Geordneter Sozialverband oder Gegenordnung?" 186–87.
6. Möller, *Regiment*, 127–132.
7. Kirchhof, *Militaris Disciplina*, 192. French officers, too, considered it their right to kill the men under their command with impunity: Meumann, "'J'ay dit plusieurs fois,'" 98.
8. See Baumann, *Landsknechte*, 104-8.; Möller, *Regiment*, 247–50.
9. On the different trial forms in the sixteenth century see Möller, *Regiment*, ch. 4; Baumann, *Landsknechte*, 103–8.
10. Möller, *Regiment*, 183–89.
11. Ibid., 185. Georg Niege, who had dropped out of his studies in theology, worked his way up through different administrative positions until he became *Schultheiß* in 1563 (Bei der Wieden, *Leben im 16. Jahrhundert*, 90), and Peter Hagendorf, who probably had no formal education beyond his schooldays, served as a juror in his regiment in the 1640s and generally had very close relations with the legal staff (Peters, *Peter Hagendorf*, 118). On experience as a decisive factor in early modern criminal justice, see Härter, "Erfahrung in der frühneuzeitlichen Strafjustiz."
12. On unenforced laws as a "structural characteristic of the early modern state" see Schlumbohm, "Gesetze die nicht durchgesetzt werden."
13. Lorenz, *Das Rad der Gewalt*, 330.
14. For example, the articles from ca. 1490 in Beck (*Artikelsbriefe*, 54–55) or the field ordinance issued in the recess of the Diet of Augsburg in 1500 (ibid., 63–64).

Making Christian Armies ∿ 69

15. Ibid., 41–43. Clerics, churches, and certain categories of noncombatants had been exempt from military violence for centuries; see Contamine, *War in the Middle Ages*, 289–90; Kaeuper, *Chivalry and Violence*, 73.

16. Beck, *Artikelsbriefe*, 18. For such an oath, see e.g., Johann Georg of Saxony, *Articuls=Brief*.

17. Hauptstaatsarchiv (HStA) Düsseldorf, Jülich-Berg II 249a. On the Anabaptist kingdom of Münster see Klötzer, *Die Täuferherrschaft von Münster*; Lutterbach, *Das Täuferreich*; and Haude, *In the Shadow of Savage Wolves*.

18. Lutterbach, *Das Täuferreich*, 78.

19. HStA Düsseldorf, Jülich-Berg II 249a, fol. 2^V.

20. HStA Düsseldorf, Jülich-Berg II 249a, fol. 1^V.

21. See Brendle and Schindling, "Religionskriege in der Frühen Neuzeit."

22. On Charles V's religious policies, see Luttenberger, "Die Religionspolitik Karls V. im Reich"; Kohler, *Karl V*; and Schilling, "Veni, vidi, Deus vixit."

23. Haug-Moritz and Schmidt, "Schmalkaldischer Bund"; Schlütter-Schindler, *Der Schmalkaldische Bund*.

24. See Brendle and Schindling, "Religionskriege in der Frühen Neuzeit," 35; Haug-Moritz, "Der Schmalkaldische Krieg."

25. The text used here is Charles V, *Römischer Kayserlicher Maiestat Declaration*. Other editions were printed under different titles.

26. Ibid., Aiii^R; Bii^R.

27. Haug-Moritz, "Der Schmalkaldische Krieg," 97.

28. See e.g., John of Saxony and Philipp of Hesse, *Bestendige vnd warhafftige / verantwortung*.

29. Regarding the differences in Maximilian I of Bavaria's military and civilian confessional policies, for example, compare Hartinger, "Konfessionalisierung des Alltags" with Kaiser, "Maximilian I. von Bayern und der Krieg" and "*Cuius exercitus, eius religio?*"

30. Edelmayer, *Söldner und Pensionäre*, 254 n117.

31. Baumann, "Süddeutschland als Söldnermarkt", 71–72.

32. See Edelmayer, *Söldner und Pensionäre*, ch. 6.

33. Bei der Wieden, "Zur Konfessionalisierung des landsässigen Adels," 311.

34. Macdonald, *Missions to the Gaels*, 50–58.

35. Grosjean, *An Unofficial Alliance*, 45, 66.

36. See Burschel, *Söldner*, 163-65.

37. Bonin, *Rechtsverfassung*, 61.

38. Charles V, *Artickell*.

39. Bonin, *Rechtsverfassung*, 61; Baumann, *Landsknechte*, 195.

40. Charles V, *Römischer Keiserlicher Maiestet bestallung*, Bi^V.

41. Ibid., Bii^R.

42. On the *Reichsartikelbrief* see Huntebrinker, "Der Reichsartikelbrief." The complete 1570 imperial ordinance including the articles of war for cavalry and infantry as well as addenda can be found in Lünig, *Corpus Iuris Militaris*, vol. 1, 58-70. The passages concerning the military in the imperial recess that accompanied the articles of war of 1570 also show that religious matters were of little importance (ibid., vol. 1, 327–332.).

43. For example, Duke Maximilian of Bavaria's articles of war (Lünig, *Corpus Iuris Militaris*, vol. 2, 778), Ferdinand III's 1642 articles, and Leopold I's revised version of 1665 still reiterated the religious regulations from the 1570 articles verbatim (ibid., vol. 1, 81–82).

44. Ibid., vol. 1, 70.

45. See Kümin, *Drinking Matters*, 81.

70 ~: *Faith in War*

46. Forster, *Catholic Revival*, 125.
47. Burschel, *Söldner*, 136–37.
48. Tallett, *War and Society*, 123. See also Oestreich, "Der römische Stoizismus und die oranische Heeresreform." The new Dutch martial law found a lot of interest in Germany and elsewhere: the articles of war were printed in translation; for example, Anon., *Kurtzer Begrieff.* Pappus annotated the Dutch legislation at length: *Holländisch Kriegs-Recht.* Alexander Leslie's *Articles and Ordinance* were essentially a translation of the Swedish model.
49. Christian IV of Denmark, *Articulsbrieff.* Citations are taken from the 1638 Glückstadt edition.
50. Ibid., Aii^R.
51. Ibid., Fii^R.
52. *Schwedisches Kriegs=Recht.* The articles were first issued for the Swedish army in 1621 and were printed in German repeatedly from 1632 onward. Also in 1632, an English translation by Watts was printed as *The Swedish Discipline.*
53. *Schwedisches Kriegs=Recht*, 4.
54. These will also be examined in Chapter 3.
55. Ibid., 8.
56. Ibid., 6.
57. Ibid.
58. The drunkenness of clerics and its effects on their duties had been discussed at least since the tenth century; see Kaiser, *Trunkenheit und Gewalt im Mittelalter*, 196–199.
59. *Schwedisches Kriegs=Recht*, 6–7.
60. See also Burschel, *Söldner*, 136–140.
61. See Möller, *Regiment*, 196.
62. For a discussion of this problem see most recently Lohsträter, "Militär und Recht," 15.
63. For a description, see Huntebrinker, *Fromme Knechte*, 40–43. I would like to thank Maren Lorenz and Jan Willem Huntebrinker for their kind help in answering my questions and their generosity in sharing their research.
64. Lorenz, *Rad der Gewalt*, 214. Here, a soldier who had drunkenly attempted to rape another soldier's wife on a Sunday morning was convicted of breaking the Sabbath in the first instance. The attempted rape, which the presiding judge initially dismissed as a "joke," finally led to a high fine.
65. Ibid.
66. See Parrott, *The Business of War*, 167.
67. See for example Kaiser, "Generalstaatische Söldner."
68. Kaiser, "*Cuius exercitus, eius religio?*" 333–36.
69. Kaiser, *Politik und Kriegführung*, 84–85.
70. *Underschiedtliche Puncta, welche in anstellung des Gottesdiensts bey der Kayß. vndt Königl. armada zu observiren weren*, in Hallwig, *Wallenstein's Ende*, vol. 2, 537.
71. Bielik, *Geschichte der K.u.K Militär-Seelsorge*, 355.
72. Kirchhof, *Militaris Disciplina*, 179.
73. Kaiser, "Ars moriendi," 332.
74. Bielik, *Geschichte der K.u.K. Militär-Seelsorge*, 18.
75. Ibid., 19.
76. These attempts by the Society of Jesus have recently received attention. In English, see the contributions in the *Journal of Jesuit Studies* special issue (2017) on the Jesuits as field chaplains. I would like to thank Nicole Reinhardt, University of Durham, for pointing its publi-

cation out to me. On the development of SJ military catechisms, see also Vincenzo Lavenia's *Il catechismo dei Soldati*.

77. On the two short-lived field missions in France, see Boltanski, "Forger le 'soldat chrétien'"; and Boltanski, "A Jesuit Missio Castrensis."
78. The account of the 1569 mission is based on Civale, "'Dextere Sinistram Vertere'".
79. Parker, *The Army of Flanders*, 145–46.
80. Bielik, *Geschichte der K.u.K Militär-Seelsorge*, 22–25.
81. Ibid., 357.
82. Gustavus Adolphus, *Schwedisches Kriegs=Recht*, 7–8.
83. Ibid., 8.
84. Autenrieth, *Samuel Gerlach*, 30–31.
85. It is possible that Chanovsky's lack of interest in Gerlach's ministry was due to the officer's Catholic sympathies. I have not been able to find solid evidence regarding Chanovsky's confessional position in 1631, but during his time as governor of Freiburg, the Jesuit "Brother Michel" seems to have been his family chaplain and in charge of the Chanovsky children; see Alzog, "Itinerarium oder Raisbüchlin des P. Conrad Burger," 352–53.
86. Autenrieth, *Gerlach*, 31.
87. Ibid., 31.
88. Ibid., 35.
89. Ibid., 36–37.
90. See ibid., 89 for a timeline of Gerlach's life.
91. Hocker, *Pastorale Castrense*, preface. The other tract was Lampe, *Der gewissenhaffte Feld-Prediger*.
92. Hocker had obtained the manuscript from Rücker's son Johann Michael, the superintendent in Windsheim, Bavaria.
93. Fronsperger, *Von Keyserlichem Kriegsrechten*, CXXXVI[R].
94. Ibid., XLI[R].
95. Alzog, "Itinerarium oder Raisbüchlin des P. Conrad Burger," 352.
96. Solms, "*Kriegsbuch*," vol. 2, 62[V].
97. Kirchhof, *Militaris Disciplina*, 133.
98. Ibid.
99. For example Fiedler, *Kriegswesen*, 75; Tallett, *War and Society*, 127.
100. Johannes a Lasco Bibliothek Emden (JALB) 503, Nr. 15. For biographical details on Northausen see Goeters, "Magister Johann Northausen," 172–184.
101. Arch. JALB 503, Nr. 15, fol. 15.
102. Arch. JALB 503, Nr. 15, fol. 15[R].
103. Goeters, "Magister Johann Northausen," 173.
104. Arch. JALB 503, Nr. 15, fol. 13[R].
105. Ibid.
106. Hocker, *Pastorale Castrense*, 8–12.
107. Ibid.
108. Ibid., 11.
109. Ibid., 444-47. The injunctions against drunkenness we have observed in the articles of war gain a new dimension against this background.
110. Fronsperger, *Von Keyserlichem Kriegßrechten*, XXXVII[V].
111. Ibid., XXXVIII[R].

72 ~: *Faith in War*

112. Solms,"*Kriegsbuch*," vol. 1, 64[R].
113. Dillich, *KriegßBuch*, 131, 211.
114. Theobald, *Heerpredigt*.
115. Ibid., Ai[V].
116. Arch. JALB 503, Nr. 15, fol. 15[R]; Northausen, *Erbermliche. . .anzeig*, 2.
117. Thodaenus, *Threni Magdæburgi*, Kiiii[R].
118. Ibid., Li[R].
119. Ibid., Lii[R]. The fact that a Lutheran field preacher served in Tilly's army calls into question the absoluteness of Peter Burschel's assessment (*Söldner*, 164) that chaplains in the armies of the Thirty Years War all shared the creed of the warlord, which has been echoed by Kaiser, "*Cuius exercitus, eius religio?*" 319 and Nowosadtko, "Die Schulbildung der Soldatenkinder," 293.
120. Autenrieth, *Gerlach*, 34.
121. Winter,"Möser's Aufzeichnungen über den Dreißigjährigen Krieg," 26–27, 31, 166.
122. Bielik, *Geschichte der K.u.K Militär-Seelsorge*, 336.
123. Hocker, *Pastorale Castrense*, 25–29.
124. Ibid., 12–13.
125. Ibid., 362–63.
126. For example Musculus, *Vermanung and den Teütschen vnnd Evangelischen Kriegßman*; Breul, *MILES CHRISTIANVS*; Anon., *Auffrichtiger Teutscher Soldaten Regul*.
127. Luther,"Whether Soldiers, Too, Can Be Saved"; Musculus, *Beruff vnd stand*.
128. Fronsperger, *Geistliche KriegßOrdnung*. The text was printed as a separate publication in 1565, although the inclusion of a register for Fronsperger's *Von Kayserlichem Kriegsrechten*, which was also printed by Georg Rabe in the same year, indicates that it was intended to be part of the military handbook. The 1566 edition of *Von Kayserlichem Kriegsrechten*, for example, included the *Geistliche KriegßOrdnung* on pages CCXXXVI[R]-CCLVI[V].
129. Ibid., II[V].
130. Two early examples are Schöpper, *Christlicher Bericht* and Behm, *Kriegesman*.
131. The Spanish translation still appeared under Possevino's name as *Platica spiritual para el soldado christiano*, the beautifully illustrated French version under Sailly's as *Guidon et pratique sprituelle du soldat chrêtien*. The Dutch text was *Verscheyden litanien tot ghebruyck des catholijken leghers*. See Lavenia,"Jesuit Catechisms for Soldiers," 600–3.
132. Puchner, *Christliche / Heilsame vnnd sehr nützliche Gebetlein*.
133. Ibid., Aiii[V].
134. Ibid., Aiv[R].
135. On German Catholic anti-papalism see Brady, *German Histories*, esp. ch. 8. The Lutheran hymn singing in Catholic parishes is mentioned by Schindling,"Neighbours of a Different Faith," 471.
136. Botvidi, *Etliche Gebete*. The book only has sporadic pagination; all page references are my own, counting the title page as page 1.
137. Ibid., 12, 15.
138. Ibid., 29–35.
139. Fabricius, *Etliche Gebet*.
140. Ibid., 1-22, 40–61.
141. Ibid., 1, 5, 23, 49, 51.
142. Ibid., 51.
143. Ibid., 62–63.

Making Christian Armies ❧ 73

144. Ibid., 67, 71–72.
145. Ericson, "The Swedish Army and Navy," 302.
146. The literature on these modes of coexistence is expanding rapidly. For just two examples see Spohnholz, "Multiconfessional Celebration of the Eucharist" and more recently Luebke, *Hometown Religion*, esp. ch. 2 and 3.

CHAPTER 3

Religion, Morality, and Military Everyday Life

> One often notices that if a person plans to excel in military life, he not only immediately changes his way of dressing but also his habits, his customs, his voice, thus setting him apart from every civilian custom.
>
> —Niccolò Machiavelli, Preface to *The Book of the Art of War*

What Machiavelli described in this quotation was a commonplace in the early modern period: there was a fundamental tension, even a contradiction, between the way a Christian man *should* behave and the way soldiers *did* behave. The first chapter has suggested that the stereotypical accusations of "godlessness" were a literary trope and the previous chapter has shown that soldiers were ultimately relatively free in how they behaved as long as their actions did not threaten the regiment. This chapter will develop a profile of military religious and moral attitudes. The guiding question is whether the specific socio-professional setting of the military was governed by a different set of norms, in the way that contemporaries feared. We will begin with a survey of religious attitudes, mainly on the basis of autobiographical accounts written by soldiers that cover the period from the 1480s to the 1640s.[1] The accounts were written either by Germans or soldiers who worked in Germany and they have been chosen to capture the potential for a variety of spiritual attitudes that men from different regional cultural backgrounds brought into the military in different locations and at different points in time. In a second step, we will take a closer look at three "typical" soldierly vices: blasphemy, magic, and sexual conduct.

Christian Soldiers

In most soldiers' accounts, religious views are framed in a language that is "Christian" rather than confessionally marked. God featured in soldiers' autobiographies in typical early modern fashion as a helper, arbiter, and punisher,

Religion, Morality, and Military Everyday Life ~ 75

and the authors habitually invoked God's grace and gave thanks for His protection.[2] Augustin von Fritsch began his life story by thanking God for protecting him "like a father for 31 years" in the armies.[3] After the carnage at Nördlingen (1634), Peter Hagendorf was the only man in his unit who had not been either wounded or killed. He noted that "the Almighty" had protected him "especially, so that I have to thank God for it in the highest [terms] for the rest of my life."[4] When recording his second marriage he asked God to grant the couple "long lasting health" and he marked a happy return after a long separation as follows: "I returned to my love in good health. Dear Lord be thanks for this, may He give his grace further."[5]

Soldiers directly attributed good and bad fortune to God's providence. During the Sack of Magdeburg (1633), a plunderer rescued the Friese family from the burning city.[6] His wife berated him for filling their hut with a horde of children and their parents instead of bringing loot, but the soldier expressed his confidence that God would reward him for his charitable deed. When he returned from a looting trip the next day laden with goods, he explicitly correlated this outcome to his saving the Frieses. Peter Hagendorf, who thanked God for his protection numerous times, also recorded how God afflicted him with a severe skin condition.[7] He did not consider all turns of events to be God's work but seems to have praised Him in situations that turned out positively against the odds. He did not thank God for his wife's convalescence after a long disease, for example, as credit was due to the healing skills of the Ingolstadt executioner's wife and to his purse, as the treatment had been expensive.[8]

God was also invoked when the authors recognized their own impotence. An anonymous former mercenary who committed his experiences to paper around 1530 is such an example. He had belonged to the *Schwarze Heer*, a mercenary band that had served the Hungarian king Matthias Corvinus in the 1480s and 1490s and was betrayed by his successor Vladislav.[9] The men had refused to fight for the new king until pay arrears were settled but had ultimately been coaxed into a campaign against the Ottomans only to be ambushed, hunted down, and hanged by their new commander and his army. When relating these events, the soldier expressed his hopes that God would punish the traitors and "take pity and have mercy" on his dead comrades.[10] He ended his account as follows:

> So the Schwarze Heer were murdered and annihilated . . . They are gone, God comfort them. AMEN. . . . I then . . . went to my father and thanked God that He protected me like this, that I helped fight such great battles and got away with a straight body . . . God give [me] longer [life].[11]

It is noticeable that the old soldier invoked God whenever he reached a point in his narrative that brought home his human helplessness, like the treason of the Hungarian king and his nobles, the massacre of his friends, and the hope

76 ❦ *Faith in War*

that God would punish the wicked and comfort the murdered in the next life. It seems that he, like most of his contemporaries, viewed God as the ultimate arbiter of justice, a belief that compensated for his very real experiences of powerlessness.

Despite their reputation for being "irreligious" and "godless," soldiers asked God for protection and the eventual administration of justice and thought His providence to be at work in their lives. The writers were very much in dialogue with the divine in what may be considered an entirely "normal" early modern manner. Other historians are more skeptical in this respect. Jan Peters, the editor of Peter Hagendorf's diary, has taken the absence of deeper religious contemplations in the text and the soldier's formulaic implorations of God to indicate that his piety was "little more than an outward norm of behavior."[12] Peter Burschel has also commented on the fact that his religiosity did not extend beyond brief religious formulas interspersed in the text.[13] However, we ought to bear in mind that, if the diary was at all intended to be read by others, it was probably written for his family and friends who did not have to be told about his religious views, nor his name, which he did not record either. Benigna von Krusenstjern has cautioned that formulaic invocations of God should not be read dismissively as mere linguistic conventions but as indicators of the writers' struggle for composure.[14] She has also pointed out that these expressions were prayer formulas, identified as such by the frequent addendum "Amen." The formulas Hagendorf used when recording the deaths of his children or his wife fit this format. When his first child was born prematurely, he noted: "my wife gave birth but the child was not mature yet and died immediately. God grant him a good resurrection. ✝ It was a young son."[15] Hagendorf mentioned the "blessed Christian baptism" of all his children, apart from the three babies who died during or soon after birth, presumably because no cleric was at hand to baptize them.[16] He also marked the deaths of eight of his ten children, his first wife, and his second mother-in-law with crosses in the text and the formula "God grant him/her a good resurrection."[17]

If we compare the formulas used by Hagendorf to those of his contemporaries, we find no qualitative difference. The nobleman Christoph von Bismarck recorded the deaths of his relatives mostly without any prayer formulas, but when he did, in a situation where three of his children died within seven days, he wrote: "God grant them all a happy resurrection."[18] The war commissary Hans Conrad Lang used a slightly more elaborate formula in which he asked for the joyous resurrection of the deceased and for God's grace and providence in bestowing a good death on "us all and everyone."[19] Neither of these diarists explicated their religious convictions and their religious integrity has not been called into question as a consequence, and to doubt Hagendorf's spiritual sincerity on this basis—and presumably that of his profession—seems unwarranted. That God was invoked in the face of danger and death should not be regarded as indicating a lower degree of piety. These instances marked decisive moments in soldiers' lives in which their own helplessness became often devastatingly apparent. In dangerous situations, God proved his providence by protecting them and when loved ones and friends died, God was the last source of hope through the promise of resurrection. Soldiers did not differ at all from their nonmilitary contemporaries in this respect.

There is more to suggest that Hagendorf's religious sensibilities were by no means unusual. His confession is, as has been variously observed, indeterminable from his diary.[20] He simply referred to the baptisms of his children as "Christian" and although he sometimes remarked on which confession was predominant in a particular region, he never expressed preference or distaste.[21] Similarly, he mentioned churches and cloisters and pilgrimage sites neutrally.[22] Even when he was forced to change sides after his capture by the Swedes or when he rejoined his old imperial regiment after two years, we find not a hint in his diary that might indicate how he felt about the confessional cause that his current warlords were proclaiming.[23]

Thanks to the combined archival ingenuity of several academic and amateur sleuths, we now know that the diary was really written by Peter Hagendorf, and we can also tell that he had his children baptized in Lutheran churches, even if he had to travel to find one.[24] He was, therefore, a conscious and conscientious Lutheran, even if he mostly served in the regiments of Catholic commanders and did not commit doctrinal self-identifications to paper. Despite its confessional ambiguity, Hagendorf's diary presents him as a man whose experience was framed and expressed in religious terms. Preternatural events were sometimes factually reported, for example, when three blaspheming gamblers were struck by lightning, when the devil appeared at another gambling table, or when the regiment marched past the Heuberg, a reputed gathering place for witches in the Swabian Alps.[25] On the other hand, he expressed his skepticism of a miraculous candle that had allegedly burned for centuries and a hint of doubt is detectable when he mentions the execution of a pretty eighteen-year-old witch in Lippstadt.[26]

Hagendorf also used the church year by way of dating and to reveal the absurdities of military life: "On Good Friday we had bread and meat in abundance, and on the holy Easter day we did not have a mouthful of bread."[27] He also used biblical imagery: when his wife fell ill and he had to transport her on horseback, he wrote, for example, "I came here like Joseph travelled in Egypt"; when he picked up his only surviving son Melchert Christoff from a schoolmaster in Altheim after the war, he expressed his happiness in another biblical image: "Thus I fetched my son out of Egypt."[28] It seems that he went to church when he had the chance and on one occasion he commented on the beauty of the church music in Mühlhausen.[29] Mühlhausen had been one of the centers of Lutheran church music since the sixteenth century and would later give an

78 ❦ *Faith in War*

up-and-coming musician named Johann Sebastian Bach his first prestigious position.[30] Amid the turmoil of war, such musical splendor was a memorable experience. The comment not only reveals that he appreciated the rare musical treat, but it is one of the few fragments of evidence contained in his diary that suggest his Lutheranism.[31] Hagendorf noted the celebrations after the Peace of Westphalia with a degree of disapproval ("as if it were Easter or Pentecost") yet recalled the details of the sermon he heard on the occasion, including the Bible passage and its content.[32] Reading his diary closely, it becomes very clear that Hagendorf was not irreligious in any way, but followed the Christian life as well as circumstances allowed.

Soldiers appear in the sources in diverse religious contexts: reading devotional literature, singing hymns, saving and christening foundlings, celebrating Christmas, and so forth.[33] Wealthier soldiers invested in their local churches. Following a narrow escape from a lynch mob, Caspar von Widmarckter obtained a "comfortable chair" in his local church to hear God's word and "not be distracted from the eternal by the temporal."[34] Augustin von Fritsch endowed an altar in a local chapel three years after he had left the military, "In praise and the glory of the most holy undivided Trinity, God Father, God Son, and God the Holy Ghost" for having protected him in "31 years of faithfully rendered military service."[35] Both the Protestant Widmarckter and the Catholic Fritsch therefore not only considered God the ultimate protector in their professional lives, but also invested parts of their revenue in church furnishings as part of their devotional practice.

Wealthy Catholic soldiers also bestowed significant endowments on religious and other institutions. The Irishman Walter Butler, who had earned infamy and promotion in the assassination of Albrecht von Wallenstein in 1634, left a fortune to spiritual orders. The Prague Franciscans were to receive 20,000 *reichsthaler* in order to train missionaries who should be sent to re-Catholicize Scotland and Ireland. The Jesuit William Lamormaini, who had agitated against Wallenstein at the Habsburg court, received 200 *thaler*, while the Irish Jesuit Peter Wadding, chancellor of the University in Prague, received three thousand *thaler* to aid poor Irish travelers.[36] Field Marshal Melchior von Hatzfeldt appointed his younger brother Franz, the prince-bishop of Würzburg (1631–42) and Bamberg (1633–42), as the executor of the will he specified on 21 July 1634.[37] Hatzfeldt left his house in Cologne with all its contents to another brother called Hermann. Franz was asked to commission a bejeweled lamp weighing 1,000 ducats for "Loreto" (probably the Basilica della Santa Casa in Loreto, not the sanctuary of that name in Prague mentioned later), as he had promised this in Italy but had not been able to fulfill this vow. Two silver lamps worth 600 *reichsthaler* apiece were to be sent to Mariazell (Austria) and to the recently dedicated Loreto Sanctuary in Prague. One thousand *reichsthaler* were to be paid out to poor, Catholic soldiers, and a minimum of 1,200 *reichsthaler* were to be used as an alms trust for an infirmary ("zum Unterhalte bresthafter Leute"). During his illness Melchior had promised a pilgrimage and donations to Altötting and asked Franz to deliver an altar he had commissioned years earlier to its destination after his death.

The notion that soldiering was a profession of anti-Christians or that military life had a de-Christianizing effect cannot be sustained, as Christian modes of thinking clearly characterize soldiers' life accounts. The evidence presented here contradicts the characterization of soldiers as irreligious, as the attitudes toward the sacred expressed in the diaries suggest that soldiers did not differ from their civilian contemporaries in any meaningful way.

Worship in War

While soldiers could pray on their own, communal worship, which was a central element of early modern religiosity, generally required the presence of clerics, as did the ceremonies that marked important stages in life like baptism, marriages, or burials, and, for Catholics, going to confession. The chronic lack of chaplains ultimately raises questions regarding the possibilities for the common soldiery to receive pastoral care. Using civilian clerics where opportunities arose was one option. We have already seen Peter Hagendorf taking his newborn children to be baptized in Lutheran parishes. Similarly, the Cistercian Conrad Burger became very popular with the French troops garrisoned close to his abbey in Kenzingen, north of Freiburg, because he spoke French. During the Lenten season of 1643 he heard so many confessions that he could buy himself a whole new suit of clothes and new shoes from the confessional fees (*Beichtpfennig*) the soldiers paid him.[38]

While on campaign, the practical limitations of religious practice in the field were considerable. Camp services often had to be held in the open field, an unfavorable acoustic setting: the parish priest's voice carried and resonated from the walls of a church, while the field chaplain's voice drifted into the open air.[39] The reliance on the spoken word in Protestant worship may consequently have been a problem in regard to preaching and bible readings, but communal singing and collective prayer provided a valuable mode of inclusion for the individual. The references to the "usual" hymns, psalms, and liturgy in the military literature surveyed in the previous chapter gain further importance in this respect, as the soldiers already knew the hymns from their civilian lives. Inclusion in worship through hymn singing was not really an option for Catholic troops, as church music "was performed by part of the body on behalf of the whole" by clergy and trained singers.[40] Singing was used to bolster morale in isolated instances, for example at White Mountain when the Irish Jesuit Henry Fitzsimon intoned the "*Salve Regina*," as the infantry began to march toward

80 ❧ *Faith in War*

the enemy.[41] MacCulloch's characterization of the hymn as the "secret weapon" of Protestantism thus takes on a new dimension when considering the use of devotional singing in the military.[42] The material and visual elements of the Catholic rite may in some ways have provided an equivalent mode of inclusion for Catholic troops. Matthias Rogg has described a painting of a pre-battle scene in which two Dominicans elevate the host while standing on dung heaps, thereby making the miracle of transubstantiation visible across distance and blessing the men from afar.[43] While this was a drastically curtailed version of Catholic rites from a liturgical standpoint, ordinary Catholics quite commonly considered only the miracle of transubstantiation and the elevation of the host to be of interest, so a digest version of the mass that only provided the highlight may actually have been welcome.[44]

Soldiers' participation in field services was witnessed by the nun Maria Anna Junius on two occasions.[45] The first field service was held on a Sunday for sappers constructing fortifications around the Heilig Grab cloister, and although the level of solemnity among the trenchers was rather low that day— Sister Junius thought their behavior "worse than [in] a Jewish school"—we get a sense of the process.[46] The preacher began to sing a hymn and then said a prayer for "his little pack of devils," followed by another hymn.[47] The second service Junius witnessed, however, met with even her approval: "Tuesday the 19th [July 1633] early at four o'clock the soldiers began to sing very beautifully again, afterward their preacher gave them a sermon, when it was over they sang again, these [soldiers] were certainly very devout."[48]

In the absence of clergy and sufficient church space, soldiers also spontaneously organized religious observances on their own. In Robert Monro's description of the Battle of Leipzig, Mackay's regiment seems to have conducted communal religious rites without the guidance of chaplains.[49] After the long siege and eventual sack of Pilsen in November 1618, Ernst von Mansfeld's victorious troops held a Protestant service in the main Catholic church of St. Bartholomaei. After the congregation of officers, soldiers, and interested Pilseners had sung Luther's hymn "A Mighty Fortress is Our God," Ernst von Mansfeld's field preacher Johann Jacob Heylmann gave a long sermon, followed by prayers and the hymn "Maintain Us, Lord, in Thy Word."[50] The church was far too small to hold all the common soldiers who wanted to partake in the official victory service and no provision had been made for the units guarding the city gates. Some soldiers outside the church began to sing "Vater unser im Himmelreich," a hymn based on the Lord's Prayer, in thanks for His protection during the assault, in which several hundred comrades had died, and the singing spread among the soldiers throughout the town.[51] The troops then sang Psalm 42 and when cannons were fired after the sermon in St. Bartholomaei, the soldiers across town also discharged their weapons in jubilation, shattering the Pilseners' windowpanes. This episode shows how the singing of familiar psalms and hymns enabled soldiers to cope with difficult spatial situations and the lack of chaplains. The spontaneous nature of this improvised act of worship also indicates the apparent desire of the soldiery to thank God for the victory and for protecting them.

Worship in the field appears to have been a pragmatic version of regular liturgy. For Protestants, the widespread practice of hymn singing made communal worship somewhat easier. As we have seen in the descriptions of Protestant field services, even Catholics commented positively on the fact that soldiers sang, and apparently sang well. The hymns also provided a means by which soldiers could give thanks to their God even in the absence of a central meeting place and without the direction of field preachers. In the Catholic context, the great prominence given to the visual could compensate for the absence of congregational singing as central sacred rites, such as the previously mentioned elevation of the host, could be witnessed by large groups and from a distance.

In the German context there is little indication of modes of devotion that were exclusive to the military or religious organizations that catered specifically to soldiers. There were soldier confraternities in the Netherlands, for example the Jesuit-led Confraternity of the Holy Sacrament, established by papal bull in 1589, a network of Confraternities of Our Lady of the Rosary with its central church in Brussels, and even a Confraternity of St. Barbara exclusively for gunners.[52] The only comparable phenomenon in the German context appears to have been the cult of Fidelis of Sigmaringen, which originated among soldiers before it spread among Catholics more widely.[53] The Capuchin Fidelis had been sent into the Swiss canton of Graubünden (Grison) with an Austrian occupying force on a dual brief of ministering to the troops and converting the Calvinist locals. While he excelled at the first part of his mission, he was killed by Calvinist peasants on 24 April 1622 alongside several hundred soldiers. Fidelis almost immediately assumed the role of a regimental saint who appeared in battles, bestowed victory on his former charges, and protected them from harm either on his own or in the company of the Virgin Mary.[54] The Sulzsche regiment in which he had ministered became a vector of his cult and spread it throughout parts of Switzerland, Austria, and southern Germany. Emperor Ferdinand III, supported by the Archbishops of Mainz, Trier, and Cologne, petitioned the Pope for expedited canonization, but despite the pope's refusal, the cult of Fidelis was kept alive within the regiment by its owner, Alwig von Sulz, and a group of veterans. It was promoted in the civilian population by the Capuchins and in some towns that had a connection to the martyr. In view of the question of confessional thinking and toleration that will be discussed in the next chapter, it should be pointed out that even in this regiment, whose colonel and much of his staff were deeply dedicated to the veneration of a monk martyred by Calvinists, the general principle of military toleration held, as even here, Protestant soldiers served alongside committed Catholics in significant numbers.[55]

82 ～ Faith in War

This examination of religious attitudes and behaviors among soldiers has not produced any evidence of military irreligiosity. In fact, there is very little that is unusual about the religious outlook and behavior of soldiers when we compare them to their civilian contemporaries. The same Christian norms that governed the civilian realm guided life in the armies, and, as has been shown, soldiers tried to follow the demands of the Christian life as best they could. This was difficult at times, but as we have seen, soldiers went to great lengths to find clerics when they needed them or spontaneously organized worship on their own. The allegation of soldierly godlessness thus appears more definitely as the literary trope we already suspect it to be. But there remain the accusations of sinful life that allegedly ran rampant in the armies. We should turn to these now.

Conflicting Norms and Deviance

The first chapter introduced us to the long list of "godless" behaviors that soldiers were allegedly indulging in. Among them were vices like excessive eating and drinking, brawling, idleness, luxurious clothing, gambling, as well as blaspheming, disorderly sexual conduct, and the use of magic. These last three transgressions will be studied here in greater detail, as these have the potential to reveal unusual religious positions that soldiers may have shared. In this endeavor, we have to be careful not to take the categorical moral norms that theologians were promoting as representative of civilian moral norms in general. The reformers of popular morality were painfully aware that they were the moral minority. Normative texts presented moral imperatives as absolute; there could be no *via media* and any aberration from that narrow path therefore had to be "unchristian," "godless," "pagan," "heretical," "idolatrous," and so forth.[56] Ordinary people frequently ignored moral and religious reformers such that moral improvement was not a straightforward top-down process in which secular and religious elites imposed a new regime onto an acquiescent populace, but an interaction that was characterized by negotiation and disagreement.

In the following, we will therefore compare moralists' accusations of soldierly vices with the behavior of soldiers as it can be reconstructed from the sources and then take the additional step of asking whether these transgressions were specific to soldiers or characteristic of popular behaviors more generally. So far, historians have usually only compared the moralists' visions of ideal Christian comportment to soldiers' behaviors, with the result that soldiers did indeed appear rather depraved. Insisting on the fact that the new programs of moral reform did *not* reflect popular norms and were *never* translated into actual majority behaviors will yield a different picture of soldiers' comportment, too. The example of *Landsknecht* fashion and especially the *Pluderhose* may serve to illustrate this point. Historians have highlighted different aspects of these fashions: Rogg has interpreted them as the wish to provoke, Burschel has used them as a measure of soldierly independence, and Huntebrinker has regarded them as an iconographical device to communicate the "morally corrupted disposition of the wearer."[57] While it is usually mentioned that neither the fashion of slashing cloth nor the *Pluderhose* were exclusively worn by soldiers but were, in fact, fashionable especially among young men of the middling to upper social echelons, this important fact is usually not discussed further.[58]

One of the tracts that often features in such discussions is Andreas Musculus's sermon against the *Pluderhose*, and it is often implied that his disgust was representative of civilian reactions to shocking soldier fashions, and secondly, that soldiers dressed like this as a deliberate affront to the values of Christian society.[59] Huntebrinker, for example, acknowledges the ambiguity of soldierly attire but concludes that the fashion was "above all" regarded as a sign of wastefulness and haughtiness.[60] By whom? *Pluderhosen* and slashed garments were the rage among young men at the time.

The very reason for the existence of Andreas Musculus's tract against the garment was a conflict between one of his deacons, Melchior Dreger, and his congregation.[61] Dreger had preached against the *Pluderhosen* but instead of taking his words to heart, the following Sunday, pranksters nailed a pair of the wicked trousers to a pillar opposite the pulpit.[62] Enraged, Musculus composed his thundering sermon against the diabolical depravity of the fashion. The theologians and their congregation clearly interpreted the *Pluderhose* differently: while for Musculus and Dreger it was an outward sign of inner depravity, Musculus had to concede that, apart from soldiers, the trousers were worn by many well-off "snot-nosed brat[s]" (*junger rotzlöffel*), especially in Lutheran territories.[63]

It seems unlikely that the wearers of slashed garments and *Pluderhosen* did so with the main intention to shock. In Ulinka Rublack's study of early modern dress, we find a series of 135 small watercolors that Matthäus Schwarz of Augsburg commissioned to document his wardrobe at many stages of his life.[64] Schwarz was a successful accountant in the Fugger firm and a veritable fashionista. Among his many outfits are several that could easily be classified as "typical" *Landsknecht* dress, with wide sleeves, bright colors, wide berets, and up to 4,800 slashes.[65] Schwarz was "dress-literate": he knew the intricacies of the changing fashions and designed his outfits to communicate certain intentions. But he was definitely not a deviant.

The *Pluderhosen* and the slashed garments should therefore be interpreted not as transgressive but merely as fashionable. Moralists like Musculus took umbrage and at times managed to convince authorities to issue chronically impotent sartorial legislation, but to the wearers of these clothes they seem to have indicated stylishness. Raising the blood pressure of the older generation

84 ❧ *Faith in War*

was probably a positive side effect of dressing in such dauntless clothes, but its primary intentions were to exhibit hipness, not degeneracy. Conflicting interpretations of moral values were consequently characteristic of society then as now, but while the hardliners have left us lengthy explications of their moral vision, it would be a mistake to regard these as representative. Most soldiers "were young men with young men's ideas of pleasure" and we should accept these ideas as equally valid.[66]

Blasphemy

Arguably the most immediately religious transgression associated with the soldiery was their alleged penchant for blasphemy. Early modern blasphemy has been examined in a number of monographs in recent years.[67] Schwerhoff and Loetz's studies have provided new insights into the pragmatics of blasphemy by applying speech act theory to uncover its communicative goals and they have identified situations in which blasphemous speech was likely to be uttered. Schwerhoff describes blasphemy as a "theatrical self-dramatization" (*theatralische Selbstinszenierung*).[68] The profanation of the sacred was often a means to a different communicative end and its purpose was to present the speaker in a certain light. As a linguistic strategy, blasphemy was characteristic of conflict situations and intended to intimidate opponents by imparting fearlessness and power in an ostentatious display of disrespect toward the sacred.[69] It had tradition among warriors: Werner von Urslingen, a fourteenth-century German mercenary captain in Italian service, for example, added to his fierce reputation by having his armor inscribed with his motto "I am the enemy of pity, God, and charity."[70] Cabantous has shown that about half of the blasphemy cases he studied in Paris also entailed physical violence and Loetz has identified blasphemy as an integral element of honor conflicts.[71] In the military context, such linguistic self-aggrandizing and posturing could therefore have been part of a belligerent bearing that complemented wild beards, daring attire, physical strength, and other hypermasculine signifiers.

There is evidence that conflict situations led soldiers to blaspheme. It is not without a certain irony that the blasphemous curses of a soldier prevented the Hessian pastor Georg Herdenius from being left stark naked by a looting party. The soldiers had already taken the pastor's cloak and one of them began to strip off his trousers, when another soldier intervened and shouted "may God's hundred-thousand sacraments defile you."[72] This outburst made his comrade back off. Here, the purpose of the soldier's blasphemous use of language was to intimidate his comrade into behaving himself. Maria Anna Junius recorded a similar, although not strictly blasphemous, attempt at verbal intimidation. When Swedish troops threatened to pillage the cloister, one soldier tried to

Religion, Morality, and Military Everyday Life ∾ 85

force the nuns to give him alcohol. The nuns had established close connections to Swedish commanders so they asked the soldier who his colonel was, presumably to complain later on. "The devil" was his reply.[73] In both instances, blasphemous or at any rate threatening speech was employed by soldiers to intimidate interlocutors, both times with the intended results: pastor Herdenius kept his trousers and the invader got his drink.

Unfavorable providence and bad luck also frequently provoked blasphemous utterances that accused God of unfairness and favoritism.[74] This type of blasphemy was often heard around the gambling table and that this "godless" behavior could provoke God's rage was also acknowledged in the military. Peter Hagendorf recalled a situation in the army camp near Löffingen when lightning killed three soldiers while they gambled and blasphemed.[75] Hagendorf did not explicitly make the connection between the soldiers' blasphemy and the divine retribution via lightning, but the implicit linkage is telling in its own right. Such stories were staples of early modern paraenesis and no explanation was necessary, as everybody knew who had killed the sinners and why.[76]

Other motivations for blasphemous curses were provocation and amusement.[77] Francisca Loetz has studied several cases in which blasphemous speech among men appeared to be a linguistic code of male bonding: the blasphemers wanted to impress their peers with their outrageously disrespectful quips about the sacred.[78] An instance of this type of blasphemy is found in a literary source. In Grimmelshausen's *Simplicissimus*, the hero witnesses the meeting between two soldiers after a long separation. One of them expresses his joy by saying: "The hail may strike you dead! . . . God's fuckrament [*Potz Fickerment*], how does the devil bring us together here."[79] While Grimmelshausen illustrated the alleged indecent speech habits of the soldiery in this instance, the scene also exhibits the bonding element of blasphemous utterances. It was strong language with which the soldiers expressed their joy of being reunited, and the comically over the top expletive "God's fuckrament" seems to be emphatic rather than blasphemous. Emphatic strong language invoking the devil is also recorded in soldiers' diaries. In Sweden, Erich Lassota and his traveling companions met an expatriate soldier from Lübeck, who told them to get onboard his boat "in the devil's name" when he realized that he was talking to Germans.[80] Augustin von Fritsch in one instance charged after an enemy, not realizing that his horse had been badly wounded, when a comrade warned, "lieutenant, by a hundred devils, back, your horse is shot."[81]

These examples of blasphemous and irreverent speech point toward more complex attitudes to the sacred than the unambiguous positions evident in contemporary moralist literature suggest. The regulations against blasphemy in the articles of war are of importance in this context. As we have seen in Chapter 2, sixteenth-century articles of war generally simply stated that blasphemy was to be avoided or criminalized it outright. While the uniformity and brevity

86 ❧ *Faith in War*

of the respective articles allows for few detailed insights into military authorities' attitudes toward blasphemy, the notion that blasphemous curses could
be excusable as slips of the tongue can be detected in some instances. A field
ordinance from the early sixteenth century (ca. 1510–20), for example, characterized blasphemy as impious, and therefore undesirable, but did not condemn
it outright. It stated that the soldiers were to refrain from blasphemy "as much
as possible," therefore leaving room for occasional slips of the tongue.[82]

In the seventeenth century, the more elaborate regulations that the crowns
of Denmark and Sweden issued for their troops in Germany also left inter-
pretative leeway and distinguished between grades of severity according to the
object of blasphemous attacks and intent. The Danish articles of war stated
that soldiers were to "refrain entirely from the abuse of God's holy name and
His word and [from] unchristian and inappropriate swearing."[83] Common offenders should receive warnings, but if they continued to blaspheme their pay
should be cut and they could face imprisonment. Should this not implement
linguistic constraint, the culprit was to be stripped down to his shirt and discharged.[84] A more serious form of blasphemy was defined as "intentional disdain and derision of God, His Word and servants."[85] This deliberate blasphemy
entailed public humiliation (*Ehrenstrafe*) or corporal punishment (or both).
Similarly, the Swedish articles of war acknowledged different degrees of blasphemy and intent. Article II stated that soldiers, drunk or sober, who showed
contempt for the Bible or spoke of it in a calumnious or derisive manner should
be sentenced to death if two witnesses could confirm the allegation.[86] While
this was seemingly unambiguous, the following articles differentiated between
circumstances and clarified procedures. Should the defendant be found guilty
of severe blasphemy, the *consistorium ecclesiasticum* was given power to pass
a death sentence.[87] If the blasphemous utterance was the result of linguistic
carelessness or levity, the first two offences entailed a fortnight in jail and a
fine to be paid into a fund for infirm soldiers; on the third offence the soldier
faced the firing squad. The fifth article acknowledged that verbal transgressions
could be prompted by "rash haste" or *Amptszorn*, which literally translates as
the "ire of (the) office."[88] If these mitigating factors applied, the culprit was to
put money into a poor relief fund or could be publicly impounded. The final
variant of blasphemous talk was defined as an intentional but frivolous abuse
of God's name, which again incurred a fine but was sharpened by public pen-
itence before the whole regiment during service. Despite the length at which
they were discussed in the articles of war, the distinctions between the various
kinds of blasphemy remain somewhat opaque. Two main factors seem to have
influenced the judgment: the severity of the blasphemous oath and whether
the utterance could be considered a slip of the tongue or indicated genuine disdain for the sacred. The situational context mattered as well. From the Swedish
military authorities' point of view, therefore, blasphemy was transgressive but

existed in different degrees of gravity, and there were situations in military life in which blasphemy was almost incidental to the profession.

I have not been able to find a case from the period in which a soldier was punished for blasphemy in the military context, and it seems that the prohibitions in the articles of war were more of a formality. The apparent absence of the prosecution of blasphemy in the military becomes more readily explicable if we compare it to trial statistics from the civilian realm: convictions purely on the grounds of blasphemy were generally rare.[89] Between 1562 and 1692, six blasphemers in Frankfurt underwent corporal punishment or were executed, about one in every twenty-two years. In Nuremberg (1503–1743) it was one conviction in every twenty-five years, in Danzig (1558–1731) one in every thirty-five years. In Zurich, a city that was exceptional in its strictness, corporal punishment and death sentences for blasphemy occurred about once every one and a half years between 1562 and 1639. Whether a blasphemer ended up in court depended on denunciations, and the laity seem to have been more thick-skinned when it came to these verbal outbreaks than the tracts of their moralizing contemporaries would lead us to believe.[90] Moralists and theologians warned incessantly that tolerating blasphemy would incur God's wrath over the entire community, but they were simultaneously aware that most people did not consider blasphemy to be particularly disturbing. Andreas Musculus was representative of his colleagues when he complained that no one reprimanded nor shunned the company of blasphemers and that secular authorities were too lax in enforcing the law in this respect.[91]

Maureen Flynn has found in her study of blasphemy in Spain that moralists thought speech gave "access to the moral center of the human being," so for "heuristic purposes . . . speech was carefully heeded by moral authorities in order to fathom the depths of the human psyche."[92] The offenders, however, did not think that their brains and mouths were that intimately connected and drunkenness, anger, levity, or habit were accepted as valid excuses for blasphemy in court.[93] A rather unagitated attitude toward the curses as such therefore seems to have been prevalent among ordinary people. It was maybe annoying and often antisocial, but few seem to have taken the threat of God's wrath seriously or to have considered the sacred dimension of the blasphemous utterance important.[94] Ultimately, it was apparently a small step from abhorrence to excusing blasphemy as a glitch or even an "endearing foible."[95]

Moralists not only lamented the laxness with which blasphemy was prosecuted, but they also perceived it to be endemic throughout society, and the list of people that were considered likely to blaspheme could be astonishingly inclusive.[96] Caspar Brunmüller, for example, declared the "horrifying vice" to be common among "rich and poor, young and old, great and small, clerical and secular, woman and man," in short, everyone.[97] The same estimation can be found in military literature. Count von Solms was especially worried about

88 ~: Faith in War

the blasphemous speech habits of the soldiery, but he too considered this to be a problem of society in general.[98] Hans Wilhelm Kirchhof stressed that blasphemy was not just a problem of the common soldiers but was even more prevalent among their superiors and that although articles of war uniformly banned it, no rule was held in "less esteem and remains inviolate."[99] Although examples of soldiers' blasphemous curses were rarely recorded verbatim, the moralist authors may well have been right to suspect soldiers of shameless linguistic habits. A seasoned warrior like Götz von Berlichingen, for example, had no problem recording one of his own blasphemous utterances in an only slightly bowdlerized way: "May God's this and that defile you in one heap."[100] A former soldier who had to defend himself for blasphemy in the Zurich court did so without any trace of guilt. He claimed that such language was entirely normal in the army and that the Zurich authorities violated his rights by prosecuting him.[101] The soldier's statement contains an important piece of evidence other than his apparent guilt-free conscience: blasphemy was common and accepted among the military and his outrage at being prosecuted for cursing by the civilian authorities suggests that he had not experienced similar strictness in the military.

Thus, while blasphemy was on the books as a punishable offence in military and civil law, the willingness to excuse blasphemous speech was widespread, if one thought it problematic at all.[102] But how can the seeming complete absence of convictions for blasphemy in the military be accounted for? As the analysis of the blasphemy clauses in the articles of war has shown, the prohibition was ubiquitous, but at least in the seventeenth century, different registers of blasphemy were acknowledged. We have also already seen that throughout the period the responsibility for the prosecution lay with the colonels and their legal staff. We therefore have to assume a laissez-faire attitude on their behalf, similar to the leniency of their civilian counterparts. A singular piece of evidence that individual colonels may have tried to improve their troops' speech habits stems from Kirchhof's collection of humorous anecdotes and therefore has to be taken with a pinch of salt. He claimed to have witnessed Colonel Ludwig von Deben, who had a reputation for piety, exhorting his men to refrain from blasphemy when a soldier farted loudly behind him. Infuriated, Deben turned around and snapped, "may God's thousand sacraments defile you, you scoundrel."[103] According to Kirchhof, the colonel's manifest inability to live up to his own ideals caused the soldiers to continue in their blasphemy.

Blasphemy seems to have been common among soldiers—as, indeed, it was throughout society—despite the fact that we find few verbatim quotations. Depending on the setting, the ostentatious disrespect had a wide range of communicative functions that ranged from intimidation to amusement. It cannot be answered conclusively whether soldiers were more prone to blaspheme than their contemporaries. It is clear, however, that blasphemy was part of masculine posturing and that a penchant for irreverent speech cannot be taken as a reliable indicator of more deeply rooted religious deviance. It was maybe impious, but due to its frequency should be regarded as a common way of expression in certain situational contexts, not as a sign of religious abnormality.

Magic

While blasphemers outrageously denounced the sacred, practitioners of magic offended through their attempts to control it. Early modern magic has been mostly studied in reference to witchcraft and the so-called "learned magic" of the elites, which frequently gives rise to the impression that magic in general was criminalized and the pursuit of a desperate minority or of eccentric intellectuals. It was not: magic was omnipresent in early modern life. It centered around the view that all of creation was permeated by forces that connected the "sublunar" world of human experience—humans, animals, plants, and inanimate matter—with the other cosmic spheres, the planets, and supernatural beings. These forces could either be manifest and observable or occult ("hidden") and undetectable with the human sensory apparatus. Occult forces were thought to follow certain principles according to which magic could be rationalized—a project that occupied natural philosophers—but ideas of how magic was thought to work were rarely pronounced outside of learned discourse. What mattered most to ordinary users of magic was that it worked. Early modern European magic can thus be described as a category of behaviors that sought to manipulate natural and supernatural forces and cosmic interconnections in order to produce specific, desired effects. In the military, magic was used for three primary purposes: to heal, to produce enhanced weaponry, and to gain invulnerability.

Although battle wounds probably seemed the most typical risk for soldiers, disease, hunger, and the physical strain of military life were far more dangerous. Johannes Pharamundus Rummel, who published his *Medicamenta Militaria* specifically as a medical self-help manual for soldiers, treated combat wounds only after offering recipes to heal diseases like fevers, plague, scurvy, typhoid, or diarrhea.[104] Skeletons of soldiers from the period prove their miserable physical condition. Examinations of the remains of men-at-arms killed at Towton in 1461 revealed that 90 percent of the men—most of whom had probably not yet reached thirty years of age—suffered from spinal injuries and 82.9 percent had developed spinal arthritis.[105] The remains found in the mass grave associated with the Battle of Wittstock in 1636 present a similarly harrowing picture.[106] A third of the men suffered from chronic sinusitis, a third had an acute stomatitis, and many skulls showed signs of long-standing parasite infestation. The skeleton of a young man, possibly a Scot, caught the archaeologists' attention because of the horrendous perimortem injuries he suffered. Closer

90 ~: *Faith in War*

examination revealed that "Individual 71" was in a very bad physical state when he died. Bone analysis indicated malnutrition throughout his lifetime and deficiency left traces all over his body: he suffered from a chronic mouth infection and chronic inflammation of the respiratory system, and chronic vitamin D deficiency had softened his bones, and, in combination with the strains of marching and carrying heavy loads, deformed his shin bones. His legs also showed signs of periostitis, possibly from ill-fitting boots. The hip and shoulder joints of the man, who probably died in his early twenties, were already significantly degenerated and an improperly healed ankle fracture meant that a bone splinter obstructed the movement of ligaments. Each step hurt and it seems miraculous that Individual 71 dragged himself into battle at all.[107]

Given soldiers' poor health, the persistent lack of medical personnel, and the high prices for treatment from surgeons who *were* available, medical self-help was an attractive option or even a necessity in the armies. We can assume that the prayers, healing charms, sacramentals, and magical remedies that were ubiquitous in early modern everyday life were also used in the military.[108] It is difficult to draw convincing analytical distinctions between "magical" and "nonmagical" healing because both magic and medicine were highly hybrid and dynamic traditions that borrowed and mixed elements from what modern observers might consider to be the disconnected realms of medicine, religion, and magic (or, worse, "superstition").[109] Medical manuals like the aforementioned *Medicamenta Militaria* presented remedies and therapies from different medical traditions, including magic, side by side, without obvious favor or prejudice. Johannes Rummel offered Galenic, Paracelsian, and magical treatment for each disease he addressed and left it up to the reader which type of cure they preferred; in Rummel's experience they all worked well.[110] Other medical authors were less explicit when they suggested magical healing methods to soldiers.[111] This may either indicate a conscious hesitancy to publicize such practices in a cultural environment increasingly hostile to magic, or suggest that the medical authors did not consider such therapies "magical" and merely recommended what had proven efficient in their medical practice. Whether explicitly or implicitly, magical practices intended to heal were propagated in print well into the seventeenth century.

The other kinds of magic that were commonly associated with soldiers, weapons magic and apotropaic magic, elicited far greater anxiety. Weapons magic was used to enhance the durability and lethality of all types of weapons and armor and drawing on occult natural and supernatural forces to ensure a particularly sturdy or powerful weapon or armor seems to have been ubiquitous.[112] *Büchsenmeister*, the frequently university-trained gunners, who often cast their own cannon, made gunpowder, and knew how to calculate ballistics, were shrouded in mystery. They made astrological calculations to determine the optimal planetary constellations in which to cast new pieces and said prayer formulas while pouring the molten metal.[113] They also often melted down church bells to gain the material for their cannons, which lent the process and the product both a sacred and a sacrilegious dimension.[114] The weapons that were most commonly enhanced through magic were swords, muskets, and pistols, or rather the balls they were loaded with. Soldiers used all manner of materials (pieces of meteorite, aetites (*Adlersteine*), parts of executioners' swords, axes, or chains, etc.) to make their swords invincible.[115] We must assume a strong oral tradition of efficient weapons charms, but building instructions for magical swords were also disseminated in print. Johannes Staricius, whose *HeldenSchatz* ("Hero's Treasure") became *the* magical military handbook of the sixteenth and seventeenth centuries, described several ways of making invincible swords.[116] A typical example took a sword blade that had already killed a man and added a hilt and pommel made from a chain with which criminals had been hanged and a grip carved from the spoke of a wheel on which a man had been broken. Materials that had been used in executions or body parts of executed men were common both in weapons magic and, as we will see shortly, in apotropaic magic. The reason was that these materials contained *spiritus vitalis*, the life force that each healthy individual possessed, which became especially virulent in the throes of death and remained in the body or was absorbed by the tools used to kill it. In German culture, executed criminals were regarded as "poor sinners" (*arme Sünder*) who atoned for all their sins in the moment of execution and assumed an almost saintly purity, thus becoming a source of sacred power, which, like their life force, lingered in their remains.[117] When harvested and transferred into weapons, this sanctified human life force of the executed potentiated the power of the bearer of such swords. Other natural forces were also harnessed, for example, when Staricius suggested using wood from a tree that had been struck by lightning to make the grip of another magical sword. Magical musket or pistol balls were relatively easy to make. Balls could be made to hit their target with supernatural surety by using lead from church windows or liturgical objects, dipping them into the blood of bats, or, again, adding ground-up body parts of executed criminals or powdered hosts to the metal or the gunpowder.[118]

The third type of magic that was associated with soldiers were apotropaic practices intended to make the user invulnerable either permanently or for a set amount of time.[119] Such enchanted men were called *fest* ("hard") or *gefroren* ("frozen"). In the early seventeenth century, the term *Passauer Kunst* ("the Passau Art") became common, following rumors that Kaspar Neithart, the executioner of Passau, had either taught soldiers how to make themselves invulnerable in an army camp outside the city in 1611 or sold them printed charms.[120]

That soldiers and many other men used magical means to protect themselves in fights was an early modern commonplace. Especially theologians,

92 ᴄ: *Faith in War*

however, strongly rejected these practices as superstitious, or worse, demonic. Luther warned against military superstition such as the invocation of certain saints, the enchanting of weapons, or the wearing of the Gospel of John (which was supposed to physically protect the wearer), as the soldiers committed the sin of unbelief, or rather, false faith in God.[121] He branded soldiers' apotropaic efforts as superstitious but still positioned them within the well-stocked store of Christian danger defense, whereas later authors across the confessional spectrum agreed on the fact that this kind of magic was demonic in nature. The Jesuit Georg Scherer's 1595 tract *Ein bewährte Kunst vnd Wundsegen* is a typical example of the Catholic position on apotropaic magic that recommended prayer, charity, and temperance as pious alternatives to the "demonic arts" and "superstitious charms" that "not only the common soldiers but also many officers and colonels habitually use."[122] Scherer's estimation is typical in so far as it clearly condemned the apotropaic magical practices of the soldiers as black magic and superstition and considered the phenomenon common to all ranks.

"Frozen" men were commonly encountered in military life. Hans Wilhelm Kirchhof told the story of a soldier called Funck who was executed in an army camp near Kassel in 1547.[123] Funck had previously stayed with a *Garthaufen* (a conglomerate of unemployed mercenaries) near Bremen and, trusting in his magic, had repeatedly started fights and wounded or killed several soldiers. During the siege of Pilsen in 1619, a soldier called Hans Fabel took a beaker of beer, walked toward the city walls, shouted abuse at the garrison, drank up, and returned to the camp, where he pulled five musket balls from his chest that the defenders had fired at him.[124] His charm did not protect Fabel from illness, however, and he died before the city was taken, which was no coincidence in the opinion of the author of the report. Such magical practices were very common and effective, but the author was also convinced that they were demonic and warned his readers that he had known many men who had made themselves invulnerable through magic and that all had lost their lives in horrific ways.[125] He also considered the use of magic to be short-sighted in regard to the afterlife and salvation, as it violated the first and second commandments, so that those who died trusting in God were carried to Heaven by angels, while the "frozen" ones were hauled off by the Devil. Augustin von Fritsch encountered invulnerable men in two situations. A lieutenant in his regiment was shot in the stomach but much to everyone's surprise only a bad bruise could be seen— Fritsch concluded that he was using the "devil-art" (*Teufelskhunst*).[126] In another situation, his unit overran a detachment of Frenchmen who were all immune to musket shot and had to be laboriously bludgeoned to death.[127]

The *Passauer Kunst* was thought to be endemic in all ranks. The imperial *Rittmeister* Levin Zanner, ironically called *Immernüchtern* ("always sober"), had to be killed with an axe after twenty musket balls had failed to harm him.[128] The English pro-Swedish propagandist William Watts reported that General

Tilly had been wounded during the Battle of Leipzig and that the Halle barber who treated his wounds had spread the rumor that that Tilly was frozen.[129] Watts rejected this thought as slanderous: "Very loath I am to leaue so base an imputation vpon so honourable a Commander; as to owe his life, all this while, vnto a devilish inchantment."[130] Watts was interested in the *Passauer Kunst* and referred to it in the first edition of the first volume of his *Swedish Intelligencer*, where he described this magical German technology in a long marginal note.[131] He stressed that such a practice really existed, that its efficacy was beyond doubt, and even introduced his readers to the German terminology.[132] To illustrate his report Watts mentioned that a soldier had braved an English detachment at Stade in Lower Saxony and although the enemy fired at least a hundred shots at him, which tore up his clothes and severed his belt, the man gathered up his breeches and walked away. While this made a good anecdote when the protagonist was an anonymous common soldier, Watts did not tolerate the rumors of magic sullying General Tilly's reputation. Tilly was known for his deep Catholic piety and despite being a formidable adversary of the Protestant cause, his enemies esteemed him highly as an honorable soldier. Watts thought only the "reprobate raskalite" of the armies would use such demonic enchantments, however, and even common soldiers rejected it if they cared for their reputation (and salvation). To associate an honorable enemy like Tilly with the *Passauer Kunst* was a gratuitous vilification even to a partisan propagandist like Watts.

The *Passauer Kunst* was denounced for religious reasons but usually without denying its efficacy. Divine justice meant that the magically bulletproof would eventually meet a dreadful end, but nobody generally denied that such charms worked and really did make the user invulnerable. In 1601, the Erfurt executioner had to decapitate a convict who was considered *vest* ("hard") and asked him not to make his life—and the condemned man's departure therefrom—unnecessarily difficult.[133] The enchanted man concurred and handed him a bundle of dried St. John's wort (*Johanniskraut*) that he had kept under his right arm and the decollation was brought to a swift end. Compared to the estimation of the contemporaries who classified the *Passauer Kunst* as demonic, the bundle of herb that the convict handed over seems rather ordinary, and we should examine its practices in more detail at this point.

The enormous scope of Johannes Staricius's *HeldenSchatz* included weather charms, magical swords and magically guided musket balls (*Freikugeln*), recipes for fortifying tonics, instructions for the transfusion of horses' strength into weary soldiers, an explanation of how to blast rocks with bacon, and a one-hour cure for dysentery. Staricius was understandably eager to protest the suspicion that he was advocating "the devilish conjunction of spirits . . . and other necromantic magic."[134] His arts were merely "natural and legitimate magic" (*Naturali legitimâque Magica*) that God had revealed to humanity and whose

94 ❧ Faith in War

use was therefore permitted. Staricius knew of many practices that protected against injury. St. John's wort, the herb that the Erfurt convict was carrying, was best picked on St. John's Day (24 June) between eleven o'clock and noon and should be worn on the body or sewn into the doublet.[135] An acquaintance of his had collected a virgin's menstrual blood with a linen cloth, wrapped this in an undershirt (Niderkleid) that had been made by another virgin, and worn it under his right arm.[136] In conjunction with a particular magical sword, Staricius suggested to make a seal or stamp from an executioner's sword and have this incorporated in a ring. The seal depicted alchemical symbols and the ring should bear the inscription "O Castiel Princeps armorum, per Deum Abraham, Isaac & Iacob." When the seal was imprinted on the forehead and the ring worn on the sword hand, the owner would be invulnerable and his opponents' blades would break. Staricius emphasized that this ritual had the decisive advantage that it did not involve speaking a magical formula. This advantage becomes apparent to the modern reader when we consider that magical rituals traditionally involved a gesture as well as a spoken formula.[137] By imprinting the seal, the gesture was made, while a simultaneously uttered prayer or spell could have led bystanders to suspect illicit magic, which was neither in the interest of the user nor of the author.

Nothemden, magical shirts that protected the wearer from injury and death, were mentioned by early modern authors, but they were very difficult to produce. The anonymous author of the Victori-Schlüssel described the production of such a garment: girls no older than seven years had to spin a yarn, weave it, and tailor a shirt using a specific cross-stitch, and afterward the shirt had to be hidden at the altar until three masses had been read over it.[138] Compared to other Nothemden this process seems almost hurried. Another instruction involved astrologers who determined an auspicious night for manufacture and no less than forty pure virgins who had to spin the yarn in the name of the Devil and embroider the finished shirt with the face of a bearded, helmeted man, as well as that of the crowned Beelzebub and two crosses.[139] Finding astrologers and forty virgins would have been possible for the right client but to have the women make the shirt in the name of Satan and apply the demonic embroidery without the event becoming public seems rather implausible.

While such shirts seem almost improbably complex, laborious, and dangerous to make, there were other means to attain invulnerability that also involved preparation but could be made from cheap materials by one person—as long as they had access to a church altar. One way to harness sacred power in order to become invulnerable was to write "I.N.R.I" on small pieces of parchment at midnight at Christmas, put them into small wheat cakes (Küchlein), and wrap them in parchment or paper before the hour was up.[140] The cakes then had to be hidden under the altar cloth until the masses on Easter, Ascension Day, and Pentecost had imbued them with their sacral powers. Before battle, the user had to commend his soul into the hands of God by saying a short formula ("In nomine Patris, & Filii, & Spiritus sancti, Amen. In manus tuas Domine commendo spiritum meum"), swallow one of the cakes, and say another formula that cited Luke 4:30 ("Iesus autem transiens per medium illorum ibat in pace: Deus meus custodiat me (Ioannem, Petrum, &c.) ab omni malo").[141] The soldier was now invulnerable for twenty-four hours. A last way to achieve invulnerability from the *HeldenSchatz* was not as complex but also needed preparation.[142] First, one had to find the skull of a convict who had been hanged or broken on the wheel that had moss growing on it. The following day the skull had to be arranged so that the moss could be scraped off and the following Friday, the moss could be harvested while saying the following formula:

> I, NN, ask today in this hour, you, my Lord Jesus Christ, son of the pure maiden Mary, to stand with me on this [battle]field and help me bind the hands of all my enemies and help me tear their steel and all their iron, Jesus, Mary's son, help me on this [battle]field. In the name of the Father, the Son and Holy Spirit, Amen.[143]

What now had to be done with the moss is unclear, but it was probably worn as an amulet like the St. John's wort or eaten.

If such painstaking preparations could not be organized in time, a consecrated host could go a long way. The main way to use the host was to make a cut in the skin, place a particle of the host in the wound, and let the sacral implant heal. What seems like a uniquely bad idea did indeed pose problems when the host would not take, but men did try.[144] Doctrinal disagreements over the nature of the eucharist notwithstanding, lay Catholics and Protestants continued to believe hosts to be rich sources of sacral power useful for magic well into the eighteenth century.[145] In 1710, the Lutheran field preacher Johannes Hocker admonished his colleagues to gather all hosts that the wind might blow off the paten during open air services specifically to prevent abuse of the host in soldiers' magical rituals.[146]

The rituals and objects described here do not fit contemporary theological condemnations of the *Passauer Kunst* as black magic. Apart from the Beelzebub embroidery on the magical shirt, a detail Kronfeld gathered from a nineteenth-century collection of legends, military apotropaic magic seems hardly "demonic."[147] On the contrary, almost all of the practices had a distinctively Christian element to them: the Gospel of John features prominently, the prescribed formulas invoke God, Christ, the Trinity, or the angel Cassiel, and many of the magical objects gained their sacral power by being hidden in the altar and the mass, or were, in the case of the host, sacraments in their own right. The *Passauer Kunst* thus belonged to the realm of popular piety and popular magic, and indeed, the weapons magic and apotropaic practices described here for the military context were the same that were used by civilians.[148] Neither

96 ~: *Faith in War*

the rituals nor the objects associated with this kind of magic were specific only to the *Passauer Kunst* but were current in other areas of popular magic as well. The opening verses of John's Gospel, for example, was the most frequently used bible passage in textual amulets and served a variety of purposes, including protection from demons or witchcraft or the treatment of a multitude of illnesses.[149] The eucharist was also a popular talisman. The moss from a skull (*usnea*) was an integral agent in early modern medicine and the idea that body parts of preferably young people who had died suddenly were medically especially potent was widespread.[150]

The denunciation as demonic by Protestant and Catholic writers alike is typical of the position on popular magic in all confessions in the sixteenth and seventeenth centuries. There were two main reasons for this: first, theologians were increasingly convinced that the Devil did, in fact, work all magic, even if the rituals seemed to rely solely on natural and sacred forces.[151] By the end of the sixteenth century, the opinion that amulets like those associated with the *Passauer Kunst could* only work if the Devil caused the effects attributed to them had become a majority opinion among theologians across the confessional spectrum. That this development occurred at the same time that amulets experienced an unprecedented popularity across Europe exemplifies the fundamental rift over magic in early modern culture very neatly.[152] The second reason that authorities wanted to curtail popular magical practices was that the use of magic was interpreted as a refusal to submit to providence and bow to God's plan. Christians were expected to humbly present their case to God in prayer and to accept the outcome obediently, not to manipulate the cosmos to force an outcome and thus tempt God's retribution.

How far the accusation of the demonic was *only* polemic cannot be conclusively answered. Staricius himself seems to have been convinced that illicit magical practices were also current in the military and he warned his readers against "idolatrous charms and other unchristian, devilish means."[153] The demonic side of the *Passauer Kunst*, if it existed, eludes us, however, and the reasons for this can be readily suggested. It would not have been opportune for an author like Staricius to advocate explicitly demonic rituals to his readership and in terms of "market value" it was advisable for the providers of magical protection to offer methods that drew their powers from the sacred and nature, rather than the demonic. That military authorities did not take the accusations of black magic particularly seriously can be inferred from the fact that rules and ordinances largely ignore the *Passauer Kunst*. Only the 1621 Swedish articles of war and their derivatives mention that conjurers and weapon enchanters should be apprehended and expelled from the army. Despite my best efforts, I have been unable to find a case in which military authorities punished soldiers or magical service providers for these types of magic. There were good reasons to turn a blind eye. Soldiers who made themselves invulnerable did not harm anybody and the ends to which magic was used remained the main popular criterion for its legitimacy or illegitimacy. Despite the misgivings of many theologians, who wanted to ban all magic irrespective of its intended application, secular authorities continued to consider beneficial and apotropaic magical practices legitimate or at least not deserving of prosecution. Secondly, magically enhanced weaponry and bulletproof soldiers, whose reality was not doubted even by the most ardent critics, must have appeared rather attractive from a military perspective.

Elite warriors could afford to engrave their armor with prayer formulas or devotional etchings, which certainly were not merely decorative but carried apotropaic significance.[154] They also had access to powerful sacred objects that, even if they did not prevent death, certainly made the prospect of dying far less daunting. Maximilian of Bavaria wore the Carmelite scapula at the Battle of White Mountain, which promised that the Virgin Mary herself would free the wearer from purgatory and escort him to Heaven the Saturday following his death.[155] Nearly a hundred years previously, Georg von Frundsberg had supposedly worn a Franciscan habit over his armor at Pavia, also in the hope that the garment would positively influence his postmortem welfare.[156] While such sacred protection was reserved for a select few, soldiers of all ranks had the option to protect or heal their bodies through magic. The appeal of apotropaic charms in particular is easy enough to understand, but magical DIY is also interesting because we can observe soldiers as active and self-determined agents in the Christian cosmos who accessed and manipulated the natural and sacred forces at their disposal for their own ends. Theologians developed qualms regarding the nature and implications of magic, but soldiers, like most of their contemporaries, could draw on magic to directly influence their fate in the deadly circumstances of their profession.

Marriage and Sexual (Mis)conduct

The last type of potentially deviant behavior to examine in this chapter is soldiers' sexual conduct and their relationships (we will examine sexual violence in the next chapter). The regulation of lay sexuality was a major preoccupation of all confessional churches throughout the early modern period. Lust was not just one of the seven deadly sins, aberrant sexuality had long been taken as a symptom of spiritual deviance. Many medieval heresies were not just branded for their theological unorthodoxy but associated with sexual eccentricities as well.[157] In the sixteenth century, Catholics made sinful sex a ubiquitous topic in the confessional, while Protestants established courts and consistories to uncover and correct the sexual proclivities of the faithful. Doctrinal differences in sexual morality only concerned the clergy: Catholic clerics were supposedly

98 ❧ *Faith in War*

celibate but Protestant pastors were expected to marry and to set new marital standards through their example. For the laity, all confessions projected the ideal of orderly sexual conduct in a church-sanctioned marriage as a central part of Christian life, and in this respect, soldiers were thought to be chronically wanting.

The role of women in early modern armies has received some scholarly attention.[158] Women were central to the daily workings of military life: they cooked, washed and mended, and cared for the sick and wounded; they trenched, plundered, and sometimes fought; they were lovers, wives, mothers, and prostitutes.[159] We have to distinguish primarily between three statuses of women in military society: "wife," "whore," and "prostitute." While the first and the third category are rather straightforward, "whores" are more difficult to define. The term used in the sources is *Hur(e)*, a semantically capacious term in early modern German that could denote a sex worker but was more broadly used derogatorily for any woman who had sex with changing partners or who was in a sexual relationship with a man but not formally married to him. In military sources (as elsewhere), we are confronted with a misogynist suspicion of women's morality, which was exacerbated by the fact that the women we are concerned with here had ended up in the armies. The fact that these women had wound up in the military context at all called their morality into question; *honorable* women did not populate the army train, it was assumed. The fact that the officer in charge of the army train was called *Hurenweybel* (maybe translatable as "whore beadle") indicates the negative view of military women in general irrespective of their individual marital status.[160]

John A. Lynn has described "whores" as "exclusive to one partner without the sanction of a formal marriage."[161] This is a good working definition if we add the possibility that women may have occasionally or temporarily also engaged in "sexual barter," for example when their relationship ended, their partner died, or when it seemed useful or necessary.[162] The problem is that we are mostly unable to look behind the term as it is used in the sources: women described as "whores" may have been sex workers, concubines, or wives. Thus, when I use "whore" in inverted commas in the following pages, it is intended to preserve this ambiguity.

We have seen in the previous chapter that the articles of war uniformly banned "whores" from the camp and the train, but a broader survey of military legal literature suggests that the issue was more complex. Military legal manuals made provisions for informal marriages.[163] As late as 1630 a legal tract detailing the *Privileges and Liberties of the Soldiery* stated explicitly that soldiers were free to "marry and court without religious rites [*Solennitet*] and customs."[164] Martial law also granted women rather liberal rights to inherit their partners' possessions. If the soldier did not have a lawful wife elsewhere, a pregnant concubine (the term used here is *Beyschlaf*) was entitled to his inheritance.[165] The legal

Religion, Morality, and Military Everyday Life ⁘ 99

status of soldiers' unmarried partners was therefore ambiguous: while these women were not supposed to exist in the first place, informal marriages were considered legitimate by some legal theorists.

At first sight, such leniency seems rather out of the ordinary in the historical context. Since the fifteenth century, questions of sexuality and, concomitantly, marriage customs had commanded the attention of moralists and authorities alike, a trend that gained momentum in the wake of the Reformation.[166] Late medieval marriage had largely been a secular affair. Marriage only became a sacrament in 1439 and a priest's involvement in the rites became officially mandatory for Catholic couples only as late as 1563.[167] Parental involvement and sanction later became a precondition for both Protestant and Catholic marriages, but clandestine marriage (*Winkelehe*), a private promise to marry once the couple had sufficient funds to set up their own household, were a persistent custom.[168] For many young people, this marriage promise was sufficient to start having sex. This practice could obviously lead to severe difficulties for the women if pregnancy ensued and the father reneged his promise.[169] This attitude toward premarital sex was widespread and one of the elements of popular "sinfulness" disciplinarians were especially eager to eradicate, albeit with only modest success. Well into the eighteenth century, premarital sex and extramarital children were incredibly common. Stefan Breit has described parishes in which one fifth of all young people appear in official records as fornicators (suggesting a greater number who did not get caught), more than a quarter of all mothers were unmarried, and half the men had children out of wedlock.[170] Families and communities tended to tolerate premarital sex and considered it part of courtship, and clandestine marriages between consenting adults—that is, fourteen years and older—were upheld in episcopal courts even against the opposition of the parents.[171] Pregnancies were also not necessarily problematic as long as the couple got married and the union was financially viable.[172] The zeal with which local religious and secular regimes prosecuted fornicators could be a significant factor, however, and as we will see shortly, unyielding authorities often cast unmarried pregnant women or unwed mothers into utterly desperate situations.

Courts were involved mainly when marriage promises were broken and the fathers or their families refused to support the mother and child. For the city of Augsburg, Lyndal Roper has shown that the pre-Reformation ecclesiastical and the reformed civic marriage court were busily occupied with disputed marriage promises, which gives an indication both of the frequency and of the unreliability of such arrangements.[173] Courts tended to push for the couple to get married in the first instance, but when the relationship had deteriorated too far they could also sentence the father to pay alimony for the child and heart balm (*Kranzgeld*) if the woman had been a virgin at the beginning of the relationship. Women who got involved with local men had the relative advantage that the

100 ❧ *Faith in War*

unwilling "husbands" could be apprehended and taken to court. Women who entered relationships with journeymen or soldiers found themselves in an even more precarious situation due to the professional mobility of their sex partners. Finally, it should be mentioned that most women who had even several children out of wedlock did eventually get married, especially if they had a dowry or could hope for an inheritance. Despite the best efforts of the churches to sensitize Christians to the sinful nature of fornication, ordinary people therefore resisted this interpretation for centuries and regarded premarital sex and pregnancies as economically risky but common behaviors among young people.

An exceptional archival find made by Fritz Wolff provides unique insights into relationships between soldiers and local women.[174] It comprises fifty-four letters written in the summer of 1625 between soldiers in Tilly's army and inhabitants of the towns of Allendorf, Schmalkalden, Eschwege, and Witzenhausen, in the border region of Thuringia and Hesse.[175] Several letters give insights into the predicament of women who had trusted soldiers' marriage promises. Anna Immick of Allendorf wrote to Batzer Wahs as she had not received word from him and was worried of being ridiculed by her friends should the soldier let her down.[176] More critically, Anna had children—whether they were Batzer's is unclear—and the local *Schultheiss* had threatened her with expulsion so her future and that of her children depended on Batzer keeping his word. A woman called Catharina had an illegitimate child with a soldier named Henß All and the young mother was in dire straits.[177] She had found shelter with her godmother (*gevatter*) in Schmalkalden but this was only a temporary solution. She tried to return to her mother in nearby Wasungen but the authorities there had demanded twenty *Reichstaler* before allowing her into the village, an exorbitant sum when she was struggling to feed herself and the baby. She was also suffering the rejection of the community and felt "despised and considered worthless by everyone."[178] All she had to rely on was the hope that the soldier would honor his promise: "I am of comforting hope and confidence . . . that you will honor your pledge and lead me to the church on the soonest [possible] day and not leave me completely stuck in squalor." She urged him to send money as soon as possible.[179] Both letters betray the insecurity the women felt. Anna and Catharina had attracted the attention of the authorities, who defended the communal alms funds from them and their babies by threatening expulsion or preventing a return to the family. Catharina's case especially makes clear that she was not allowed to live with her mother because the village officials in Wasungen feared that she would not be able to support herself, which is why they demanded the money as a form of insurance. They did not, however, bar her primarily because she had had a baby out of wedlock, and her mother and godmother seem to have been willing at least to support her. The illegitimate child was an economical liability, possibly even a catastrophe, but there is no indication that religious or moral considerations played a role in these cases.

Anna and Catharina's situation was especially grim because they were single mothers. In this respect, Lene Möllerin from Schmalkalden was comparatively lucky as she did not mention a pregnancy or a child when she wrote to her "dearest lover" (*liebsten Bulen*) Ebertt.[180] Lene reminded Ebertt of their vows, and confirmed that she was still interested in marriage and expected a clear answer from him. In contrast to the other women, Lene does not seem to have been overly distressed. She did not beg Ebertt to keep his word and ignored his request for a love token, flatly stating that the occasion did not permit it. All she wanted was clarity. Maria Braunß, on the other hand, was bitterly disappointed by Hanß Thomas von Kalbach's behavior: he, too, had promised marriage but did not even say goodbye or leave a love token.[181] Another woman was left heartbroken after "Monsieur Rischardt" had stopped writing, which she took to mean that he had "locked her out of his heart."[182] There is no indication that these women suffered social ostracization for their relationships with the soldiers, but their heartbreak is an important reminder that relationships were not just economic and social arrangements but also had an emotional dimension.

A girl called Liese, however, was harassed for her relationship with the imperial cavalryman Hans Merdt, who apparently had been billeted in her father's house in Schmalkalden.[183] After the imperial troops had left about two months previously, the enemy, the Danish crown and Ernst von Mansfeld's army, had begun recruiting infantry in the region. A letter from Merdt to Liese had fallen into the hands of several young men drinking in a tavern, many of whom had just enlisted. The new recruits practiced being soldiers by shooting off their mouths; one wished that "the devil would throw away all cavalrymen," while another hoped that no imperial cavalryman would ever lay eyes on the town of Schmalkalden again.[184] One man even came to Liese's door and tried to intimidate her. Local women also picked on her: Anna Borggräffin said that she would rather date a "sheep dog" than a cavalryman.[185] Someone else mocked that Merdt should have prayed a rosary rather than write letters, which appears to be a pointed comment about him serving in a Catholic army. The letter shows how profoundly the atmosphere in Schmalkalden had changed within a couple of months: the Schmalkaldeners had lived with the imperial troops in apparent harmony for about two years but the departure of Tilly's troops and the arrival of the Danish and Mansfeldian recruiters created a markedly different climate. The local men who joined the ranks began to hassle those who were associated with their new "enemies" and women like Liese bore the brunt of their drunken belligerence.

Contrary to the common trope, it was not just "silly" or "wanton" girls who were duped by soldiers' promises. Entire families were deceived. One unnamed man sent a furious, enraged letter to Johannes Klein, a soldier who had apparently promised marriage to the sender's sister and was the father of her child.[186] The family and indeed the whole community knew of the relationship, as the lovers had "run all over town and courted in the park." The engagement seems to have been official and met with the family's approval, because the soldier is addressed as *Gevatter*, a term used to indicate a close relationship between non-blood relatives. Certain details are missing but it seems that Klein had taken the pregnant woman with him when the regiment went on campaign, she had given birth outside of the city boundaries, and was now refused reentry by the authorities. This is suggested by the brother's indignant remark that he and his family could have cared for mother and child had she stayed at home, implying that this was not an option now. Klein's behavior was reprehensible in any case, but what seems to have infuriated the brother especially was that the soldier had lied to them. If Klein had only wanted sex, the brother wrote, he could have sought out the local prostitutes. Instead, he had abused their friendship and trust and turned his sister into a "bawd" (*dirn*). In this case, no one accused the young mother of misconduct or wantonness, nor do we find any indication that the family found her behaviors problematic. Johannes Klein had betrayed them all and the brother swore that he would shout his accusations on Judgement Day.

These desperate examples make us wonder why women entered into relationships with soldiers in the first place. Ulinka Rublack has emphasized "the violence that soldiers, more than other men, employed in their wooing of women."[187] Her sources, trial records, certainly contribute to the impression that sexual violence was predominant. In contrast, none of the letters preserved in Marburg suggest that the women were pressured into having intimate relations with their military partners. This does not rule out the possibility of coercion, but there is no evidence for it either. We should also not ignore the potential appeal such relationships could hold. For some women, marrying a soldier promised a way out of unhappy family or employment situations. In one of the letters, a woman asked her husband to send her a passport so that she could join him on campaign because she could no longer bear the "heartache" that her parents were causing her.[188] Gercke Hoffmeyer's daughter Maria seems to have eloped with a lieutenant after she had caused strife in the family.[189] The letter is unclear in many respects but it seems that Maria had scammed money from her brothers Thomas and Otto. Her father informed her that she had "fallen from grace" with her brothers and that God's grace was her last resort now. In this situation, entering a relationship with a soldier appears to have allowed the young woman to escape the family crisis she had caused. A case recorded in Wesel suggests that soldiers could offer a way out of an unhappy marriage: Evert von Hesen's wife ran off with a soldier and stole money from her husband before she left.[190] While we do not learn details about the circumstances it is fair to assume that the marriage was unhappy and that the new lover's professional mobility made him a welcome escape vehicle.

Finally, the letters also suggest a less calculating reason that women got involved with soldiers: love. Many letters do not speak of hardships other than the pains of separation from the beloved.[191] One woman wrote: "*Ach*, my dearest darling and sustainment [*auffenthaltung*] of my young life, I know not when I will see you again, but I ask you, my dearest darling, that you will keep my heart secluded in yours, as only to you I have utterly and completely surrendered myself."[192] Love is also evidenced in the letters written by soldiers. From the army camp near Bielefeld, Hanns Mohs wrote a love letter to his wife Catharina Hardtmann who had stayed behind with her family. He implored her to write as soon as possible because he was pitifully lovesick. "My dearest darling, I had not thought that love was so great," he wrote, "I will nevermore be happy until I can come to you."[193] He also asked her to greet her family and everyone he knew in Allendorf and sent her his love "9000000000000000000 hundred thousand times." Catharina's equally passionate reply has also been preserved and she expressed her love and the anguish of separation in a poem:

> Oh God, what must those who love suffer . . . and must not tell anyone what suffering they carry in their heart . . . You I have chosen for myself no one I like better in my heart You are my most beautiful love, that is why I write you this letter. Oh *Gott*, shall my heart not break, loving you and not being allowed to speak of it . . .[194]

Hanns and Catharina were clearly in love and the letters show that the soldier had been welcomed into the family and integrated into the community.

While the letters provide valuable snapshots, diaries allow us to follow soldiers' relationships over time. Peter Hagendorf was married twice, first to Anna Stadlerin and after her death in 1633 to Anna Maria Buchlerin.[195] While Hagendorf's affection to his wives is indisputable, he also casually recorded two incidents in his time as a widower when he took girls as loot.[196] It is unclear if he raped the girls; referring to the second kidnapping, he wrote obliquely that he was "sorry to let her go because [he] did not have a wife at that time." There is no indication that Hagendorf, who comes across as a caring husband and father when he had families, thought the kidnapping of the women to be morally questionable. The girls were human loot and taking hostages was legitimized by martial custom. That he let the girls leave after a short while suggests that they represented only a momentary solution to him, and two months after the second abduction he married Anna Maria in Pforzheim.

With his keen sense for finance, Sydnam Poyntz seems to have valued his wives—their names he did not mention—in terms of wealth and thrift. His first wife, "a rich Merchants [*sic*] Daughter" who died during childbirth after two years of marriage, met his approval not least because she left him a rich inheritance and "was of an humble condition and very housewifely."[197] His second wife was of a "higher birth," which he did not mind, but her concomitant higher "spirit" and lifestyle he found less agreeable. She "spent at home" what he "got abroad."[198] Poyntz, who profiteered from his own plundering, experienced

104 ❧ *Faith in War*

the "true tryall of fortunes mutabilitie" when his second wife and child were killed and his possessions pillaged by soldiers in his absence.[199] Other soldiers only married after they had retired. Aged forty-three, Jürgen Ackermann, for example, married Elisabeth Lambrecht, who was twenty-two years his junior and bore him eleven children.[200]

The analysis of the letters and the diaries presents a varied picture of gender relations in the military. Some letters document the profound problems that arose for women who got involved with soldiers. The unfortunates who became pregnant could face dire repercussions when the fathers did not honor their marriage promises and their families could not take care of them. Contrary to Ulinka Rublack's case study of Konstanz, where she found evidence that merely keeping company with soldiers could call a woman's reputation into doubt, this attitude is not noticeable in the letters.[201] There is the isolated case of Liese, who became the target of ridicule and harassment for her relationship with a soldier, but in numerous instances the women's friends and family members sent their regards and good wishes to the soldiers. This suggests that the men were well integrated and liked in the community. Cases in which women were duped by false promises and those that seem to suggest sincerity on behalf of the soldiers are roughly balanced in this sample. This indicates that entering a relationship with a soldier was not just motivated by desperation and that Rublack's estimation that soldiers "sought women for pleasure, not permanent ties" has to be qualified in its generalization.[202] Some soldiers did trick women into sexual relationships or change their minds but others proved to be sincere, committed, and in love. We should also be mindful of the possibility that some of the men who had stopped writing or had not returned had died in the meantime. The committed relationships we have encountered here speak against a simple equation of soldiers with sexual predation, but the basic fact remains that soldiering offered great sexual license and soldiers' professional mobility presented an easy escape from the consequences of reckless sexual behavior.

Religious considerations or lines of argument are saliently absent from the letters. It seems, therefore, that the relationships were not conducted in the light of piety or sin, or at least they were not negotiated in this way. The deserted women did not describe their plight in terms of spiritual anguish but had material and immediate social repercussions to deal with or were merely disappointed by a broken promise. God's help was at times implored but none of the women expressed their fear of having offended Him with their sexual conduct. Nor did they accuse the soldiers of having violated *religious* norms, but principles of common decency and trustworthiness. The church was mentioned once but only as the place where a marriage would be officiated.[203] Therefore, while marriage discipline was officially phrased and preached in religious terms and while the imperative of an orderly sex life was a Christian norm, the pressure to conform was experienced and expressed in social and economic terms. Finally, there is no indication that officers or military authorities had any role in the way the soldiers conducted their sexual life. One could have imagined requests from abandoned women asking officers for assistance in bringing their erstwhile lovers to heel but there is not evidence in this sample. It seems that the women had no hopes that military authorities would care about their plight or the sexual conduct of their soldiers. All the women could do was write letters and hope.

Conclusion

This chapter set out to examine religious and moral norms in the military. In contrast to their reputation as godless deviants, the examination of military autobiographical accounts has shown that soldiers' religious modes of thinking can be considered entirely normal for the early modern context. They perceived the sacred and divine in unequivocally Christian terms and followed the ritual demands of Christian life when circumstances permitted it. They also apparently had a penchant for blasphemy, which their detractors interpreted as one of the clearest expressions of soldiers' religious deviance. It has been argued here that blasphemy served a variety of purposes, ranging from intimidation to amusement, but that it was not generally indicative of religious deviance. The examination of the articles of war has indicated that blasphemy was considered a complex issue, as martial law recognized different degrees of severity and intent. It seems, however, that, similar to the situation in the civilian realm, it was generally ignored in the military context.

The magic that soldiers used to heal, enhance weapons, or make themselves invulnerable belonged to the wider context of early modern popular magic. Soldiers, like their civilian contemporaries, performed rituals that allowed them to access and direct natural and sacred powers in ways that produced these effects. That the ubiquity of magical practices—used habitually and often without an awareness of doing something illicit—coexisted with the ever more categorical demonization of all magical practices by religious and secular authorities is characteristic of the "Age of Ambiguity." The employment of natural and especially sacred forces to help with survival in a deadly environment was maybe not compatible with the ideal of meek submission to God's plan, but it shows an intimate interaction with the sacred, and is certainly not indicative of irreligion.

The assessment of sexual conduct has provided evidence that counters the dominant view that soldiers in general were brutal sexual predators. Although they are only snapshots of relationships, the letters examined allow a more balanced view than court records, for example, as their existence did not rest on the premise that things had gone awry and had to be settled by a magistrate.

106 ❧ *Faith in War*

Many of the letters betray the hardship of unwed mothers who had been deserted. Other examples indicate, however, that committed relationships could equally develop from military–civilian encounters. What is more, soldiers here appear not just as terrifying outsiders but as men who were welcomed into friendship circles, families, and beds. Religion, however, seems to have played a marginal role at best in the way soldiers and women (who wrote most of these letters) conducted their relationships, or at any rate wrote about them. Notions of "sin" are noticeably absent from the letters.

Where does this leave us on our quest to understand early modern military religion? It seems fair to abandon the notion that soldiers were "irreligious" or were "de-Christianized" by the military environment. The military experience had no perceivable degenerative impact on lay Christian values or on the way that soldiers perceived their relationship with God. One aspect that increasingly characterized religious communal life and individual identities has not yet been discussed, however, and that is confession. Especially in this period of European history, defined as it was by religious pluralization and sectarian strife, confessional thinking and its impact on military everyday life must be examined, and we will turn to this complex issue in the next chapter.

Notes

1. Tettau, "Erlebnisse eines deutschen Landsknechts"; Ulmschneider, *Götz von Berlichingen*; Schönhuth, *Leben und Thaten*; Bei der Wieden, *Leben im 16. Jahrhundert*; Staden, *Wahrhafftig Historia*; Schottin, *Tagebuch des Erich Lassota*; Gräf, *Söldnerleben*; Westenrieder, "Tagebuch des Augustin von Fritsch"; Volkholz, *Jürgen Ackermann*; Peters, *Peter Hagendorf*; Poyntz, *The Relation of Sydnam Poyntz*; Monro, *Monro His Expedition*; Turner, *Memoirs of His Own Life*; Raymond, *Autobiography of Thomas Raymond*.
2. See for example Ulmschneider, *Götz von Berlichingen*, 52, 56, 67, 76–77, 140–41; Staden, *Wahrhafftig Historia*, passim; Peters, *Peter Hagendorf*, 139, 146, 160.
3. Westenrieder, "Tagebuch des Augustin von Fritsch," 105.
4. Peters, *Peter Hagendorf*, 146.
5. Ibid., 148, 160.
6. Hoffmann, *Geschichte der Stadt Magdeburg*, vol. 3, 177.
7. Peters, *Peter Hagendorf*, 174.
8. Ibid., 170, 175.
9. Tettau, "Erlebnisse eines deutschen Landsknechts," 43-46.
10. Ibid., 9, 16.
11. Ibid., 17.
12. Peters, *Peter Hagendorf*, 233.
13. Burschel, "Himmelreich und Hölle," 191.
14. Krusenstjern, "Seliges Sterben," 471–72.
15. Peters, *Peter Hagendorf*, 136.
16. Ibid., 136, 142, 151, 162.
17. Ibid., 136 (twice), 139, 142, 151, 156, 162, 170, 183.
18. Schmidt, "Das Tagebuch des Christoph von Bismarck," 74.

Religion, Morality, and Military Everyday Life ~ 107

19. Pfeilsticker, *Tagebuch des Hans Conrad Lang*, for example 7, 10, 11, 12, 14.
20. Peters, *Peter Hagendorf*, 233, 241; Kaiser, "*Cuius exercitus, eius religio?*" 342; Burschel, "Himmelreich und Hölle," 191.
21. Peters, *Peter Hagendorf*, 172, 174, 186.
22. Ibid., for example 142, 161, 186.
23. Ibid., 40, 48.
24. Medick, *Der Dreißigjährige Krieg*, 135–36.
25. Peters, *Peter Hagendorf*, 148, 163, 167.
26. Ibid., 156, 137.
27. Ibid., 136, 157.
28. Ibid., 170, 187.
29. Ibid., 172.
30. Wolff, *Johann Sebastian Bach*, 104–5.
31. As proposed by Müller ("Das Leben eines Söldners," 48–49) and now confirmed by Juliana da Costa José and others; see Medick, *Der Dreißigjährige Krieg*, 135–36.
32. Peters, *Peter Hagendorf*, 187.
33. Hümmer, "Bamberg im Schweden-Kriege," 142–43, 155; Volkholz, *Jürgen Ackermann*, 43; Friesenegger, *Tagebuch*, 23.
34. Gräf, *Söldnerleben*, 93.
35. Westenrieder, "Tagebuch des Augustin von Fritsch," 187.
36. Carve, *Reysbüchlein*, 54–55.
37. Krebs and Maetschke, *Aus dem Leben*, vol. 2, 237–38.
38. Alzog, "Raisbüchlin", vol. 2, 84.
39. Johannes Hocker remarked on the vocal strength required from a field preacher in his manual for chaplains (*Pastorale Castrense*, 11).
40. Box, *Make Music to Our God*, 6.
41. Chaline, *Bataille*, 311.
42. MacCulloch, *Reformation*, 36.
43. Rogg, *Landsknechte*, 146.
44. Forster, *Catholic Germany*, 77.
45. Hümmer, "Bamberg im Schweden-Kriege," 49–50, 142–43.
46. Ibid., 49.
47. Ibid.
48. Ibid., 142–43.
49. Monro, *Monro His Expedition*, part II, 63.
50. Anon., *Warhaffter Bericht*, 53.
51. Ibid.
52. Parker, *Army of Flanders*, 146.
53. This section relies solely on Ilg, "Fidelis von Sigmaringen."
54. Ibid., 313–14.
55. Ibid., 330.
56. Auffarth, "Alle Tage Karneval?" 79–80.
57. Rogg, *Landsknechte*, 19; Burschel, *Söldner*, 42; Huntebrinker, "Soldatentracht," 96.
58. For example Rogg, *Landsknechte*, 19.
59. Musculus, *Vom Hosen Teuffel*. An anonymous song in which an old *Landsknecht* complained about the new fashion was printed in the same year: Anon., "Ein new Klagliedt."
60. Huntebrinker, "Soldatentracht," 96.
61. See Rublack, *Dressing Up*, 110, for a discussion of the sermon.

108 ❦ *Faith in War*

62. Stambaugh, *Teufelbücher*, 274.
63. Musculus, *Vom Hosen Teuffel*, 21, 31.
64. Rublack, *Dressing Up*, 33–46.
65. Ibid., 51, 53, 56.
66. Lynn, *Women, Armies and Warfare*, 40.
67. Cabantous, *Blasphemy*; Loetz, *Mit Gott handeln*; Schwerhoff, *Zungen wie Schwerter*; Nash, *Blasphemy*.
68. Schwerhoff, "Starke Worte," 248; Schwerhoff, *Zungen wie Schwerter*, 279–288.
69. Schwerhoff, *Zungen wie Schwerter*, 221, 259; Loetz, *Mit Gott handeln*, 272–301.
70. Caferro, *John Hawkwood*, 5.
71. Cabantous, *Blasphemy*, 107, 114–15.
72. Georg Herdenius, letter to superintendent Konrad Dieterich (1622), in Herrmann, *Aus tiefer Not*, 52.
73. Hümmer, "Bamberg im Schweden-Kriege," 213–14. There was a colonel by the name of Teuffel in Swedish services, but he had died three years previously at Breitenfeld.
74. Loetz, *Mit Gott handeln*, 452.
75. Peters, *Peter Hagendorf*, 148.
76. See for example Schwerhoff, *Zungen wie Schwerter*, 59–60; Walsham, *Providence*, 78–81.
77. Loetz, *Mit Gott handeln*, 340-358.
78. Ibid., 332, 340–41, 347–351.
79. Grimmelshausen, *Simplicissimus Teutsch*, 96.
80. Schottin, *Tagebuch des Erich Lassotta*, 134.
81. Westenrieder, "Tagebuch des Augustin von Fritsch," 123.
82. Beck, *Artikelsbriefe*, 113–117.
83. Christian IV, *Articulsbrieff*, Aii[V].
84. Ibid.
85. Ibid.
86. *Schwedisches Kriegs=Recht*, 5.
87. Ibid.
88. Ibid.
89. The following statistics are taken from van Dülmen, "Wider die Ehre Gottes," 25.
90. Schwerhoff, *Zungen wie Schwerter*, 138–39; Loetz, *Mit Gott handeln*, 327–337.
91. Musculus, *Vom Gotslestern*, 61, 69, 76.
92. Flynn, "Blasphemy," 34–35.
93. Loetz, *Mit Gott handeln*, 329.
94. Ibid., 298, 327.
95. Schwerhoff, *Zungen wie Schwerter*, 53.
96. Cabantous, *Blasphemy*, 82.
97. Brunmüller, *Von dem Erschrockenlichen*, v–vi.
98. Solms, "*Kriegsbuch*," 15[V]-16[V], 18[R].
99. Kirchhof, *Militaris Disciplina*, 67–68.
100. Ulmschneider, *Götz von Berlichingen*, 126.
101. Loetz, *Mit Gott handeln*, 317.
102. Ibid., 298.
103. Kirchhof, *Wendunmuth*, part I, 53, 63–64.
104. Rummel, *Medicamenta Militaria*.
105. Holst and Sutherland, "Towton Revisited," 109.

Religion, Morality, and Military Everyday Life ∾ 109

106. Eickhoff and Jungklaus, "Die Medizinische Versorgung", 122–129.
107. Eickhoff et al., "Die Schlacht von Wittstock.", 159–60.
108. I have examined magical healing in the military in "Magische Medizin und Schutzzauber." On popular magical healing in Germany see Ruff, *Zauberpraktiken als Lebenshilfe*, ch. 4; Labouvie, *Verbotene Künste*, 95–110.; and with a wider European focus, Bever, *The Realities of Witchcraft*, 273–303.
109. The notion of a "magico-religious continuum" suggested by Stephen Wilson and Kathryn A. Edwards seems very convincing and could for present purposes be expanded to a "magico-religious-medical" continuum. Wilson, *The Magical Universe*, XXVI; Edwards, "The Early Modern Magical Continuum."
110. Rummel, *Medicamenta Militaria*, Axi^{V}.
111. For example Raymund Minderer, town physician of Augsburg and Bavarian court physician, who explained the production of several magical plasters and amulets in his *Medicina Militaris*.
112. On weapons magic in early modern Europe see most recently Ludwig, "Der Zauber des Tötens" and Tlusty, "Invincible Blades."
113. Eichberg, "Gespenster im Zeughaus," 10. An example in which a new mortar was forged in the name of the Trinity can be found in Dudík, *Tagebuch des feindlichen Einfalls der Schweden*, 345.
114. According to military custom, master gunners were owed either all bells or just the tocsin in every place that was taken by storm; see Fronsperger, *Von Kayserlichem Kriegßrechten*, CIV^{V}; Lünig, *Corpus Iuris Militaris*, vol. 1, 4.
115. See Tlusty, "Invincible Blades," passim.
116. Staricius, *HeldenSchatz*, 69–70, 87, 97.
117. See Tlusty, "Invincible Blades," 663.
118. Ludwig, "Der Zauber des Tötens," 38–39.
119. For a fuller account of military apotropaic magic see Funke, "'Naturali legitimâque Magica.'" For other recent studies see Tlusty, "Invincible Blades"; Kaiser, "Ars moriendi"; and Bei der Wieden, "Niederdeutsche Söldner." Older studies include Bächtold's *Deutscher Soldatenbrauch* and Kronfeld's *Der Krieg im Aberglauben*, as well as the lemma "Festmachen" in the *Handwörterbuch des deutschen Aberglaubens (HDA)*, vol. 2, 1353–1368.
120. Kronfeld, *Krieg im Aberglauben*, 88; Bächtold, *Deutscher Soldatenbrauch*, 22. The anonymous author of the *Victori-Schlüssel* supported this chronology when he wrote in 1631 that this magical vogue began "over twenty years ago" (Aii^{V}).
121. Luther, "Whether Soldiers, Too, Can be Saved," 135–36.
122. Scherer, *Ein bewerte Kunst vnd Wundsegen*, Aii^{R}.
123. Kirchhof, *Militaris Disciplina*, 62–63.
124. Anon., *Warhaffter Bericht*, 17.
125. Ibid., 18.
126. Westenrieder, "Tagebuch des Augustin von Fritsch," 156.
127. Ibid., 163.
128. Abelinus, *Theatrum Europæum Vierdter Theil*, 629–30.
129. Watts, "The Famovs Victorie of Leipsich." The battle account starts with a new pagination after *The Swedish Discipline*.
130. Ibid., 32.
131. Watts, *The Swedish Intelligencer—The First Part*, 127.
132. Ibid.
133. Staricius, *HeldenSchatz*, 91.

110 ~: *Faith in War*

134. Ibid., 54.
135. Ibid., 75.
136. Ibid., 76.
137. See e.g., Bacon, "Versuch einer Klassifizierung altdeutscher Zaubersprüche und Segen," 226.
138. Anon., *Victori-Schlüssel*, Aiv[R].
139. Kronfeld, *Der Krieg im Aberglauben*, 90. A contemporary English anthology of supernatural events (Bromhall, *An History of Apparitions*, 89) also mentions an *Indusium Necessitas*, or *Nothembt*, whose fabrication is identical to that described by Kronfeld.
140. Staricius, *HeldenSchatz*, 92.
141. Ibid.
142. Ibid., 93–94.
143. Ibid.
144. See for example Byloff, *Volkskundliches aus Strafprozessen*, 40–41; Tlusty, "Invincible Blades," 670.
145. Scribner, "The Reformation, Popular Magic, and the 'Disenchantment of the World,'" 478; van Dülmen, *Kultur und Alltag*, vol. 3, 60–61.
146. Hocker, *Pastorale Castrense*, 447.
147. Kronfeld (*Der Krieg im Aberglauben*, 90) cites J. Gebhart, *Österreichisches Sagenbuch* (Pest, 1863).
148. See, for instance, the Bavarian anti-magic law of 1611 that described and prohibited most of the practices portrayed here (*Landtgebott wider die Aberglauben, Zauberey, Hexerey und andere sträffliche Teufelskünste*, paragraphs 9–21) or Tlusty's hypermasculine civilian users of weapons and apotropaic magic, which could all conceivably have occurred in the military as well ("Invincible Blades," passim).
149. See Skemer, *Binding Words*, 87–88.
150. Sugg, "'Good Physic but Bad Food.'"
151. Rider, "Common Magic," 310–11.
152. Baldwin, "Toads and Plague," 227–28.
153. Staricius, *HeldenSchatz*, 77.
154. This includes Protestants like Gustavus Adolphus, who had his breastplate decorated with silver angels and the word *IEHOVA* (depicted in Langer, *Hortus Bellicus*, 141).
155. Schreiner, "Sygzeichen," 70–76.
156. Baumann, *Frundsberg*, 217.
157. Crawford, *European Sexualities*, ch. 2.
158. Most recently Ailes, *Courage and Grief* and Lynn, *Women, Armies and Warfare*. See also Hagemann and Pröve's edited collection of essays, which provides a varied overview of many aspects of military gender relations (*Landsknechte, Soldatenfrauen und Nationalkrieger*). See also Irsigler and Lassotta, *Bettler und Gaukler*, 210-214.; Rublack, "Wench and Maiden," esp. 11-18; Engelen, "Warum heiratete man einen Soldaten?"; Jansson, "Soldaten und Vergewaltigung." For a global overview of women in the military since antiquity see Hacker and Vining, *Companion to Women's Military History*.
159. See Kroener, "'. . . und ist der jammer nit zu beschreiben,'" 286–87; Lynn, *Women, Armies and Warfare*, ch. 3.
160. See for example Fronsperger, *Kriegs Ordnung Vnd Regiment*, LIII[R]–LIII[V].
161. Lynn, *Women, Armies and Warfare*, 67.
162. On the concept of sexual barter see Hájková, "Sexual Barter in Times of Genocide."

Religion, Morality, and Military Everyday Life ~ 111

163. Kirchhof described regular marriages held at churches or by the field preacher when a soldier wanted to wed a dead comrade's widow or "another wench" (*Dierne*). Kirchhof, *Militaris Disciplina*, 133.
164. Rennemann, *Privilegia Vnd Freyheiten der Soldatescha*, 17.
165. Junghans von der Olnitz, *KriegsOrdnung*, I[V]; Anon., *Regiments Capitulation*, K[R].
166. On the "reformation" of the household see Roper, *Holy Household*. Regarding marital discipline see esp. ch. 4. See also Robisheaux, *Rural Society*, 95–116.; Muir, *Ritual in Early Modern Europe*, 37–41.; Greyerz, *Religion und Kultur*, 182–190.
167. Muir, *Ritual in Early Modern Europe*, 37.
168. Roper, *Holy Household*, 159–64.; Greyerz, *Kultur und Religion*, 184.
169. Rublack, *Magd, Metz' oder Mörderin*, 200.
170. Breit, *Leichtfertigkeit und ländliche Gesellschaft*, 238.
171. Harrington, "Shifting Boundaries and Boundary Shifters," 206.
172. Loetz, "Probleme der Sünde," 209.
173. Roper, *Holy Household*, 157–64.
174. Wolff, "Feldpostbriefe aus dem Dreißigjährigen Kriege."
175. Huntebrinker (*Fromme Knechte*, 292-314) seems to have been the only historian since Wolff to use the letters until they were recently edited by Silke Törpsch and published on Markus Meumann's Thirty Years War internet platform (https://thirty-years-war-online. net/quellen/briefe, retrieved 12 January 2024). Given the threat of impermanence of online resources like these, I am using the reference codes of the Marburg state archive.
176. Staatsarchiv (StA) Marburg Best. M 1 Nr. 275, fol. 9[R].
177. Ibid., fol. 62[R].
178. Ibid.
179. Ibid.
180. Ibid., fol. 53[R].
181. Ibid., fol. 68[R].
182. Ibid., fol. 51[R].
183. Ibid., fol. 66[R].
184. Ibid., fol. 67[R].
185. Ibid.
186. Ibid., fol. 50[R].
187. Rublack, "Wench and Maiden," 12.
188. StA Marburg Best. M 1 Nr. 275, fol. 25[R].
189. Ibid., fol. 7[R].
190. Bambauer and Kleinholz, *Geusen und Spanier*, 345.
191. StA Marburg Best. M 1 Nr. 275, fols. 52[R], 54[R], 65[R].
192. Ibid., fol. 45[R]–45[V].
193. Ibid., fol. 12[R].
194. Ibid., fol. 13[R]-13[V]. Catharina's poem was not an original, however, as another letter (fol. 16) contains the same poem. I have not been able to find out where the piece was borrowed from.
195. Peters, *Peter Hagendorf*, 142–43, 148.
196. Ibid., 145, 147.
197. Poyntz, *The Relation of Sydnam Poyntz*, 125.
198. Ibid., 125–26.
199. Ibid., 127–28.

112 ❧ *Faith in War*

200. Volkholz, *Jürgen Ackermann,* 54–55.
201. Rublack, "Wench and Maiden," 13–15.
202. Ibid., 11.
203. StA Marburg Best. M 1 Nr. 275, fol. 62[R].

CHAPTER 4

Confession
Conflict, Indifference, Coexistence

When examining the religious dimension of military life in sixteenth and seventeenth-century Europe, we are faced with a curious conundrum: the wars that were waged frequently had a confessional dimension—more pronounced in some conflicts than in others—yet the armies who fought these wars, certainly in the Holy Roman Empire, were confessional composites, comprised of Protestants and Catholics. This led to a fundamental tension: at the same time that military force was a means to enforce genuine or pretended confessional goals, religious coexistence was a fact of military everyday life. The questions this chapter seeks to answer are how confessional conflict manifested itself, how characteristic it was in military society, and how it was resolved. We will thus have to place the exceptional occasions in which unambiguously religious violence occurred in relation to the toleration, or rather, the confessional indifference, that was so typical of army life. To appreciate and understand this complex problem, we must also analyze the norms that guided early modern military violence more generally and examine the peculiarly unemotional character of enmity among professional soldiers.

In the following, close reading of individual historical scenes in which confessional violence occurred is favored over theoretical abstractions. The material examined in this chapter documents acts of violence that range from taunts to iconoclasm and the torture and murder of adherents of a different confession. This methodology is influenced by the groundbreaking work of Natalie Zemon Davis and her analysis of the "rites of violence" of sixteenth-century France and the analysis of religious violence that followed.[1] Davis departed from the then predominant interpretation that religious riots were mere reflections of "real," material problems arising from economic or social strife and showed the genuinely religious motivation and the theological logics behind the violence. Barbara Diefendorf, like Denis Crouzet, has stressed the importance of preachers and the pervasiveness of their violent message throughout all social strata.[2] She also identified a small, extremist, and self-selecting faction of Catholics in the militias that actively inflicted violence, while the majority of Catholics did not join in the slaughter even if they condoned it.[3] The observation that only a small minority of Catholics engaged in bloodshed is of great importance because it points toward a major quandary: if the logics of religious pollution and violent cleansing were inherent in early modern religious thinking and if action was encouraged and demanded by clerical leaders, then why did not *more* people follow these imperatives? If religious violence against Christians of other confessions was not only legitimate but required, why was there not *more* religious violence in early modern Europe?

The question becomes even more urgent when we turn to the military, whose central function was violence and whose members were doubly legitimated to act violently against confessional enemies through their profession as well as their faith. The initial focus of this chapter will be on the patterns, or "rites," of military religious violence, asking what such behaviors can tell us about the confessional outlook of the perpetrators and their knowledge of confessional difference. The previous chapters have shown that military authorities phrased legal codes in universally Christian, rather than confessional terms, that religious literature aimed at soldiers also predominantly conveyed common Christian values, and that soldiers were active Christians in a typical early modern fashion. How can we understand religious violence committed by soldiers—individually or in groups—in view of the unconfessional and latitudinarian attitudes that dominated everyday life in the armies? Finally, we have to ask why religious violence was such a rare occurrence in military society and what norms outweighed or blunted impulses to engage in confessional conflict.

The historiography presents contradictory evaluations of such questions. On the one hand, we can remind ourselves of the negative postulates regarding military religiosity that have been examined in the first chapter. The general consensus among historians maintains that religion did not concern soldiers, that they were morally substandard, and even that the military milieu had a "de-Christianizing" effect on soldiers.[4] We now know that this was not the case. On the other hand, Johannes Burkhardt has claimed that confession was a strong motivator for the armies of the Thirty Years War.[5] A number of historians have diagnosed latent confessional tensions in the armies.[6] As we have seen, military authorities generally tried to gloss over confessional differences and that expediency took priority over confessional issues. This allows us to deduce two things: firstly, there appears to have existed enough confessional sentiment among soldiers to make such latitudinarian legislation necessary. Secondly, the defusing of conflict potential seems to have worked from the perspective of the authorities. But the argument for high confessional tensions rests on circumstantial evidence. Bonin deduced confessional strife from stipulations in martial law, not from reports of actual events. Baumann based the assertion that the "different creeds of the soldiers posed a significant problem of order" on Bonin's earlier statement.[7] Kaiser similarly argued for the existence of confessional conflict from articles of war that forbade religious disputations.[8] Burschel, finally, does not provide an example of *confessional* conflict but cites a case in which it seems that *national* discord led to a mass brawl between Spanish and German troops. In short, there is little direct evidence for confessional conflict among soldiers.

Ralf Pröve's observations that confessional intolerance was branded "unchristian" in the military context in the later seventeenth and eighteenth centuries stand in marked opposition to these assertions of serious confessional tensions.[9] I will argue that these tolerant attitudes in fact existed throughout the sixteenth and seventeenth centuries, not just in unconfessional military structures but also in everyday life. Confessional thinking—or the absence thereof—is related to soldiers' attitudes toward the enemy in general, a dimension of army life that has yet to be studied in greater detail for the wider European military context. Civilian perceptions of war and atrocities have been thoroughly researched and a few articles have addressed the military perspective, but our understanding of soldiers' attitudes toward the enemy remains rudimentary.[10] Barbara Donagan has examined the "Web of Honor" that bound enemies to mutually honorable treatment for the specific context of the English Civil War.[11] She has found that despite confessional and political differences, "shared standards of honor survived between military enemies" who treated one another as honorable gentlemen and Christians, not as Parliamentarians or Royalists.[12] Notions of enmity therefore have to be studied to provide the context for the findings on confessional attitudes. The specific conditions of early modern warfare, it is argued, help to account for the widely unemotional nature of enmity in the period.

Historians tend to associate the military closely with princely enforcements of confessional policies. Kaspar von Greyerz and Kim Siebenhüner have pointed out that the "main agents of religious violence were secular and ecclesiastical authorities."[13] In this view, soldiers feature as executors of policies but their own attitudes toward religious violence remain opaque. But was it really the case that early modern soldiers were merely carrying out orders or did they shape events through their behavior? What can we say about their personal investment in these actions? The following discussion will concentrate on these questions and analyze the motivations behind specific occurrences of religious violence. Acts of religious violence tended to be recorded in detail, allowing for nuanced reconstruction, but, as we will see, printed reportage was often biased and relied heavily on literary topoi that superimposed confessional patterns onto soldiers' behavior. Eyewitness accounts receive special attention here and although many of these were written by the victims, we can often glimpse soldiers as individuals who exhibit differing attitudes toward confessional difference and religious violence through their actions if we read these

116 ᴄ: *Faith in War*

texts closely. Through a close reading of specific situations in which religious violence occurred, we may thus encounter soldiers not just as an amorphous force executing orders, but as individual agents who influenced events through their behavior, which in turn was shaped by their religious beliefs.[14]

The Sack of Rome is a good place to start. It was a well-documented catastrophe that produced several detailed reports and numerous eyewitness accounts that allow a good reconstruction of group and individual behavior.[15] On 6 May 1527 Emperor Charles V's army, consisting of German, Spanish, and Italian contingents, overpowered the papal defenders and sacked the eternal city. Only ten years before, Martin Luther had sparked a heretical movement in a German backwater that had spread like wildfire and Italian commentators were already referring to the German *Landsknechte* simply as "Lutherans" (*Luterani*) or "heretics" (*Eretici*).[16] In the months leading up to the Sack of Rome, the *Landsknechte* had shown their distaste for the Church and its symbols in the region of Piacenza. Somewhat intrigued by the new sect, Luigi Guicciardini, a Florentine official, reported:

> they did no other damage, than to destroy the images in the churches and cast the holy relics to the ground along with all the sacraments except for the Eucharist. For this alone these Lutherans showed reverence. But the other things that with good reason the modern Church reveres are despised by the Lutheran sect, and they broke them to pieces and trod them underfoot.[17]

The commander of the imperial troops, the Duke of Bourbon, also recognized the Lutheran element.[18] Before the assault, he allegedly gave a speech in which he appealed to the anticlericalism and anti-Catholicism of the *Landsknechte* by promising them "the incredible wealth of vicious and ridiculous prelates."[19] Many of the Lutheran *Landsknechte* did not need such encouragement: they had left home to fight for the emperor and now, after months of hunger and misery, they found themselves attacking the seat of the papal Antichrist.[20]

For a mercenary captain like Sebastian Schertlin, the Sack of Rome was a golden day for purely financial reasons. His description of events, void of any recognition of the religious significance or the suffering, is noteworthy for its bluntness: "The sixth day of May we took Rome by storm, struck dead about 6,000 men inside, plundered the whole city, took anything we found in all churches and on the ground, and husbanded strangely."[21] He also came straight to the point when he reported the capture of Pope Clement and twelve cardinals: "What great lamentation was among them, they cried heartily, we all got rich."[22] His account does not indicate that he found it remarkable that he as a Catholic should arrest the pope.[23]

The soldiers began to loot. Bourbon had managed to avert a mutiny among the Spanish contingents by distributing what little money he could find, but the *Landsknechte* had not been paid in months and they were starving. Ambrosius von Gumpenberg, a German merchant living in Rome, described the haunting sight of his compatriots as they entered the city. The *Landsknechte* "had their weapons in their right hand, in the other a piece of bread that they had taken from bakeries or houses during their entry, which they ate running, like mad beasts dying from hunger."[24] All soldiers, regardless of confession, began to plunder churches and the cardinals' palaces. But the *Landsknechte* also engaged in the abuse and humiliation of clerics, iconoclasm, and the purposeful desecration of churches, which the witnesses attributed to their Lutheran convictions. Not only did they treat the many relics they found with heightened disrespect, but they also began to actively destroy or deface the material manifestations of the old faith:

> They committed shameful acts on the altars and in the most sanctified places in contempt of contemporary religion. Many sacred images and sculptures that had once been worshipped with vain ceremonies were burned and broken by iron and fire. Crucifixes were shattered by shots from arquebuses and lay on the ground; the relics and calvaries of saints lay among the dung of men and animals. . . . There was no sin or villainy that these mad and impious Lutherans did not commit.[25]

While the Spaniards shocked the Romans with their uninhibited and inventive cruelty, especially when it came to the torturing of captives to extract ransoms, the Germans' fierce attack on the church interiors and sacramentals almost caused the troops to turn against each other. Not that the Catholic soldiers had any scruples about stealing liturgical vessels, reliquaries, or breaking into the sarcophagi and tombs of popes and cardinals in search of valuables. But it seems from Guicciardini's report that Catholics perceived the behavior of the "mad and impious" Lutherans not merely as plundering but as an attack on what these objects symbolized: the Catholic faith, its images, and its rites. These attributed intentions appear to have made the German soldiers' actions seem more offensive than the plundering of the other troops. Most relics were merely discarded as useless, while others were treated as historical artifacts and taken as souvenirs. One *Landsknecht* affixed the Holy Lance to his pike to parade it through town, Sebastian Schertlin took the enormous rope with which Judas was said to have hanged himself home to Schorndorff as a keepsake, and Saint Veronica's handkerchief was removed from the reliquary and appeared for sale in taverns soon afterward.[26]

The *Landsknechte* also left a record of their religious interpretation of the events and when the forces finally departed, Rome and the Vatican were covered in Protestant graffiti. Some of the soldiers carved the name "Luther" into walls, another showed off his Latin skills ("*Vivat Lutherus*"), while others gave clear expression to their hatred of the Pope, Rome, and all that it stood for. The portrait of Giovanni di Medici, the later Pope Leo X, suffered a pike stab

118 ~: *Faith in War*

to the face.[27] As Volker Reinhardt has noted, making the connection between the cardinal in Rafael's fresco and Luther's early adversary and recognizing his likeness demonstrated "a lot of [skill in] iconology and genealogy."[28] A fresco showing the Holy City in the Villa Farnesina had "Babylon" written over it, echoing the reformers' identification of Rome with the Whore of Babylon and the seat of Antichrist. A soldier called Dietwart wrote "God bless you, Bourbon," presumably thanking the Duke for this chance to personally deliver a blow to orthodoxy, while an anonymous German wrote "Why should I, who is writing this, not have to laugh? The *Landsknechte* made the Pope run!" In these brief statements one can detect not only the professional but also the confessional pride of the Lutheran soldiers who were raging in the very heart of Catholicism.

Among the many riches that fell into the hands of the imperial troops were also the clothes of the cardinals and liturgical vestments.[29] The soldiers used the vestments to impersonate and ridicule the clergy in carnivalesque performances. During the siege of Castel Sant'Angelo where the pope and a number of cardinals had fled, a German knight, Wilhelm von Sandizell, and his men mockingly "played Vatican."[30] Sandizell dressed up as the Pope, complete with the actual papal tiara, while his soldiers dressed in cardinals' hats and scarlet vestments, bowing and genuflecting before him and kissing his hands and feet. The pretend pope then held up a chalice, blessed the entourage, and drank health to Clement, which was answered by the "cardinals" downing cups of wine. They shouted that they wanted to make "right pious" (*recht fromme*) popes and cardinals now, ones who obeyed the emperor and did not start wars and cause bloodshed. Finally, they hollered in the direction of the real pope in the castle that they wanted to put Martin Luther in his place and the entire group started chanting "*Luther Bapst!*"[31] Processions like this, in which *Landsknechte* dressed up as popes or cardinals, administering mock blessings from communion chalices, became a regular sight for the next few weeks. In one situation, soldiers dressed a mule in clerical vestments and tried to force a priest to feed it the eucharist, killing him when he refused.[32] Guicciardini and another eyewitness, Jacopo Buonaparte, report a more elaborate case of clerical abuse in a rather bizarre mock funeral. A group of German soldiers—Buonaparte stressed that they were "all Lutherans" (*tutti luterani*)—dragged Cardinal Numalio from his bed and carried him through the city singing his obsequies.[33] They finally brought the cardinal into a church and held a funeral sermon in which they detailed Numalio's sexual habits, a humiliation that was rejected as calumny by Buonaparte but given some credence by Guicciardini, who only refrained from characterizing the cardinal's carnal appetites as "criminal" out of respect for his office.[34] After the soldiers had lifted up a slab from the church floor and forced the cardinal into this "grave" for a while, they either lost interest in their game or ran out of drink and returned to the cardinal's palace to feast.

The Sack of Rome and its aftermath have been described in detail because in this event we can witness the full spectrum of military religious violence typical of the period before 1650. The looting of churches, iconoclasm, the mockery and parody of the other confession, and the abuse and killing of its adherents all occurred, often simultaneously or in a cascade of events, in many different contexts and constellations across Europe. Most of the soldiers' energy in Rome was invested in looting churches, but one ought to be careful not to overstate the religious significance of such events. Plundering churches had a long tradition among Christian warriors and although the articles of war banned the practice, it was a military custom that was difficult to root out.[35] That factors other than religious zeal frequently underlay attacks on religious sites, objects, or persons must be taken into account here, the most frequent being avarice, hunger, and destitution. During the Sack of Rome, half-starved mercenaries piled into the city and their first objective was to steal a piece of bread. For the context of the Thirty Years War, Bernhard Kroener has shown that plundering mainly occurred when the military provisioning system had broken down, and it seems that this observation is more widely applicable to the phenomenon of military looting.[36] In Rome, it was the indiscriminate looting that unified the conquerors across national and confessional lines and much if not most of the plundering can be attributed to nonreligious incentives. Thus, while churches and clerics feature frequently as sites or victims of military violence, their religious nature was not necessarily of primary importance.

As was the case during the Sack of Rome, where Catholics and Lutherans looted side by side, there is not much evidence to indicate that soldiers spared churches of their own confession or those of their employers. Three examples from the Thirty Years War illustrate this: the imperial—and thus at least nominally Catholic—troops that ransacked the churches in the Bavarian villages of Aschering and Traubing in 1633 did not shrink back from the tabernacles, which they forced open to steal the holy vessels, discarding the hosts in nearby fields.[37] In early August 1634, Spanish-Burgundian horsemen plundered the monastery of Andechs—"friends," as its abbot Maurus Friesenegger bitterly noted.[38] Likewise, Dr. Georg Herdenius, the Lutheran pastor of Echzell in Hesse, lamented the loss of a number of books after the village was plundered by Christian of Brunswick's Protestant troops.[39] After they had pillaged the church, some of the soldiers turned their attention to the church library, and Herdenius noted that there were many students from Hesse among the Brunswick soldiers and that it was these former students who stole his books. None of these instances of plundering seem to have been informed by religious hatred, but by material desires or, in the case of the book thieves, also intellectual ones. What these examples indicate is that confessional allegiance or association *as such* neither exacerbated nor limited looting, which indicates that the specific situation and the individuals involved had a significant influence on such events.

120 ❧ *Faith in War*

Ultimately, however, trying to neatly distinguish between "religious" and "profane" motives is an artificial endeavor. For a soldier, plundering a church could simultaneously satisfy his material needs *and* offer a chance to express confessional hatred. A Catholic Polish soldier, for example, left a note in a plundered and burnt-out parsonage insulting the pastor as a "scoundrel" (*Scelm*) and a thief. He stated that the pastor did not deserve to preach in a church that had been built as a Catholic house of worship and that Lutherans had no business using it for their apostate services. The soldier ended his note with "Martinus Luther, scoundrel, dog's cunt [*Hundsfort*], and you are [a] dog's cunt."[40] Likewise, pastor Nikolaus Moterus's church and parsonage in Rosdorf, Hesse, provided ample spoils for plundering soldiers.[41] While the paradisiacal abundance of food was welcome, the soldiers wanted to find the owner as well (Moterus had gone into hiding), and swore they would kill the "blasphemous Lutheran pastor" and string him up.[42] Verbal intimidation like this was often heard and intended to frighten locals into submission, but in this case, these were no hollow threats: while Moterus was fortunate enough to escape, the soldiers apprehended his colleague in the neighboring village of Beerfelden, crushed his hip, cut off his genitals, and sneered that he would not sing "Maintain us, Lord, by Thy Word" for much longer.[43] Apart from the apparent joy they gained from torturing the "heretic," the soldiers here also betrayed their perception of a typical Lutheran religious practice, hymn singing, and showed that they were acquainted with the title of at least one of Luther's hymns.

Plundering and confessional violence could therefore go hand in hand, and while it is important to emphasize the possibility of different incentives coinciding, we should now approach instances that appear to have arisen from a more decidedly religious motivation. The—admittedly rough—gauge that remains is the question of how soldiers profited from acting out violence in a particular set of circumstances. Those situations where soldiers seem to have had little or nothing else to gain from their behavior other than satisfaction of confessional hatred, where their actions would not make sense without a religious motivation, suggest that we are dealing with "real" religious violence. Religious violence should be defined broadly in this context, ranging from "milder" instances such as interrogation or intimidation of members of another denomination to the defiling or destruction of religious sites, iconoclasm, and the torture and killing of clergy or members of a different creed. In this way we will first examine attacks on the material manifestations of the religious "other," followed by discussions of intimidation, humiliation, torture, and the killing of humans.

Instances of iconoclasm and the desecration of churches are less ambiguous expressions of confessional thinking than plundering. But where lies the difference between irreverence and desecration? Mere destruction does not seem to be a reliable criterion, because soldiers of all confessions destroyed churches of all confessions. What we are looking for is an element of confessional malice to speak of desecration or iconoclasm. Churches had been customarily plundered before the Reformation, that is, before the possibility of confessional violence even arose. During the Middle Ages, troops had frequently attacked the sacred images of vanquished opponents to demonstrate power.[44] Guy Marchal has shown that images did not possess a universal sanctity before the Reformation but were frequently associated with particular towns or communities, and thus became religious party symbols.[45] In mocking and attacking these specific images, soldiers did not express their defiance of the sacred in general but proved that *this* image was impotent.

As we have seen above, this tradition persisted as Catholic soldiers of the confessional age continued to break into Catholic churches to steal monstrances, reliquaries, and other church treasure. Concurrent with the ostentatious display of power was a material incentive, as the soldiers mostly discarded the sacramentals, the hosts and relics, which suggests that they were after the precious containers, not the contents. Contemporaries noted such irreverence with indignation, but they seem to have considered this "normal" church theft that was not uncommon.[46] The same kind of behavior caused greater abhorrence, however, when it became known that the church breakers belonged to another confession, as was the case with the Lutheran *Landsknechte* in Rome. In such an instance, it was apparently assumed that the offenders were not just thieving and destroying but had committed their trespass in order to insult the other confession. The difference between irreverence and desecration or iconoclasm was thus a matter of intention and often only *perceived* intention. Despite the Italian commentators' assumption that all Germans were infected by Luther's heresy, not all of them necessarily turned against the religious objects in Rome on a distinct confessional impulse; many may have sought to irreverently emphasize their power or simply to loot.

In other circumstances, the destruction of religious objects and the desecration of religious sites were more unambiguously motivated by confession and are interesting in so far as the perpetrators acted not against individuals but against *symbols* of the other confession. Aggression was consequently directed at the material manifestations of religion, something that not only requires varying degrees of abstraction but also seems to have no other purposes than to express one's subjective dislike of the religious objects one destroys and to inflict spiritual anguish on those who venerate these items. Throughout the sixteenth century, iconoclasm was more a symptom of radical reformations in civilian communities and was predominantly carried out by members of these communities.[47] In certain contexts, such as the Sack of Rome or the early stages of the Thirty Years War, however, instances of military iconoclasm were recorded. The desecration of churches was a catastrophe for the local faithful and caused abhorrence, but there was no consensus regarding what kind of behavior could be justified by military custom and what constituted sacrilege within

122 ❧ Faith in War

the military either. On rare occasions, troops could cause one another to retaliate against the desecration of sacred spaces and objects. One such episode is recorded between imperial and Bohemian troops during the early stages of the Thirty Years War in the western Bohemian region of Tachov (Tachau). The author of the *Acta Mansfeldiaca* interpreted the relentless plundering of a cloister by Mansfeld's men as an act of revenge for the behavior of an imperial unit operating in the area that had allegedly desecrated not just every Lutheran church it came across, but had also disturbed graves. It appears from the account that it was the violation of the churches and graves that provoked the Protestant soldiers to ransack Tachov's abbey and its church especially thoroughly: everything the soldiers found was carried off, including two carts of lard, the brewing pan, cartloads of books, textiles, the bells, and all ornaments from the cloister and the church. The organ pipes were melted to cast ammunition.[48]

While they could have a discernible confessional motivation, acts of iconoclasm were not necessarily born out of mortal hatred. On the contrary, soldiers usually had a lot of fun smashing holy objects and in many instances we find elements of levity in soldierly behavior that seem to have had their models in the rites of inversion that characterized carnival.[49] Mock processions, at times so convincing that spectators mistook them for the real thing, were common in fifteenth and sixteenth-century Europe, as were burlesque caricatures of church ritual and the hiding of holy objects.[50] Although they were often motivated by serious misgivings, these popular traditions allowed the expression of discontent in a derisive manner, which is not to say that these occasions did not tip over into violence. Laughter and derision were ubiquitous in Reformation polemics.[51] Aquinas had deemed only *eutrapelia* (benevolent laughter as opposed to malicious Schadenfreude) to be proper hilarity for a Christian. Monastic rules had frowned upon clerical laughter and Protestant reformers also promoted a pious earnestness.[52] At the same time, however, both Protestant print and sermons employed caricature and ridicule of the old religion from the beginning. Similarly, Loyola frowned upon laughter or provoking laughter, but the Society of Jesus used caricature and mockery heavily in its attempts to ridicule "heretics."[53] Laughing at the misguided and the enemy asserted one's superiority and we find this kind of behavior among soldiers throughout the period, often in the context of iconoclasm and desecration. Peter Blickle has characterized iconoclasm as a "proxy phenomenon" (*Stellvertreterphänomen*) that was associated with revolutionary upheavals and civil strife.[54] Just as revolutionaries might smash the religious symbols of the old order, soldiers could employ these rites for their own purposes: by getting their hands on and debasing the sacred images of their opponents, they could prove their power and derive enjoyment from the scandal they caused.

When the rebel troops laid siege to Pilsen in 1618 only months after the Bohemian Revolt had broken out, they were not just attacking a city but the symbol of foreign Catholic oppression of the indigenous Hussite and Protestant faiths.[55] As the trenches moved toward the city walls, the cloisters and Catholic churches surrounding the town were captured by the Protestant attackers and the soldiers not only looted the buildings but devised ways to make the Catholic defenders destroy their own holy objects.[56] Some soldiers took a crucifix from a church, draped the Savior in a soldier's coat, and hoisted him up above the trenches, causing the Pilsen garrison, who mistook the figure for an enemy, to fire at their own "idol." When the crucifix was shot to pieces, the soldiers dragged a statue of the Virgin Mary into the trench, dressed her in an apron, and repeated the procedure. The statue was destroyed in the same way as the crucifix and a Protestant eyewitness gleefully remarked that had the Pilseners' "saint-munching mothers known this, they would've bawled their eyes out."[57] Likewise, a marked air of mirth characterized the iconoclasm in Prague's castle church on Christmas 1619. Supervised by Frederick V's Calvinist court preacher Abraham Scultetus, who had lobbied the king for the removal of the "idols," the cleansing of the church was partly carried out by officers who set the tone of the event.[58] Frederick had ordered the images' removal in order to put an end to Catholic idolatry and laborers had been brought in to take them down.[59] The workers, presumably in accordance with their instructions, began to lower the statues and crucifixes carefully to the ground when the officers stepped in and ordered them to drop the "idols" from a height so that they would smash.[60] To the soldiers, the mere removal of the offensive art was not enough; they wanted to see it destroyed. An officer called Barbistorff approached one of the broken crucifixes, kicked the figure of Christ, and mocked: "Here you lie, you poor one, . . . help yourself."[61] The scene is reminiscent of the legionaries taunting Christ for his seeming impotence in the passion narratives, but it cannot be determined from the report whether this was a conscious reenactment of the events on Golgotha.[62] Nevertheless, while the legionaries proved to themselves and others that they were killing a man, not a God, Barbistorff wanted to expose the object he kicked as a blasphemous image made by idolaters. The sniggering soldiers also illustrated that the Virgin Mary and St. John were not worthy of veneration when they arranged the saints' statues in a sexually explicit manner.[63] In this situation, the soldiers turned a stripping of a church into full-blown iconoclasm. That Frederick did not order the destruction but merely the removal may have been informed by a desire to not alienate his new subjects too much, or it may have been recognition of the artistic value of the pieces.[64] It has been noted that iconoclasts were anxious about the possibility of being led into idolatry by the presence of images, and a simultaneity of revulsion and recognition of their potential influence is evident in the actions of the officers who shattered and degraded the figures. On the one hand, the artworks were rejected as "idols," unchristian, and worthy of destruction; on the other, they were not merely discarded as trumpery and their importance

124 ~: *Faith in War*

was in a sense emphasized by the energy invested in destroying them.[65] It was this need to prove that there *really* was no connection between the image and its divine or saintly prototype that motivated early modern iconoclasm in general.[66] Scultetus apparently did nothing to stop the soldiers, but the fact that he did not mention how the images were treated in a sermon defending the removal as a theological imperative suggests that he did not (publicly) approve of the events.[67] The mention of the events in the *Theatrum Europaeum* equally concealed the destruction and merely reported that the Winter King had the idolatrous images removed from sight or covered, which may suggest that these authors, too, were uncomfortable with what had actually occurred.[68]

The ornamental wealth of Catholic churches and the religious significance of material objects in Catholicism offered ample opportunity for desecration, but even the sparseness of Calvinist churches could be despoiled. A defilement scandal occurred during the Spanish occupation of predominantly Calvinist Wesel in June 1616. During the night preceding the Corpus Christi procession, Spanish soldiers broke into the main Calvinist church and comprehensively debased it. They cut off the bell cords and used them to hang a dead cat from the pulpit candleholder.[69] They also tore the bible stand off the pulpit and smeared the pulpit with human feces before doing the same to the church benches, so that, as the Calvinist citizen Arnold von Anrath commented, no believer could sit down without making themselves dishonorable.[70] That the soldiers were ritually polluting the church is clear, but the meaning of the dead cat in this context is puzzling. Given the taboo surrounding carcasses, the dead animal may merely have been intended as an addition to the excrement with which the church was coated. There may have been a deeper, demonic meaning to this arrangement, as well, because soldiers of the Spanish army frequently seem to have equated Protestantism, specifically Calvinism, with devil-worship. In Maastricht, a Spanish soldier who was pleading for his life with his Calvinist captors declared, "I believe in devils, like you all" (*Credo en Diablos, corno* [*sic*] *voz otros*).[71] Another Spanish soldier disrupted a Calvinist service in Wesel and summarized his assessment of the situation by shouting "*Diabol*[o]."[72] The dead cat may therefore have been intended to signify the diabolical nature of Calvinism, and the close association of cats with demons and witchcraft as well as the use of bell cords in popular magic make it possible that the soldiers were attempting some kind of magical ritual.[73] That there was something menacing specifically about the cat would help explain Arnold von Anrath's otherwise cryptic final remark on the episode: "What significance this will further have, time will tell, because of the cat."[74]

The soldiers revealed precise knowledge of the defining elements of the Calvinist faith as they specifically targeted the pulpit, the focal point of a Reformed service, and the bible stand, which carried significant symbolism due to the central importance of Scripture in Calvinism. Regardless of the intended or perceived meaning of the dead cat, the soldiers had fully achieved their goal and the disgusted burghers confronted the Spanish governor. His reply ("es wehr ihm ledt solches zu horen") is ambiguous and can either mean that he was "tired" of hearing about such things or that he was "sorry" to hear this.[75] In either case, he promised to have the case investigated and to hang the culprits in the church portal if they could be found. It was not only the Calvinist citizens of Wesel who were scandalized over the defilement; indignation extended across confessional divisions. The following day, a Jesuit condemned the act during the Corpus Christi procession but, by way of explanation, mentioned a church desecration by Dutch soldiers that involved an aspersorium or stoup and possibly more human waste.[76] The ritual pollution of the Calvinist church could therefore have been an act of revenge for a previous desecration of a Catholic one. One gains the impression that the soldiery's confessional sensibilities were so heightened at this point in time—be it by the important Catholic feast of Corpus Christi, a previous sacrilegious act on behalf of the Protestant enemy, or both—that they engaged in acts of religious violence that led to condemnation from the Spanish governor of Wesel, and even from the Society of Jesus, a body not commonly known for its squeamishness in the confessional struggle. The desecration of the church remained a unique event during the fifteen-year occupation and it is noticeable that the accentuation of confessional identities was situational and fluctuated throughout the year. The soldiers became predominantly confessional actors in the days leading up to Corpus Christi when they were busily involved in the preparations and the processions themselves.[77] If we cut through the confessional bias of the Calvinist chronicler who described these activities, the Spanish troops appear as devout Catholics who invested time and effort into turning the "heretic" city into a place of Catholic worship for Corpus Christi. But once the holiday was over, their Catholic identity faded into the background until the coming year and confession did not color the interface of soldiers and civilians in the meantime.

Scenes of iconoclasm and desecration can therefore provide good evidence about the religious views of the soldiers involved: these men manifestly had a clear sense of themselves as agents of their denomination when they engaged in such activity. This finding stands in contrast to the unconfessional attitudes described later in this chapter, and we will have to evaluate this seeming contradiction below. For now, it is important to note that the scenes also demonstrate that soldiers had a clear understanding of the doctrinal and material elements that defined the denomination they were attacking. This is a valuable insight into soldiers' religious perceptions in so far as it demonstrates not only awareness of the differences in ritual and theology, but also that some were evidently so repulsed by these objects that they felt the need to destroy or desecrate them.

Let us turn from attacks on the material manifestations of other denominations to the mockery, abuse, and killing of believers. During the Sack of

126 ❧ Faith in War

Rome, this took the shape of carnivalesque mock processions in which the *Landsknechte* dressed up in liturgical vestments and caricatured Catholic ritual. In contrast to regular carnival processions, the German troops enacted a carnival "with an edge" in Rome: here, they wore real liturgical vestments, not imitations, abused actual relics, and killed priests when they refused to play along. These men had grown up with the rituals of the old faith as well as the rites of inversion and knew them inside out, which was reflected in their ability to parody Catholic ritual and probably also the gusto with which they did.

Taunts, mockery, and the joyous bullying of adherents of another confession persisted throughout the period. Catholic troops that had been sent to Breisach on the Rhine in August 1587 to enforce counter-reformation policies mocked Protestant ritual. The soldiers swaddled two dogs like babies and baptized them in the Protestant church, much to the horror of the locals who were then forced to provide food and drink to celebrate the event.[78] Insulting the confessional other with religiously charged slurs is a rather clear indicator of confessional identity, as the confessional slight simultaneously functions as a demarcation and affirmation of the speakers' own convictions. Furthermore, by reducing the addressee to their religious allegiance, creed alone becomes the distinguishing element and the focal point of conflict, which overrides all other difference or commonalty. During the siege of Pilsen, the defenders called the besiegers "horse thieves" and "cow thieves" but also "Lutheran dogs," to which Mansfeld's troops retorted "sons of whores," "nun keepers" (*Nonnen Hütter*; "nuns' pimps" might convey the intended meaning more accurately), or "perjurious, seal and letter breaking sons of priests."[79] While the garrison's denigration of the attackers as Lutheran "dogs" is rather straightforward, some of the Protestant besiegers' insults were implicit but indicative of an acute understanding of the religio-political situation. The accusation of being seal- and letter-breakers related to the Letter of Majesty (1609), issued by Rudolph II and initially confirmed by emperor Matthias, which granted the Bohemian and Silesian estates freedom to decide on the confession in their territories, a privilege whose revocation had proven of significant consequence in the events leading up to the Bohemian Rebellion.[80] Accusing the Catholic defenders of this injustice was thus a confessional as well as a political statement, which shows that, in this instance, the Protestant Bohemian propaganda was echoed by common soldiers passing time during the siege. The comparatively subtle slur "priest's son" managed to simultaneously draw into disrepute the legitimacy of the son as well as deny the alleged father's vow of celibacy. The missing necessary constituent in their opponents' births, the "whore" mothers, were also not forgotten. "Priest's son" was consequently a denigration of the addressees' provenance, but it also had a confessional dimension. That the soldiers insulted their enemies on the grounds of their denomination shows that the garrison were identified as agents of Catholic duplicity and simultaneously that the jeerers considered themselves to be Protestant soldiers, fighting to right the wrongs worked against the Bohemian estates.

The pleasure of intimidation became evident when imperial troops came to Zwingenberg in Hesse in 1635, as they enjoyed mocking the Lutheran locals and forced several of the villagers, among them the pastor David Stumpf, to drink to the pope's health.[81] For the soldiers, knowing full well that the frightened villagers were at their mercy, it was an *amusing* display of power. For Pastor Stumpf it was a humiliation that he struggled to come to terms with. He tried to alleviate the insolence by restyling the toast as a "civil" and "social" act (*civiles gesellschaftswerk*), presumably to deprive it of its religious dimension, while at the same time affirming that they had only toasted the pope "in keeping with their confession" (*salva confessionis nostrae forma*). Such situations, marked by the desire to exhibit superiority, could and did tip over into full-blown acts of violence. We have already encountered soldiers who mocked, mutilated, and killed a pastor while looting. Moreover, instances in which small groups of soldiers abused civilians on the grounds of their confession seem not to have been infrequent.

Sexual violence against women was certainly common but it does not seem to have followed confessional patterns. That soldiers raped was taken as a given in early modern Europe and, to soldiers, it was a privilege that came with victory. The rape of women (but not, as far as I am aware, of men) and the threat that "the children in the womb" would not be spared was made especially in the context of sieges, when the besiegers tried to convince the defenders to surrender in time.[82] Stories about raped civilians were also told with various intentions. Erika Kuijpers has recounted the story of a maidservant who is raped by two soldiers.[83] The soldiers are so moved by her cries that they stop their assault and propose to marry her. The woman then chooses one and during the ensuing engagement celebration, she reveals where her employers hid their valuables, which the soldiers then steal. Kuijpers suggests that to contemporaries, the central message of the story was not about sexual violence at all; it was a warning to employers not to tell their domestics their secret hiding places. Apart from the indifference toward sexual violence against lower-class women, Birgit Emich has cautioned against taking descriptions of sexual violence, even eyewitness accounts, at face value when it comes to rape. Emich examined reports of rape relating to the Sack of Magdeburg and found that Catholic reports uniformly underlined the sexual dissolution of the female Protestant victims, while Protestant commentators repeatedly mention women who, like Lucretia, killed themselves to escape rape and preserve their honor.[84] Early modern accounts of rape were thus focused on the way the victim reacted, and this perspective makes it very difficult to deduce the intentions of the rapist. Rape was a common form of military violence but there is no good evidence that confession was a criterion when soldiers sexually assaulted women. There

128 ~: *Faith in War*

is the case of Colonel Gerrit von Nuyß, who apparently tried to chat up women by bragging about how he had once strangled sixteen beguines in one night, but such crassness seems to have been rather unique and it is important to highlight that he killed, not raped, his victims.[85]

Confessional propaganda endlessly related situations in which soldiers allegedly killed civilians on the grounds of their confession, but in most cases it is indeterminable whether religious hatred was really the motivation or whether this was an interpretation or an invention of the respective authors. The propaganda machines of all churches exaggerated enemy violence and embellished or invented confessional cruelty, which makes it often difficult to ascertain the extent to which massacres or murders were religiously motivated. The Sack of Magdeburg (20 May 1631), for example, is considered one of the defining moments of the Thirty Years War and is to this day remembered as the epitome of unrestricted confessional cruelty and destruction.[86] Hans Medick has provided a compelling portrayal of the atmosphere leading up to the fall of the city and the recognition among contemporaries that they witnessed an important historical event.[87] Contemporary broadsheets and pamphlets reporting the siege and the sack employed the image of the Maid Magdeburg who was finally forced to wed her bridegroom Tilly.[88] From a Catholic perspective, the horrors of Magdeburg had been brought about by the city's obstinate refusal to obey imperial orders and its fervent adherence to Lutheranism. The Premonstratensian Zacharias Bandhauer prefaced his eyewitness account with a long description of the city's unreasonableness, which in his view flowed directly from the Lutheran heresy.[89] Bandhauer even attributed the suicide of a family who had drowned themselves in a well to Lutheran stubbornness.[90] Catholic commiseration with the Protestant victims was in short supply. One Jesuit who followed the troops into the city forced inhabitants to say a prayer to the Virgin Mary before he would attempt to save them. Pope Urban VIII himself sent a congratulatory letter to Count Tilly, which declared joyously that the victors had been able to "wash their hands in the blood of the sinners" (*potuisti lavare victrices manus in sanguine peccatorum*).[91] For the Catholic victors, Magdeburg was a great prize militarily as well as religiously and hopes were high that the Protestant stronghold would become a masterpiece of counter-reform. Tilly announced that Magdeburg would henceforth be called "Marienburg" in honor of the Virgin Mary and only five days after the catastrophe, a great procession made its way through the ruins, attended by the commanders, officers, and a great number of clerics, all singing the "*Te deum*."[92]

Reports that followed the catastrophe of Magdeburg attributed the exceptional violence of the imperial soldiers to religious hatred. Both Kaiser and Medick have pointed out that while horrific scenes doubtlessly unraveled on 20 May and the following days, it is less certain that the violence was in fact motivated religiously.[93] If we consider Arnold Mengering's report of the sack, the problem becomes evident. In his account, Mengering, who had been driven from his position as minister in Halle and found employment as court preacher in Dresden in 1631, had the soldiers indulge in their hatred of "heretics" and legitimize their atrocities by the victims' Protestantism.[94] He relates an anecdote in which one soldier brags to his comrades about having impaled more than twenty Magdeburg infants on his pike. When the other—clearly horrified—soldiers ask him if he is not afraid of God's punishment for this atrocity, the soldier replies that his only regret is not having killed more children in this manner "as they were heretics' children and not worth anything better."[95] It seems doubtful that this lurid scene actually took place as it is too reminiscent of topoi of violence that we find throughout early modern Europe. The impaling of children is a recurrent image in narratives of violence that dates back to antiquity and became associated specifically with the Ottomans after the Fall of Constantinople (1453). Jürgen Luh has shown that commentators used precisely this image to communicate the experience of unbridled violence and to relate horrors that were indescribable.[96] Kaiser has described a similar topos—not sparing the fetus in the womb—in the same way, namely as a *chiffre* of extreme and illegitimate violence, so we have to understand such descriptions not as reflections of actual events but as metaphors.[97] Still, it becomes clear that even horrific acts of violence could conceivably be justified in a manner that was plausible for early modern civilians and soldiers alike. The scene is also noteworthy for an important methodological observation, however. As readers and interpreters, we are captivated by the barbarity of the child impaler and it would be easy to take his atrocity as yet another instance of soldiers' religious violence and move on. But if we widen our focus, even this probably literary story shows that the killer's behaviors and his justification are atypical and not shared by his comrades. They do not commend him for his efforts to exterminate heresy, they confront him, appalled by the evil he has done. They even fear that his actions might incur divine retribution, which shows that they do not accept his religious legitimization. So, while our attention is drawn to the killer, we must not overlook his comrades when we analyze situations like this, especially when we are trying to form a picture of how "typical" or "characteristic" religious violence was in the military. Their reaction highlights that acts of religious violence were not accepted as the norm by the majority of soldiers, and when we ask how representative religious violence was of soldiers' behavior, we should emphasize their revulsion and condemnation over the murderous fanaticism exhibited by the single soldier.

Another example, also taken from Mengering's account, further illustrates the potential for confessional deformation in the interpretation of events. Mengering described an abduction of Magdeburg children to the army camp, where the girls were allegedly either raped or sold and the boys transferred into the care of Catholic monasteries to be raised as monks.[98] He attributed the

130 ᏼ *Faith in War*

treatment of the girls to the sexual depravity of the soldiery, while the transportation of the boys to the monastery on the other hand was presented as a counter-reformation machination devised to destroy the future Magdeburg Protestantism. But there are possible alternative interpretations. It is likely that many of the children that were taken to the camp were captives, but this did not necessarily mean that they were mistreated. If we consider the fate of the Friese family who were captured and rescued by a soldier from Nuremberg, a different version of events becomes thinkable. The soldier looked out for the Frieses not out of mere charity but also because he had been promised a handsome ransom. The family knew that being one soldier's loot provided relatively good protection against others and they pleaded with the man to take them as his prisoners. The soldier treated the several children kindly and the eldest son Johann Daniel expressed his deep gratitude years later when he recorded his family's ordeal: "He was a mild-hearted, god-fearing man. [May] the Lord repay him forever for what he did for us! We will never forget the benefactions he accorded to us and will still know how to praise them on Judgment Day."[99] In these circumstances, being taken captive could be a desirable position for civilians, as it placed the vulnerable townsfolk under the protection and in the care of their military captors. Secondly, it seems that during the Sack of Magdeburg children who had lost their parents were sent into the care of clerics regardless of confession. Jacobus Schwanenberg, for example, the Protestant field preacher of Henrik Holk's regiment, looked after many solitary children in his quarters in nearby Olvenstedt.[100] The transfer of the boys to the monasteries may therefore have been motivated by a wish to ensure their welfare, rather than by the confessional impetus of wanting to turn heretics into Catholics.

The confessional interpretation of the Sack of Magdeburg exemplifies the difficulties historians face when dealing with such events. The soldiers' behavior was recorded within a confessional framework, and especially in printed accounts, it is difficult and often impossible to see behind the propagandistic interpretations and exaggerations of atrocities. If we turn to the actual behavior of the soldiery in this particular instance, however, the interpretation of the events changes fundamentally, as there is little evidence that the soldiers themselves saw the Sack of Magdeburg in confessional terms.[101] Two Lutheran soldiers, Peter Hagendorf and Jürgen Ackermann, took part in the sack and recorded the event in their diaries, and the entries show that the horrors of Magdeburg also affected veterans. Hagendorf, who had been fighting in wars at least since 1624, was shot twice during the assault and noted: "I felt sorry from the bottom of my heart that the city burned so horribly."[102] To him, Magdeburg was undeniably a catastrophe, but no confessional interpretation is evident in his account. Likewise, captain Jürgen Ackermann was moved by the many dead and wounded from his company and he pondered God's "strange omnipotence and punishment" as he looked at the burning city, but his meditation, again, has no confessional dimension.[103] If either man had wanted to insert a confessional reflection in his account, a better occasion than Magdeburg would be hard to imagine, and yet they remained silent on the topic.

The experiences of the Lutheran pastor Christoph Thodaenus during the sack provide further evidence that most imperial soldiers did not act on confessional grounds but simply looted. Thodaenus encountered plunderers who spared him because he was a pastor, some who wanted to kill him because he was a pastor, and others who wanted to kill him *although* he was a pastor.[104] Even though he was repeatedly addressed with the slur *Pfaffe*, which was applicable to clerics of all confessions, no plunderer made a specific comment about him being a *Lutheran* pastor. One soldier was about to bludgeon Thodaenus with his mace when his comrade intervened and said, "what do you want to do, you see that he is a preacher."[105] The two soldiers were looting together, which suggests familiarity, but they clearly had different views on how to treat clerics. Thodaenus, his wife, and their maidservant were ultimately saved by the Spanish colonel Joseph de Ayñsa. Ayñsa not only berated a soldier for mistreating the pastor but also placed the "heretic" under his personal protection and proved open to mostly friendly theological discussions in the following days.[106] It was only on the way out of the city that Thodaenus reports that some Croat soldiers tried to get to him because they recognized him as a Lutheran preacher.[107] For the most part, therefore, the soldiers seem to have been after plunder, and while they reacted differently to Thodaenus's habit, few exhibited a particular hostility that could be linked to confessional hatred.

The discrepancy between the way the Sack of Magdeburg was experienced, described, and remembered by civilians and the way in which soldiers seem to have behaved could not be greater. While civilians interpreted the sack and the ensuing military violence in unambiguously confessional terms, the soldiers apparently did not: to them it was a looting opportunity or a monstrous cataclysm, but there is no indication that they were motivated by confessional hatred or, in the case of the Lutherans Ackermann and Hagendorf, that the sack caused them to reflect on the role they were playing in this catastrophe. We consequently have to be even more careful when labeling acts of violence "religious," as not every instance that was experienced or interpreted in this way by civilians was necessarily motivated by confessional hatred on behalf of the soldiers. This finding also raises questions regarding the influence a specific situational context had on the violence it produced. One might have expected that a confessionally charged situation like the siege of Magdeburg would have affected the behavior of the soldiers. The commanders of the victorious forces, Tilly especially, were known enemies of Protestantism, so soldiers inclined toward confessional violence might have perceived license to indulge themselves. But while Magdeburg witnessed horrific scenes of violence that civilians *attributed* to confessional hatred, when we analyze soldiers' behavior, it seems doubtful that it was, in fact, confessionally motivated. Close examination of soldiers' actual behavior in the recorded instances examined here (rather than of the situational context) is therefore crucial, as only individual behavior allows us to determine if a given act of violence was religiously motivated.

Turning away from the specific example of Magdeburg, there is, however, one specific group in which attitudes seem to have been markedly different: in the Spanish army, the perception that the enemy were heretics seems to have been rather common. The Spanish army seems exceptional in so far as confessional thinking actually appears to have had an impact, which stands in marked contrast to the general indifference to confessional and political categories that we will examine in the second half of this chapter. While the acts of religious violence described above were isolated events, the evidence for confessionally motivated violence in the Spanish army is rather dense across time and appears in many different contexts. The Black Legend—the systematic distortion, exaggeration, and invention of Spanish Catholic atrocities by Protestant propagandists—has to be taken into account here and heightened suspicion is called for when we deal with allegations of Spanish cruelty.[108] However, as Henry Kamen has pointed out, the Black Legend was "a legend, not a myth," and Benjamin Keen has posited that "the so-called Black Legend is substantially accurate, if stripped of its rhetoric and emotional coloration" and therefore "no legend at all."[109] Propaganda does not account for the frequency with which Spanish religious violence occurs in the sources because, as we will see, the kind of violent behavior reported is not uniform enough to suggest a mere trope; it exhibits distinctive variations on a common theme, namely the persecution of heresy.

The Spanish Army of Flanders was mainly deployed in northwestern Europe to fight the Dutch Revolt but frequently operated in the German lands of the Holy Roman Empire in aid of the Austrian Habsburgs and their Catholic allies. In the sixteenth century, these incursions were generally limited to the border regions of the Rhineland and Westphalia, but during the Thirty Years War, Spanish troops fought throughout the Empire. The Netherlands from the 1520s to the 1570s have been described by William Monter as the "epicentre of heresy executions" in Europe and when the Duke of Alba first led his army into the Netherlands in 1567, his men were already convinced that the "expedition was directed specifically against heresy."[110] While Alba initially considered his enemies to be political rebels rather than heretics, by 1571 he was imploring the Vatican to send more inquisitors so that more heretics could be burned.[111] From the beginning, the Spanish army frequently suspended martial law and custom when they encountered heretics, real or assumed.[112] The Spanish incursion into imperial territory in 1598-99 and the treatment of the Calvinist Count Wirich von Daun-Falkenstein and his troops is a good example.[113] The Spanish army entered the lower Rhine region in September

1598 under its commander Francisco de Mendoza, the Admiral of Aragon.[114] The immediate reason for Mendoza's incursion was the need to find winter quarters for his troops, but Mendoza's other declared objective was to eradicate Protestantism.[115] Along the way, Spanish troops attacked especially Protestant estates and despite Count Daun's protestation of neutrality, Mendoza laid siege to his castle Broich near Mülheim. An accord was negotiated but as soon as Daun's soldiers marched out of the castle, they were taken to a nearby field and massacred. The count himself was taken captive and killed while taking a walk some days later.[116]

In the Empire, the reaction to the invasion and Count Daun's murder was a grand display of impotence: the estates sent letters of protest to Mendoza and to the emperor, Rudolph II, who wrote indignant letters to Mendoza and the acting Governor General of the Habsburg Netherlands, Albert of Austria, who in turn abdicated all responsibility and blamed Mendoza.[117] Unfazed, the Admiral of Aragon continued to threaten cities and potentates including the Bishop of Paderborn, Dietrich von Fürstenberg.[118] In this particular letter, Mendoza stated bluntly that he had entered the Empire for want of pay and food and that there was little chance that he could keep the "hungry and naked soldier" from pillaging Fürstenberg's diocese, because it was known among the soldiery that Lutherans lived and preached in the bishop's dominions.[119] To ensure that the "innocent" (read: "Catholics") among Fürstenberg's subjects were spared the "whip" (*flagellum*) of the "*miles Catholicus*," the bishop should ensure that no Protestants were found once—not *if*—Mendoza's men arrived.[120] Otherwise, the Admiral assured him that all Lutherans would be hanged and everyone, regardless of confession, plundered.

Mendoza thus not only invaded the Empire without authorization but began to dictate religious policy to the Catholic rulers whose territories he illegally raided. While this behavior is indicative of a peculiar arrogance and betrays Mendoza's ability to predict correctly that he would get away with his gross insubordination, the episode also shows that he saw the revolt in the Netherlands in religious terms. He evidently regarded the problem as less political than religious in nature, which would explain why he so readily ignored territorial boundaries. The threat Mendoza was fighting was not so much uniquely Dutch but generally Protestant, and the rebels' Protestant German neighbors had to be treated in much the same way as the Admiral's nominal enemy. This view, as we will see, was apparently not limited to the commanders but was shared by many Spanish soldiers of all ranks and expressed also in the way they acted out religious violence.[121]

Spanish religious violence is especially conspicuous because it often imitated elements of heresy trials. During the Cologne War (1583–88), allied Spanish and Bavarian troops took the city of Bonn by accord in late January 1586 and the Spanish colonel Don Juan Manrique de Lara arrested and inter-

134 ~: *Faith in War*

rogated the town's reformed preacher Magister Johannes Northausen.[122] The army's behavior toward the inhabitants of Bonn and especially the abuse of the ministers was criticized even from within its own ranks. Colonel Wolff von Erlach, a Protestant in Bavarian service, wrote a letter to the Duke of Württemberg in which he condemned the events at Bonn and attributed them either to Manrique's instigation or to general "papist tyrannical bloodthirstiness."[123] Erlach was certainly keen on marring the reputation of his rival Manrique but the Protestant soldier's concern for the welfare of the preachers seems to have been genuine. He had previously tried to hire Northausen as his personal field preacher, a proposition the latter had fatefully rejected because he feared a Catholic trap.[124] Northausen's ordeal is remarkable not only for its dreadfulness but also for the amount of information we can extrapolate from it regarding the religious mindset of the Spanish colonel. Northausen was taken to Manrique, who began to interrogate the preacher in the presence of a few other soldiers and officials.[125] Not only did he call the new faith a "pseudo-religion" (*ein vermeinte Religion*) that was engaging in empty ritual; more importantly, he maintained, Protestantism had no tradition, which further undermined its claim to being a "real" religion.[126] The Catholic Church, in contrast, boasted the unbroken apostolic succession, which Manrique regarded as irrefutable proof of orthodox supremacy. Despite his dismissive attitude toward the new faith, Manrique seems to have appreciated the opportunity to examine a Protestant in person and the discussion went on to topics such as the communion and other sacraments as well as the definition of "heretic."[127] Eventually, however, he declared the silliness of Protestantism proven and repeatedly offered the preacher the choice between death and conversion. When Northausen refused Manrique had him thrown into the River Rhine.

The scene illustrates that the colonel was thoroughly immersed in confessional thinking and that he saw the violence he administered in confessional terms. What makes his behavior especially conspicuous is his imitation of the procedure of heresy trials. Ecclesiastical law pertaining to heretics was well defined and envisioned several stages that had to be passed through before an individual was branded a heretic and had to suffer the consequences.[128] The heretical thought stood at the beginning, followed by an accusation of heresy and a trial in which the contested ideas were examined and their unorthodoxy explained. Then the heretic was admonished to recant and return to orthodoxy and only when they exhibited lasting obstinacy (*pertinacia*) did they face execution. Colonel Manrique followed this procedure in every way: he first established the nature of the heresy, debated the heretical beliefs of the accused, repeatedly offered the chance to recant, and only ordered the execution when Northausen's *pertinacia* had become evident again and again.

The episode in Bonn is well documented and one might object that the confessional mindset of an individual colonel can hardly be taken as representative.

But the view among Spanish soldiers that they were fighting heretics seems to have been rather widespread and was often reflected in the way they dealt with the corpses of their enemies: they had the tendency to burn dead Protestants. After the sack of Neuss (1586), the Protestant town commander Friedrich Hermann Clout was killed in his bed, his corpse draped in tar wreaths, hung out of a window next to the body of Clout's preacher Christoph Fetzer, and partially burned.[129] Similarly, Wirich von Daun was left unburied for several days before the soldiers returned to burn his body in a nearby hut.[130] One of the authors reporting this outrage felt that the body had been cremated to express "public *despect*, mockery and ignominy of all Protestant estates" and while this may well have been the intention, the idea that Daun was a "heretic" influenced how this contempt was expressed, namely by fire.[131] Soldiers thus imitated the ritual burning of heretics that the Catholic Church practiced in the way that they dispatched with their Protestant enemies. This connection was rarely made explicit (at least it was not reported), but when Spanish troops poured gunpowder on the bodies of killed Swedish troops, they did explain their reasoning: "because they are heretics, they must be persecuted and burned with fire."[132]

The unusual confessional aggression of some Spanish soldiers may at least partially be explained by the specific background of religious warfare in the Iberian Peninsula. Until the conquest of Granada in 1492, the *Reconquista* had nurtured a crusading mentality that had dissipated in the rest of Europe. It had also given rise to a class of nobility, the *hidalguía*, who had earned their nobility in the wars against the Muslims and to whose self-image religious warring was central. It has recently been argued that the brutality of the colonization of the Americas can be interpreted as a continuation of the way the *Reconquista* had been fought, and it seems plausible that similar sentiments were still harbored by the *hidalgos* and other Spaniards who fought in the Low Countries and Germany.[133] In Spanish accounts of the Netherlands and literary depictions, the image of Flemings as greedy, feckless drunks gave way to characterizations that emphasized heresy and rebelliousness as the Revolt progressed, but even so, a differentiation between the heretical rebel and the easily misguided general populace tended to be maintained.[134] The self-evaluation as divinely commissioned defenders of the Catholic faith was also expressed in military accounts and this image seems to fit the kinds of violent behaviors of Spanish soldiers that we have observed in this chapter quite neatly.[135]

Still, despite this *comparatively* greater confessional aggression evident among some segments of the Spanish army, we should be cautious not to overstate this impression, as cross-confessional cooperation and coexistence was a feature here, too. As we have already seen, Philip II retained the services of numerous Lutheran German military enterprisers, and the governors of the Low Countries were willing to accommodate Lutheran commanders and troops

136 ❧ *Faith in War*

during their service against the Dutch rebels.[136] The Spanish army also simply adopted the patents, contracts, and articles of war that were in use in the Holy Roman Empire for the German troops in its service, so that the same unconfessional framework we have observed was recreated in the Spanish context.[137] That mutinous Spanish soldiers deserted and served in the Dutch army further suggests that they, too, could integrate into a Protestant army.[138] The memory of the *Reconquista* and its role in the self-image of military men from the Iberian Peninsula may thus go some way to explain why Spaniards appear to have been more likely to engage in confessional violence than other Europeans, and the way they performed these acts of violence strongly suggests a confessional motivation. But, as always, we must remind ourselves that although confessional violence was *comparatively* more common among Spanish soldiers, it remained an atypical form of behavior.

Where does this discussion of military religious violence leave us? The imitation of heresy trial procedures makes the ad hominem violence of Spanish troops particularly salient and the specific variations on this common theme lend the reports credibility. In contrast, sources that merely allege that soldiers killed out of confessional hatred make it impossible to ascertain whether this really was the case or the authors' interpretation, and the tendency to employ literary topoi calls into doubt their accuracy. There remains a fundamental problem, however, as rejecting the truthfulness of sources that invoke such tropes of violence ignores the possibility that soldiers were influenced in their behavior precisely by such reports. It is thinkable that soldiers, who were of course familiar with such tropes, may have thought that this was an appropriate way to behave and imitated them, but I cannot think of a way of resolving this issue given the nature of the material.

Scenes of religious violence allow insights into soldiers' religious attitudes that are difficult to document otherwise. These incidents show that the soldiers involved exhibited confessional attitudes, apparently had a religious motivation, and betrayed an often precise knowledge of confessional differences in doctrine and religious practice. The wide spectrum in which military religious violence could manifest itself also shows that confessional antagonism could be expressed in degrees of severity. The pattern that emerges confirms scholarship on religious violence in other contexts: Catholic soldiers appear to have been more prone to attack persons, while the desecration and destruction of sacred places and objects seems to have been more closely associated with Protestant violence. This pattern can only be considered a tendency, however, as we have also seen Protestant soldiers killing Catholics and Catholic soldiers debasing a Calvinist church. The likeliness with which a Catholic soldier killed a Protestant for purely religious reasons or vice versa cannot be gauged. The reason that the impression arises that (Spanish) Catholics were more prone to killing Protestants may be an effect of their imitation of Church ritual that makes their actions more conspicuous and more clearly *identifiable* as religiously motivated. Protestant soldiers who may have killed Catholics for religious reasons did not do so in ways that signaled a confessional motivation. Thus, while the examination of confessional violence yields good insights into the religious mentality of the soldiers involved, it is important to bear in mind that the acts themselves influence our ability to categorize them.

There are many instances in which soldiers inverted confessional dichotomies, for example during the Sack of Rome when Lutheran *Landsknechte* protected nuns from rape by Catholic troops.[139] Situations in which soldiers began to argue with each other over the treatment of members of a different denomination are also telling, since they show that soldiers' personal interpretations of what was legitimate violence differed. The case of pastor Herdenius, who only avoided being left stark naked by a looting party because one soldier objected to stripping a cleric and intimidated his comrades with blasphemous curses, has already been described in the previous chapter.[140] Similarly, the nun Maria Anna Junius witnessed how two Catholic soldiers in Swedish service began to fight over whether or not to plunder a Catholic convent.[141] Even in situations that were charged with confessional antagonism like the Sack of Magdeburg, confession was no reliable predictor of behavior. Not all Catholics reacted with indifference to the suffering of the Protestant population and over six hundred women found refuge in the Unser Lieben Frauen cloister where they were protected by imperial troops.[142] Others called after Father Sylvius, a Premonstratensian who guided groups of women to safety in his blood-smeared white habit, "look, there goes the priest [*pfaff*] with his whores."[143] Christoph Thodaenus's experience proves that the imperial troops behaved in entirely different ways toward the people they came upon while looting, and it bears repeating that it was a Spanish colonel who rescued the Lutheran pastor and his household. Confessional categories consequently did not predictably determine how soldiers behaved or whom they turned against; religious violence was not an institutional or professional behavior but individual and attitudinal in its occurrence and character.

Confessional attitudes could thus be expressed through acts of religious violence, but we should not conclude that confessional categories *as such* influenced the occurrence of religious violence in a meaningful way beyond introducing the potential for conflict. It is, in fact, rather difficult to find instances that can be labeled confidently as "religious" violence. The scenes we have examined so far have been selected from a vastly greater sample in which most cases appeared to be devoid of confessional motivations. We should return to a question that was raised at the beginning of this chapter: why was there not more confessional violence in a context in which actors not only had the possibility to legitimize it, but engaged in violence against adherents of other confessions without exhibiting partisanship?

138 ❦ Faith in War

The Role of Confession in Soldiers' Lives

Whether implicitly or explicitly, fighting for one's confession is commonly considered to be a significant criterion in establishing soldiers' religious sensibilities, and the lack of evidence indicating that this was often the case has contributed to the impression of soldiers' religious faultiness. Confessional perceptions of persons and events are generally absent from military autobiographical accounts, which has led historians to characterize soldiers' spirituality as "pragmatic," "unideological," and "mechanistic."[144] There seems to be a general sense of disappointment over the fact that military autobiographers did not commit more explicit religious statements to paper and did not gnaw more overtly on the bones of doctrinal contention. But the characteristic absence of confessional modes of thinking does not necessarily indicate a lack of religiosity. To make a dominating confessional identity and perception the litmus test for religious sincerity seems to place unrealistic expectations on military religiosity, especially as the lower ranks did not always have control over which side they fought for. The situation is to some extent different for officers. Brage Bei der Wieden has shown that some Lower Saxon Lutheran mercenary leaders managed to negotiate a semi-official clause with Margaret of Parma, the Spanish governor in the Netherlands, exempting them from fighting fellow Lutherans, but not, however, Calvinists.[145] Such confessional conscientiousness is mostly extremely difficult to prove because contracts were overwhelmingly concerned with military, financial, and logistical matters. It may have been the case that confession was a factor in mercenary leaders' choice of sides, but such considerations are not reflected in the documents. Kaiser has described cases in which officers converted to their employers' confession, seemingly to further their careers, but these instances indicate a *lack* of confessional allegiance and therefore the inversion of the type of behavior Bei der Wieden describes.[146] Pangs of conscience resulting from fighting coreligionists rarely manifest themselves and Albrecht von Freiberger's mutiny is an exceptional case. The Lutheran Freiberger served as *Obristleutant* in Wallenstein's army and in March 1634 mutinied and tried to reform Troppau (Oppava, Moravia-Silesia).[147] Probably influenced by Wallenstein's assassination the previous month, he had finally become convinced that the emperor sought to exterminate Protestantism—after eighteen years in imperial service.

Evidence for confessional thinking in soldiers' autobiographies is scarce and mostly incidental. Captain Georg Niege composed a poem on the Augsburg Interim (1548), the "whore-child" as he and other dissatisfied Lutherans called it. But this explication of his views on imperial religious policies was not part of his autobiographical account, in which he barely mentions the Interim.[148] Confessional sentiment is otherwise entirely absent in the description of his military life. English and Scottish mercenaries who fought in the Thirty Years War are conspicuous in so far as they all commented on the confessional dimension of the conflict. Sydnam Poyntz deliberated at some length about his religious convictions but the reason for this candor appears to be due to his unusual biography. Born in Surrey in 1607, he was raised a Protestant, ran away from an apprenticeship, spent 5–6 years in Ottoman captivity, converted to Catholicism upon his escape, fought in Germany first on the Protestant side, then for the Emperor, and was scouting for employment back home when he wrote his life account in 1636-37.[149] There were considerable twists in Ponytz's career and if we read his *Relation* as the self-advertisement of a Catholic mercenary looking for employment in late 1630s Britain, he was well advised to explain himself. Poyntz described his conversion in some detail. Former Ottoman slaves were open to the suspicion of having converted to Islam in order to alleviate the conditions of their captivity. The Viennese Franciscans who sheltered Poyntz after his escape were no exception and tried to ascertain if he still "had any sparke of Christianity" in him or if he had become "a Turke."[150] He had not, but while his Protestant prayers had sustained him in servitude, the friars' "wonderfull humility and charity" moved him to convert to Catholicism "wherein by Gods grace" he intended to die.[151] Poyntz's account of his conversion is to the point and seems to have been consciously written for an English readership with its anti-Catholic bias. He acknowledged the prejudice by referring to the Roman Church as "Papistry" but explained his conversion by the friars' humility and charity, virtues in every Christian context, albeit ones Protestants did not generally associate with Catholics. He thus presented his attraction and dedication to Catholicism purely as a matter of pious practice and avoided the delicate subject of Catholic politics.

The Scot James Turner described his decision to fight in the German wars in religious terms. Before he joined the army, he spent a year learning about doctrinal differences between Catholicism and Presbyterianism with the declared intent to fortify himself in his faith.[152] He went to fight for the Swedish/Protestant cause when he procured an ensignship in James Lumsden's regiment, which was levied for the "thrice famous Gustavus Adolphus, King of Sueden" in 1632.[153] Robert Monro gave a rather thorough confessional interpretation of the war in Germany in several instances.[154] Words like "papist" are used frequently and the Protestant cause is highlighted throughout.[155] Of the autobiographical accounts examined here, Monro's is the most consciously written for a broad (Protestant) audience, and we have to assume that the clear confessional stance was at least in part influenced by his intended readership. His confessional comments usually pertain to political situations and the main actors Gustavus Adolphus II, the emperor, or General Tilly. Confession is also used to highlight individual depravity in this account. Field Marshal Holk's "barbarous crueltie," for instance, is emphasized by stating that the Protestant commander made "no conscience of Religion" and "shewed lesse compassion then the *Papists* did."[156] When talking about strictly military affairs and his personal encounters with the enemy, however, confessional commentary is absent,

140 ~: *Faith in War*

and Monro's authorial commitment to the Protestant cause did not preclude him from forming close friendships with Catholics like John Hepburn.

These examples are exceptional, as affirmations of confessional identity and motivation are generally rare in military autobiographies. Götz von Berlichingen did not address the confessional upheavals of his time at all; he even related his controversial involvement in the Peasants War without mentioning religion.[157] Nothing in his memoirs betrays the fact that he was one of the first German knights to introduce the Reformation in his estates as early as 1522.[158] The only allusion to his Lutheranism was made in connection to his trial by five councilors of the Swabian League, whom he thought biased because they were "not of [his] faith."[159] It is difficult to extrapolate religious convictions from the gunner Hans Staden's account of his travels to Brazil and his captivity by the Tupinambá.[160] The whole narrative is a "homily of redemption and faith" and was revised and "improved" by a Lutheran professor of medicine, Johannes Dryander, on Staden's request.[161] The account is littered with references to and implorations of God's grace and protection but it is indeterminable whether these reflect Staden's actual behavior or were added either by himself or his pious editor Dryander. Despite the latter's involvement, however, there are no confessional comments. We can infer from his circumstances that Staden was a solitary Protestant among Catholic sailors and colonists but there is no indication that this caused any problems. Moreover, he repeatedly mentioned joining in Catholic communal prayer and that he prayed with other Christians during his captivity, yet he never commented on the fact that they were bridging the doctrinal divide in doing so. The young noble soldier Erich Lassota's religious views are a conundrum. His diary of the campaign in Spain and Portugal (1580–83) reads like a pilgrimage account. He visited a vast number of devotional sites around Santiago de Compostela and elsewhere, described the interiors of dozens of Catholic churches, explained the legends behind religious sites and miraculous statues, traveled with his colonel's Catholic chaplain, and went to confession, all of which seems to indicate a fervent Catholic.[162] Yet he later remarked that his Swedish captors *mistook* him for a Catholic, which implies that he identified as a Protestant.[163] If he had converted in the meantime, he did not mention it in his diary. Caspar von Widmarckter's account is a last case in point. The only time he makes a confessional remark is in relation to a dispute with his "papist" neighbors.[164] Without this single aside, evidence for Widmarckter's Protestantism would be entirely circumstantial. As these examples suggest, confessional self-identification or comment in military autobiographical accounts is mostly random, almost accidental. While civilian commentators often clearly positioned themselves as confessional beings and interpreted events and motivations in confessional terms, confessional self-identification and in fact any confessional commentary is generally and saliently absent in military narratives.

The same observation holds for confessional conflict among soldiers, as none of the diaries provides any evidence for internal arguments over confession. We may suppose that the silence can be partially explained by the nature of the genre as it recorded military lives rather than spiritual journeys. Yet we find seemingly random comments, for instance, on the fashion among Polish nobles to gel their hair with egg whites, marmot behavior and women's goiters in the Alps, Westphalian beer, witches and pumpernickel, the abundance of rosemary in the Champagne, the delights of Parmesan cheese, or the construction of a Würzburg mill.[165] All of this makes the silence surrounding confessional matters even more pronounced.

Another partial explanation may be adduced from the research into confessional identities. Ulrike Ludwig has shown that even the funeral sermons for elite men who experienced the Reformation and converted to Lutheranism did not mention this experience, which shows that the Reformation was not yet seen as an epochal event in the later sixteenth century.[166] In Germany, a pronounced confessional way of thinking only became more evenly widespread in the later seventeenth century and beyond. Until then, ignorance or indifference to the finer points of doctrine was not uncommon.[167]

That the English and Scots soldiers described confessional differences more explicitly than their German counterparts may be due to the fact that Monro and Poyntz, at least, were writing for a British public. Given the more homogeneously Protestant situation in England and Scotland, it is possible that they found confessional diversity they encountered in Germany more noteworthy than the German diarists, who were more accustomed to heterogeneity both within and outside of the army. For the German soldiers, multiconfessional milieux were a fact of life that may have been too ordinary to comment on. What speaks against the suggestion that the German diarists were confessionally indifferent or confused is that they clearly behaved according to confessional norms in their private lives, as we have seen in the previous chapter. Their confessional indifference only applied to their professional lives as soldiers. There exist, therefore, clear discrepancies not just in the unambiguously confessional way that wars were presented in propaganda and experienced by civilians and how most soldiers described the same events—in unconfessional terms—but also in how the same soldiers described their professional conduct and their private religious behavior. This difference must be accounted for and it seems that it arose from the military experience itself.

Motivation and Unemotional Enmity

In the period we are studying, the lines between friend and enemy were inherently blurry and ideological categories became widely meaningless amid

142 ❧ *Faith in War*

the ever-changing fortunes of war. In order to understand this phenomenon better, we should consider military mentalities in a wider context, especially with a view to motivation and enmity. Few soldiers fought for religion, that much seemed certain to contemporaries, but it was rarely discussed within the military. Wilhelm von Kalkum genannt Lohausen, a Calvinist officer from the Rhineland who served a number of Protestant potentates in the Thirty Years War, addressed the issue in a discourse he penned while he was an imperial prisoner of war after the Battle of Lutter (27 August 1626). He saw the professional attitude to serve the highest bidder irrespective of their cause as a great threat to soldiers' spiritual obligations. Lohausen urged soldiers to evaluate their service in religious terms, to abstain from wars that "went against God, his church, law, and justness," and not to burden their consciences with such offenses. Anticipating replies from his comrades that the high-flying affairs of religious politics were impossible for them to judge, Lohausen gave a sharply negative response. Anybody smart enough to lead soldiers in war had sufficient brains to determine if the cause one was serving threatened one's religion: "I reply to you, brother in arms, whom God has granted the grace and the knowledge to lead [a military unit], the same gracious God will have doubtlessly given you enough wit to recognize what goes against His commandment, law, and justness, especially His church, your religion and conscience" and to avoid these engagements.[168] Addressing all soldiers, nobles as well as commoners, he added: "if you think about it properly, God will have granted you one and all sufficient wit and you also will have learned that you should not serve against your faith and religion, or your conscience and fatherland in church or school, or from your parents, guardians, and relatives."[169] Claiming that religious politics were too complicated was a sorry excuse to Lohausen. But even in this context, Lohausen phrased his admonition in Christian terms: soldiers should not serve against the interests of their faith, but he did not specify which confession he adhered to himself or comment negatively on other creeds.

This unideological attitude of professional soldiers was often alleged but rarely admitted. James Turner is the only soldier from the sample who described how the military experience turned a religious warrior into a "mercenary." Turner was enticed to fight for the Protestant cause by the propaganda he read at home in Scotland. He also wrote candidly about how his experience in Germany changed his outlook. When he returned to Britain in the early 1640s, political and religious categories were apparently no longer important to Turner and he joined the Covenanter army rather by accident but "without any reluctance of mind."[170] Turner explained that he had internalized "a very dangerous maxime" in Germany, "which was that so we serve our master honnestlie, it is no matter what master we serve." He had developed a "mercenary" mentality and fought "without examination of the justice of the quarrel, or regard of my duetie to either prince or countrey."[171] He never swore the Covenant although he "wold have made no bones to take, sueare and signe it and observe it, too."[172] He was never asked to do so. His experiences on the Continent had convinced him that he could do whatever his masters asked without it affecting his conscience.[173] Turner's admission is valuable for its frankness. With hindsight, it seems, Turner was mildly uncomfortable with his younger self's loss of ideological investment, yet the matter-of-factness with which he explained himself suggests that he was not necessarily ashamed of this period in his life.

Other soldiers, if they provided insight into their motivation to follow the drum at all, had more mundane reasons. Peter Burschel has shown that the rank and file were predominantly recruited from the urban and rural underclass and he comes to the concise conclusion that "destitution made the mercenary."[174] In light of the diaries we may add "dissatisfaction" with one's present situation to the motives. Georg Niege seems to have wanted to escape the stuffiness of the Marburg faculty of theology, as we have already seen. Wayward Werner von Bert, an embarrassing relative of the Wesel chronicler Heinrich von Weseken, wanted to escape an apprenticeship that did not suit him.[175] Sydnam Poyntz also deemed his apprenticeship "little better than a dogs life" and he ran away from his master thinking that "to live and dy a souldier would bee as noble in death as Life."[176] A romantically naïve view of military life, fantasies of glory and riches, and the wish to improve one's lot in life therefore seem to have played a large role in many young men's decisions to enlist. The Englishman Thomas Raymond, who had joined the army of the United Provinces and briefly served in the Rhineland, soon had enough of soldiering as "the life of a private or comon soldier is the most miserable in the world."[177] Raymond loved a comfortable bed and dryness, both rarities in Flanders, but for a while, a military career seemed his only option: "seeing no other way to make out a fortune, being a yonger brother . . . , I buckled my selfe to the profession."[178] Raymond had to make a living, ideally a "fortune," and the army seemed to promise him just that.

These economic or pragmatic reasons to enlist are also reflected by the fact that changing sides was mostly described as a matter of course. Jürgen Ackermann had served for about six years under Protestant commanders when he decided to change sides.[179] After his unit surrendered Wolfenbüttel to Count Pappenheim's regiment in 1627, Ackermann switched sides and his captain even wrote him a letter of recommendation and helped him secure a post with the enemy. Nothing in his account implies that the Lutheran Ackermann felt any compunction about deserting the Protestant cause. He had fought for years without getting paid and after the imperialists had chased his regiment through Central Europe, he decided that changing sides offered better prospects. Peter Hagendorf fought in Venetian service against Pappenheim's regiment in 1625 and although Hagendorf's side sustained heavy casualties from the enemy's artillery, this earned his professional respect rather than hatred. The Pappen-

144 ❧ *Faith in War*

heimer were clearly a good regiment to serve in and Hagendorf joined their ranks two years later in Ulm.[180] In 1633, his unit had to surrender Straubing to the Swedes and the lower ranks were pressed into Swedish service. There is no indication in his account to suggest that Hagendorf thought this turn of events important and the narrative seamlessly continues in the first person plural; only the names of his new commanding officers and the name of his new regiment are mentioned.[181] Henceforth, "we" denotes his Swedish regiment, while his former employers are the "imperialists" or "Bavarians."[182] After the Swedish defeat at Nördlingen in 1634, Hagendorf and his boy servant simply returned to Pappenheim's regiment and his old captain reinstated him to his rank of corporal.[183] The captain had also been captured at Straubing and was probably ransomed or exchanged. There seems to have been no resentment over the fact that Hagendorf had fought on the other side in the meantime; it was just a reality of military life. Hagendorf's career is typical for the experience of the rank and file in that it was often fate that determined on which side soldiers found themselves. This fact of sixteenth and seventeenth-century warfare seems to have precluded sustained loyalty to a particular side and its official cause and apparently led to a perception of "friend" and "foe" as transitional categories.

This instability meant that soldiers often found themselves fighting acquaintances, friends, and relatives who served the enemy. During the War of the Bavarian Succession (1504), Götz von Berlichingen was grudgingly obliged to fight on the Bavarian side, although he would have rather joined his brothers in the Palatinate's army.[184] Still, the fact that the brothers were fighting in opposing armies neither caused Götz to dishonor his obligations nor does it appear to have caused him moral discomfort. Erich Lassota was captured when he served the Polish king elect Maximilian in his ill-fated campaign to gain the Polish throne. After he and other nobles were paroled, two companies of horse escorted them out of Poland, one of which was commanded by a cousin of Lassota's.[185] Family bonds therefore frequently extended across enemy lines.

The diaries confirm Burschel's observation that soldiers generally saw the enemy as a "purely factual category."[186] They also indicate that Barbara Donagan's analysis of the nonpolitical and unconfessional nature of honor as a moral imperative among British military men is also generally applicable to the German context.[187] Violence was considered legitimate within the limits of what was strictly necessary to obtain victory but avoidable brutality and breach of bipartisan trust were condemned as illegitimate.[188] However fluid such notions may have been, military professionals had a keen sense of what constituted appropriate use of force and conduct in war. Given that both sides heeded the obligation to fight honorably and fairly, the enemy was treated with a degree of consideration that can be baffling to the modern observer.[189] We frequently find references to accords and quarter. Augustin von Fritsch, for example, frequently asked enemies to surrender *before* fighting began, evidently with the intention to avoid violence through negotiation.[190] Fighting in war is characterized in the diaries as a professional, unemotional encounter that entailed a certain amount of violence within clear boundaries set by the objective that had to be achieved. Once the objective had been realized, violence was generally expected to cease.[191] By and large, soldiers succeeded in limiting violence by fostering a professional, objective, and pragmatic attitude.[192] Importantly, these notions, which had their roots in chivalric norms of violence, were shared by nobles and common soldiers alike during the early modern period. The only occasion, for example, on which Hagendorf expressed hatred of enemy soldiers in a string of insults was when he recalled how the Spanish troops gave no quarter after the Battle of Nördlingen (1634).[193] The Spaniards killed with a relentlessness that disgusted him apparently especially because they did not stop after the battle was won. He disapproved of unnecessary violence and tellingly one of the few instances in which he did not shroud violence in euphemisms was when he recounted how he had badly injured another NCO in a fight.[194] Such frankness is singular in Hagendorf's account and may suggest that in this context he could not justify his behavior with his professional capacity as a soldier. He had seriously wounded a comrade in a brawl, a circumstance that could not be palliated.

Fair conduct in war included sparing surrendering enemies and this convention was generally honored in the international military community regardless of confession or confessional allegiance. The pragmatic principle was mutually beneficial: the vanquished kept their lives and the victors could speedily and cheaply replenish their ranks or let the captive ransom himself.[195] For individual units it was important to have a reputation for honoring this convention so that their enemies accorded them the same consideration when necessary. This rationale becomes evident when Augustin von Fritsch relates how his company besieged a contingent of French and German troops.[196] An honorable surrender was negotiated but as the fortification was being handed over, Fritsch's superiors declared the accord void and ordered the execution of the unwitting enemy.[197] Fritsch and his men refused as they anticipated being employed at the siege of Koblenz and feared that the French troops there could avenge the atrocity if it became known.[198] They managed to save the lives of the German enemies by impressing them into the regiment, but could not prevent the execution of two officers or the massacre of the French rank and file by cavalry troops that were brought in specifically for this purpose. Fritsch and his men's worries were justified. They were indeed sent to Koblenz, where the French captured a captain who would have been hanged had he not been able to convince his captors that his unit had honored the accord and refused to massacre their compatriots.[199]

This episode elucidates some crucial aspects of military attitudes toward the enemy: the attempts to avoid unnecessary bloodshed have already been noted,

146 ~: *Faith in War*

but here, the importance of honoring martial customs and the necessity for a unit to maintain a reputation for trustworthiness become evident. The reaction of the French toward the captured captain shows that they did not consider all imperial troops to be collectively responsible for the murder of their compatriots. Their thirst for vengeance was directed only against the particular detachment that had done the killing. Massacres of prisoners were recognized as an atrocity also by those who committed them, as can be gleaned from the example of a soldier who had been involved in the slaughter of Swedish deserters that had tried to join the imperial force at Forchheim in the summer of 1634.[200] The reasons behind this stark violation of military custom are unclear, but as it was a time of famine, the imperial commander may have been unable to feed additional men. Whatever his motives, the event caused revulsion among his own troops. In conversation with the nun Maria Anna Junius, one of the men struggled to defend himself for obeying the order to "cut down so many valiant men who begged so piteously for their life and said how long they had served the Emperor but had been captured by the Swedes."[201] The soldier could not justify the atrocity by the victims' status as "enemy" deserters: the blame lay squarely with his colonel and he tried to exculpate himself by pointing toward the consequences for his own life had he disobeyed orders.

The pragmatic imperatives to limit violence also kept emotions low, and while this is a valid generalization, the occasions on which these norms were violated were revenged mercilessly. Garrisons that did not surrender and thereby forced the besiegers into suicidal assaults could not expect quarter.[202] Colonel Monro described the taking of Breitenburg castle after which the enemy killed the Scottish defenders and everyone within in a murderous fury.[203] Monro characterized the event as a "monstrous and prodigious massacre" and admonished his readers "to forbeare the like" as revenge could be taken "in a Christian manner, without making Beasts of ourselves."[204] However, Monro held the garrison commander Dunbar's unreasonable refusal to surrender directly responsible for the escalation of violence. This interplay of behavior is more explicit when he relates the failed last-minute attempt of General Major Knyphausen to surrender Neubrandenburg after he had previously rejected the offer of an accord.[205] Knyphausen's surrender came "too late" and many of his men were put to the sword. Monro commented on the "crueltie and inhumanitie" of the conquerors but stated that Knyphausen's lack of judgment had "brought himselfe and others to the slaughter."[206] Hatred therefore had to develop dynamically; it did not arise merely from serving on opposing sides.

While these pragmatic and unemotional notions of enmity have so far been described in cultural terms, modern psychological studies suggest further explanations for the apparent reluctance to kill outright and the importance of situational buildup of aggression in early modern warfare. Transposing psychological observations made in one historical context into a different one is risky business, but at least in general terms, the preconditions considered necessary for nonpsychopathic individuals to kill effectively can structure our analysis of early modern military violence.[207] Most of the distancing elements that have been identified (cultural distance, moral distance, social distance, and mechanical distance) were not—or not consistently—present in premodern warfare. Cultural distance between soldiers was often negligible and diminished quickly. Soldiers shared a professional ethos and despite doctrinal differences, we have seen that they also shared common Christian values. Given the international makeup of the armies, we also find surprisingly little evidence for communication problems. Soldiers apparently quickly learned to adapt to changing linguistic situations, be it by the use of a dictionary, by learning the language from locals, or out of the sheer necessity that forced Sydnam Poyntz to learn Turkish and almost forget his English.[208] Ethnic or (proto-)national distance may have played a role but, as we have seen in the example of the German-French contingent above, soldiers of different ethnicities also fought in the same units. The unideological mindset that has been described and the awareness that the changing fortunes of war meant that the categories of "friend" and "enemy" were inherently ambiguous precluded preexisting moral distance.[209] It developed, however, when military ethics were contravened. Illegitimate acts of violence and the deaths of comrades created personal enmity and a moral gulf, which manifested itself, for example, in the wholesale slaughter of obstinate garrisons. Social distance existed primarily vertically in the military hierarchy but less so horizontally between combatants who met on the battlefield. On the other hand, the predominance of men from the higher social strata in the cavalry and the prevalence of commoners in the infantry did constitute a social differentiation. Regarding the execution of the French POWs described by Fritsch, it may therefore be telling that the infantry troops refused to massacre other foot soldiers—their own "kind," as it were—while the horsemen apparently readily obeyed the order.[210] Social distance was probably more effective in facilitating killing down the social hierarchy rather than upward, as the potentially gratifying act of killing a social superior was counterbalanced by the prospect of a hefty ransom if the life was spared. Low-ranking commoners' lives were often literally worthless.[211]

The modern technologies that create mechanical distance between the killer and the target were only emerging in our period and soldiers had to dispatch the enemy mostly at close quarters. The small elite of gunners and their assistants fought from the greatest distance and even they struggled with guilt.[212] Arquebuses and muskets had an effective range of maybe 150 meters in the sixteenth century and about 215 meters during the Thirty Years War, but they were usually discharged at a far shorter distance.[213] Psychologically, firing these guns may be considered relatively easy, as the soldier shot at the enemy from a distance and aiming with precision was impossible. Pike formations clashed at

148 ~: *Faith in War*

a distance of about 4–5 meters, so that the opponent was clearly visible.[214] Part of the pike techniques involved thrusting the pike into the face, neck, or other unprotected parts of the opponents' bodies, which not only involved strength and skill but also required overcoming a deep human resistance to stab another person.[215] Below the reach of the pike, soldiers had to engage in hand-to-hand combat, which is the most intimate and emotionally difficult way of killing: the more intimate, the greater the psychological resistance in healthy humans to kill another human being unless the act is preceded by significant buildup of hatred toward the target. The situation is different when soldiers experience a "combat high," the release of large amounts of adrenaline that causes extreme exhilaration and often entails uninhibited killing, which is what we see when soldiers had survived high-risk assaults or breeched city walls.[216] But combat high arose during battle—when the strategies to limit violence had failed—and under these circumstances, men had to kill or die, whether they were "high" or not.

The nature of early modern warfare thus generally precluded a dehumanization of the enemy, which prevented the development of the psychological distance that allows sane individuals to kill efficiently. Simultaneously, the absence of dehumanization helps to account for the great importance placed on surrendering and giving quarter, as these practices prevented the use of potentially traumatic violence. Enemy relations do not even appear to have been generally characterized by hatred; on the contrary, it seems that enemies were united in a bipartisan interest in limiting violence, which manifested itself in pragmatic and unemotional attitudes and behaviors. Political and religious categories also widely lost meaning for military men and consequently confessional considerations mattered little if at all in this professional setting. Huntebrinker has observed that relationships and loyalties were built between the soldiery, their officers, and the field commanders and were usually detached from absentee warlords or their professed ideological causes.[217] It seems that enemies treated one another in much the same way: fair conduct of war mattered, not its causes. This unemotional attitude not only extended across confessional boundaries but could include non-Christians as well. Jürgen Luh has shown that the same conventions described here were also mutually observed between Christians and Muslims in Eastern Europe.[218] Refuting notions that the Ottoman wars were informed by an "ideology of annihilation," Luh argues that Christian propaganda of the "barbarous Turk" had no impact on the way that Christian soldiers dealt with their Muslim opponents. The "Web of Honor," to borrow Barbara Donagan's term again, was therefore an integral part of a European military culture that bound soldiers across religious and political fault lines.[219] This insight helps to account for the unconfessional tenor of soldiers' autobiographical accounts. They recorded their experiences in the same way they conducted war, according to principles that were detached from confession. It also suggests the reason that authors mostly mentioned their confessional identity incidentally or not at all: it may have mattered to them personally, but it was irrelevant to the experience they recorded.

Religious Coexistence

It has been repeatedly mentioned that all armies in the period were confessional composites, but we have yet to understand how religious coexistence functioned in practice and what its dynamics were. An absence of sufficient direct evidence in the diaries and other sources poses a significant obstacle to this endeavor. Religious coexistence was too unproblematic and too mundane to produce a paper trail, which is an important, if not exactly satisfying, insight. It is, in fact, bitterly frustrating for historians because we struggle to argue from documentary silence.[220] As we have seen in this chapter, we are very well equipped to analyze conflict, because conflict tends to produce sources. Conflict is not just much more readily remembered than peaceful encounters, it also demands action and, ideally, resolution and each one of these stages of conflict invites documentation. The sources reflect this inherent imbalance, as conflict situations are more likely to be recorded than peaceful encounters, which are usually documentary nonevents.[221] The countless daily interactions between soldiers of different confessions that did *not* end violently were simply not recorded.[222] The fact that we read about all kinds of quarrels between soldiers arising for all manner of reasons but that none of the military diarists mention confessional arguments strongly suggests that differences of faith just did not commonly affect relationships between professional soldiers. The scholarship on civilian religious coexistence and conflict provides some possible clues as to why confessional plurality may not have posed a great problem in the military.[223] Religious coexistence was a fact of life and in many if not most German urban and rural communities, two or more confessions lived together in a predominantly peaceful if not always happy manner. Picturing Reformation Europe and its inhabitants as riven with confessional division is as common as it is inaccurate. Confessional plurality did not inevitably cause irreconcilable conflict among communities. Zealotry and divisiveness could be countermanded by the universal Christian social imperatives of neighborliness and charity and the ideal of the common good, maxims that bound members of a community "in relations of solidarity and mutual dependence that were dangerous as well as painful to break."[224]

If these values were important in settled communities, they were even more vital in the chronically endangered communities of the military. In living circumstances characterized by instability and unpredictability, hunger, cold, and violence, the necessity of maintaining group cohesion had to override confes-

150 ～ *Faith in War*

sional divisions.[225] We can also assume that the conflict potential as such abated as personal relationships were established and acquaintance, friendship, and shared experiences created interpersonal bonds. Deaccentuating confessional divisions was therefore a matter of survival for soldiers, and one major factor facilitated this latitudinarian mindset: the confessionally divisive policies that often introduced strife in multiconfessional civilian settings were absent in the military. Thomas A. Brady has argued that the "primary agents of religious violence . . . were not the religious communities but the rulers who tried to coerce their subjects into religious conformity."[226] As we have seen, military authorities anxiously avoided policies that highlighted confessional differences and might have bred dissent. Soldiers were therefore left to their own devices in negotiating confessional diversity and it seems that they did so very successfully.

The characteristically tolerant attitudes among military men were lamented by confessionalizing agents, who saw solidarity and friendship across denominational lines as a threat. The Jesuits who hoped to missionize the Spanish army of Flanders and the papal troops in France in the second half of the sixteenth century identified the mixed composition of the armies, transconfessional sociability between soldiers, and their tendency to read heterodox books as main sources of impiety.[227] Antonio Possevino raised this point on several occasions in his spiritual tract for Catholic soldiers and urged them to draw an uncrossable boundary between themselves and their heretical comrades. Any contact with "infidels and heretics" was a threat and he demanded that captains stop hiring non-Catholics to prevent pollution.[228] Lorenzo Lenzi, bishop of Fermo and commissioner of the papal army during the French expedition of 1569-70, was given detailed instructions to police the religious conduct of the entire army, including that of the officers, to prevent any dealings, conversations, or disputations between Catholics and Protestants and to confiscate any books banned by the Church, regardless of the rank of the owner.[229] Tolerant attitudes were thus considered endemic in the military by those to whom intolerance was a religious imperative, which is an important insight, but it does not appear that their efforts to destroy coexistence were successful. For that, they would have needed the support of the commanders, and as we now know, military rationales demanded toleration.

A few situations in which confessional differences were bridged peacefully may help us understand how this military mode of coexistence worked in practice. Robert Monro's clearest self-identification as a member of the Presbyterian Kirk is embedded in a tale in which he and the Swedish chancellor Axel Oxenstierna disputed the merit of the different confessions based on the alcohol they produced.[230] Both attended a dinner that became increasingly cheerful due to the liberal intake of Zerbster beer.[231] This was a Calvinist product and Monro's favorite, as it was "the wholsomost for the body, and cleerest from all filth or barme, as their Religion is best for the soule, and cleerest from the dregs of superstition."[232] Monro gave the Lutheran chancellor his appraisal, to which Oxenstierna replied: "no wonder it taste well to your palat, being it is the good beere of your ill religion."[233] They then debated "the good wine of a worse religion" that was produced by Catholics around Mainz and Oxenstierna quipped that "he liked the wine and the beere better than both the Religions." Monro concurred on the excellence of papist wine and contemplated how living in the Calvinist Palatinate would allow him to "drinke good Rhinish wine" without compromising his religion for the rest of his life. In Monro's long account this is the only point at which confessional differences are openly discussed, or rather, are the topic of drunken banter. The Lutheran Oxenstierna and the Presbyterian Monro were conscious of their confessional differences but this did not inhibit sociability. They did not dodge the potentially difficult topic, nor did Monro show much deference to the chancellor in this matter; they joked about their religious differences. Both positioned themselves clearly, and Oxenstierna even referred to Monro's "ill religion," but they defused the topic through humor.

It might be argued that a few jokes over good beer are not indicative of much, but Monro's relationship with John Hepburn, briefly mentioned above, shows that confessional differences did not prohibit long and close, even loving, friendships. Hepburn was a Catholic who made a career in different Protestant armies until he accepted a French commission in 1633, and Monro's description of their friendship is rather touching in its warmth. They were "oft Camerades of danger together" and through their long acquaintance became "Camerades in love": they met at college, traveled in France together as teenagers, and were reunited when Monro arrived in Germany in August 1630.[234] Monro served as Hepburn's second in command for a while and remembered not just the "love" his friend showed him but also his wise counsel. To Monro, his friendship with Hepburn was nothing short of an ideal:

> Nothing therefore, in my opinion, more worthy to be kept next unto Faith, then this kinde of friendship, growne up with education, confirmed by familiarity, in frequenting the dangers of warre, and who is more worthy to be chosen for a friend, then one who hath showne himself both valiant and constant against his enemies, as the worthy Hepburne hath done.[235]

It is difficult to imagine a fuller celebration of friendship. That Hepburn was also a "papist," the slur Monro usually used for Catholics, did not diminish their affection and neither did it seem to compromise Monro's faith, the importance of which he affirmed in the same breath in which he extolled the virtue of this friendship. This example shows *Omgangsoecumene* quite powerfully: shared experiences, friendship, and the "camaraderie of danger" simply made confession a nonissue.

The Dominican nuns of the Heilig Grab Kloster witnessed that soldiers' love of music could also bridge the confessional divide. In late February 1633, they

152 ❦ *Faith in War*

were visited by Wilhelm von Kalkum genannt Lohausen, a Calvinist general-major in the Swedish army, who arrived with a group of officers and the prior of the Bamberg Carmelite cloister. After lunch, Lohausen requested that the nuns sing compline for him. This was not uncommon: many officers from the Swedish and Saxon-Weimar armies, including Duke Bernhard himself, liked to visit the cloister and listen to the Dominicans' music.[236] But much to the nuns' bewilderment, Lohausen did not just listen but joined them in the choir and sang along.[237] He enjoyed himself tremendously but asked them to spare him the "Salve Regina," as the Marian hymn was just "too much." A Calvinist soldier joining nuns in singing Catholic devotional song is an extraordinary transgression of confessional boundaries. Lohausen evidently appreciated not only the beauty of the music but also the spirituality it promoted, except for the "Salve Regina" whose overt Marian focus offended his reformed sensibilities. That Lohausen could not only judge the religious meaning of the songs but was able to perform them suggests that this was not the first time he had partaken in Catholic devotion. Lohausen later commended the nuns for their piety and their impeccable *imitatio Christi* and therefore recognized common Christian ideals despite differences like devotion to the Holy Virgin.[238] We have already encountered Lohausen in this chapter when he insisted on soldiers' personal responsibility for assuring that their service did not pose a threat to their confession or their conscience. He was no lukewarm Christian but a committed Calvinist whose intellect and piety earned grudging recognition from the Bamberg Jesuits as well as an ebullient funeral sermon from the Lutheran superintendent of Rostock Constantin Fiedler upon Lohausen's death in 1640.[239] Fiedler detailed the strict spiritual regime to which Lohausen subjected not just himself but his wife, his household, and the soldiers under his command.[240] Considering Lohausen's reputation for his principled Reformed faith and his behavior toward the nuns of the Heilig Grab Kloster, as well as the apparently friendly relationship with the Carmelite prior who accompanied him, we should question the notion that toleration was a sign of religious pragmatism or, worse, hypocrisy, or that intolerance was a mark of religious sincerity. "Toleration" actually seems too negative a term in this instance, because Lohausen's attitude toward Catholics clearly went beyond nonconfrontation: despite their misguided veneration of the Virgin, he appreciated the Dominicans as virtuous Christians whose worship he not only respected but participated in. For Lohausen and other early modern Christians, soldiers or civilians, deep personal confessional piety did not preclude the recognition that members of other confessions could also be good people with whom they shared the most important Christian values; we just do not get to witness it often.[241]

A few months later, a unit of Swedish horse was detailed to guard the same convent. When the nuns celebrated their evening service, a placid battle of the hymns ensued: "As we sang the *Salve Regina*, [the soldiers] also began to sing, their preacher stood in their midst, and all the soldiers around him sang their Lutheran songs very beautifully."[242] That the Protestant soldiers intoned their Lutheran songs while the sisters sang the "*Salve Regina*" does not seem coincidental; it appears that the Marian hymn prompted the soldiers to answer in the Lutheran mode. That the soldiers, or at least their preacher, recognized the "Salve" shows again that practices of the religious other were still common cultural currency in the first half of the seventeenth century. The episode also illustrates how confessional identity could be asserted in a nonviolent, not even markedly antipathetic manner. Anna Maria Junius, finally, could acknowledge the Lutherans' devotion and appreciate the beauty of their singing, just as the Calvinist Lohausen had enjoyed evensong.

What do these scenes tell us about religious coexistence? As such situations were rarely recorded it must remain uncertain how far the behavior of the soldiers in these instances can be regarded as representative. If we consider, however, that hundreds of thousands of soldiers daily dealt with religious diversity over one and a half centuries, among themselves, across enemy lines, and in encounters with the population, it seems that confession was mostly offset by other norms and necessities in everyday life. We reach epistemological limitations when trying to assess behaviors that were not usually recorded, but the absence of confessional conflict among soldiers in the military diaries speaks loudly. We can, however, suggest factors that may have facilitated confessional coexistence. The guiding interest in group cohesion and survival certainly counterbalanced doctrinal division and the absence of divisive interference from above gave troops the freedom to negotiate confessional diversity. We can also point toward modes of behavior that could defuse the potential for conflict. These included humor, friendship, focusing on shared Christian values rather than divisive doctrinal elements, appreciating the other confession's worship, or asserting a confessional identity in a nonconfrontational manner, for example by singing or by joking about booze. There were many ways in which soldiers could and did avoid confessional strife.

The latitudinarian values that Ralf Pröve has described for the later seventeenth and eighteenth centuries were therefore present throughout the early modern period. There is also evidence that this characteristic of the military experience had a lasting effect on former soldiers. Jürgen Ackermann, for example, retired from his military career in Protestant and Catholic service around 1636 and bought a farm in Kroppenstedt, southwest of Magdeburg. With his military experience and connections, Ackermann was frequently sent to negotiate with military authorities and deal with passing troops on behalf of the small town.[243] While the townspeople appreciated and depended on his negotiating skills, his unconfessional pragmatism caused problems at least once. Ackermann had arduously but successfully negotiated a safeguard for the community with imperial commanders and returned only to have his efforts slighted by the

154 ～ *Faith in War*

mayor, who sourly remarked that the privilege had been accorded to Catholics. Ackermann snapped, "even if they were Turks and they wanted to do us good, why wouldn't one accept it."[244] Here, civilian and (ex-)military notions regarding the importance of confession clashed. The mayor's objections to striking a deal with Catholics were incomprehensible to the veteran Ackermann, who was primarily interested in the protection of the community's livelihood and had little patience with the mayor's doctrinaire gripes.

Conclusion

In this chapter we set out to examine the role of confession in military everyday life. Religious violence did occur, and soldiers not only revealed their own confessional identity in these instances but also exhibited a clear understanding of the defining elements of the confession they were attacking. This further substantiates the impression we gained in the previous chapter, which portrayed soldiers as active Christians, and it also proves that soldiers were not confessionally confused: they had a well-defined sense of where the fault lines of doctrine and worship ran, which enabled them to commit religious acts of violence with considerable precision. But the examination of attitudes toward the enemy and the influence of confessional thinking on military everyday life shows that soldiers who attacked the other confession were a small minority. Military autobiographical accounts show that confessional self-positioning is rare and mostly incidental and that soldiers described their experience in unconfessional terms. Distinctly military notions of enmity help account for the subordinate role confession played in the military realm. Dehumanization of the enemy was impeded by the specific conditions of combat and the fluctuating composition of the armies in general. The intimacy of killing and the instability of the categories "friend" and "enemy" contributed to the tendency among early modern soldiers to limit bloodshed. Soldiers' attitudes toward the enemy were largely unaffected by confessional considerations and the imperative to conduct war fairly in accordance with military custom compelled all Christian soldiers. Enemies generally encountered one another in this universally accepted moral framework as professional Christian soldiers, not as champions of a confessional cause. These examinations of notions of enmity have been taken to explain why confession is widely undetectable in military diaries. It appears that confession and ideology had no impact on the experiences that were recorded, which is why they are not reflected in soldiers' accounts. It bears repeating that this should not be taken to indicate the authors' lack of sincerity regarding their personal faith; all we can say is that they did not reflect on confessional matters when they recorded their professional lives as soldiers.

The dynamics of confessional coexistence are the most difficult to reconstruct, which is mainly due to the fact that sources in general are more likely to record conflict than its absence. We therefore often argue from silence, but the few instances in which the peaceful negotiation of confessional differences becomes observable imply that doctrinal fissures could be overcome with relative ease. Apart from the common interest in survival that united soldiers both in the same army and across enemy lines, humor, friendship, emphasizing common Christian values, or unconfrontational affirmations of personal beliefs made coexistence possible. The absence of a biased legal framework and divisive confessional policies created a social context in which confessional coexistence could be negotiated in freedom.

Overall, then, confessional differences did not normally affect the conduct of war and religious coexistence was an elemental characteristic of military society. But we still have to place the atypical acts of religious violence in relation to the predominant inclination to overlook confessional differences in the military. It seems that religious violence in the military context was caused by a small minority whose deeds were recorded not least *because* they were uncharacteristic and shocking. This fundamental documentary imbalance in the sources toward the exceptional and the violent distorts our view by lending acts of religious violence an artificial salience that can lead us to overestimate the effects of confessional hatred on everyday encounters.

The simultaneity of religious violence and religious coexistence in the military is not contradictory but indicative of a plurality of attitudes toward confessional matters in early modern culture more widely. The doctrinal fragmentation of Western Christendom introduced the *potential* for confessional conflict but there was no *inevitability* of confessional conflict and violence. Moreover, whether religious violence occurred or not appears to have depended crucially on the individuals involved, who chose to act out religious violence, refrain from it, stop it, or simply overlook confessional categories altogether. Confessional militancy was easy to demand and propagate for those who did not risk their lives; those who did were mainly interested in survival.

The discrepancy between the demands of religious hardliners, the rhetoric of confessional propaganda, and the way civilians experienced war, on the one hand, and the confessional indifference that characterized the armies on the other is consequently a problem of perspective. The fact that confession played such a marginal role in soldiers' experience and the conduct of war does not indicate spiritual deficiency. It only shows that confessional ideology was mostly meaningless in the way that they led their professional lives, which is a fine but crucial point. Stuart Carroll has drawn attention to the dynamic relationship between micropolitics and confessional relations, and the example of the military proves that these parameters were also of great importance for the containment of strife in professional settings.[245] Like many other communities,

156 ❦ *Faith in War*

the international military community functioned according to principles that were either unaffected or could be detached from confessional issues. As martial law did not make confessional demands, other principles such as military rank, patronage, merit, friendship, and the values of honorable conduct could govern military life.

The relationship between agency and structure also becomes evident, as it was still up to the individual soldier to keep the peace. The effortlessness with which men and women from diverse social, geographical, and religious circumstances coexisted in the military shows that people of the confessional age had a much greater aptitude to accommodate difference than we tend to give them credit for. Military drill taught recruits how to use their weapons but they did not attend workshops on toleration when they joined the army. They consequently must have already possessed the ability to handle confessional differences before they became soldiers. Confessional hostility and strife were not automatic or universal features of life in the post-Reformation; ordinary Christians from all over Europe coexisted with one another with such ease that they did not even comment on how they accomplished this.

Notes

1. Davis, "The Rites of Violence"; Richet, "Aspects socio-culturels des conflits religieux"; Crouzet, *Les Guerriers de Dieu*; Diefendorf, *Beneath the Cross*.
2. Diefendorf, *Beneath the Cross*, 48, 146; Crouzet, *Les Guerriers de Dieu*, part I, 201, 205, 233–240, part II, 295-297.
3. Ibid., 162, 177.
4. Tallett, *War and Society*, 128.
5. Burkhardt, *Der Dreißigjährige Krieg*, 134.
6. Bonin, *Rechtsverfassung*, 61; Baumann, *Landsknechte*, 195; Burschel, *Söldner*, 161; Kaiser, "*Cuius exercitus, eius religio?*" 319.
7. Baumann, *Landsknechte*, 195; Bonin, *Rechtsverfassung*, 61.
8. Kaiser, "*Cuius exercitus, eius religio?*" 319.
9. Pröve, "Reichweiten und Grenzen der Konfessionalisierung," 82–87.
10. On the civilian perspective see the contributions in Meumann and Niefanger, *Ein Schauplatz Herber Angst*; Krusenstjern, Medick, and Veit, *Zwischen Alltag und Katastrophe*; Asche and Schindling, *Das Strafgericht Gottes*; and with particular attention to religion, Greyerz and Siebenhüner, *Religion und Gewalt*. See also Roeck, "Der Dreißigjährige Krieg und die Menschen im Reich." The military perspective is examined by Kaiser, "*Ärger als der Türck*"; Burschel, "Himmelreich und Hölle"; and Pröve, "Violentia und Potestas."
11. Donagan, "The Web of Honour."
12. Ibid., 388.
13. Greyerz and Siebenhüner, *Religion und Gewalt*, 19.
14. This way of analyzing scenes of violence is heavily influenced by Randall Collins's microsociological theory of violence as laid out in *Violence*.

15. On the Sack of Rome see Gregorovius, *Geschichte der Stadt Rom*, vol. 8, 514–57; Schulz, *Der Sacco di Roma*; Hook, *The Sack of Rome 1527*; Chastel, *Le Sac de Rome, 1527*; Reinhardt, *Blutiger Karneval*. Primary sources are edited in Guicciardini, *The Sack of Rome*; Milanesi, *Il sacco di Roma*; Reißner, *Historia*, 116[R]-138[R].; Schönhuth, *Leben und Thaten*, 7–8.

16. Römling, "Ein Heer ist ein großes gefräßiges Tier," 74n.

17. Guicciardini, *The Sack of Rome*, 38.

18. Baumann, *Frundsberg*, 274–75, 280.

19. Ibid., 87.

20. Gregorovius, *Geschichte der Stadt Rom*, 514, 519. On the identification of Antichrist with the papacy and its use in popular reformation print see Scribner, *For the Sake of the Simple Folk*, ch. 6.

21. Schönhuth, *Leben und Thaten*, 7.

22. Ibid.

23. Schertlin only officially converted in 1546; see ibid., 33.

24. As cited by Römling, "Ein Heer ist ein großes gefräßiges Tier," 68.

25. Guicciardini, *The Sack of Rome*, 114–15.

26. Gregorovius, *Geschichte der Stadt Rom*, 535; Hook, *The Sack of Rome*, 173.

27. The graffiti are described and depicted in Chastel, *Sac de Rome*, 123–126.

28. Reinhardt, *Blutiger Karneval*, 95.

29. Guicciardini, *The Sack of Rome*, 113.

30. Adam Reißner gives Sandizell's name (*Historia*, 122[R]) but the events are related in greater detail in another contemporaneous report: Anon., *Wahrhafftige vnd kurtze Bericht ynn der Summa*, ci[R]-ci[V]. According to the anonymous source, the *Landsknecht* procession made its way through the whole city and performed these "rites" in front of several houses in which high-ranking clerics were imprisoned.

31. Reißner, *Historia*, 122[R]-122[V].

32. Guicciardini, *The Sack of Rome*, 109.

33. Buonaparte, "Il sacco di Roma," 378. See also Gregorovius, *Geschichte der Stadt Rom*, 542.

34. Giucciardini, *The Sack of Rome*, 108–9.

35. For instances of late antique and medieval military church plundering and iconoclasm see Schnitzler, *Ikonoklasmus*, 91-95; Marchal, "Das vieldeutige Heiligenbild," 320–21.

36. See also Kroener, "Kriegsgurgeln, Freireuter und Merodebrüder," 57–60.

37. Friesenegger, *Tagebuch*, 31.

38. Ibid., 49.

39. Georg Herdenius, letter to superintendent Konrad Dieterich (1622), in Herrmann, *Aus tiefer Not*, 52.

40. As quoted in Kaufmann, *Dreißigjähriger Krieg und Westfälischer Friede*, 106.

41. Nikolaus Moterus, letter to Landgrave Ludwig (1621), in Herrmann, *Aus tiefer Not*, 33–34.

42. Ibid., 34.

43. Ibid., 30–31. Such incidents were not just rumors. Another pastor only escaped an encounter with a squadron of Croats with his manhood intact because a colonel intervened (Kaufmann, *Dreißigjähriger Krieg und Westfälischer Friede*, 109).

44. Schnitzler, *Ikonoklasmus*, 91-95.

45. Marchal, "Das vieldeutige Heiligenbild," 329–30.

46. See for example the matter-of-fact mentioning of the theft of holy vessels by imperial troops by the abbot Friesenegger (*Tagebuch*, 31.)

47. On iconoclasm across early modern Europe, see the contributions in Blickle et al., *Macht und Ohnmacht der Bilder*. See also Schnitzler, *Ikonoklasmus*.

158 ~: Faith in War

48. Anon., "Acta Mansfeldiaca post pugnam Pragensem," 52–56.
49. The carnival rites described by Scribner are in many instances identical with the contemporaneous events in Rome (Scribner, "Reformation, Carnival and the World Turned Upside-Down," 304-9). The literature on carnival and the carnivalesque following, expanding on and criticizing the original ideas of Mikhail Bakhtin, is too vast to recapitulate here. See Aaron Gurevich's overview of Bakhtin's studies ("Bakhtin and his Theory of Carnival").
50. Scribner, "Reformation, Carnival and the World Turned Upside-Down"; Schindler, *Widerspenstige Leute*, 138-151.
51. See for example Verberckmoes, "The Comic and the Counter-Reformation" and the contributions in Auffarth and Kerth, *Glaubensstreit und Gelächter*.
52. Verberckmoes, "The Comic and the Counter-Reformation," 82; Auffarth, "Alle Tage Karneval?" 83.
53. Verberckmoes, "The Comic and the Counter-Reformation," 79, 83.
54. Blickle, "Bilder und ihr gesellschaftlicher Rahmen," 2.
55. Wilson, *Europe's Tragedy*, 275.
56. Anon., *Warhaffter Bericht*, 32.
57. Ibid.
58. Scultetus explained and defended the removal in his apologetic autobiography: *Historische Erzehlung*, 109-12.
59. Jessen, *Der Dreißigjährige Krieg*, 83.
60. Anon., *Reformation der königlichen Schloßkirchen zu Prag*, 1. See also Louthan, "Breaking Images and Building Bridges"; Wolter, *Deutsche Schlagwörter zur Zeit des Dreißigjährigen Krieges*, 158–59.
61. Anon., *Reformation der königlichen Schloßkirchen zu Prag*, 1.
62. Matthew 27:28–40, esp. 38–40; Mark 15:29–30; Luke 23:36–37.
63. Anon., *Reformation der königlichen Schloßkirchen zu Prag*, 1.
64. On Calvinist appreciation of Catholic "idols" as art see Veldman, "Bildersturm und neue Bilderwelten," esp. 282.
65. Roeck, "Macht und Ohnmacht der Bilder," 33–34.
66. This is a central contention of David Freedberg's work on iconoclasm, most recently summarized in *Iconoclasm*, ch. 6.
67. Scultetus, *Kurtzer / aber Schrifftmäßiger Bericht*, esp. Aii[R].
68. Abelinus, *Theatrum Europaeum*, 280.
69. The event was related in the chronicles of the Wesel burghers Arnold von Anrath and Heinrich Weseken: Bambauer and Kleinholz, *Geusen und Spanier*, 120–21, 362.
70. Ibid., 121.
71. Anon., *Franckenthalische Belägerung*, 12.
72. Bambauer and Kleinholz, *Geusen und Spanier*, 356.
73. "Katze," in *HDA*, vol. 4, 1107–24. Burying a dead cat under a doorstep, for example, would attract evil to the house, so it could be that the soldiers had something similar in mind for the church and the congregation (ibid., 1115–16). See also Darnton, *The Great Cat Massacre*, 92–93; "Glocke," in *HDA*, vol. 3, 868–76, esp. 871–72.
74. Bambauer and Kleinholz, *Geusen und Spanier*, 121.
75. Ibid.
76. The passage is incomplete: "doch es wehre daher kommen, das 6 Uhr von ... (Porta zu Embrich) in ein Wey-Kessel ge... und darnah Schwartzel darin gethan wehre." Bambauer and Kleinholz, *Geusen und Spanier*, 362.

Confession 〜 159

77. Ibid., 42, 93-95, 114, 145–46, 159, 240.
78. Anon., *Newe Zeitung*, Aii^V (my own pagination).
79. Anon., *Warhaffter Bericht*, 19.
80. See Wilson, *Europe's Tragedy*, 113-15, 269-74.
81. David Stumpf, letter to superintendent Dr. Simon Leisring (1635), in Herrman, *Aus tiefer Not*, 128–29.
82. Emich, "Bilder einer Hochzeit," 227; Kaiser, "Ärger als der Türck," 177.
83. Kuijpers, "Between Storytelling and Patriotic Scripture," 183–84.
84. Emich, "Bilder einer Hochzeit," 226.
85. Bambauer and Kleinholz, *Geusen und Spanier*, 387–88.
86. For a detailed history of the events leading up to and including the sack see Hoffmann, *Geschichte der Stadt Magdeburg*, 18–181. Other studies include: Medick, "Historisches Ereignis und zeitgenössische Erfahrung"; Kaiser, "Excidium Magdeburgense" and "Die 'Magdeburgische' Hochzeit"; with a special focus on General Tilly, see Elsner, "Magdeburg."
87. Medick, "Historisches Ereignis und zeitgenössische Erfahrung."
88. See Rublack, "Wench and Maiden," regarding the metaphorical equation of a free city with a virgin or maiden in early modern German print. For an example see Anon., *Copey eines Schreibens Auß Magdeburgk*.
89. Klimesch, "Zacharias Bandhauer's deutsches Tagebuch," esp. 245–67.
90. Ibid., 280.
91. See Kaiser, "Die 'Magdeburgische' Hochzeit," 209. Diefendorf has observed similar behavior in the French context (*Beneath the Cross*, 103). The papal letter is cited in Kaiser, "Excidium Magdeburgense," 48–49.
92. Mengering, *Letzte Belagerung*, 61–62.
93. Kaiser, "Die 'Magdeburgische' Hochzeit," 210; Medick, "Historisches Ereignis und zeitgenössische Erfahrung," 405.
94. Mengering, *Letzte Belagerung*, 41.
95. Ibid.
96. Luh, "Religion und Türkenkrieg," 200–1.
97. Kaiser, "Ärger als der Türck," 164.
98. Mengering, *Letzte Belagerung*, 51–52.
99. Hoffmann, *Geschichte der Stadt Magdeburg*, 177.
100. Thodaenus, *Threni Magdaeburgici*, Liii^R.
101. Kaiser has also made this point in "Die 'Magdeburgische' Hochzeit," 210–11.
102. Peters, *Peter Hagendorf*, 138.
103. Volkholz, *Ackermann*, 17.
104. Thodaenus, *Threni Magdaeburgici*, Jii^R–Liiii^V.
105. Ibid,. Ki^R.
106. Ibid., Ki^V-KiiiR., Kiiii^V.
107. Ibid., Kiii^R.
108. On the Black Legend, see Swart, "The Black Legend"; Maczkiewitz, *Der niederländische Aufstand*, 256-264; Keen, "The Black Legend Revisited."
109. Kamen, *Empire, War and Faith*, 143; Keen, "The Black Legend Revisited," 719.
110. Monter, "Heresy Executions," 49; Kamen, *The Duke of Alba*, 79.
111. Kamen, *The Duke of Alba*, 94, 166. On Alba's rule see also van der Lem, *Revolt in the Netherlands*, ch. 3.
112. Maczkiewitz, *Der niederländische Aufstand*, 258.

160 ❧ Faith in War

113. Anon., *Kurtze vnd warhafftige Anzeig*, Aiii[R]-Aiv[R].
114. See Arndt, *Das Heilige Römische Reich und die Niederlande*, 124-129.
115. Ehrenpreis, "Wir sind mit blutigen Köpfen davongelaufen . . .", 48, 51–52.
116. Anon., *Kurtze vnd warhafftige Anzeig*, Aiii[R]-Aiii[V].
117. The documents were collected and printed the following year: Anon., *Hispanischer Arragonischer Spiegel.*
118. Mendoza's letter to the bishop was printed with Fürstenberg's letter to the town of Paderborn: Mendoza, *Des Hispanischen Kriegsvolcks Obersten.*
119. Ibid., Aii[R].
120. Ibid.
121. Unless names are given, it is impossible to determine whether soldiers described as *Spanier* were actually native Spaniards or came from the Low Countries, the Empire, or elsewhere. Straddling has described native Spaniards as "an ever-contracting minority" in Philip IV's armies so that "by the 1640s, less than one in four of the men enlisted . . . was a native of the peninsula" (*Spain's Struggle*, 251).
122. Northausen, *Erbermliche...anzeig*. On the accord of Bonn see Lossen, *Der Kölnische Krieg*, vol. 2, 459-72.
123. Cited in Lossen, *Der Kölnische Krieg*, vol. 2, 473n.
124. Northausen, *Erbermliche...anzeig*, 3.
125. Ibid., 8–9.
126. Ibid., 9.
127. Ibid., 10-13.
128. See Angenendt, *Toleranz*, 239.
129. Anon., *Warhafftige: Zeytungen / Von der Belegerung / vnnd eynemung / der Statt Neuß*, Aiiii[R]. See also Gilliam, "Neuss und der Kölner Krieg," 22.
130. Anon., *Kurtze vnd warhafftige Anzeig*, Aiii[R].
131. Ibid., Aiii[V].
132. Heilmann, *Kriegsgeschichte*, vol. 2, part 1, 496n.
133. Cervantes, *Conquistadores*, 55-61.
134. Rodríguez-Pérez, *The Dutch Revolt through Spanish Eyes*, 37, 48, 69–70.
135. Ibid., 86-88.
136. Edelmayer, *Söldner und Pensionäre*, ch.6.
137. Ibid., 226–27.
138. Parker, *Army of Flanders*, 165.
139. Chamberlin, *The Sack of Rome*, 173.
140. Herdenius, letter to superintendent Dieterich, in Herrmann, *Aus tiefer Not*, 51.
141. Hümmer, "Bamberg im Schweden-Kriege," 213–14.
142. Klimesch, "Zacharias Bandhauer's deutsches Tagebuch," 277–80.
143. Ibid.
144. Peters, *Peter Hagendorf*, 233; Müller, "Das Leben eines Söldners," 49, Tallett, *War and Society*, 128.
145. Bei der Wieden, "Zur Konfessionalisierung des landsässigen Adels," 311–12.
146. Kaiser, "Cuius exercitus, eius religio?" 327.
147. Mann, *Wallenstein*, 1100–1; Polišenský, *Thirty Years War*, 200–1; see also Kaiser, "Cuius exercitus, eius religio?" 329–30.
148. Bei der Wieden, *Leben im 16. Jahrhundert*, 62–63.
149. Poyntz, *The Relation of Sydnam Poyntz*, passim. Poyntz stated his unsuccessful attempts at finding employment (ibid., 130). Regarding the suspicion of conversion to Islam toward former Turkish slaves see Ulbrich, "'Hat man also bald ein solches Blutbad,'", 96.

150. Poyntz, *The Relation of Sydnam Poyntz*, 54.
151. Ibid.
152. Turner, *Memoirs of His Own Life*, 3.
153. Ibid., 4.
154. Monro, *Monro His Expedition*, for example: Part II, 67–68, 77, 86, 89, 94, 106, 114–15, 116, 119, 122, 124, 126, 136, 154, 156, 164, 168.
155. Ibid., Part II, 89, 94, 100, 104, 106, 114.
156. Ibid., 156.
157. Ulmschneider, *Götz von Berlichingen*, 122–28.
158. On Berlichingen's Lutheranism see Franz, *Bauernkrieg*, 194.
159. Ulmschneider, *Götz von Berlichingen*, 133.
160. Staden, *Historia*, Cii^V, Div^V.
161. Whitehead and Harbsmeier, *Hans Staden's True History*, XXI; Staden, *Historia*, Aiii^R.
162. Schottin, *Tagebuch des Erich Lassota*, 41-43, 50-56.
163. Ibid., 147.
164. Gräf, *Söldnerleben*, 102.
165. Ulmschneider, *Götz von Berlichingen*, 57; Gräf, *Söldnerleben*, 126; Peters, *Peter Hagendorf*, 137, 153, 165.
166. Ulrike Ludwig, "Erinnerungsstrategien in Zeiten des Wandels."
167. See for example Lehmann, "Grenzen der Erklärungskraft der Konfessionalisierungsthese," 246; Greyerz, "Konfessionelle Indifferenz."
168. Kalkum genannt Lohausen, *Zweiter Discours*, 507–8.
169. Ibid., 508.
170. Turner, *Memoirs of His Own Life*, 14.
171. Ibid.
172. Ibid., 16.
173. Ibid.
174. See Burschel's detailed discussion of the social composition of armies in *Söldner*, 54–87. On motivation see also Huntebrinker, *Fromme Knechte*, 100-103.
175. Bambauer and Kleinholz, *Geusen und Spanier*, 324.
176. Poyntz, *The Relation of Sydnam Poyntz*, 45.
177. Raymond, *Autobiography of Thomas Raymond*, 43.
178. Ibid., 44.
179. Volkholz, *Jürgen Ackermann*, 10–11.
180. Peters, *Peter Hagendorf*, 132, 135.
181. Ibid., 143.
182. Ibid., 145.
183. Ibid., 146.
184. Ulmschneider, *Götz von Berlichingen*, 74.
185. Schottin, *Tagebuch des Erich Lassota*, 108.
186. Burschel, "Himmelreich und Hölle," 191.
187. Donagan, "Web of Honour," passim, esp. 367, 387–88.
188. See Pröve, "Violentia und Potestas," esp. 40–41.
189. See Fiedler, *Kriegswesen*, 166.
190. Westenrieder, "Tagebuch des Augustin von Fritsch," 142, 143, 144.
191. The exception being the state of "prima furia," a temporary state of berserker-like arousal comparable to the modern concept of a "combat high" (see below), for example after breaching a wall, in which it was accepted that soldiers would kill indiscriminately until they had calmed down.

162 ~: *Faith in War*

192. See also Donagan, "Web of Honour," passim.
193. Peters, *Peter Hagendorf*, 146.
194. Ibid., 165.
195. See Kroener, "Der Soldat als Ware." On the practice of impressing prisoners see Redlich, *The German Military Enterpriser*, vol. 1, 480; Burschel, *Söldner*, 158-159; Tallett, *War and Society*, 128-131.
196. Westenrieder, "Tagebuch des Augustin von Fritsch," 152-154.
197. Ibid., 153.
198. Ibid., 154.
199. Ibid., 158.
200. Hümmer, "Bamberg im Schweden-Kriege," 190–91.
201. Ibid., 191.
202. For similar observations regarding the English Civil War see Donagan, "Web of Honour," 368-71.
203. Monro, *Monro His Expedition*, part I, 39–40.
204. Ibid.
205. Ibid., part II, 27–28.
206. Ibid., 28.
207. Grossman, *On Killing*, 160.
208. Peters, *Peter Hagendorf*, 131; Turner, *Memoirs of His Own Life*, 6; Poyntz, *The Relation of Sydnam Poyntz*, 53–54. The owner of the copy of Wallhausen's *Manuale Militari* held at the Staats- und Universitätsbibliothek Dresden also amended and extended the glossary of military technical terms at the end of the book and began his personal dictionary on the blank pages. Pastor Thodaenus mentioned that a soldier he encountered spoke only broken German, but this did not hamper communication (Thodaenus, *Threni Magdæburgici*, Ki[v]).
209. See Kroener, "'Kriegsgurgeln, Freireuter und Marodebrüder,'" 60.
210. Redlich has described a very similar case (*The German Military Enterpriser*, vol. 1, 481).
211. Contamine, *War in the Middle Ages*, 257.
212. See Leng, "Gründe für berufliches Töten."
213. Ortenburg, *Waffe und Waffengebrauch*, 55–56.
214. Ibid., 45.
215. Grossman, *On Killing*, 121-33. Humans prefer to slash or bludgeon.
216. Ibid., 234–35. Due to the taboo surrounding the joy of killing, it is difficult to gauge how common combat high is, but as a neurobiological process we can assume that it is and was not uncommon.
217. Huntebrinker, *Fromme Knechte*, 316.
218. Luh, "Religion und Türkenkrieg."
219. Donagan, "Web of Honour."
220. See also Walsham, *Charitable Hatred*, 169.
221. Kaiser, "Die Söldner und die Bevölkerung," 81.
222. See Kaiser, "Ärger als der Türck," 182, for a similar estimation.
223. Greyerz et al., *Interkonfessionalität*; Kaplan, *Divided by Faith* and *Reformation and the Practice of Toleration*; Christman and Plummer, *Topographies of Tolerance and Intolerance*.
224. Kaplan, *Divided by Faith*, 76.
225. For a fuller account of the terrible living circumstances in the armies, see Chapter 5 of this book and Funke, "Magische Medizin und Schutzzauber," esp. 57-64.
226. Brady, "Limits of Religious Violence," 141.

227. Civale, "'Dextere sinistram vertere,'" 566-67.
228. Possevino, *Il Soldato Christiano*, 34-39.
229. Civale, "'Dextere sinistram vertere,'" 567.
230. Monro, *Monro His Expedition*, part II, 47–48.
231. I think that Monro was referring to beer from Zerbst, the capital of the then Reformed principality of Anhalt-Zerbst. Zerbster beer was also generally positively reviewed in Heinrich Knaust's roughly contemporary beer guide: Knaust, *Fünff Bücher*, 57.
232. Monro, *Monro His Expedition*, part II, 47–48.
233. Ibid., 48.
234. Ibid., 75. I would like to thank Steve Murdoch, who kindly alerted me to this passage and to Hepburn's religion.
235. Ibid.
236. Hümmer, "Bamberg im Schweden-Kriege," 125–26.
237. Ibid., 115.
238. Ibid., 118.
239. Fiedler, *Miles Christianus*.
240. Ibid., Ii^V-Iii^R.
241. I am thinking here for example of the deep friendship between Arnoldus Buchelius and Caspar Barlaeus that Judith Pollmann has examined so memorably (*Religious Choice in the Dutch Republic*, esp. ch. 6).
242. Hümmer, "Bamberg im Schweden-Kriege," 142.
243. Volkholz, *Jürgen Ackermann*, 47, 49–50, 51–52.
244. Ibid., 52.
245. Carroll, "The Rights of Violence."

CHAPTER 5

Dying, Death, and Burial in the Military

In this final chapter we will examine what characterized dying, death, and burial in the military sphere and how far attitudes and practices differed from the civilian context. Much has been written about the importance of death, dying, and burial in early modern culture but our knowledge of how these themes were dealt with in the military is still rudimentary.[1] We will begin with an overview of the culture of death in the civilian context. Funeral sermons given for soldiers provide a good starting point for the study of military dying culture as these texts were very specific regarding the circumstances of death and, importantly, offered qualitative evaluations of the death described. We will then move on to examine theological advice given to soldiers in spiritual literature regarding the preparation for death under the adverse circumstances of military life. Military attitudes toward dying and death will be surveyed next, and finally we will analyze military funerary rites.

Dying Well in Early Modern Culture

Early modern dying was both an intricate and an important matter: "[t]here were procedures to follow, people to meet, tasks to be performed and property to be dispersed."[2] The soul's welfare in the netherworld was a primary concern for the individual and to most people dying well was the ultimate determiner of postmortem standing. Conscious preparation for the transition to the next life was indispensable, as was the adherence to the rules laid out by the *ars moriendi* literature that had begun to circulate in the late Middle Ages. The most important goal was to die well; a bad death was greatly feared.[3] In contrast to the bad, sudden death, the good death was anticipated and dealt with by the individual. Five temptations had to be overcome in the hour of death (loss of faith, despair, impatience, vainglory, and avarice) and deathbed procedures were aimed at helping the dying person to do this.[4] Friends and family

Dying, Death, and Burial in the Military ∿ 165

gathered around the bed to aid the dying, Catholics praying for their souls, Protestants praying for faith and steadfastness. Dying went well when *moriens* had put their worldly affairs in order, stoically endured the pains of illness, accepted death, said the necessary prayers, and passed on calmly. After the Reformation, Catholics and Lutherans continued to place great importance on the moment of death. The Calvinist doctrine of double predestination meant that the soul's fate had been determined at the beginning of time, so deathbed comportment could not have an influence in this regard, but to Calvinists, death still meant the imminent revelation of this predestined fate. The deathbed was thus a liminal space, where the netherworld reached into the world of the living and Christians of all denominations could hope to glean their loved ones' destinies in the next life from the way they died.

Local dying customs and individual attitudes betray at times significant variation.[5] Marc Forster has found that seventeenth-century Catholics in southwestern Germany rejected the sacrament of extreme unction, as they feared that receiving it would seal their fate and remove the chance of recovery.[6] In England, both Catholics and Protestants were convinced that they could control their own salvation by concentrating their thoughts on the divine in the final moment before death, a notion that was unknown in *any* official creed.[7] Calvinism's official funerary minimalism and the separation of the living from the dead met with resistance among the Reformed population. David Luebke has described how Westphalian Calvinists ignored official Reformed doctrine and asserted themselves against the Catholic clergy in their determination to be buried in the Catholic churchyard, as they considered extramural burial demeaning and were intent on remaining part of their community also in death.[8] So, while general patterns of good dying were widely shared, local and regional attitudes could be varied and resilient against demands of doctrinal conformity.

Burial practices were also subject to custom and varied depending on place and situation. With their lower population densities, rural parishes could usually inhume the dead individually in the churchyard. When these filled up, bones that were dug up when new graves were made were transferred to charnel houses, which had become common in Germany in the thirteenth century.[9] What mattered was that the body had first been interred in sacred ground proximate to the sacral radiance of the relics housed in the church altar and that, when space was needed for later generations, their remains stayed in the community. In urban settings, individual burial was limited by space and for many ordinary town dwellers, their last journey ended in a mass grave.[10] Burial often became rather hurried in times of plague and the rites performed were frequently stripped down or suspended entirely.[11] We know too little about how people rationalized the denial of customary burial rites and what effect this was perceived to have on the souls of the dead. In Catholic contexts, much could be done for the benefit of the deceased after the event through the sub-

166 ❦ Faith in War

sequent consecration of the grave pits and the reading of masses. Protestants, however, had little more than faith to console them after a loved one had received a plague burial. So, while the good death and decent burial were commonly of great concern, the quality of death and burial was determined by the situation in which it occurred.

Several specifics of military life raise doubt regarding the likeliness that soldiers would die well according to early modern norms. Dying needed tranquility and comfort in one's last hours, but both were scarce commodities in soldiers' lives and dying in battle obviously precluded the possibility of composing one's thoughts in the moment of death. We have already seen that chaplains were never available in sufficient numbers, so many soldiers died without professional spiritual assistance. So how did soldiers cope with these unpromising prospects for their own departures from this life?

Funeral Sermons for Soldiers

The most detailed insights into how certain soldiers died are given in funeral sermons. "Certain" has to be emphasized: the individuals honored with these sermons and their subsequent publication were few and disproportionately privileged in life as in death. But the deathbed rites of the military elite can serve as a good entry point into a discussion of military death, because the detailed attention these deaths received contrasts starkly with the indifference toward the majority of the military dead. We will examine the deaths of three noblemen: the unequivocally "good" death of Friedrich Wilhelm von Wallendorf, the violent, potentially "bad" death of Johann Dietrich von Haugwitz, and finally the execution of Bernhard von Miltiz. The circumstances of their deaths were recorded by clerics and later published in booklets including the sermons given at their funerals, their *curricula vitae*, and related texts, in Miltiz's case a consolatory letter (*Trostschrift*) that his mother had written to her son and a prayer that the condemned man had composed while awaiting execution.[12]

Friedrich Wilhelm von Wallendorf died an impeccable death by any standard. Born in 1609, he and one of his cousins had joined the Bubenheim regiment under Werner von Tilly in 1626.[13] Much to his superiors' delight, Wallendorf proved to be a diligent, hardworking soldier, while superintendent Wilhelm Eggelinck, who authored the funeral sermon, was impressed by the young officer's piety. His parents had raised him in accordance with the "pure Lutheran catechism" and the eighteen-year-old performed a model death.[14] Wallendorf fell ill with a fever and although two of his cousins serving in the same regiment paid for medical treatment, he died. When Wallendorf realized that he would surely die, he called for superintendent Eggelinck and confessed his sins. Eggelinck read him edifying passages from Scripture and prayed with

Dying, Death, and Burial in the Military ∾ 167

him until Wallendorf died the following day. It is noteworthy that a superintendent, a high-ranking Protestant officeholder, attended to Wallendorf. Jean Tserclaes and Werner von Tilly had enforced re-Catholization in the Lower-Saxon Circle, to which Ahlden, the town where Wallendorf died, belonged. That Wallendorf nevertheless had access to a Lutheran cleric as he lay dying indicates not only his high birth but also shows, again, the general acceptance of confessional difference among soldiers. In his sermon, the superintendent comforted Wallendorf's family and friends with the assurance that he had not died "like a godless [man], without any remorse and anguish for his sins: but as a blessed, penitent, faithful Christian."[15] Wallendorf's had not been a "bad," "quick death," he had died "in faithful meditation" and "passed on gently."[16] Finally, the young man had received an honorable burial with "persons of nobility and officers as well as a great number of soldiers" in attendance. Wallendorf had managed to meet the high demands of death etiquette: he had accepted his death, was attended to by a cleric, confessed his sins, said the appropriate prayers, passed on calmly in the presence of relatives, and received an honorable burial. Such a death left nothing to be desired.

Johann Dietrich von Haugwitz met a far less peaceful end: he was shot by quartermaster Johann Burckelau in a quarrel over horse fodder.[17] His regimental chaplain, Johann Jacob Angermüller, used the occasion of Haugwitz's funeral to remind the attending soldiers of their spiritual obligations in no uncertain terms. Angermüller centered his sermon on Psalm 90:12 ("So teach us to number our days, that we may apply our hearts unto wisdom"). Like King David, cavaliers should strive to "die well" ("ευθανασιαν", euthanasian), as Haugwitz's death was a divine *monstrum* that showed how suddenly a soldier's life could end.[18] Angermüller preached sardonically against the lack of concern with postmortem matters among the cavalry, stating not only that the cavalryman's god was most frequently "his belly" but also that he had personally heard from many soldiers that they would rather be at a large banquet in Hell than in Heaven, while others did not even believe in the resurrection.[19] Throughout the sermon, Angermüller shamed his congregation, who apparently compared rather unfavorably to a man like Haugwitz. Not only had he been a model soldier, courageous and "magnanimous" ("μεγαλόψυχος", megalopsychos), and in his early twenties already a veteran of the battles of White Mountain and Fleurus, Haugwitz had also been a model Christian. He had attended Angermüller's sermons whenever possible, making him "a curious exception to our cavalrymen, both noble and common," and the chaplain had seen him read his prayer book many times.[20] He did have his character flaws, but Haugwitz had readily confessed and rued his deficiencies.[21] Regarding Haugwitz's quick and potentially bad death, Angermüller assured his congregation that, in this exceptional case, the factors that might cast doubt over the welfare of Haugwitz's soul could be ignored. His death *was* sudden, but the chaplain asserted that in

168 ❧ *Faith in War*

this instance St. Augustine's dictum *non male moritur qui bene vixit* applied.[22] The Lord would surely forgive that it had been Haugwitz who had challenged the quartermaster to the duel, as his anger was caused by the injustice of Burckelau's rude and insubordinate behavior.

Compared to the calm, orderly death of Friedrich von Wallendorf, it is important to underline that Angermüller could still present Haugwitz's death as a "good" one, despite its inauspicious circumstances. In contrast to the perfect death performed by Wallendorf, Johann von Haugwitz's departure from this world displayed elements that could raise concerns regarding his soul's welfare. The suddenness with which he met his fate and the resulting lack of preparation, the anger that had made him challenge the quartermaster, and his spiritual "infirmities" were all factors that could, in principle, have detrimental effects on his salvation. His pious comportment during his life outweighed these, however, such that the way he had departed from this life lost importance.

Even more remarkable is the funeral sermon of Bernhard von Miltitz, who was executed for killing another nobleman in Dresden in 1614.[23] In contrast to Haugwitz's life and death, the former being exemplary, the latter less so, the inverse was true of Miltitz's case: he was a convicted murderer facing execution but had rediscovered piety just in time to perform a perfect death. Born into a Junker family in 1587 he had served in Hungary, Denmark, and other theatres of war and was apparently en route to another engagement in Scandinavia when he committed the murder.[24] He initially fled the city but, much to the satisfaction of Paul Reich, a deacon at Dresden's Kreuzkirche who attended to Miltitz while he awaited execution and gave his funeral sermon, the killer returned of his own accord to face his punishment.

Miltitz appears to have accepted the verdict and the prospect of his execution calmly. Reich recounts Miltitz's fantasies of becoming an advocate against "ire and faction" among nobles should he obtain a pardon, but the convict seems not to have squandered too much hope on this unlikely prospect and instead prepared himself for death.[25] In prison, Miltitz copied Bible passages and prayers as a means of meditation and composed prayers of his own including one that was printed alongside the sermon. He asked God's mercy, expressed his confidence in dwelling with Him eternally, and commended his mother into God's care.[26] On the morning of the execution, Miltitz confessed his sins and received communion. When it was time to die, the young man bound his own hands, walked willingly and without assistance to the place of execution, knelt confidently, commended his soul into God's hands, and seems to even have rejoiced at the prospect of being with Christ.[27]

An execution offered an ideal opportunity to perform a good death. Miltitz was in control of all his faculties until the end, and he could produce written evidence of his faith, write and recite prayers, and impress with his composed demeanor and active compliance. The description given in Reich's account is reminiscent of a religious play. With the deacon's help, Miltitz managed to transform the "theatre of horror," to borrow Richard von Dülmen's term, into a "theatre of piety."[28] It is neither exceptional nor surprising that convicts facing execution embraced the endeavors of the clergy to prepare them for death and strengthen their faith. In contrast to modern concepts of capital punishment that generally regard the moment of death as the point in which retribution is made, in premodern times penitent convicts became "poor" sinners who suffered their cleansing punishment in front of an often-sympathetic public. If judges, clerics, executioners, and convicts played their role well, an execution was not a mere act of revenge but an awe-inspiring, edifying event. As long as the delinquents accepted the role of the penitent sinner, they could not only expect comfort and sympathy but also act as moral exemplars. Bernard von Miltitz's performance fully satisfied deacon Reich, who composed his funeral sermon around Ezekiel 33:11 ("As I live, saith the Lord GOD, I have no pleasure in the death of the wicked; but that the wicked turn from his way and live").

What do these three accounts of military deaths show us? The funeral sermons use the same language of the good death that was common in the civilian context and the same criteria applied to civilian and military deaths. It is striking, however, that while the circumstances of these deaths could not be more different, all three were described as "good" deaths. One could somewhat cynically account for this by pointing to the elevated social and military status of the deceased and assume considerable pressure to present these deaths positively. This may have been a factor, but an eagerness to please the congregations does not sufficiently explain why the preachers interpreted these heterogeneous deaths as "good." Chaplain Angermüller for one seems not to have been exactly cowed by his congregation when he attacked their lack of piety and morality in Haugwitz's funeral sermon. What these examples indicate is that the precepts of the *ars moriendi* were in fact far more elastic than is often assumed and that, in practice, clerics and lay people alike had some leeway in negotiating even imperfect deaths. The tenets of dying etiquette were valid in the military context, but it seems that the reality of military life and the likeliness of a sudden, quick death led chaplain Angermüller to emphasize the importance of a pious life, which could outweigh a "bad" death.

The sermons do not testify only to the norms of the clerics, as Wallendorf and Miltiz both deliberately followed the same norms to die their good deaths. Evidence from military diaries provides further evidence that the authors evaluated death in the same terms as their civilian contemporaries. Caspar von Widmarckter, for example, mentioned death frequently and distinguished between death in battle, which he did not judge either way, and the explicitly good death of his ensign Hans Friedrich von Harstall who died of a fever "blessed in God and [in a] Christian [manner]."[29] Augustin von Fritsch also described

170 ❧ *Faith in War*

the good death of Colonel Melchior von Reinnach, who "passed on blessedly in the Lord" when he succumbed to a gunshot wound.[30] That the notion of dying well was shared by soldiers shows that a traditionally well-managed death was also an ideal in the military. In the context of the army, however, such placid departures could not be counted on, as the "bad" death was constantly lurking.

Preparing for a "Bad" Death

In military life, comfort was rare especially for the lower ranks, and whether they died in battle or in the squalor of the camps, neither situation was conducive to dying well.[31] Soldiers, Hans Wilhelm Kirchhof wrote from experience, "march in the frost and cold, rain and foul weather in wet clothes and shoes . . . they suffer bitter hunger . . . They lie in the filth, mess, lice and stench, tangled and on top of each other."[32] These were the conditions in which many soldiers met their end. Trying to avoid death was the obvious reaction and in this respect, the efforts to heal and protect through magic and to limit violence among enemies that we have examined in previous chapters gain an additional urgency.

Most authors who wrote about military dying envisioned a death on the battlefield in which the pivotal moment of death, which according to the *ars moriendi* ought to be calm and composed, was experienced engulfed in violent chaos. Meditative prayer and passing on calmly in these circumstances were impossible, especially as death increasingly came in the form of a shot, fired from a distance and suddenly killing the unsuspecting victim. The solution to the problem was prayer before the engagement. Communal prayer had been customary throughout the Middle Ages and into the early modern period; warriors knelt down before an engagement, and prayed to God, the Virgin, and the saints for victory and their intercession. In preparation for death, Catholic field preachers heard dying confessions and administered the last sacraments. The nun Maria Anna Junius mentions that an officer who was dying on a battlefield near her convent called for a preacher who heard his last confession, which shows that at least some preachers went into battle.[33] The chronic shortage of military clerics also meant, however, that the preachers who were present could only attend to a minority, so many men died without their spiritual comfort. While this problem was especially noticeable in the context of battles, the burden on the preachers was also enormous in other situations. Abbot Maurus Friesenegger described how a field preacher had to hear thirty confessions in one day in late December when a great number of his flock were dying from hunger and cold.[34] In the past, soldiers themselves had at times adopted the role of priests, as was the case before the Battle of Pontvallain (1370) when the men made the sign of the cross over their bread rations and used them for com-

Dying, Death, and Burial in the Military :~ 171

munion, heard each other's confession, and prayed together.[35] While maybe unusual, Robert Monro's description of how his Scots regiment prepared for the Battle of Leipzig is reminiscent of this, as here, too, the soldiers seem to have conducted their religious rites without the guidance of clerics:

> As the Larke begunne to peepe, the seventh of September 1631. having stood all night in battaile a mile from *Tillies* Armie, in the morning, ... having before meditated in the night, and resolved with our Consciences; we begunne the morning with offering our soules and bodies, as living Sacrifices unto God, with Confession of our sinnes, lifting up our hearts and hands to Heaven, we begged for reconciliation in Christ, by our publique prayers, and secret sighes, and groanes; recommending our selves, the successe, and event of the day unto God, our Father in Christ; which done by us all, we marched forwards in Gods name ...[36]

Communal prayer and, in the Protestant context, hymn singing was a practicable option to counter fear, although the main intention seems to have been to ask for protection from death rather than to prepare for it. When the Protestant troops readied for battle at Drakenburg in 1547, the whole force knelt down three times and prayed for God's assistance.[37] Then, Luther's suitably martial hymn "A Mighty Fortress is Our God" was sung. Finally, when the time for battle had come and the soldiers marched toward their enemy, they sang "In Peace and Joy I Now Depart," another hymn of Luther's with a consoling orientation toward the netherworld.[38] The choice of hymns seems to have been intended to bolster the men's morale through the celebration of God's protection against the "evil foe" and secondly to soothe their fears when it came to fighting and dying so that they might die "peacefully," if not "joyously." As was the case with hymns used during services, the hymns sung here were not specifically military.[39] The words fit the occasion of battle, because of their at times martial overtones and reliance on military language, but they were common Lutheran fare that the soldiers had learned in their civilian lives.

Indeed, hymns or prayers that were written specifically for the use of the soldier are rare. Martin Luther composed one of the first prayers for soldiers to prepare themselves for death.[40] Luther warned that soldiers should not hope for salvation as warriors but as Christians; their profession was thus superseded by the emphasis on the individual's faith and personal accountability. The prayer is void of implorations for victory or, in fact, anything that is not directly concerned with the individual speaker's salvation. The context in which it is spoken—by a soldier before battle—is assigned to the background. The individual character is further emphasized by Luther's suggestion to add the Lord's Prayer or the creed and "[i]n doing so commit body and soul into God's hands, draw [one's] sword, and fight in God's name."[41] Just before battle, in Luther's view, the soldier should consequently ignore the situation as far as possible and fight and potentially die in direct communication with the Lord. This is

172 ᴧ: *Faith in War*

the closest soldiers could be expected to approximate the pious contemplation befitting the dying in less adverse circumstances.

Luther's prayer was included in later military publications, most notably in Leonhart Fronsperger's *Spiritual War Regime*, but the focus in theological tracts shifted away from final contemplation to godly living.[42] Andreas Musculus did not concern himself with last things in his 1558 theological handbook for soldiers; he gave his readers instructions on how to *live* in a way that did not threaten salvation.[43] He suspected most soldiers of leading a "disorderly life" but such "evil, wild, and scurrilous sows" were no concern of his; he was addressing the few pious warriors who abstained from this "devilish life."[44] Providing that his readers had ascertained that the warlord they were serving had a just cause to go to war and that it was not waged against Protestantism, it was a soldier's moral conduct that determined his chances in the netherworld; it was not how soldiers died but how they lived that mattered. That this emphasis on a pious life spent in preparation for a sudden death found its way into the military realm was already evidenced in chaplain Angermüller's funeral sermon for Johann Dietrich von Haugwitz. It was a position commonly held in the military and not specific to Protestants. The Catholic Lazarus von Schwendi, a soldier and councilor to the emperors Charles V, Ferdinand, and Maximilian II, also cautioned soldiers to live piously because they "know no certain time of their life and death but stand in constant danger" of death.[45] The key to Heaven therefore lay in the soldier's life, not his death: the *ars bene vivendi* became a substitute for the *ars moriendi*, and this notion was also promoted in religious literature aimed at soldiers.[46]

Being prepared for death and remaining alert to the suddenness with which a soldier's life could end remained of tantamount importance in the military and this notion was shared at least by the military elites. Caspar von Widmarckter felt that his busy life distracted him from contemplating its end and after a narrow escape from death, he purchased a seat and two grave sites in his local church.[47] Robert Monro also explained in cautionary passages that soldiers "ought ever to be well prepared, having death ever before their Eyes, they ought to be the more familiar with *God*, that they might be ever ready to embrace it."[48] He warned "foolish men" that battle was not where most soldiers met their end but rather that "some die, through one kinde of death, and some by another; so that we ought ever be prepared and ready, not knowing how, when, or where to die . . . Our care then should be still, to meditate on the end, that it may be good, and then doubtlesse we shall die well."[49]

The *ars moriendi* was in many ways a practical solution to the problem that different sets of norms were constantly tugging at people to behave in sometimes contradictory ways. The norms of male honor, which often had to be established and defended through violence, were diametrically opposed to the Christian imperatives of peaceful forbearance, for example. The military profession was at its core in conflict with these religious norms but, as we have seen in the first chapter, soldiering was also considered necessary for the defense of Christian society so long as soldiers adhered to the strictures of Christian warfare. Fighting Christians could only ever be a normative compromise, however, and in this respect, soldiering was typical of the normative ambiguity that characterized early modern culture as a whole. Leading a life in exclusive accordance with religious norms was impossible for anybody but monastics or nuns and even they grappled with these demands. The *ars moriendi* offered a way out: by following religious norms exclusively just before death, the individual could still bring a life in which other sets of norms may have predominated to a happy, God-pleasing end.[50]

Military Attitudes toward Death

Outside of theological advice literature, soldiers were associated with a defiant attitude toward death. In the sixteenth century, the *Landsknecht* was frequently depicted in the *danse macabre* genre and in a type of broadsheet illustration that showed soldiers in conversation with Death.[51] The soldiers in these images are noteworthy for their confident, even cocky demeanor in the face of Death. A pen and ink drawing by Hans Baldung (around 1503) shows the scene in an almost comic form.[52] The *Landsknecht* is leaning casually on a pole weapon, half turning toward the Reaper who looks not very "grim" in this depiction. The soldier's facial expression is void of fear; he looks rather bored. Death, on the other hand, is smiling, his body fully turned toward the *Landsknecht*. In other depictions of the "Death and moriens" type, Death leads or drags the unfortunates away by their arms or clothes: in Baldung's drawing, Death feels the fine cloth of the *Landsknecht's* cape and seems almost awestruck. While Baldung took the motif to the extreme, soldiers were frequently portrayed as unbothered in the face of death. The soldier rarely attempts to flee but surrenders to Death fatalistically.[53] Albrecht Dürer's broadsheet of 1510, admonishing the reader to be prepared for death at all times, also uses the *Landsknecht* in the image to illustrate the omnipresence of mortal danger.[54] Again, the *Landsknecht* leans casually on his halberd, calmly looking at the hourglass Death holds up to him. In contrast to the calm acceptance is another, rather rare, motif in which the soldier puts up a fight with Death. These fights are full-on engagements with Death, who often exchanges his customary scythe for military weapons.[55] The soldiers' reactions to Death as portrayed in art are exceptional: collected acceptance, even shoulder-shrugging on the one hand, and resorting to a fierce fight on the other, but in either case fearlessness is a characteristic response.

While the *Landsknecht* therefore featured prominently in art, common soldiers' deaths were of little interest in written sources. The suffering of the pop-

174 ❧ *Faith in War*

ulace and the deaths of commanders received much attention, but few cared about the dying of the rank and file. It may have been their low social status and the stigma attached to soldiering or the voluntary nature of the profession that widely precluded compassion, but the degree to which soldier death evades the modern eye is extraordinary. Warlords and commanders rarely showed interest in the deaths of their troops. When Tilly's troops massacred the Scottish garrison of Neu Brandenburg in early 1631, the Swedish king sent Donald Mackay, the owner of the regiment, a letter in which he expressed his regret about his loss. But this was not a letter of condolence, as Gustavus Adolphus matter-of-factly ordered Mackay to replenish the ranks of his three regiments as soon as possible.[56] Robert Monro, who was serving under Mackay but had been dispatched elsewhere and thus escaped the slaughter, showed more empathy for his dead comrades. He noted the "crueltie and inhumanitie" of the imperial troops in not giving quarter to the Scots who "fought valiantly to the last man."[57] Typically, Monro mentioned the names of the officers killed but the rank and file remained anonymous and amorphous. In battle reports and other news media the names of killed noble officers were often meticulously listed. In an account of the Swabian League's Württemberg campaign of 1519, the event of legendary mercenary leader Georg von Frundsberg having his beret shot off his head was as important as the fact that many of the League's men had been shot that day.[58] An author reporting the events in Bohemia in late 1618 stated that an attack on the retreating imperialists resulted in only twenty dead on the rebels' side and that "apart from a lieutenant on horse, no one noble" died.[59] On the enemy side, over a thousand men had been lost through death, desertion, or capture, among them seven or eight nobles, all but an anonymous captain listed by name and rank.

Indifference toward the suffering of the rank and file was thus the norm, but in some instances the military elites did commiserate. Colonel Caspar von Widmarckter was not overly concerned with his men's welfare and in his campaign diary, diplomatic and organizational matters and personal misfortunes, for example when a Piedmont ox stepped on his foot and the colonel lost a toenail, took precedence over pondering his men's lot.[60] In some instances, however, Widmarckter was moved to record the dire living conditions of the common soldiers, for example when the army was stuck in Brusasco: "the whole time I saw nothing but squalor, misery, and disease among the soldiers in the excessively stinking quarters."[61] When the army was finally ordered to march on Montiglio after six days, the colonel expressed pity with the sick men, many of whom "died miserably while marching."[62] Widmarckter finally arranged to have the sick cared for in two villages, but as soon as the healthy troops moved on, the villagers drove the dying soldiers into the countryside or tortured them to death.

It did not take treacherous villagers to kill sick soldiers; often the lack of concern or incompetence of their superiors was deadly enough. A letter sent to

Dying, Death, and Burial in the Military :~ 175

the imperial colonel Wilhelm von Westphalen in 1641 shows that his inability or unwillingness to take care of his men had become known to his outraged superiors. General Wahl had received a letter in which field marshal Melchior von Hatzfeld vented his anger over the fact that the officers had allowed several hundred soldiers to "starve and croak" (*verrecken*) in a "pitiless manner."[63] Hatzfeld had ordered the distribution of the sick over all imperial garrisons in the region to ensure their care and Wahl had passed specific orders down to Westphalen, who had failed to organize the transport such that five hundred men had been left to die in Paderborn. Wahl's fury is plain from the letter and Hatzfeld wrote that whoever was responsible would have to justify himself before God. In this instance, the unnecessary deaths of hundreds of men provoked harsh condemnations from high-ranking officers. Such sympathy appears to have been rare, however, and maybe also undesirable for men who had to cultivate an unemotional attitude toward those they sent into battle.

It is striking how comparatively little one reads about death in military literature. The horrors of the battlefield are hardly ever described at length and when Kirchhof attempted this he cautioned the reader that a realistic portrayal of a battle defied both language and imagination.[64] Mostly extolling the joys of *Landsknecht* life, songs, too, only rarely shed light on the deadly side of the soldier's experience. References to the gore of battle were not an infrequent interjection, however, even in lyrical contexts that praised the valor and bravery of the *Landsknecht*. The former *Landsknecht* and songwriter Jörg Graff called the battlefield the "judge's book" into which the combatants wrote the sentences until "the blood runs into the shoes."[65] Wading through blood became a common formula to describe the carnage of battle. In a Low German song about the Battle of Milan (1521), the author contrasted the short duration of the battle with the amount of blood that was spilled: "The battle lasted only a short time / From 3 o'clock until dinner time / One saw a lot of blood being shed / One saw many a *Landsknecht* stand there / in the blood up to his feet."[66] While in these two songs the blood on the ground was shed by the vanquished, it becomes a memento mori in a song about the Battle of Pavia (1524): "In the blood we had to walk / it came up over our shoes, up over our shoes / merciful God, acknowledge the misery / or else we have to perish also."[67]

The reality of battle caused mass panic and the chaotic retreats of whole regiments are frequently described phenomena. In his scathing report on the Protestants' defeat at White Mountain, Christian von Anhalt, the field commander of the Bohemian army, sharply condemned the mass flight among the common soldiery that had completely dissolved the battle formation, but showed unusual empathy in blaming the cruel treatment their officers had inflicted on them.[68] Anhalt's subordinate Count Thurn was less willing to blame the officers and instead rehearsed the old litany of the soldiery's "unchristian, unheard-of godless lifestyle" with which they had invoked God's wrath "thousandfold."[69]

176 ◊ *Faith in War*

It was not just the demoralized, destitute, and hungry soldiery who panicked in the face of death. The horrors of the battlefield also affected the nobility, the supposed warrior caste. In his account of the Battle of Breitenfeld (1631), Sydnam Poyntz described the panic that grabbed the Duke of Saxony and his nobles. With the Catholic cavalry and some of Tilly's infantry approaching, the battle became heated around the Saxon regiments and in Poyntz's estimation Duke John George proved a coward when he fled the battlefield.[70] The romantic vision of chivalrous, knightly combat that was still entertained by the nobility did not prepare the young men for the grisly reality of the battlefield: "being young Cavalliers and Gallants, and who had never seene a battaile fought, and seeing themselves drop, and the bullets fall so thicke, and their Duke gonne, threw away their Armes, and fled."[71] While Poyntz had observed the Duke's and his nobles' cowardice with cynicism, John George's final order to hang all men who fled from the battlefield filled the Englishman with disgust because "hee deserved it best, for hee fled hymself first."[72] Poyntz's unusually defiant criticism of his former warlord and those above his station becomes more readily understandable when bearing in mind that John George had broken one of the greatest taboos in the early modern military code of honor. If a commander decided to join his troops in battle, he was *never* to leave the field before the fighting was over, not even when wounded.[73] Instead it was considered the commander's and the officers' duty to fight and die with their men. Kirchhof composed a template for a prebattle speech for commanders to give to their troops, which ended: "I will not desert you while I [still] have one warm drop of blood [in me], my breath, or a single vein may stir. *In summa*, on this day and on this field I will stay alive with you or die honorably."[74] Cowardice was a disgrace for the rank and file, for a commander it was unforgivable.

The likeliness of one's own death is never pondered at great length in the military memoirs. We find very few and mostly laconic descriptions of narrow escapes in soldiers' accounts, which allow an admittedly rough sketch of how soldiers viewed the prospect of their own death. For a born warrior like Götz von Berlichingen, death was not the worst outcome. When he had his hand shot off, his initial reaction was to plead with God to let him die, as he thought that his loss had rendered him useless for his vocation.[75] Looking back on his life, however, Berlichingen later thanked and praised the Lord for having protected and helped him through almost six decades of undeterred, single-handed warring.[76] For less dedicated warriors avoiding death was the top priority. Cowardice was both a punishable offence and a source of dishonor. Peter Hagendorf is exceptional when he candidly describes spending an assault on Straubing hidden in a hedge and entering the city when the fighting was over.[77] The outcome certainly justified his passive role: only nine men of his three hundred strong regiment had survived the assault and Hagendorf was

Dying, Death, and Burial in the Military ∾ 177

promoted from corporal to *Wachtmeister*, as no one of that rank was still alive. Hagendorf's decision to sit in his hedge until the attack was over shows that he did not wish to die in what the veteran may have correctly predicted to be a high-risk attack. The serious wounds he had suffered during the storming of Magdeburg the year before may also have taught him caution.[78] He had survived the storm unscathed but was shot twice, in the stomach and through the armpits, after entering the city. After the surgeon had treated him he was taken back to his hut "half-dead." Instead of giving more information about his state or contemplating the likeliness of his impending death, however, he laments the fate of the city, which "burned so horribly."[79] Jürgen Ackermann, who was also at Magdeburg, narrowly escaped being shot. After the assault, he began to loot but when he smashed in a door with an axe, a man fired a musket from the inside, barely missing Ackermann and killing the man next to him. Ackermann wryly remarked that after this he was "fed up with breaking down doors" and started looking for plunder elsewhere.[80] Neither Hagendorf nor Ackermann stated the likeliness of their death explicitly but whether this was because they did not ponder the danger or did not consider their thoughts on dying to be worthy of being recorded remains uncertain.

Peter Hagendorf's diary reveals his priorities in this situation and it seems that he distinguished between the professional deaths of soldiers, including himself, and the illnesses and deaths of his family. After he had been taken back to his hut, his wife went into the burning city to loot, leaving their sick daughter Elisabet with her husband. When news reached the camp that the houses were collapsing and the looting women were likely to have died Hagendorf noted: "my wife grieved me more than my own damage because of the sick child."[81] Even in his own critical situation, the soldier's familial worries overrode concerns about his own life. Elizabet's two siblings had died shortly after birth, but she was about two and a half years old now and her father may have hoped that she would survive infancy. If these were his hopes, they were sadly disappointed a few weeks later.

Hagendorf's consideration for his wife and child stands in marked contrast to the at times callous description of the deaths of soldiers. He soberly recorded the high fluctuation of captains during the siege of Magdeburg when one after the other was shot.[82] Amusement is detectable when he records that the soldier and his wife in the hut next to his tent had their legs "shot off close to the arse" by a cannon during the siege of Compie.[83] Nothing indicates that he considered the impact the cannonball could have had on him and his family had it taken a slightly different trajectory. When it came to his loved ones, however, Hagendorf showed no indication of callousness. The death of every child was recorded throughout the diary, giving the name and adding the formula "may God grant him/her a joyous resurrection" and a cross in the margin. The

178 ❦ Faith in War

death of his first wife Anna Stadlerin grieved him especially and he composed an "obituary" for her and their children:

> God grant her and the child [Barbara, born the same year, died just before her mother] and all her children a joyous resurrection, Amen. For in the eternal, blessed life we will see each other again. So now my wife has passed away with her children. Their names are these: Anna Stadlerin from Traunstein in Lower Bavaria. Children: The first did not [live long enough to] get a baptism the other three, however, all received the blessed, Christian baptism.
> The mother
> Anna Stadlerin ✠
> The children
> The first NN ✠
> Anna Maria ✠
> Elisabet ✠
> Barbara ✠
> God grant them eternal rest, 1633.[84]

This passage is the most detailed insight we gain into Hagendorf's attitude toward death and it is testimony of a family man's grief. The hope of being reunited with his wife and children in the next life, the emphasis he placed on the fact that apart from the prematurely born boy all his children had been baptized, and the invocations of God to rest their souls and resurrect them are all sentiments one would expect from a seventeenth-century father and husband.[85] The passage also implies his hope to enter Heaven, as this is where he would be reunited with his wife and children. There is no bravado or defiance. A detail that Marco von Müller has observed in the manuscript further illustrates how deeply affected Hagendorf was by the deaths in his family.[86] The private obituary for his family contrasts with the remainder of the diary, as Hagendorf's usually steady hand deteriorates in this passage, suggesting that he was still deeply distressed by his losses when he produced the clean copy of his diary years after their deaths.

Despite the scarceness of detail in the sources, certain general trends of military attitudes toward death may be suggested. Firstly, the omnipresence of death made the topic relatively uneventful. Military writers only recorded details when the situations were especially noteworthy for their gravity, cruelty, or novelty. This implies an acceptance of the fact that death was part of their occupation. The evidence from Peter Hagendorf's diary supports this interpretation, as he seems to have felt wholly differently about death in his professional environment and his private context. The lack of reflection on the soldiers' own mortality is more difficult to account for. It is plausible that the soldiers thought their deliberations about death not particularly interesting. They presumably knew how they felt about death and must have made their peace with it or ignored it.

Burial

The last element of military death to be considered is burial. Again, the sources are surprisingly tacit on the topic and for the most part, the dead seem to vanish from sight. Often, we hear of soldiers' burials only if the circumstances were interesting for other reasons. It is for the perceived slyness of the Jesuits that the burial of a soldier named Berndtt was recorded, for example.[87] Berndtt, who served the United Provinces near Wesel on the Lower Rhine, was captured by the Spanish and, in captivity, a Jesuit promised him that his life would be spared if he converted to Catholicism. Berndtt complied but was hanged nevertheless. His newly wed wife requested and received her husband's body from the governor, and, after Jesuit intercession, she was allowed to bury him in the churchyard. Arnold von Anrath, a Calvinist Wesel citizen, recorded this episode as another instance of what he perceived to be Catholic duplicity; the mention of the soldier's burial by his wife in consecrated ground is fortunate but rare.

Not even religious literature such as victory sermons mentions the dead.[88] Military ordinances that policed life in the army in varying degrees of detail are also tacit in respect of dying or burial. While dying itself was admittedly difficult to regulate, it is remarkable that articles of war and other texts that planned military life laid out rules regarding where to slaughter and bury animals but not what should be done to dead humans.[89] This may be explained by the fact that the articles of war were predominantly aimed at the personnel, whereas the burial of the dead was an organizational task that fell under the responsibility of the commanders and their subordinates. Military manuals should therefore contain relevant passages but, again, finding directives as to what should be done with the dead is very difficult, as before the eighteenth century military authors paid little attention to burial.[90] Lazarus von Schwendi dedicated four lines of his hundred-page *Kriegsdiskurs* (1577) to the fallen. Under the heading "what is to be done after victory" Schwendi encouraged the victor to perpetuate what he deemed the old tradition of celebrating mass on the battlefield to thank God and pray for the slain.[91] Afterward, high-ranking officers and nobles should be buried "with honor," the rest, friend *and* foe, in pits on the battlefield. Schwendi's emphasis on burying the officers honorably is important as it implies that the way the rank and file were buried was less than honorable.

Noble officers were usually buried individually in churches or churchyards of their confession. The bodies of officers killed in a skirmish between Dutch and Spanish troops near Mülheim on the Ruhr in 1605, for example, were taken westward to the Rhine to be buried. The Dutch dead were buried in the Calvinist main church in Wesel, while the Spanish officers were taken to Duisburg.[92] If possible, noblemen were buried with all due splendor and rites, but

180 ❧ *Faith in War*

even for the nobility, arranging an appropriate burial could be difficult. Heinrich Julius von Veltheim tried to have his brother Adrian Hildebrand's remains transferred home for six years after he had been killed at Lützen.[93] If officers came from far away, funeral arrangements were made close by. A Spanish officer by the euphonic name of Julius Caesar de Cacciis, hailing from Milan and shot at Frankenthal, was buried in Worms in 1621. His Latin epitaph gave a brief curriculum vitae and stated that Julius Caesar had died "pro defendenda Catholica Religione, contra Lutheranos & Calvinistas."[94]

The bodies of fallen officers were usually exchanged, as was the case with the remains of Wolfgang Endres Stieber, who died at Budweis in 1618.[95] In exceptional situations, they became the target of mutilation. When Martin Schenk von Niedeggen drowned in an ill-fated attempt to take Nijmegen in 1589, the citizens pulled his body from the river, took him to the city hall, and had the punishment for high treason administered on the dead body: they cut off his penis and stuffed it into his mouth, cut out his heart, quartered the body, and skewered his head on a pike.[96] After the sack of Breitenburg (*Bredenberg*) castle, the victors, who had sustained heavy casualties, searched the castle for the body of the garrison's commander, Major Dunbar, "and having found it, they ript up his breast, tooke out his heart, sundered his gummes, and stucke his heart into his mouth."[97] Robert Monro accounted for the defilement of the corpse by the fact that the besiegers had lost more than a thousand men after Dunbar had refused to surrender in a previous parley and had thus forced the attackers into a deadly assault.

The rank and file ideally ended up in mass graves. Bernardino de Mendoza, writing his *Theorica y practica de guerra* (1595) after a distinguished career in Flanders, portrayed the burial of the fallen as a moral obligation of the commander.[98] The victor was to give thanks to the Lord and reward the sacrifice of the dead by burying them "with all honor and solemnitie" as well as "rewarding their sonnes, & heires, according to the qualitie of their service."[99] The German translation goes into greater detail regarding the commander's obligation to the soldiers' kin and adds a rare dimension of empathy with the families of the common soldiery who would "lament that they have incurred the greatest damage, especially because the fatherly heart cannot be compensated with money."[100] Hans Wilhelm Kirchhof viewed such a degree of care for the fallen with nostalgia. In his own experience, the dead were simply left on the battlefield and the peasants who buried them did so negligently; dumped in shallow ditches, the corpses became fodder for wild animals.[101] An etching attributed to Christian Richter, though unrelated, illustrates Kirchhof's description.[102] Strewn about on the ground lie the corpses of six soldiers, some dressed, some naked. Two dogs tear at the flesh of a naked man in the foreground while large birds feed on the remaining corpses, with more birds descending from the sky. The sarcastic caption reads: "This is the gown of honor and the last pay, take

Dying, Death, and Burial in the Military ∾ 181

Hans Huhn away and carry him off at last."[103] The illustration and the caption are unambiguous in their message: being stripped naked, left unburied, and preyed on by animals is the appropriate, deserved end for a soldier.

It seems that these and other descriptions describe a gruesome reality. The frequency with which rotting, naked corpses occur in the sources and the art of the time suggests that armies indeed left behind trails of bodies. In the early stages of the Bohemian rebellion, a news pamphlet reported the many naked dead soldiers who lay in the forests and lined the roads between Neuhaus and Budweis.[104] Only extraordinarily hideous scenes moved contemporaries to express commiseration with the military dead. After the imperial besiegers of the Palatinate city of Frankenthal had been routed, their camp was set on fire, resulting in the death of many ill and wounded soldiers who had been left behind. In this instance, the author reporting the events commented on the lamentable sight of the many "fresh dead" lying about.[105] Importantly, however, leaving the dead behind unburied was not shrugged off as yet another military digression from the norm. Some civilians may have felt Schadenfreude and probably a sense of justice in seeing their erstwhile tormentors left to rot, bereft of Christian burial and their last honors. For the most part, however, contemporaries, civilian and military, were appalled at such a degree of neglect and even for a seasoned soldier, the sight of abandoned corpses was harrowing. When Caspar von Widmarckter moved his troops to Brusasco in 1617, he was shocked by the state of the area and especially by the fact that it was "full of dead [bodies] a great number of which were not half buried, others not at all, many were still half alive."[106]

If not out of respect for the dead, corpses had to be removed to allow the local population to return to their daily lives. This may have been immediately apparent in villages and towns—and even here it could take a while until the dead had been removed—but when battlefields were to be restored to their normal use, the rotting corpses had to be buried as well. Negligence affected the surrounding areas in very real terms. In 1606, the Wesel knackers went through the town to kill all dogs, as there were a high number of reports regarding canine rabies. The townsfolk thought the dogs had infected themselves by eating the corpses of Spanish and Dutch soldiers that had not been buried deep enough the year before.[107]

Burial was not just down to the assiduousness of the respective commanders but often a question of mere possibility. Fleeing armies could not stop to bury their dead and the victors were often overstrained by the effort. Robert Monro stressed the importance of according fallen comrades the honor of burial "as becomes Christians" and admonished his readers to recover the dead and wounded "with the hazard of our own lives," but pointed to a lack of time that might preclude such considerations.[108] It seems that usually little distinction was made between the dead in respect of which side they had died for. Uni-

182 ❧ *Faith in War*

forms were only beginning to appear during the Thirty Years War, so affiliation was often difficult to determine, especially as the dead were routinely stripped naked. Burial is another instance in which the solidarity among mercenaries could become evident, and a song from 1622 contained the line "We will bury them in the ground without any mockery, may God have mercy on them" when describing the treatment of the enemy dead.[109] A compromise approach of sorts was taken after the Battle of Wittenweier in 1638. The victorious Bernhard, Duke of Saxe-Weimar, held a banquet on the battlefield when the fighting had ended, before the dead were buried. This task was begun the following day and the news report stated that the duke's killed men were all buried along with enemies recognizable as "noble officers."[110] All other enemy dead, nonnoble officers and the rank and file, were left above ground because, according to the report, the victors did not have sufficient manpower to bury every body, a rather weak excuse given the several hundred prisoners of war that are mentioned a few lines earlier. In some situations, the living just proved very thick-skinned regarding the decomposing bodies littering the locale. After the Sack of Rome, a plague broke out among the German contingents and claimed about five thousand men, and Sebastian Schertlin blamed the outbreak of the plague on the many dead bodies that were still unburied almost two months after the city had been taken.[111] Burial was time-consuming, and after the attack on Frankfurt on the Oder in April 1631, it took six days to bury the corpses. Respect for the dead suffered in these situations and Robert Monro, present at Frankfurt, observed that "in th' end they were cast by heapes in great ditches, above a hundred in every Grave."[112]

One would expect that chaplains were present at these mass burials but the sources do not mention them. It seems, then, that the dead were mostly buried without religious rites, which is extraordinary in the context of early modern funerary culture. The civilian modes of burial most similar to the military mass grave were urban pauper burial and the plague pit. In the civilian context, however, clergy were usually present at the interment or, in Catholic locales, could bestow rites on the dead when an opportunity arose afterward.[113] But plague victims dying without sacraments and burials without rites scandalized contemporaries—a marked contrast to the military context in which burial without rites seems to have been accepted without comment. Interment in a military mass grave was an anonymous and unsentimental affair, which may explain why clerics were not mentioned in this context whether or not they were present. But that military funeral traditions for individuals were also devoid of religious rites is striking.[114] Hans Wilhelm Kirchhof described military burial customs. When a soldier died, his comrades made a bier from pikes and carried the body to a grave outside the camp. The procession was headed by fife and drums and the dead man's comrades, family, and friends followed the dead man. The fife and drum and the interment were the only necessary constituents of military burial; there is no mention of a chaplain or of any religious element. Kirchhof does refer to exceptional cases in which the congregation said the Lord's Prayer and sang psalms, but these were explicitly optional additions at the discretion of the mourners.[115] This fundamentally secular rite seems peculiar in comparison to the funerary customs of the established churches, but it is not dissimilar to a popular trend in the early stages of the Reformation that has been described by Craig Koslofsky.[116] The reformers initially failed to back up their attack on "papist" funerary rites with suggestions regarding how a God-pleasing interment should be conducted. Much to the shock of the Wittenberg theologians, some communities began to bury their dead either in an extremely simplified manner or entirely without ceremonies. The rejection of intercession for the dead and the reformers' message of *sola fide* was interpreted so radically at times that bodies were buried in a completely deritualized manner at night "like senseless beasts, like dogs," as a shocked Catholic priest wrote.[117] The population could prove hostile to the perpetuation of the old rites, which were associated with clerical greed, and although the wholesale rejection of all ceremony was deemed offensive also by the reformers, in Koslofsky's estimation those who "buried their dead very simply probably thought they were showing greater respect to the dead than did the 'superstitious' ceremonies of the established churches."[118] Popular anticlericalism could therefore be reflected in the way the dead were treated. Such anticlerical sentiments predated the Reformation and were expressed already in a *Landsknecht* song from around 1510, in which the speaker states that the simple, martial accompaniment of the drum to his grave is "nine times" more preferable than "all the shavelings' [*Pfaffen*] muttering."[119] The song, attributed to the former *Landsknecht* Jörg Graff, is full of bravado in addressing the dangers of military life, especially being wounded, and it is difficult to discern to what degree the sentiment expressed here is a sign of anticlericalism or a martial pose. The *Landsknecht* in the song is not opposed to funerary rites as such but rather rejects the traditional, "civilian" funeral in favor of the distinctly military burial ceremony with fife and drum. In this sense, the sentiment expressed may be less an attack on the "shavelings" than a deliberate emphasis on the military way of life and its customs, very much in line with the other calculated diversions from civilian society and its norms including dress, demeanor, and deliberate blasphemy.

Even high-ranking soldiers made provisions for their funerals that emphasized their military status through their simplicity. Field marshal Melchior von Hatzfeld, a man whose orthodox Catholicism is rather undisputed, stipulated that his body should be taken to Eger in his baggage wagon "without pomp" and remain there for a while in the church of the discalced Franciscans.[120] If his brother Franz, the prince-bishop of Würzburg and Bamberg, thought it appropriate, he wanted to be buried there as well, in which case a donation

184 ⁓ *Faith in War*

should be made for the annual celebration of a memorial mass. His funeral was to be conducted in silence, but whether this referred to just the interment itself or precluded any prayers surrounding this act cannot be gleaned from his will.

While this silent interment was explicitly demanded beforehand, musical accompaniment and burial during the day seem to have been regarded as honorable. Kirchhof described with disdain that military authorities frequently banned both daylight burial and the musical accompaniment to maintain morale when men were dying in great numbers. Instead, the dead were put in the ground hastily and quietly at night.[121] Silence, darkness, and the absence of rites were the marks of the dishonorable "donkey burial" (*Eselsbegräbnis* or *sepultura asina*) that placed the deceased on the level of animals and was "reserved for criminals, suicides, notorious drunkards and other dishonest people" before the late seventeenth century.[122] In terms of practice and symbolism, burying dead soldiers silently during the night excluded them from the communion of Christians and assigned them to the status of outcasts and beasts. Civil authorities took similar measures in times of plague but contemporaries did not readily accept public health concerns as sufficient reasons to excuse such a stark deviation from honorable burial customs. In 1564, Hieronymus Weller, a superintendent in Electoral Saxony, sharply criticized the Freiberg town council for ordering the burial of plague victims at night and without ceremonies because "the hygiene benefits of the burial ordinance were far outweighed by the immense dishonor and disturbance caused by burial without ceremony at night."[123] It seems that Kirchhof was moved to reject the military authorities' practice of nocturnal burial by similar sensibilities. The cultural and social implications of denying soldiers daylight burial speak loudly. While burial at night was usually an extension of a criminal's punishment, soldiers were disgraced with nocturnal burial purely on the grounds of their profession and for reasons of military expedience. The low social status of the soldier thus found its expression also in the way in which his body was disposed of. Hastily and silently interred at night, he shared the criminal's final disgrace. The reasoning of the military authorities for letting bodies disappear during the night is straightforward enough but how those who faced such a disgrace dealt with the prospect cannot be determined.

We must assume that the soldiers' families and other train followers were buried in the same mass graves as the soldiers, but the sources do not mention them either. Despite the meticulousness with which Peter Hagendorf recorded the deaths of his wife and children, the diary does not give any indication regarding where and how his family were buried. Anna Stadlerin, his first wife, died in a hospital in Munich while Hagendorf was on campaign and he did not record what happened to her body or that of their baby daughter Barbara, who had died while Anna was rambling through Bavaria in search of her husband's regiment.[124] The military elite could afford to give their loved ones

Dying, Death, and Burial in the Military :~ 185

distinguished funerals, like Colonel Salomon Adams, who had his newborn daughter Anna Sophia buried in Magdeburg Cathedral in 1633, where her sandstone epitaph is preserved in the courtyard.

Until recently, no early modern military mass graves were known in the territories of the former Holy Roman Empire and questions concerning the state of the bodies, causes of death, how the corpses were arranged, or if they were indeed naked as the written and pictorial sources suggest had to be left unanswered. In 2007, 2008, and 2011, however, three mass graves from the Thirty Years War were discovered near Wittstock (Brandenburg), Alerheim (Bavaria), and Lützen (Saxony-Anhalt).[125] The finds tell different stories of military burial; the Wittstock and Lützen sites suggest different degrees of orderliness in the way the dead were treated, while the Alerheim pit evidences neglect. The Lützen grave contains the skeletons of forty-seven men who were buried in a pit measuring 3.5 m by 4.6 m and 2.5–3 m deep.[126] The victorious Swedes had ordered the authorities of the Lützen *Amt* to send two hundred men to bury the dead on the battlefield.[127] The way the bodies were deposited in the grave suggests that teams carried bodies from all directions and laid or dropped them into the pit without any particular order, so that the bodies were orientated differently, mostly on their backs, and their limbs were not adjusted in a particular position but rested where they fell.[128] The last two bodies that were laid into the grave had their arms outstretched at a right angle in the pose of the crucified Christ. The grave in Wittstock was dug for the remains of soldiers killed on 4 October 1636, which claimed between six and eight thousand victims.[129] The grave was the most orderly of the three and contained 110–25 bodies, closely packed into a pit measuring 6 m by 3.5 m, orientated east–west. In the bottom layers, the bodies had been stacked in two rows, heads pointing outward in a north–south orientation. To maximize the use of space, corpses were laid on top of the arms of the neighboring bodies and individual bodies were interspersed at a right angle on the legs of the layer below. The bodies in the top six layers were stacked in the grave, heads pointing eastward, bodies overlapping so that the heads of the men below rested between the legs of the men that were laid on top of them.[130] Most of the bodies were naked when they were put into the grave, but iron hooks and eyelets as well as a few buttons found with twenty-four skeletons indicate that these men were buried in some form of garment, probably their undershirts.[131] The third find, the Alerheim "bone pit" (*Knochengrube*), is a dump rather than a grave. It contained the remains of about eighty-five soldiers and boys who fell in the Battle of Alerheim (3 August 1645).[132] No coherent skeletons could be recovered as the bodies had been inhumed in an advanced state of decomposition. It had taken at least six weeks after the battle before the local count had found four men willing to carry out the gruesome task of interring 1,965 corpses and an unspecified number of horse cadavers "piece by piece" (*stuckweiß*) for 130 gulden.[133]

186 ❦ *Faith in War*

The graves substantiate the diverging descriptions of postmortem treatment in the written sources. The men who fell at Wittstock were buried in an organized effort by members of the Swedish army soon after the battle had been won. The careful way in which the bodies were placed in the grave may indicate a greater sense of dignity that the men who buried the bodies accorded the dead. In contrast, the bodies at Lützen were buried by the local population and the way that the dead were dragged, thrown, dropped, and stamped down into the grave suggests a less than respectful attitude toward them. The bone pit at Alerheim was just a clearance of cadavers that had been rotting in the summer heat for close to two months because nobody was willing to bury the corpses littering the fields and adjacent villages. But especially the Wittstock grave highlights another aspect of military funerary culture. Analysis of strontium isotopes from their tooth enamel has shown that the men came from all over Europe: Scandinavia and the Baltic, Scotland, Germany, Italy, and possibly Spain.[134] All had been buried in the same pit, irrespective of the side, or the cause, for which they had died. In this sense, the mass graves are powerful manifestations of the international character of the early modern military community. Catholics, Lutherans, and Calvinists shared their hope for salvation, albeit in different confessional modes, they had fought with and against one another, and in the end they also shared their grave.

Conclusion

The examination of attitudes to dying, death, and burial has revealed arguably the clearest deviations from civilian norms we have encountered in this study. While the historiography of death tends to agree on the importance of a good death and honorable burial in early modern culture, the military dealt with these matters in a flexible, pragmatic, and often negligent way. While the ideals of dying well were shared by soldiers, the evidence from the funeral sermons shows that even traditionally bad deaths could be interpreted in a favorable light, such that the evaluation of good and bad deaths was far more elastic than normative tracts on dying etiquette and historians working with these sources suggest. Soldiers had to live with the knowledge that their deaths were unlikely to meet the high standards of the *ars moriendi*. The solution that was offered by theologians was to stress the importance of a Christian lifestyle and constant contemplation of death, while the actual circumstances in which the soldier died were deemphasized. This was a new approach to death in the sixteenth century, but it bears repeating that the sanctification of life in preparation for death was not unique to the military but had originated among pious civilians.

Soldiers' attitudes toward death are difficult to extrapolate, but the bold defiance in the face of death that artists and songwriters attributed to soldiers is not typically reflected in other sources. In fact, many instances are described in which individuals and units reacted with panic and flight to impending death. From the perspectives of the military elites and civilian accounts it appears that the suffering and deaths of the common soldiers elicited little commiseration. In autobiographical accounts, the likeliness of the author's own death was usually ignored, but it seems that soldiers distinguished between deaths of military personnel, which were mostly treated with indifference or coarse humor, and the deaths of family members, which affected soldiers as much as anyone else.

Funerary rites remain opaque, as the scant evidence is conflicting. Whereas the consensus was that burying the dead was a necessity, if not a Christian obligation, in many instances corpses were neglected and left to rot. The chronic shortage of field preachers can explain why burial had to happen without religious ceremony, but the secular nature of military burial rites that have been described remains puzzling. It has been suggested that the declericalized military funeral may have been related to other popular movements against religious ceremonies that were fueled by anticlericalism. Conversely, it is possible that, in this instance, the comparison to the civilian context draws attention to seeming inconsistencies that were not perceived as such by soldiers themselves. They may have just accepted that these burial customs were contingent on their status as warriors. But how this was rationalized and whether it was thought to influence the afterlife remains uncertain. We can only note that the presence or absence of clerics at funerals was considered of no great importance in the military context. It also remains unclear how soldiers coped with the prospect of being interred haphazardly, or worse, not being buried at all.

When health, the strategies to limit violence, and magic failed, soldiers died as they had lived. They had to negotiate the norms and values surrounding death under unfavorable conditions. As in life, dead soldiers could be a burden to the civilian population, who had to endure the failures of an overstretched and inefficient military system to remove the bodies they left behind. Finally, the international community of Christian warriors continued to exist also in death, when men of all confessions, from all over Europe, friends and enemies, were laid to rest in the same pit.

Notes

1. The pioneering French studies are: Ariès, *Essais sur l'histoire de la mort* and *Geschichte des Todes*; Chaunu, *La Mort a Paris*; Vovelle, *La Mort et l'Occident*. See also Houlbrooke's collection of essays *Death, Ritual and Bereavement* and his monograph *Death, Religion and the Family*; Llewellyn, *The Art of Death*; Cressy, *Birth, Marriage and Death*; Holtz, "Die Unsicherheit des Lebens"; Koslofsky, *The Reformation of the Dead*; Harding, *The Dead and the Living*; Marshall, *Beliefs and the Dead*; Ohler, *Sterben und Tod im Mittelalter*; Kellehear, *A Social History of Dying*; Luebke, "Confessions of the Dead." Specifically for the military context

188 ❧ *Faith in War*

see Pietzcker, "Die Todesvorstellung im Landsknechts- und Soldatenlied"; Krusenstjern, "Seliges Sterben," esp. 483-87; Kaiser, "Ars moriendi."

2. Kellehear, *Social History of Dying*, 89.
3. Holtz, "Die Unsicherheit des Lebens," 137.
4. See Morgan, "Of Worms and War", 128.
5. Kaiser, "Ars moriendi," 324.
6. Forster, *Catholic Revival*, 108–9.
7. Wunderli and Broce, "The Final Moment before Death."
8. Luebke, "Confessions of the Dead."
9. Kenzler, "Religion, Status and Taboo," 150.
10. Ohler, *Sterben und Tod im Mittelalter*, 148; Muir, *Ritual*, 56.
11. Bergdolt, *Der schwarze Tod*, passim; Cohn, "The Black Death," 42–43.
12. Reich, *Leichpredigt*.
13. Eggelinck, *Majestät Brieff*, Hi[R].
14. Ibid., Giiii[R].
15. Eggelinck, *Majestät Brieff*, Hii[V]–Hiiii[R].
16. Ibid.
17. Angermüller, *Christliche Leichpredigt*. The circumstances of Haugwitz's death are related on pages Gii[V]-Giii[R].
18. Ibid., Bi[V], Giiii[R].
19. Ibid., Biiii[V].
20. Ibid., Gi[V]-Gii[R].
21. Ibid.
22. Ibid.
23. Reich, *Leichpredigt*.
24. Ibid., DiiiR-DivV.
25. Ibid., Diiii[R].
26. Ibid., Diiii[R]-Diiii[V]., Eiii[V]–Eiiii[R].
27. Ibid., E[R].
28. Van Dülmen, *Theater des Schreckens*.
29. Gräf, *Söldnerleben*, 143.
30. Westenrieder, "Tagebuch des Augustin von Fritsch," 171.
31. For the period of the Thirty Years War, see Outram, "The Socio-Economic Relations of Warfare," esp. 156–159.
32. Kirchhof, *Militaris Disciplina*, 108–9.
33. Hümmer, "Bamberg im Schweden-Kriege," 59.
34. Friesenegger, *Tagebuch*, 37.
35. Contamine, *War in the Middle Ages*, 299.
36. Monro, *Monro His Expedition*, part II, 63.
37. Bei der Wieden, *Leben im 16. Jahrhundert*, 54.
38. Luther, "In Peace and Joy I Now Depart."
39. See Chapter 2.
40. Luther, "Whether Soldiers, Too, Can Be Saved," 136–37.
41. Ibid., 136.
42. Fronsperger, *Geistliche KriegßOrdnung*, xv[V].
43. Musculus, *Beruff vnd Stand*. The insistence on a pious, repentant life was a characteristic of Lutheran orthodoxy (Holtz, "Unsicherheit des Lebens," 138).
44. Musculus, *Beruff vnd Stand*, Ciiii[R]–Ciiii[V].
45. Schwendi, "Kriegsdiskurs," 278.

Dying, Death, and Burial in the Military ∶∾ 189

46. See for example Puchner, *Christliche*, Biiii^V, E^R–Eiii^R.
47. Gräf, *Söldnerleben*, 93.
48. Monro, *Monro His Expedition*, part II, 7.
49. Ibid., part II, 48.
50. Thiessen, "Das Sterbebett als normative Schwelle," 648.
51. See Rogg, *Landsknechte*, 213–22.
52. Ibid., 214.
53. See for example the anonymous "Totentanz" depicted in Miller and Richards, *Landsknechte*, 57.
54. Albrecht Dürer, "Keyn ding hilfft fur den zeytling todt," depicted in Rogg, *Landsknechte*, 215.
55. See also the woodcuts by Wolfgang Strauch, "Landsknecht und Tod" (ca. 1555), in Strauß, *German Singleleaf Woodcut*, 21, and Jacob Binck, "Landsknecht kämpft mit dem Tod" (undated), in Blau, *Landsknechte*, part I, 121.
56. Letter from Gustavus Adolphus II to Donald Mackay, 15 March 1631. National Archives of Scotland (NAS), GD84/2/181.
57. Monro, *Monro His Expedition*, part II, 23–24.
58. Anon., *Des hochloblichen schwebischen punds Hörzug*, 7.
59. Anon., *Zwo warhaffte Zeitungen auß Böhmen*, Aii^V–Aiii^R.
60. Gräf, *Söldnerleben*, 136.
61. Ibid., 133.
62. Ibid., 134.
63. Letter from General Wahl to Colonel Westphalen, 24 January 1641, in Neuwöhner, *Im Zeichen des Mars*, 180.
64. Kirchhof, *Militaris Disciplina*, 147.
65. Jörg Graff, "Ein schön Lied."
66. Anon., "Dat ledlin van der slacht to Meiland," in Meinhardt, *Schwartenhals*, 62–63.
67. Anon., "Der Landsknecht Trommelreihen auf die Pavier Schlacht," in ibid., 72.
68. Anhalt, "Abschrift der Liste von des Feinds Macht," 501–504.
69. Jessen, *Der Dreißigjährige Krieg in Augenzeugenberichten*, 90.
70. Poyntz, *The Relation of Sydnam Poyntz*, 58.
71. Ibid.
72. Ibid., 59.
73. Schwendi, "Kriegsdiskurs," 231.
74. Kirchhof, *Militaris Disciplina*, 144.
75. Ulmschneider, *Götz von Berlichingen*, 77.
76. Ibid.
77. Peters, *Peter Hagendorf*, 53, 143.
78. Ibid., 47, 138.
79. Ibid.
80. Volkholz, *Jürgen Ackermann*, 16.
81. Peters, *Peter Hagendorf*, 47, 139.
82. Ibid., 138.
83. Ibid., 155.
84. Ibid., 142–43.
85. The Brandenburg squire Christoph von Bismarck used a very similar formula when recording the deaths of his children from the plague: "God grant them a peaceful rest and a joyous resurrection to the eternal life on Judgment Day" (Schmidt, "Tagebuch des Christoph von Bismarck," 76).

190 ❧ *Faith in War*

86. Müller, "Das Leben eines Söldners," 41–42.
87. Bambauer and Kleinholz, *Geusen und Spanier*, 20.
88. See for example Sabinus, *Eine Predigt Von der Victori*; Anon., *Victori-Schlüssel*; Theobald, *Heerpredigt*.
89. Christian IV, *Articuls Brieff*, Ei^V.
90. Fleming discussed the advantages of, as well as the cultural stigma attached to, cremation and briefly addressed burial etiquette (see below) in two and a half columns of *Der Vollkommene Teutsche Soldat* (375–76).
91. Schwendi, "Kriegsdiskurs," 235. The same advice is given in Dillich's *Kriegßbuch*, 298.
92. Bambauer and Kleinholz, *Geusen und Spanier*, 303.
93. Kannemann, *Christliche Leichenpredigt*, 43.
94. Anon., *Franckenthalische Belägerung*, 16. According to the account, this declaration of religious motivation moved the Worms Jesuits to scratch out the offending epitaph. What would turn into the Thirty Years War was, after all, not supposed to be openly labeled a "religious" war.
95. Anon., *Zwo warhaffte Zeitungen auß Böhmen*, Aiii^R.
96. Bambauer and Kleinholz, *Geusen und Spanier*, 27; Preuß, "Martin Schenk von Nideggen," 136.
97. Monro, *Monro His Expedition*, part I, 39.
98. Mendoza, *Theorica y practica de guerra*. An English translation, *Theorique and Practice of Warre*, was published in 1597, and a German translation, *Theorica et Practica Militaris*, in 1619.
99. Mendoza, *Theorique and Practice of Warre*, 115.
100. Mendoza, *Theorica et Practica Militaris*, 151.
101. Kirchhof, *Militaris Disciplina*, 146.
102. Richter (?), *Soldatenbüchlein*, etching 24, in Bussmann and Schilling, *1648*, vol. 3, 162.
103. Ibid.
104. Anon., *Zwo warhaffte Zeitungen auß Böhmen*, Aiii^R.
105. Anon., *Franckenthalische Belägerung*, 14.
106. Gräf, *Söldnerleben*, 133.
107. Bambauer and Kleinholz, *Geusen und Spanier*, 302–3.
108. Monro, *Monro His Expedition*, part II, 25.
109. Pietzcker, "Die Todesvorstellung im Landsknechts- und Soldatenlied," 4.
110. Anon., *Relation Oder gründliche Erzehlung*, Aiv^R.
111. Schönhuth, *Leben und Thaten des [...] Sebastian Schertlin*, 7.
112. Monro, *Monro His Expedition*, part II, 35.
113. See Bergdolt, *Der schwarze Tod*, 82. Bergdolt also makes the important point that clerics and monks died in such vast numbers because they did *not* forsake their flocks (ibid., 163). See also Harding, "Whose Body?" 183–84.
114. Olnitz, *Kriegs Ordnung*, I^R; Kirchhof, *Militaris Disciplina*, 179–80.
115. Kirchhof, *Militaris Disciplina*, 179–80.
116. Koslofsky, *Reformation of the Dead*, 86–89.
117. Ibid., 91.
118. Ibid., 92.
119. As quoted in Burschel, *Söldner*, 266.
120. Krebs and Maetschke, *Aus dem Leben*, 237–38.
121. Kirchhof, *Militaris Disciplina*, 180.
122. See Koslofsky, *Reformation of the Dead*, 101–2, 133.

Dying, Death, and Burial in the Military ✒ 191

123. Ibid., 134.
124. Peters, *Peter Hagendorf*, 36–37.
125. Descriptions and forensic analyses of the three graves and their contents can be found in several contributions to Meller and Schefzik, *Krieg*.
126. Friedrich and Schröder, "Das Massengrab in Lützen."
127. Stahl, "Nach der Schlacht von Lützen," 389.
128. Nicklisch et al., "Die 47 Soldaten aus dem Massengrab"; Friedrich and Schröder, "Das Massengrab in Lützen," 402.
129. Eickhoff, Grothe, and Jungklaus, "Söldnerbestattungen des Dreißigjährigen Krieges." I would like to thank Anja Grothe for her help and for providing me with copies of the articles she and her colleagues have published.
130. Ibid., 105–6.
131. Eickhoff, Grothe, and Jungklaus, "Memento Mori," 29.
132. Berg-Hobohm, "Ein anderer Blick auf die Schlacht von Alerheim"; Misterek, "Ein Massengrab aus der Schlacht von Alerheim."
133. Misterek, "Ein Massengrab aus der Schlacht von Alerheim," 366–67.
134. Eickhoff, Grupe, and Jungklaus, "Freund und Feind in einem Grab."

Epilogue

On 14 July 1650, Ottavio Piccolomini, the Duke of Amalfi, imperial pleni-potentiary, and generalissimo of the imperial army, staged a grand spectacle to celebrate the conclusion of the Nuremberg Execution Congress (*Nürnberger Executionstag*). It had assembled in the spring of the previous year to implement the Peace of Westphalia, which had been signed in May 1648. The Peace, which had taken years to negotiate, had left some important issues unresolved, one of the most pressing being the demobilization of the armies. The crowns were bankrupt but the troops—maybe a quarter of a million soldiers in the spring of 1648 and still probably 160,000 men and their families two years later—were owed vast sums in pay arrears and would not simply go away.[1] Queen Christina of Sweden and her military command were concerned that they might lose control over the army altogether and the threat by senior commanders in autumn 1649 to go rogue and occupy territories in their own right was taken very seriously.[2] On the other hand, the emperor and Sweden were hesitant to dismiss their troops because they were seen as the guarantors that the other side would honor their obligations according to the peace treaties.

The negotiations in Nuremberg had been led by Piccolomini on behalf of the Empire and for Sweden by Carl Gustav, Count Palatine of Zweibrücken, heir presumptive to the Swedish throne, and current commander in chief of the Swedish army, who, due to his inexperience in international diplomacy, was supported by field marshal Carl Gustav Wrangel, the incumbent governor general of Swedish-occupied Pomerania. Piccolomini and Wrangel had grown up in the war. Born into a Tuscan noble family in 1599, Piccolomini had already fought at White Mountain in 1620, and gained fame for his performance at Lützen (1632) and infamy for his involvement in the assassination of Albrecht von Wallenstein in 1634.[3] For the remainder of the war, he fought for both Habsburg houses, was made a count of the Empire in 1638 and Duke of Amalfi as well as a Spanish Grandee in 1639, and finally became commander in chief of the imperial army just before the war ended.

Wrangel had been born into a Baltic German family in 1613. His father Hermann had already been a Swedish general in the Polish wars and during the first few years of Sweden's involvement in Germany. Carl Gustav had spent his entire adult life as a successful soldier and briefly had been a naval commander in Swedish service before he succeeded Lennart Torstenson as Swedish generalissimo in 1646. His wife Anna Margareta's life had been dramatically affected by the war despite her noble descent.[4] Born into the Haugwitz family in Calbe in 1622, she had been orphaned when she was eight. Her parents had fallen on hard times and Anna Margareta and her four brothers and sisters ended up in the care of relatives who were struggling amid the chaos in the archbishopric of Magdeburg in 1630. Her siblings died and despite her Lutheran baptism, Anna Margareta was placed in the Marienstuhl cloister in Egeln, southwest of Magdeburg. In 1633, she met Elisabeth Juliana von Erpach, Countess Löwenstein, the widow of a Swedish colonel who had been killed earlier that year. The countess became her foster mother, and the women spent the following years in the Swedish army camp of Johann Banér until Anna Margareta met and married Carl Gustav Wrangel in 1640. The marriage was a happy one and at the end of her life she would feel blessed to have given birth to eleven living children who had all been baptized, five of whom reached adulthood.[5]

Her husband's namesake, the Count Palatine of Zweibrücken, had been born the same year as her.[6] His father Johann Casimir had fought on the losing side at White Mountain, which had prompted the family's exile in Sweden, as Carl Gustav's mother Katharina was Gustavus Adolphus's sister. He had been born in Nyköping Castle and despite his father's commitment to Calvinism, he was raised Lutheran, not least because this smoothed a potential ascent to the Swedish throne should Princess Christina die without issue. He had gathered experience as an officer in the concluding years of the war and had successfully negotiated the Swedish withdrawal from Bohemia, but his international diplomatic skills were yet untested when he arrived in Nuremberg on 4 May 1649 to negotiate the demobilization of the armies. The chief negotiators in Nuremberg thus all had been intimately affected by the war and experienced the effects of confessionalism at first hand.

The negotiations proved arduous and threatened to collapse at several stages over the next fourteen months. But while the official business was hard-nosed, private diplomacy was conducted in the evenings at carousals and banquets. Piccolomini had paid a first private visit to the Swedish chief negotiator a few days after he had arrived in Nuremberg, and over the following months, Ottavio and the two Carl Gustavs spent many evenings drinking. The count palatine had become used to this kind of sociability in Prague, where the negotiating enemy officers had frequently visited each other in their quarters on either side of the Vltava in the evenings.[7] In Nuremberg, major diplomatic accomplishments were celebrated with official banquets while setbacks were followed up by more private dinners where mutual goodwill could be demonstrated and strained relations repaired.[8] After the diplomats had finalized the interim recess in Sep-

194 ∾ *Faith in War*

tember 1649, the count palatine held a lavish banquet with 150 guests in the Nuremberg town hall, which had been decorated splendidly for the occasion.[9] That evening ended in a little burlesque: Carl Gustav and Piccolomini dressed up (or rather, "down") as military officers, Wrangel and Karl Ludwig of the Palatinate—the son of the "Winter King"—as NCOs, and they marched to the castle, where they fired some cannons and were comically demobilized by an imperial colonel. The following day, a magnificent fireworks display marked the end of the celebrations.[10]

In the following spring, negotiations reached a nadir to which the Swedish delegation reacted with further feasts. Wrangel, who had to leave for Pomerania in March 1650, invited the diplomats to a big banquet for his "valediction," but even this did not move matters forward. After threatening to end negotiations and depart, the Swedes finally managed to shift the imperial position toward a compromise, and they celebrated this success with a party in the countryside billed as a "dinner of familiarity" (*Vertraulichkeitsmahl*).[11] Sumptuous feasts in elaborate, purpose-built settings, often in combination with firework displays, became a regular occurrence at the Execution Congress in the fourteen months it sat in session. But the spectacle with which Piccolomini celebrated the eventual ratification of the main recess on 14 July 1650 was the most splendid and ambitiously organized by far.[12]

Piccolomini chose the rectangular firing range (ca. 165 m x 50 m) just outside the city as the site for his event.[13] On one end, he had a large wooden structure erected that had a large octagon at its center, about 17 m in diameter, from which two long rectangular side buildings extended on either side. This was the "House of Peace," and it was decorated with greenery and flowers, and adorned with the busts of Roman emperors and a huge imperial eagle perched atop the central cupula. The coats of arms of the Empire, France, and Sweden hung above the main portal of the central building. On the opposite end of the square, a wooden castle, the "House of Discordia," had been built. A tall column, painted to look like stone, stood between the two structures, about 30 m in front of the castle; on its top stood an allegory of Peace.

The 123 guests arrived in the afternoon, admired the buildings and the decorations, and were then ushered to their seats along three long tables by imperial colonels. The seating plan followed the hierarchy of imperial and international rank: in the middle of the table in the central octagon sat Carl Gustav and Piccolomini, next to them Wrangel and Alexander Erskine, the chief administrator ("president") of the Swedish army, and the imperial negotiators Isaac Volmar and Johann Crane, then followed the representatives of the Electors, and so forth.[14] At the tables in the two side buildings, noble men and women dined with Swedish and imperial officers. After Piccolomini's Jesuit confessor said a benediction, the guests ate and then the toasts began. They drank to the good friendship between the Empire, France, and Sweden, then to the emperor and the two royal majesties, then to the kings of Spain, Hungary, and Bohemia, then to the health of the archduke of Austria, Piccolomini, and the count palatine; the fifth, sixth, and seventh toasts were dedicated to the electors, the imperial princes, and the imperial cities. Finally, they toasted Wrangel and "all brave soldiers" of the Swedish crown, then the generals and the "valiant soldiers" of his imperial majesty.[15] Each toast was followed by gun salutes from cannon that had been set up near the wooden castle and across the River Pegnitz.

As dusk fell, the spectacle began. A large tent was carried onto the firing range and actors began to perform three dramatic scenes, the first of which saw Discordia, portrayed as a snake-haired hag, appear and complain that after a sojourn in England (where Charles I had been executed the previous year) she had now returned to Germany to find it in a dreadful state of harmony. Her plan to reignite conflict was foiled by the allegories of Concord, Peace, and Justice, who praised the audience for their commitment to reconciliation and goodwill.[16] The second scene portrayed a dialogue between a shepherd and a soldier whose initial haughtiness soon gave way to despairing fear of peacetime; he only knew war and had learned nothing that might be of use to him as a civilian. Finally, Discord reappeared on the ramparts of her castle and her son, Mars, performed a monologue in which he portrayed himself as a divine scourge, and after a pyrotechnically enhanced show battle, Discord lay in the smoking ruins of her castle, while Peace reigned triumphant on his column.

The Thirty Years War and with it the period of European inter-Christian confessional war was thus concluded in a manner that paralleled the way in which soldiers had conducted these conflicts for almost one and a half centuries: they ignored confession. Instead of the doctrinal intransigence that had caused such terrible strife across Europe, Christianized dramatizations of Greco-Roman allegories of vices and virtues entertained the guests. A Jesuit spoke a benediction, but while his exact words are unknown, we may assume that he did not lob sectarian grenades during the peace banquet. The celebration was predominantly organized according to the political hierarchy of the Holy Roman Empire, but not according to confessional differences or the side individuals had fought on. Protestants and Catholics, former allies and enemies all sat at the same tables, ate and drank merrily, and celebrated the peace.

Given that the preceding chapters have addressed a variety of questions and themes, it seems more appropriate to "take stock" than to "conclude." The book set out to examine religious attitudes that were characteristic of the military in the Reformation period and the time of religious pluralization that ensued. We have seen that the role of religion and religious mentalities were more complex than is usually allowed. Soldiers and civilians did not differ fundamentally in their religious beliefs. In contrast to certain areas of the civilian realm, however, confession did not play a significant role in the military. Soldiers' lives were predominantly unaffected by confessional considerations regarding who

196 ~: *Faith in War*

they fought with, for, or against. Military authorities tried to regulate religious matters and foster Christian behaviors, but were generally intent on providing an unconfessional legal and organizational structure. At the same time, universally Christian mindsets and values underpinned military society. In this respect and others, this book has provided a historiographical link between pre-Reformation warfare and the "tolerant" military attitudes that have been described for the later seventeenth century and beyond. It appears that confessional mindsets were not developed after the Thirty Years War; they had never been a characteristic of military life in the first place.

These insights also have implications for our perception of the period in general. Firstly, it affects the way we conceptualize "confessional" wars, as evidently, confession neither had much of an impact on the professional lives of the men who fought them nor on the way they conducted war. Secondly, there are consequences for the way we perceive of early modern confessional differences and their influence on everyday life. Despite doctrinal pluralization and change, we should not lose sight of the fact that, fundamentally, the same common Christian values lay at the core of all confessions. Precisely these shared principles and beliefs were amplified and fostered in the military, both on a structural level and in everyday life. The notion that confessionalism was *the* determining principle that shaped society and culture in the period is thus patently false. Confessional policies invariably ceded to the *ratio belli* and, while it was a grudging toleration on behalf of the warlords, the fact remains that confessionalization was generally not pursued and had no measurable impact on the military as a socio-professional environment.

It would be tempting to present the military as a "vector of toleration" in early modern society, but that would probably go too far.[17] The military setting made it possible for early modern Europeans to widely ignore confession as a factor of social (and antisocial) interaction, but it did not teach them how to coexist. People who joined the armies already had the wherewithal to lead "tolerant" lives because confessional oppositions lost meaning too easily for such dichotomies to have been deeply ingrained. It is important to stress again that this was not due to military society being confessionally confused or ill informed. All the soldiers whose beliefs we can reconstruct in any detail were conscious confessional Christians in their personal lives and even those individuals who engaged in confessional violence knew precisely what distinguished the faith they were attacking from their own. The military thus did not *make* people "tolerant," but by removing confession as a social principle, the military context shows that confessional divisions were not a fundamental aspect of early modern society and culture, but the effect of particular settings in which they became inscribed—or not. In this and other respects, for example regarding deathbed etiquette, the preceding chapters have spoken to the pervasive ability to negotiate putative axioms of early modern religion and culture in different contexts.

The great complexity of at times contradictive ideas and behaviors has become evident throughout. By the same token, categories like "Catholic," "Protestant," "confessional," "enemy," and so forth have proven to be only of limited use as they threaten to conceal cultural diversity. Approaching the early modern military under the premise of formal confessional and theological categories, for example, must lead to the conclusion that soldiers were abnormal in this respect because their behavior cannot be categorized in these terms. By paying attention to what the sources actually tell us and by remaining vigilant regarding our own presuppositions, however, we can hope to encounter the past more fully in its convolution and its contradictions. It is crucial not to gloss over these contradictions and inconsistencies because, while it may not make for neat arguments, it arguably yields a more representative view of the past.

Notes

1. Burkhardt, *Der Dreißigjährige Krieg*, 215; Wilson, *Europe's Tragedy*, 769.
2. Parker, *The Thirty Years War*, 168.
3. On Piccolomini's career see Alessandra Becucci, "Ottavio Piccolomini (1599–1656)."
4. Anna Margareta Wrangel penned an account of her life that was printed in her funeral sermon: Gerthen, *Christ=Gebührliche Klag= Trost= und Ehren=Gedächtnuß*, Bi[V]–Ciii[R]. See also Ailes, *Courage and Grief*, 17-22.
5. Gerthen, *Christ=Gebührliche Klag= Trost= und Ehren=Gedächtnuß*, Biiii[R].
6. "Karl X. Gustav," in *Allgemeine Deutsche Biographie*, vol. 15, 360–64.
7. Hengerer, *Kaiser Ferdinand III*, 271.
8. Laufhütte, "Das Friedensfest in Nürnberg 1650."
9. Schleder, *Theatrum Europæum VI*, 937–941.
10. Laufhütte, "Das Friedensfest in Nürnberg 1650."
11. Ibid.; see also the note in Schleder, *Theatrum Europæum VI*, 1048.
12. Ibid., 1071ff; Anon., *Das Kaiserliche Friedens Freudenmahl*; Anon., *Tempel des Friedens*.
13. A scale plan is included in Schleder, *Theatrum Europæum VI*, between pages 1078 and 1079.
14. Ibid., 1079.
15. Ibid., 1081.
16. Laufhütte, "Das Friedensfest in Nürnberg 1650."
17. Alec Ryrie planted this thought in my head when I presented in the History of Christianity lecture series at Durham in 2016.

Bibliography

Primary Sources

Manuscript Sources

Hauptstaatsarchiv Düsseldorf:
HStA Jülich-Berg II 249a.

Johannes a Lasco Bibliothek Emden:
Documents relating to Johannes Northausen: Arch JALB 503, Nr. 15.

National Archives of Scotland:
Letter from Gustavus Adolphus II to Donald Mackay, 15 March 1631 GD84/2/181.

Staatsarchiv Marburg:
Letters between soldiers and civilians, Summer 1626. Best. M 1 Nr. 275.

Printed Sources

Abelinus, Johann Philipp. *Theatrum Europæum*, vol. 1. Frankfurt a. M., 1635.
———. *Theatrum Europæum Vierdter Theil*. Frankfurt a. M., 1643.
Alzog, J., ed. "Itinerarium oder Raisbüchlin des P. Conrad Burger, Conventual des Cisterzienser=Klosters Thennenbach und Beichtiger des Frauen=Klosters Wonnenthal vom J. 1641 bis 1678." *Freiburger Diözesanarchiv* 5 (1870): 247–359.
Anhalt, Christian von. "Abschrift der Liste von des Feinds Macht und Anzahl an Kriegsvolck." In *Quellen zur Vorgeschichte und zu den Anfängen des Dreißigjährigen Krieges*, edited by G. Lorenz, 501–11. Darmstadt, 1991.
Angermüller, Johann Jacob. *Christliche Leichpredigt / vnd Bußpredigt / Bey dem Adelichen Begräbniß / Des weiland WolEdlen / Gestrengen / vnd Mannhaften Johann Dietterichen von Haugwitz [...] gehalten*. Leipzig, 1624.
Anon. "Acta Mansfeldiaca post pugnam Pragensem." In Anon., *Bayrischer Feldtzug Welcher Gestalt der Hertzog in Bayern alle Flecken / Schlösser / Dörffer vnd Städt / im Ländtlein ob der Enß / Oesterreich vnd Böheimen eingenommen vnd erobert habe*. N.p., 1621.
Anon. "Acta Maximiliani." In *Das frühe Christentum bis zum Ende der Verfolgungen*, edited by P. Guyot and R. Klein, vol. 1, 166–77. Darmstadt, 1997.

Bibliography · 199

Anon. *Das Kaiserliche Friedens Freudenmahl.* N.p., 1650.
Anon. "Ein new Klagliedt eines alten deutschen Kriegsknechts wider die grewliche vnd vnerhörte Kleidung der Pluderhosen." In *Der Schwartenhals—Lieder der Landsknechte*, edited by Albert Meinhardt, 24–25. Heidenheim, 1976.
Anon. "Von dem König aus Frankreich" (ca. 1525). In *Der Schwartenhals—Lieder der Landsknechte*, edited by Albert Meinhardt, 12–13. Heidenheim, 1976.
Anon. *Auffrichtiger Teutscher Soldaten Regul, Oder Kurtze Erinnerung an den Teutschen Evangelischen Kriegßmann.* N.p., 1620.
Anon. *Copey eines Schreibens Auß Magdeburgk// darinnen kürtzliche doch gewisse/ und unpartheiische Relation zubefinden.* Eisleben, 1631.
Anon. *Des hochloblichen schwebischen punds Hörzug im landt zu Wirtenberg.* N.p., 1519.
Anon. *Ein Lied für die Landsknecht gemacht.* N.p., 1546.
Anon. *Franckenthalische Belägerung.* Frankenthal [?], 1621.
Anon. *Hispanischer Arragonischer Spiegel.* N.p., 1599.
Anon. *Kurtze Relation, Was massen die Meuterey vnnd Vnerhörte Verrhäterey / schändtlich Vbergebung der Statt Bonn [. . .] sich zugetragen.* Edenberg [?], 1584.
Anon. *Kurtze vnd warhafftige Anzeig vnd bericht / Was sich innerhalb drey Monaten nechsthin in dem Niderländischen Westphelischen Creiß verloffen.* N.p., 1599.
Anon. *Kurtzer Begrieff / Der Kriegs Ordnung / So vnter den Herrn Staden [. . .] gehalten wird.* Rinteln, 1625.
Anon. *Lacrymæ Germaniæ: OR, The Teares of Germany.* London, 1638.
Anon. *Newe Zeitung [. . .] welcher gestaldt die Papisten durch die vngehewren Gülgische Kriegsgurgel das Euangelium Jesu Christi [. . .] zu Brysich am Reyn [. . .] grewlich verfolget.* N.p., 1587.
Anon. *Reformation der königlichen Schloßkirchen zu Prag.* Prague. 1621.
Anon. *Regiments Capitulation Und Bestallungs Brieff Der Cavaglieria [. . .] Benebens Der Infanterien.* Erfurt, 1632.
Anon. *Relation Oder gründliche Erzehlung, Wie die Ernstliche FeldtSchlacht [. . .] nahend dem Dorff Wittenweyher [. . .] sich Erstlich zugetragen.* N.p., 1638.
Anon. *Tempel des Friedens und gegenüber gesetztes Castel des Unfriedens.* N.p., 1650.
Anon. *The Invasions of Germanie.* London, 1638.
Anon. *Victori-Schlüssel.* N.p., 1631.
Anon. *Warhaffter Bericht / Von der Belägerung vnd mit gestürmter hand Eroberung der Stadt Pilsen inn Behem.* N.p., 1618 [?].
Anon. *Wahrhafftige vnd kurtze Bericht ynn der Summa. Wie es yetzo [. . .] ynn eröberung der Stad Rom ergangen ist.* N.p., 1527.
Anon. *Warhafftige: Zeytungen / Von der Belegerung / vnnd eynemung / der Statt Neuß.* Augsburg 1586.
Anon. *Zwo warhaffte Zeitungen auß Böhmen.* N.p., 1618.
Augustin, Caspar. *Der newen Cornet vnd Fahnen / welche in Augspurg der Außgewählten Burgerschafft gegeben worden.* Augsburg, 1633.
Bacon, L. W., and N. H. Allen, eds. *The Hymns of Martin Luther.* New York, 1883.
Bambauer, Klaus, and Hermann Kleinholz, eds. *Geusen und Spanier am Niederrhein: Die Ereignisse der Jahre 1586–1632 nach den zeitgenössischen Chroniken der Weseler Bürger Arnold von Anrath und Heinrich von Weseken.* Wesel, 1992.
Beccarie de Pavie, Raimond de. *Kriegs=Practica.* Frankfurt a. M., 1619.
Behm, Martin. *Kriegesman, Das ist: Gründlicher Vnterricht, wie sich ein Christlicher Kriegsman verhalten solle.* Leipzig, 1593.

200 ~: *Bibliography*

Bei der Wieden, Brage, ed. *Leben im 16. Jahrhundert: Lebenslauf und Lieder des Hauptmanns Georg Niege.* Berlin, 1996.

Botvidi, Johannes. *Etliche Gebete / Welche im Schwedischen Kriegslager gebräuchlich.* N.p., 1630.

Breul, Tilemann. *MILES CHRISTIANVS: Christlicher Kriegsman.* N.p., 1573.

Bromhall, Thomas. *An History of Apparitions, Oracles, Prophecies, and Predictions.* London, 1658.

Bruhns, Alfred, ed. *Tagebuch der Truchsessischen Wirren im Herzogtum Westfalen 1583/84.* Brilon, 1987.

Brunmüller, Caspar. *Von dem Erschrockenlichen [. . .] laster dem Gottslesteren.* N.p., 1560.

Buonaparte, Jacopo, "*Il sacco di Roma.*" In *Il sacco di Roma del MDXXVII: Narrazioni di contemporanei,* edited by Carlo Milanesi, 245–408. Florence, 1867.

Carve, Thomas. *Reysbüchlein / Deß Ehrwürdigen Herrn Thomæ Carve Jrrländers.* Mainz, 1640.

Charles V. *Die Peinliche Gerichtsordnung Kaiser Karls V.,* edited by Friedrich-Christian Schroeder. Stuttgart, 2000.

———. *Artickell wie sich die kriegslewt Edell vnnd vnedel ym zug wider den Turcken vorhalden sollen.* N.p., 1541.

———. *Römischer Keiserlicher Maiestet bestallung [. . .] auff den jetzigen Zugk des 1544. Jars.* N.p., 1544.

———. *Römischer Kayserlicher Maiestat Declaration: Wider Hertzog Friderichen Churfürsten von Sachsen unnd Landtgraff Philipsen von Hessen.* Regensburg, 1546.

Clairvaux, Bernard of. *In Praise of the New Knighthood—A Treatise on the Knights Templar and the Holy Places of Jerusalem.* Translated by Conrad Greenia, introduction by Malcolm Barber. Trappist, KY, 2000.

Christian IV. *Articuls Brieff.* Glückstadt, 1638 [1625].

Dillich, Wilhelm. *KriegßBuch.* Kassel, 1608.

Droste, Heiko, and Arne Losman, eds. *Jöns Månsson Teitt, Kriegszüge mit Gustav II Adolph, 1621–1632.* Retrieved 18 January 2024 from http://www.fh-augsburg.de/~harsch/germanica/Chronologie/17Jh/Teitt/tei_kri0.html.

Dudík, Beda, ed. *Tagebuch des feindlichen Einfalls der Schweden in das Markgrafthum Mähren während ihres Aufenthalts in der Stadt Olmütz 1642–1650, geführt von dem Olmützer Stadtschreiber und Notar Magister Friedrich Flade.* Vienna, 1884.

Eberlin von Günzburg, Johann. *Mich wundert das kein gelt ihm land ist.* N.p., 1524.

Eggelinck, Wilhelm. *Himmlischer Majestät Brieff.* Braunschweig, 1627.

Erasmus of Rotterdam. "A Complaint of Peace Spurned and Rejected by the Whole World." In *Collected Works of Erasmus,* vol. 27, translated by Betty Radice, edited by A. H. T. Levi, 292–322. Toronto, 1986.

———. "Education of a Prince." In *Collected Works of Erasmus,* vol. 27, translated by Neil M. Cheshire and Michael J. Heath, edited by A. H. T. Levi, 203–88. Toronto, 1986.

———. "Julius Excluded from Heaven: A Dialogue." In *Collected Works of Erasmus,* vol. 27, translated by Michael J. Heath, edited by A. H. T. Levi, 168–97. Toronto, 1986.

———. "Dulce bellum inexpertis." In *Collected Works of Erasmus,* vol. 35, translated by Denis L. Drysdall, edited by J. N. Grant, 399–439. Toronto, 2005.

Fabricius, Jacob. *Etliche Gebet / so Königl. Majest. Zu Schweden Kriegsheer neben den Psalmen Davids vnnd der Christlichen Litaney / von den Feld Predigern gebrauchet / vnd der Soldatesca fürgebettet werden.* Augsburg, 1632.

Feyerabend, Sigmund, ed. *Theatrum Diabolorum.* Frankfurt a. M., 1575.

Fiedler, Constantin. *Miles Christianus, Ein Christlicher Kriegsmann, Das ist, Leich und Ehren Predigt* [...] *Bey der Volckreichen vnd Ansehnlichen Begrebnuß* [...] *Herrn Wilhelm von Calcheims, genandt Lohausen* [...] *gehalten.* Rostock, 1640.

Fleming, Hannß Friedrich von. *Der Vollkommene Teutsche Soldat.* Leipzig, 1726.

Frauenholz, Eugen von, ed. *Lazarus von Schwendi: Der erste Verkünder der allgemeinen Wehrpflicht.* Hamburg, 1939.

Franck, Sebastian. *Das Kriegbüchlin des frides.* Ulm [?], 1539.

Friesenegger, Maurus. *Tagebuch aus dem 30jährigen Krieg.* Edited by W. Mathäser. Munich, 2007.

Fronsperger, Leonhart. *Fünff Bücher: Von Kriegß Regiment vnd Ordnung.* Frankfurt a. M., 1555.

———. *Kriegs Ordnung Vnd Regiment samt derselbigen befehl.* Frankfurt a. M., 1564.

———. *Von Kayserlichem Kriegsrechten Malefitz vnd Schuldhändlen.* Frankfurt a. M., 1565.

———. *Geistliche KriegßOrdnung.* Frankfurt a. M., 1565.

———. *Von Kayserlichem Kriegsrechten Malefitz vnd Schuldhändlen.* Frankfurt a. M., 1566.

Gerthen, Johann Henrich. *Christ=Gebührliche Klag= Trost= und Ehren=Gedächtnuß Der Weyland Hochgebohrnen Gräffin und Frauen / Frauen Annæ Margrethæ Wrangelin.* Stockholm, 1673.

Guicciardini, Luigi. *The Sack of Rome.* Translated by James H. McGregor. New York, 1993.

Gräf, Holger Th., ed. *Söldnerleben am Vorabend des Dreißigjährigen Krieges. Lebenslauf und Kriegstagebuch 1617 des hessischen Obristen Caspar von Widmarckter.* (Beiträge zur Hessischen Geschichte 16). Marburg, 2000.

Graff, Jörg. "Ein Schön Lied / von der Kriegsleut Orden" (ca. 1520). In *Der Schwartenhals—Lieder der Landsknechte,* edited by Albert Meinhardt, 9–10. Heidenheim, 1976.

Grimmelshausen, Hans Jacob Christoffel von. *Simplicissimus Teutsch.* Edited by Dieter Breuer. Frankfurt a. M., 2005.

Gustavus II Adolphus, *Schwedisches Kriegs=Recht.* Strasbourg, 1644.

Hallwig, Hermann, ed. *Wallenstein's Ende, Briefe und Acten.* 2 vols. Leipzig, 1879.

Herrmann, Fritz, ed. *Aus tiefer Not: Hessische Briefe und Berichte aus der Zeit des Dreißigjährigen Krieges.* (Hessische Volksbücher 26–27). Friedberg, 1916.

Hocker, Johann Ludwig. *Pastorale Castrense Oder Nützlich= und treuer Unterricht Vor neu=angehende Feld=Prediger.* Frankfurt a. M., 1710.

Hümmer, F. K., ed. "Bamberg im Schweden-Kriege." *Bericht des Historischen Vereins für die Pflege der Geschichte des ehemaligen Fürstbistums Bamberg* 52 (1890): 1–168; 53 (1891): 169–230.

Jessen, Hans, ed. *Der Dreißigjährige Krieg in Augenzeugenberichten.* Munich, 1971.

Junghans von der Olnitz, Adam. *KriegsOrdnung / zu Wasser vnd Landt.* Cologne, 1598.

Kalkum genannt Lohausen, Wilhelm von. *Zweiter Discours Von kriegs rechtmessigen endursachen.* Printed with: Wilhelm von Kalkum genannt Lohausen. *C. Crisp. Sal. Von Catilinischer rottierung und Jugurthischem Krieg.* Bremen, 1629.

Kannemann, Peter. *Christliche Leichenpredigt über das schöne Trostsprüchlein.* Halberstadt, 1639.

Kirchhof, Hans Wilhelm. *Militaris Disciplina.* Edited by Bodo Gotzkowsky. Stuttgart, 1976.

———. *Wendunmuth.* Edited by Herman Österley. Tübingen, 1869.

Kleinholz, Hermann, ed. *Die Protokolle des Presbyteriums der reformierten Gemeinde in Wesel 1612–1624.* Wesel, 2012.

202 ~: Bibliography

Klimesch, P. P., ed. "Zacharias Bandhauers deutsches Tagebuch der Zerstörung Magdeburgs 1631." *Archiv für Kunde österreichischer Geschichts-Quellen* 16 (1856): 239–319.

Knaust, Heinrich. *Fünff Bücher, Von der Göttlichen vnd Edlenn Gabe der Philosophischen, hochthewren vnd wunderbaren Kunst, Bier zu brawen.* Erfurt, 1614.

Krebs, Julius, and Ernst Maetschke, eds. *Aus dem Leben des kaiserlichen Feldmarschalls Grafen Melchior von Hatzfeldt.* Vol. 2, *1632–36.* Breslau, 1926.

Lampe, Johann Christoph. *Der gewissenhaffte Feld-Prediger.* Braunschweig, 1707.

Leslie, Alexander. *Articles and Ordinance of Warre.* Edinburgh, 1640.

Lorenz, G., ed. *Quellen zur Vorgeschichte und zu den Anfängen des Dreißigjährigen Krieges.* Darmstadt, 1991.

Lünig, Johan Christian, ed. *Corpus Iuris Militaris.* 2 vols. Leipzig, 1723.

Luther, Martin. "Against the Robbing and Murdering Hordes of Peasants." In *Luther's Works*, vol. 46, *The Christian in Society III*, edited by R. C. Schultz and H. T. Lehmann, 45–55. Philadelphia, 1967.

―――. "Whether Soldiers, Too, Can be Saved." In *Luther's Works*, vol. 46, *The Christian in Society III*, edited by R. C. Schultz and H. T. Lehmann, 93–137. Philadelphia, 1967.

―――. *Gesamtausgabe, Tischreden.* Vol. 2. Weimar, 1913.

―――. *Gesamtausgabe, Tischreden.* Vol. 4. Weimar, 1916.

―――. "In Peace and Joy I Now Depart." In *The Hymns of Martin Luther*, edited by L. W. Bacon and N. H. Allen, 58. New York, 1883.

Machiavelli, Niccolò. *The Book of the Art of War.* Edited and translated by Peter Bondanella and Mark Musa. London, 1979.

Maximilian I of Bavaria, *Landtgebott wider die Aberglauben, Zauberey, Hexerey und andere sträffliche Teufelskünste.* Munich, 1611.

Meinhardt, Albert, ed. *Der Schwartenhals—Lieder der Landsknechte.* Heidenheim. 1976.

Mendoza, Bernardino de. *Theorica y practica de guerra.* Madrid, 1595.

―――. *Theorique and Practice of Warre.* Translated by Edward Hoby. London, 1597.

―――. *Theorica et Practica Militaris.* Translated by Lucas Jennis. Frankfurt a. M., 1619.

Mendoza, Francisco. *Des Hispanischen Kriegsvolcks Obersten / Don Francisci de Mendoza Copey Schreibens An den Bischoff zu Paderborn.* Erfurt, 1599.

Mengering, Arnold. *Perversa Ultimi Seculi Militia Oder Kriegs-Belial.* Meissen, 1641.

―――. *Letzte Belagerung und jammerliche Erober- und Zerstörung der alten Stadt Magdeburg.* Magdeburg, 1689.

Milanesi, Carlo, ed. *Il sacco di Roma del MDXXVII: Narrazioni di contemporanei.* Florence, 1867.

Minderer, Raymund. *Medicina Militaris.* Augsburg, 1627.

Monro, Robert. *Monro His Expedition With the Worthy Scots Regiment.* London, 1637.

Musculus, Andreas. *Vom Hosen Teuffel.* In *Teufelbücher in Auswahl*, edited by Ria Stambaugh, vol. 4, 1–31. Berlin, 1978.

―――. *Vom Gotslestern.* In *Teufelbücher in Auswahl*, edited by Ria Stambaugh, vol. 4, 33–79. Berlin, 1978.

―――. *Vom beruff vnd stand der Kriegsleuth.* Frankfurt (Oder), 1558.

Musculus, Wolfgang. *Vermanung and den Teütschen vnnd Evangelischen Kriegßman.* N.p., 1546.

Northausen, Johannes. *Erbermliche Aber warhaffte vnnd Instrumentirte anzeig vnnd beschreibung / was nach der Verrätherischen auffgebung der Statt Bonn der Bischoff zu Lüttig / durch seine befelchshabere gegen einem frommen Kirchen diener da selbst fürnemmen lassen.* N.p., 1584.

Pape, Ambrosius. *Bettel vnd Garteteuffel.* Magdeburg, 1586.

Pappus von Tratzberg, Petrus. *Holländisch Kriegs-Recht / vnd Articuls=Brieff.* Strasbourg, 1643 [1632].

Peters, Jan. *Peter Hagendorf—Tagebuch eines Söldners aus dem Dreißigjärigen Krieg.* 2nd edn. Göttingen, 2012.

Pfeilsticker, Karl. *Tagebuch des Hans Conrad Lang, Bürgers von Isny und Beisitzers von Biberach, Ulm und Memmingen, weiland Kriegskommisär in kaiserliche, schwedischen und spanischen Dienstenaus den Jahren 1601–1659.* Isny, 1930.

Possevino, Antonio. *Il Soldato Christiano.* Macerata, 1583.

———. *Platica spiritual para el soldado christiano.* Antwerp, 1588.

Poyntz, Sydnam. *The Relation of Sydnam Poyntz.* Edited by A. T. S. Goodrick. London, 1908.

Puchner, Stephan. *Christliche / Heilsame vnnd sehr nützliche Gebetlein / Neben einem bericht / wie ein Kriegsman sich verhalten sol damit er Christlich leben vnd selig Sterben könne.* Berlin, 1616.

Raymond, Thomas. *Autobiography of Thomas Raymond and Memoirs of the Family of Guise of Elmore, Gloucestershire.* Edited by G. Davies. London, 1917.

Reich, Paul. *Leichpredigt: Bey dem Leichbegengnüs des Weiland Edlen Juncker Bernhard von Miltitz [. . .] gethan.* N.p., 1615.

Reißner, Adam. *Historia der Herren Georg und Kaspar von Frundsberg.* Frankfurt a. M., 1572.

Rennemann, Andreas. *Privilegia vnd Freyheiten der Soldatescha.* N.p., 1630.

Richter, Christian [?]. *Soldatenbüchlein.* N.p., 1642.

Rummel (Rhumelius), Johannes Pharamundus. *Medicamenta Militaria Dogmatica, Hermetica et Magica. Das ist: Außerlesene und experimentirte Kriegs Artzney.* Nuremberg, 1632.

Sabinus. *Eine Predigt Von der Victori.* N.p., 1620.

Sachs, Hans. "Der Teuffel lest kein Landsknecht mehr in die Helle faren." In *Die deutsche komische und humoristische Dichtung seit Beginn des XVI. Jahrhunderts bis auf unsere Zeit*, edited by I. Hub, vol. 1, 57–60. Nuremberg, 1854.

Sailly, Thomas. *Guidon et pratique sprituelle du soldat chrêtien.* Antwerp, 1590.

———. *Verscheyden litanien tot ghebruyck des catholijken leghers.* Antwerp, 1595.

Saxony, John of, and Philipp of Hesse. *Der Durchleüchtigst vnd Durchleüchtigen Hochgebornen Fürsten vnnd Herren / Hernn // Johanns Friderichen Hertzogen zu Sachssen [. . .] Vnd Herrn Philipsen / Landgrauen zu Hessen [. . .] Bestendige vnd warhafftige / verantwortung.* N.p., 1546.

Saxony, Johann Georg of. *Articuls=Brief / Darauff [. . .] Johann Georgen / Hertzogen zu Sachssen [. . .] Die Hochdeutzschen Knechte [. . .] schweren sollen.* N.p., 1631.

Scherer, Georg. *Ein bewerte Kunst vnd Wundsegen.* Ingolstadt, 1595.

Schleder, Johann Georg. *Theatrum Europæum VI.* Frankfurt a. M., 1663.

Schmidt, Georg. "Das Tagebuch des Christoph von Bismarck aus den Jahren 1625–1640." *Thüringisch-Sächsische Zeitschrift für Geschichte und Kunst* 5 (1915): 68–98.

Schönhuth, Ottmar F. H., ed. *Leben und Thaten des weiland wohledlen und gestrengen Herrn Sebastian Schertlin von Burtenbach, durch ihn selbst deutsch beschrieben.* Münster, 1858.

Schöpper, Jacob. *Christlicher Bericht: Wie sich ein Christlicher Kriegesman in einem Christlichen / gebürlichem vnnd notwendigem Kriege Christlich und gebürlich halten sol.* Erfurt, 1587.

Schottin, Reinhold, ed. *Tagebuch des Erich Lassota von Steblau. Nach einer Handschrift der von Gersdorff-Weichaschen Bibliothek zu Bautzen herausgegeben und mit einer Einleitung und Bemerkungen begleitet.* Halle, 1866.

204 ❧ Bibliography

Schwendi, Lazarus von. "Diskurs und Bedenken über den Zustand des hl. Reiches von 1570." In *Lazarus von Schwendi: Der erste Verkünder der allgemeinen Wehrpflicht*, edited by Eugen von Frauenholz, 161–91. Hamburg, 1939.

———. "Kriegsdiskurs." In *Lazarus von Schwendi: Der erste Verkünder der allgemeinen Wehrpflicht*, edited by Eugen von Frauenholz, 192–287. Hamburg, 1939.

Scultetus, Abraham. *Kurtzer / aber Schrifftmäßiger Bericht / Von den Götzen Bildern*. Heidelberg, 1620.

———. *Historische Erzehlung Von dem Lauff des Lebens [. . .] D. Abraham Sculteti*. Emden, 1628.

Solms, Reinhard von. "*Kriegsbuch*." N.p., 1559.

Spangenberg, Cyriacus. *AdelsSpiegel*. Schmalkalden, 1594.

Staden, Hans. *Wahrhafftig Historia vnnd beschreibung einer Landtschafft [. . .] in der Newen welt America*. Frankfurt a. M., 1557.

Staricius, Johannes. *HeldenSchatz*. Frankfurt, 1615.

Stickel, Burkhard. *Tagebuch*. In *Schwäbische Landsknechte* (Schwäbische Lebensläufe 11), edited by Helmut Breimesser and Helmut Christmann, 117–44. Heidenheim, 1972.

Tertullian. *Of the Crown*. In *Tertullian Vol I.: Apologetic and Practical Treatises*, edited by C. Dodgson, 158–86. Oxford, 1842.

Tettau, W. J. A. von, ed. "Erlebnisse eines deutschen Landsknechts (1484–1493) von ihm selbst beschrieben." *Mittheilungen des Vereins für die Geschichte und Alterthumskunde von Erfurt* 4 (1869): 1–51.

Theobald, Zacharias. *Heerpredigt Auß dem schönen Gebet deß theuren Feld Obristen Judæ Maccabæi*. Friedberg, 1618.

Thodaenus, Christoph. *Threni Magdæburgi*. Hamburg, 1632.

Turner, James. *Memoirs of His Own Life and Times*. Edinburgh, 1829.

Ulmschneider, Helgard, ed. *Götz von Berlichingen: Mein Fehd und Handlungen*. Sigmaringen, 1981.

Vincent, Philip. *The Lamentations of Germany*. London, 1638.

Volkholz, Robert, ed. *Jürgen Ackermann: Kapitän beim Regiment Alt-Pappenheim*. Halberstadt, 1895.

Wallhausen, Johann Jacob von. *Kriegskunst zu Fuß*. Leuwarden 1630 [1615].

Watts, William. "The Famovs Victorie of Leipsich." In *The Swedish Discipline*. London, 1632.

———. *The Swedish Discipline*. London, 1632.

———. *The Swedish Intelligencer—The First Part*. London, 1632.

———. *The Svvedish Intelligencer—The Second Part*. London, 1632.

———. *The Swedish Intelligencer—The Third Part*. London, 1633.

Weinsberg, Herman von. *Das Buch Weinsberg*. Online edition: *Die autobiographischen Aufzeichnungen Hermann Weinsbergs—Digitale Gesamtausgabe*. Retrieved 18 January 2024 from www.weinsberg.uni-bonn.de.

Westenrieder, Lorenz von, ed. "Tagebuch des Augustin von Fritsch (Obersten und Commendanten der Stadt Weyden) von seinen Thaten und Schicksalen im dreyßigjährigen Kriege." In *Beyträge zur vaterländischen Historie, Geographie, Staatistik, und Landwirthschaft*, vol. 4, 105–91. Munich, 1792.

Whitehead, Neil L., and Michael Harbsmeier, eds and trans. *Hans Staden's True History. An Account of Cannibal Captivity in Brazil*. Durham, NC, 2008.

Winter, Franz, ed. "Möser's Aufzeichnungen über den Dreißigjährigen Krieg." *Geschichtsblätter für Stadt und Land Magdeburg* 9 (1874): 11–69; 165–220.

Secondary Literature

Abric, Jean Claude. "Central System, Peripheral Core: Their Functions and Roles in the Dynamics of Social Representations." *Papers on Social Representations* 2, no. 2 (1993): 75–78.

Ailes, Mary Elizabeth. *Courage and Grief: Women and Sweden's Thirty Years War*. Lincoln, NE, 2018.

Angenendt, Arnold. *Toleranz und Gewalt: das Christentum zwischen Bibel und Schwert*. Münster, 2007.

Ariès, Phillippe. *Essais sur l'histoire de la mort en occident du Moyen Age a nos jours*. Paris, 1975.

———. *Geschichte des Todes*. Munich, 1982.

Arndt, Johannes. *Das Heilige Römische Reich und die Niederlande 1566–1648*. Cologne, 1998.

Asch, Ronald G. *The Thirty Years War: The Holy Roman Empire and Europe 1618–48*. Basingstoke, 1997.

Asche, Matthias. "Krieg, Militär und Migration in der Frühen Neuzeit: Einleitende Beobachtungen zum Verhältnis von horizontaler und vertikaler Mobilität in der kriegsgeprägten Gesellschaft Alteuropas." In *Krieg, Militär und Migration in der Frühen Neuzeit*, edited by Matthias Asche et al., 11–36. Münster, 2008.

Asche, Matthias, and Anton Schindling, eds. *Das Strafgericht Gottes: Kriegserfahrungen und Religion im Heiligen Römischen Reich Deutscher Nation im Zeitalter des Dreißigjährigen Krieges*. Münster, 2001.

Asche, Matthias, et al., eds. *Krieg, Militär und Migration in der Frühen Neuzeit*. Münster, 2008.

Auffarth, Christoph. "Alle Tage Karneval? Reformation, Provokation und Grobianismus." In *Glaubensstreit und Gelächter: Reformation und Lachkultur im Mittelalter und in der Frühen Neuzeit*, edited by Christoph Auffarth and Sonja Kerth, 79–105. Münster, 2008.

Auffarth, Christoph, and Sonja Kerth, eds. *Glaubensstreit und Gelächter: Reformation und Lachkultur im Mittelalter und in der Frühen Neuzeit*. Münster, 2008.

Autenrieth, Bernd. *Samuel Gerlach: Feldprediger, Hofprediger, Prälat (1609–1683). Ein schwäbischer Pfarrer zwischen Mecklenburg, Holstein, Danzig und Württemberg*. Stuttgart, 2000.

Bächtold, Hans. *Deutscher Soldatenbrauch und Soldatenglaube*. Strasburg, 1917.

Bacon, Isaac. "Versuch einer Klassifizierung altdeutscher Zaubersprüche und Segen." *Modern Language Notes* 67 (1952): 224–32.

Bainton, Richard H. *Christian Attitudes toward War and Peace: A Historical Survey and Critical Re-Evaluation*. Nashville, 1960.

Baldwin, Martha R. "Toads and Plague: Amulet Therapy in Seventeenth Century Medicine." *Bulletin of the History of Medicine* 67, no. 2 (1993): 227–47.

Barudio, Günther. *Der Teutsche Krieg*. Frankfurt a. M., 1998.

Bauer, Franz J. "Von Tod und Bestattung in alter und Neuer Zeit." *Historische Zeitschrift* 254, no. 1 (1992): 1–31.

Baumann, Reinhard. *Georg von Frundsberg, der Vater der Landsknechte*. Munich, 1984.

———. *Landsknechte: Ihre Geschichte und Kultur vom späten Mittelalter bis zum Dreißigjährigen Krieg*. Munich, 1994.

206 ❧ *Bibliography*

———. "Süddeutschland als Söldnermarkt". In *Söldnerlandschaften. Frühneuzeitliche Gewaltmärkte im Vergleich*, edited by Benjamin Hitz and Philippe Rogger, 67-83. Berlin, 2014.

Beck, Wilhelm. *Die ältesten Artikelsbriefe für das deutsche Fußvolk. Ihre Vorläufer und die Entwicklung bis zum Jahre 1519*. Munich, 1908.

Becker, Wilhelm Martin. "Ludwig V." *Neue Deutsche Biographie* 15 (1987): 391–92.

Becucci, Alessandra. "Ottavio Piccolomini (1599–1656): A Case of Patronage from a Transnational Perspective." *International History Review* 33, no. 4 (2011): 585–605.

Bedürftig, Friedemann. *Der Dreißigjährige Krieg*. Darmstadt, 2006.

Behringer, Wolfgang. *Witchcraft Persecutions in Bavaria: Popular Magic, Religious Zealotry and Reason of State in Early Modern Europe*. Cambridge, 1997.

Bei der Wieden, Brage. "Niederdeutsche Söldner vor dem Dreißigjährigen Krieg: Geistige und mentale Grenzen eines sozialen Raums." In *Krieg und Frieden: Militär und Gesellschaft in der frühen Neuzeit*, edited by Bernhard R. Kroener and Ralf Pröve, 85–107. Paderborn, 1996.

———. "Zur Konfessionalisierung des landsässigen Adels zwischen Weser, Harz und Elbe." *Archiv für Reformationsgeschichte* 89 (1998): 310–19.

Berg-Hobohm, Stefanie. "Ein anderer Blick auf die Schlacht von Alerheim: Massengrab aus dem Dreißigjährigen Krieg entdeckt." *Denkmalpflege Informationen* 140 (2008): 21–22.

Bergdolt, Klaus. *Der schwarze Tod in Europa: Die große Pest und das Ende des Mittelalters*. Munich, 2000.

Bergen, Doris L., ed. *The Sword of the Lord: Military Chaplains from the First to the Twenty-First Century*. Notre Dame, 2004.

Bever, Edward. *The Realities of Witchcraft and Popular Magic in Early Modern Europe: Culture, Cognition and Everyday Life*. Basingstoke, 2008.

Bicheno, Hugh. *Crescent and Cross: The Battle of Lepanto 1571*. London, 2003.

Bielik, Emerich. *Geschichte der K.u.K Militär-Seelsorge und des Apostolischen Feld-Vicariates*. Vienna, 1901.

Black, Jeremy. *A Military Revolution? Military Change and European Society, 1550–1800*. London, 1991.

Blau, Friedrich. *Die Deutschen Landsknechte, ein Kulturbild*. Wolfenbüttel, 2008.

Blickle, Peter. "Bilder und ihr gesellschaftlicher Rahmen. Zur Einführung." In *Macht und Ohnmacht der Bilder: Reformatorischer Bildersturm im Kontext der europäischen Geschichte*, edited by Peter Blickle, André Holenstein, Heinrich R. Schmidt, and Franz-Josef Sladeczek, 1-7. Munich, 2002

———. *Die Revolution von 1525*. Fourth revised edition Darmstadt, 2006.

———. *Der Bauernkrieg: Die Revolution des Gemeinen Mannes*. Munich, 2006.

Blickle, Peter, Thomas A. Brady Jr., and H. C. Erik Midelfort, eds. *The Revolution of 1525: The German Peasants' War from a New Perspective*. Baltimore, 1981.

Blickle, Peter, André Holenstein, Heinrich R. Schmidt, and Franz-Josef Sladeczek, eds. *Macht und Ohnmacht der Bilder: Reformatorischer Bildersturm im Kontext der europäischen Geschichte*. Munich, 2002.

Boltanski, Ariane. "Forger le 'soldat chrétien': L'encadrement catholique des troupes pontificales et royales en France en 1568–1569." *Revue Historique* 669, no. 1 (2014): 51–85.

———. "A Jesuit Missio Castrensis in France at the End of the Sixteenth Century: Discipline and Violence at War." *Journal of Jesuit Studies* 4, no. 4 (2017): 581–98.

Bonin, Burkhard von. *Grundzüge der Rechtsverfassung in den Deutschen Heeren zu Beginn der Neuzeit*. Weimar, 1904.

Bourke, Joanna. *An Intimate History of Killing: Face-to-Face Killing in Twentieth-Century Warfare*. London, 1999.

Box, Reginald. *Make Music to Our God: How We Sing the Psalms*. London, 1996.

Brady, Thomas A., Jr. "Limits of Religious Violence in Early Modern Europe." In *Religion und Gewalt: Konflikte, Rituale, Deutungen (1500–1800)*, edited by Kaspar von Greyerz and Kim Siebenhüner, 125–51. Göttingen, 2006.

———. "From Revolution to the Long Reformation: Writings in English on the German Reformation, 1970–2005." *Archiv für Reformationsgeschichte* 100 (2009): 48–64.

———. *German Histories in the Age of Reformations 1400–1650*. Cambridge, 2009.

Breit, Stefan. *Leichtfertigkeit und ländliche Gesellschaft: Voreheliche Sexualität in der Frühen Neuzeit*. Munich, 1991.

Bremer, Kai. "Zur Rhetorik und Semantik des Begriffs 'Religionshändel' in der konfessionellen Polemik." In *Süß scheint der Krieg den Unerfahrenen: Das Bild vom Krieg und die Utopie des Friedens in der Frühen Neuzeit*, edited by Hans Peterse, 25–33. Göttingen, 2006.

Brendle, Franz, and Anton Schindling, eds. *Religionskriege im Alten Reich und in Alteuropa*. Münster, 2006.

———. "Religionskriege in der Frühen Neuzeit. Begriff, Wahrnehmung, Wirkmächtigkeit." In *Religionskriege im Alten Reich und in Alteuropa*, edited by Franz Brendle and Anton Schindling, 15–52. Münster, 2006.

———. *Geistliche im Krieg*. Münster, 2009.

Breuer, Stefan. "Probleme und Problemverlagerungen bei Max Weber, Gerhard Oestreich und Michel Foucault." In *Soziale Sicherheit und Soziale Disziplinierung: Beiträge zu einer historischen Theorie der Sozialpolitik*, edited by Christoph Sachße and Florian Tennstedt, 45–69. Frankfurt a. M., 1986.

Brockmann, Thomas, and Dieter J. Weiss, eds. *Das Konfessionalisierungsparadigma: Leistungen, Probleme, Grenzen*. Münster, 2013.

Brunner, H., ed. *Der Krieg im Mittelalter und in der Frühen Neuzeit: Gründe, Begründungen, Bilder, Bräuche, Recht*. Wiesbaden, 1999.

Burkhardt, Johannes. *Der Dreißigjährige Krieg*. Frankfurt a. M., 1992.

Burschel, Peter. *Söldner im Nordwestdeutschland des 16. und 17. Jahrhunderts*. Göttingen, 1994.

———. "Himmelreich und Hölle, Ein Söldner, sein Tagebuch und die Ordnungen des Krieges." In *Zwischen Alltag und Katastrophe: Der Dreißigjährige Krieg aus der Nähe*, edited by Benigna von Krusenstjern, Hans Medick, and Patrice Veit, 181–94. Göttingen, 1999.

———. *Die Erfindung der Reinheit: Eine andere Geschichte der Neuzeit*. Göttingen, 2014.

Bussmann, Klaus, and Heinz Schilling, eds. *1648: War and Peace in Europe*. 3 vols. Münster, 1998.

Byloff, Fritz. *Volkskundliches aus Strafprozessen der Österreichischen Alpenländer mit besonderer Berücksichtigung der Zauberei- und Hexenprozesse 1455 bis 1850* (Quellen zur Deutschen Volkskunde 3). Berlin, 1929.

Cabantous, Alain. *Blasphemy: Impious Speech in the West from the Seventeenth to the Nineteenth Century*. New York, 1998.

Caferro, William. *John Hawkwood: An English Mercenary in Fourteenth-Century Italy*. Baltimore, 2006.

208 ❧ *Bibliography*

Canning, Joseph, Hartmut Lehmann, and J. M. Winter, eds. *Power, Violence and Mass Death in Pre-Modern and Modern Times*. Aldershot, 2004.

Carroll, Stuart. *Blood and Violence in Early Modern France*. Oxford, 2006.

———. "The Rights of Violence." In *Ritual and Violence: Natalie Zemon Davis and Early Modern France* (Past and Present Supplement 7), edited by Graeme Murdock, Penny Roberts, and Andrew Spicer, 127–62. Oxford, 2012.

Cervantes, Fernando. *Conquistadores: A New History*. London, 2020.

Chaline, Olivier. "The Battle of White Mountain (8 November 1620)." In *1648: War and Peace in Europe*, vol. 1, edited by Klaus Bussmann and Heinz Schilling, 95–101. Münster, 1998.

———. *La Battaille de la Montagne Blanche: Un mystique chez les guerriers*. Paris, 1999.

Chamberlin, E. R. *The Sack of Rome*. London, 1979.

Chambers, D. S. *Popes, Cardinals and War: The Military Church in Renaissance and Early Modern Europe*. London, 2006.

Chastel, André. *Le Sac de Rome, 1527, du premier maniérisme à la contre-réforme*. Paris, 1984.

Chaunu, Pierre. *La Mort a Paris: XVIe, XVIIe et XVIIIe siècles*. Paris, 1978.

Christman, Victoria. *Pragmatic Toleration: The Politics of Religious Heterodoxy in Early Reformation Antwerp, 1515–1555*. Rochester, NY, 2015.

Christman, Victoria, and Marjorie Plummer, eds. *Topographies of Tolerance and Intolerance: Responses to Religious Pluralism in Reformation Europe*. Leiden, 2018.

Civale, Gianclaudio. "'Dextere sinistram vertere': Jesuits as Military Chaplains in the Papal Expeditionary Force to France (1569–70). Discipline, Moral Reform and Violence." *Journal of Jesuit Studies* 4, no. 4 (2017): 559–80.

Cohn, Samuel K., Jr. "The Black Death: The End of a Paradigm." In *Power, Violence and Mass-Death*, edited by Joseph Canning, Hartmut Lehmann, and J. M. Winter, 25–66. Aldershot, 2004.

Collins, Randall. *Violence: A Micro-sociological Theory*. Princeton, 2008.

Contamine, Philippe. *War in the Middle Ages*. Translated by Michael Jones. Malden, MA, 1984.

Corvisier, André. *L'Armée Française de la fin du XVIIème siècle au ministère de Choiseul: Le Soldat*. 2 vols. Paris, 1964.

Coster, Will, and Andrew Spicer, eds. *Sacred Space in Early Modern Europe*. Cambridge, 2005.

Cramer, Kevin. *The Thirty Years' War and German Memory in the Nineteenth Century*. Lincoln, NE, 2007.

Crawford, Katherine. *European Sexualities, 1400–1800*. Cambridge, 2007.

Cressy, David. *Birth, Marriage and Death*. Oxford, 1997.

Crouzet, Denis. *Les Guerriers de Dieu: La violence au temps des troubles de religion (vers 1525–vers 1610)*. Paris, 1990.

Cunningham, Andrew, and Ole Peter Grell. *The Four Horsemen of the Apocalypse: Religion, War, Famine and Death in Reformation Europe*. Cambridge, 2000.

Darnton, Robert. *The Great Cat Massacre and Other Episodes in French Cultural History*. New York, 1984.

Davis, Natalie Zemon. "The Rites of Violence: Religious Riot in Sixteenth-Century France." *Past & Present* 59 (1973): 51–91.

Delbrück, Hans. *Geschichte der Kriegskunst*. 4 vols. Berlin, 1900–20.

Demandt, Alexander. *Geschichte der Spätantike*. Munich, 1998.

Diefendorf, Barbara. *Beneath the Cross: Catholics and Huguenots in Sixteenth-Century Paris.* New York, 1991.

Duchardt, Heinz, Patrice Veit, and Pierre Monnet, eds. *Krieg und Frieden im Übergang vom Mittelalter zur Neuzeit: Theorie—Praxis—Bilder (Guerre et Paix du Moyen Age auf Temps Modernes: Théories—Pratiques—Représentations).* Mainz, 2000.

Dülmen, Richard van. *Theater des Schreckens.* Munich, 1985.

———. *Kultur und Alltag in der Frühen Neuzeit,* vol. 3, *Religion, Magie, Aufklärung 16.–18. Jahrhundert.* Munich, 1994.

———. "Wider die Ehre Gottes: Unglaube und Gotteslästerung in der frühen Neuzeit." *Historische Anthropologie* 2, no. 1 (1994): 20–38.

Dixon, C. Scott. "Urban Order and Religious Coexistence in the German Imperial City: Augsburg and Donauwörth." *Central European History* 40, no. 1 (2007): 1–33.

———. "Introduction: Living with Diversity in Early Modern Europe." In *Living with Religious Diversity in Early Modern Europe,* edited by C. Scott Dixon, Dagmar Freist, and Mark Greengrass, 1–20. Farnham, 2009.

Dixon, C. Scott, Dagmar Freist, and Mark Greengrass, eds. *Living with Religious Diversity in Early Modern Europe.* Farnham, 2009.

Donagan, Barbara. "The Web of Honour: Soldiers, Christians, and Gentlemen in the English Civil War." *Historical Journal* 44 (2001): 365–89.

———. *War in England 1642–1649.* Oxford, 2008.

Edelmayer, Friedrich. *Söldner und Pensionäre: Das Netzwerk Philipps II. im Heiligen Römischen Reich.* Vienna, 2002.

Edwards, Kathryn A. "The Early Modern Magical Continuum: Magic's Ties to Religion and Folklore in Europe, ca.1400–1700." *Groniek: Historisch Tijdschrift* 220 (2019): 323–38.

Ehlert, Hans. "Ursprünge des modernen Militärwesens: Die Nassau-oranischen Heeresreformen." *Militärgeschichtliche Mitteilungen* 38, no. 2 (1985): 27–55.

Ehrenpreis, Stefan. *"Wir sind mit blutigen Köpfen davongelaufen ... " Lokale Konfessionskonflikte im Herzogtum Berg 1550-1700.* Bochum 1993.

———, ed. *Der Dreißigjährige Krieg im Herzogtum Berg und in seinen Nachbarregionen* (Bergische Forschungen 28). Neustadt a. d. Aisch, 2002.

Eichberg, Henning. "Gespenster im Zeughaus: Aspekte militärisch-technischer Rationalität im 17. Jahrhundert." *Militärgeschichtliche Mitteilungen* 40, no. 2 (1986): 9–23.

Eickhoff, Sabine, Anja Grothe, and Bettina Jungklaus. "Memento Mori—Söldnerbestattungen der Schlacht bei Wittstock 1636." *Archäologie in Deutschland* 1 (2009): 26–29.

Eickhoff, Sabine, Anja Grothe, and Bettina Jungklaus. "Söldnerbestattungen des Dreißigjährigen Krieges: Ein Massengrab bei Wittstock." *Ostprignitz-Ruppin Jahrbuch* (2008): 103–12.

Eickhoff, Sabine and Bettina Jungklaus. "Die Medizinische Versorgung." In *1636: Ihre Letzte Schlacht. Leben im Dreißigjährigen Krieg,* edited by Sabine Eickhoff and Franz Schopper, 119-129. Stuttgart, 2012.

Eickhoff, Sabine, Anja Grothe, Hilja Hoevenberg, Bettina Jungklaus, Hans Günter König and Joachim Wahl. "Die Schlacht von Wittstock." In *1636: Ihre Letzte Schlacht. Leben im Dreißigjährigen Krieg,* edited by Sabine Eickhoff and Franz Schopper, 130-163. Stuttgart, 2012.

Eickhoff, Sabine, Gisela Grupe, and Bettina Jungklaus. "Freund und Feind in einem Grab." In *1636: Ihre Letzte Schlacht. Leben im Dreißigjährigen Krieg,* edited by Sabine Eickhoff and Franz Schopper, 178–80. Stuttgart, 2012.

210 ~: *Bibliography*

Eickhoff, Sabine, and Franz Schopper, eds. *Schlachtfeld und Massengrab*. Wünsdorf, 2014.

Elias, Norbert. *The History of Manners: The Civilizing Process*. New York, 1978.

Elsner, Tobias von. "Magdeburg—Opfertod und Kriegsverbrechen." In *"Der du gelehrt hast meine Hände den Krieg": Tilly. Heiliger oder Kriegsverbrecher?* edited by Markus Junkelman, 59–62. Altötting, 2007.

Emich, Birgit. "Bilder einer Hochzeit: Die Zerstörung Magdeburgs 1631 zwischen Konstruktion, (Inter-)Medialität und Performanz." In *Kriegs / Bilder in Mittelalter und Früher Neuzeit*, edited by Birgit Emich and Gabriela Signori, 197–235. Berlin, 2009.

Engelen, Beate. "Warum heiratete man einen Soldaten? Soldatenfrauen in der ländlichen Gesellschaft Brandenburg-Preußens im 18. Jahrhundert." In *Militär und ländliche Gesellschaft in der frühen Neuzeit*, edited by Stefan Kroll and Kersten Krüger, 251–73. Hamburg, 2000.

Ergang, Robert. *The Myth of the All-Destructive Fury of the Thirty Years War*. Pocono Pines, PA, 1956.

Ericson, Lars. "The Swedish Army and Navy during the Thirty Years' War: From a National to a Multi-National Force." In *1648: War and Peace in Europe*, vol. 1, edited by Klaus Bussmann and Heinz Schilling, 301–7. Münster, 1998.

Estèbe, Janine. "The Rites of Violence: Religious Riot in Sixteenth-Century France. A Comment." *Past & Present* 67 (1975): 127–30.

Ferry, Patrick T. "Confessionalization and Popular Preaching: Sermons Against Synergism in Reformation Saxony." *Sixteenth Century Journal* 28, no. 4 (1997): 1143–66.

Fiedler, Siegfried. *Kriegswesen und Kriegführung im Zeitalter der Landsknechte*. Koblenz, 1985.

Flynn, Maureen. "Blasphemy and the Play of Anger in Sixteenth Century Spain." *Past and Present* 149 (1995): 29–56.

Forster, Marc R. *The Counter-Reformation in the Villages: Religion and Reform in the Bishopric of Speyer*. Ithaca, NY, 1992.

———. "The Elite and Popular Foundations of German Catholicism in the Age of Confessionalism: The *Reichskirche*." *Central European History* 26, no. 2 (1993): 311–25.

———. "The Thirty Years' War and the Failure of Catholicization." In *The Counter Reformation*, edited by David M. Luebke, 163–97. Malden, MA, 1999.

———. *Catholic Revival in the Age of the Baroque: Religious Identity in Southwest Germany, 1550–1750*. Cambridge, 2001.

———. *Catholic Germany from the Reformation to the Enlightenment*. Basingstoke, 2007.

Forster, Marc R., Bruce Gordon, Joel Harrington, Thomas Kaufmann, and Ute Lotz-Heumann. "Religious History beyond Confessionalization." *German History* 32, no. 4 (2014): 579–98.

Franz, Günther. *Der Deutsche Bauernkrieg*. Darmstadt, 1965.

Freedberg, David. *Iconoclasm*. Chicago, 2021.

Freytag, Gustav. *Bilder aus der Deutschen Vergangenheit*, vol. 3, *Aus dem Jahrhundert des großen Krieges (1600–1700)*. Leipzig, 1907.

Friedrich, Susanne, and Olaf Schröder. "Das Massengrab in Lützen." In *Krieg: Eine Archäologische Spurensuche*, edited by Harald Meller and Michael Schefzik, 399–404. Halle a. d. Saale, 2015.

Frost, Robert I. "Confessionalisation and the Army in the Polish-Lithuanian Commonwealth, 1550–1667." In *Konfessionalisierung in Ostmitteleuropa: Wirkungen des religiösen Wandels im 16. und 17. Jahrhunderts in Staat, Gesellschaft und Kultur*, edited by Joachim Bahlcke and Arno Strohmeyer, 139–60. Stuttgart, 1999.

Frijhoff, Willem. "La coexistence confessionnelle: Complicités, méfiances et ruptures aux Provinces-Unies." In *Histoire vécue du peuple chrétien*, vol. 2, edited by Jean Delumeau, 229–57. Toulouse, 1979.

———. *Embodied Belief: Ten Essays on Religious Culture in Dutch History*. Hilversum, 2002.

Funke, Nikolas. "'Naturali legitimâque Magica' oder 'Teufflische Zauberey'? Das 'Festmachen' im Militär des 16. und 17. Jahrhunderts." *Militär und Gesellschaft in der Frühen Neuzeit* 13, no. 1 (2009): 16–32.

———. "Magische Medizin und Schutzzauber im frühneuzeitlichen Militär." In *Krank vom Krieg: Umgangsweisen und kulturelle Deutungsmuster von der Antike bis zur Moderne*, edited by Nikolas Funke, Gundula Gahlen, and Ulrike Ludwig, 53–76. Frankfurt a. M., 2022.

Gäbler, Ulrich. *Huldrych Zwingli: Leben und Werk*. Zurich, 2004.

Geyl, Pieter. *The Revolt of the Netherlands 1555–1609*. London, 1958.

Gilliam, Helmut. "Neuss und der Kölner Krieg." In *Neuss und der Kölner Krieg*, edited by Max Tauch, 9–25. Neuss, 1986.

Goldammer, K. "Der cholerische Kriegsmann und der melancholische Ketzer: Psychologie und Pathologie von Krieg, Glaubenskampf und Martyrium in der Sicht des Paracelsus." In *Psychiatrie und Gesellschaft: Ergebnisse und Probleme der Sozialpsychiatrie*, edited by H. Ehrhardt, D. Ploog, and H. Stutte, 90–101. Bern, 1958.

Goeters, Johann F. G. "Magister Johann Northausen, Bonns reformierter Pastor in der Zeit des Truchsessischen Krieges, und seine Gemeinde." *Bonner Geschichtsblätter* 42 (1992): 171–95.

Gordon, B., and P. Marshall, eds. *The Place of the Dead: Death and Remembrance in Late Medieval and Early Modern Europe*. Cambridge, 2000.

Gräf, Holger Th. *Söldnerleben am Vorabend des Dreißigjährigen Krieges: Lebenslauf und Kriegstagebuch 1617 des hessischen Obristen Caspar von Widmarckter* (Beiträge zur Hessischen Geschichte 16). Marburg, 2000.

Gregorovius, Ferdinand. *Geschichte der Stadt Rom im Mittelalter vom V. bis zum XVI. Jahrhundert*. Vol. 8. Stuttgart, 1872.

Grell, Ole Peter, and Bob Scribner, eds. *Tolerance and Intolerance in the European Reformation*. Cambridge, 1996.

Greyerz, Kaspar von. *Religion und Kultur: Europa 1500–1800*. Göttingen, 2000.

———. "Konfessionelle Indifferenz in der Frühen Neuzeit." In *Konfessionelle Ambiguität: Uneindeutigkeit und Verstellung als religiöse Praxis in der Frühen Neuzeit*, edited by Andreas Pietsch and Barbara Stollberg-Rilinger, 39–61. Heidelberg, 2013.

Greyerz, Kaspar von, Hartmut Lehmann, Thomas Kaufmann, and Manfred Jakubowski-Tiessen, eds. *Interkonfessionalität—Transkonfessionalität—Binnenkonfessionelle Pluralität: Neue Forschungen zur Konfessionalisierungsthese*. Heidelberg, 2003.

Greyerz, Kaspar von, and Kim Siebenhüner, eds. *Religion und Gewalt: Konflikte, Rituale, Deutungen (1500–1800)*. Göttingen, 2006.

Grochowina, Nicole. *Indifferenz und Dissens in der Grafschaft Ostfriesland im 16. und 17. Jahrhundert*. Frankfurt a. M., 2003.

Grosjean, Alexia. *An Unofficial Alliance: Scotland and Sweden 1569–1654*. Leiden, 2003.

Grossman, Dave. *On Killing: The Psychological Cost of Learning to Kill in War and Society*. New York, 1995.

Gunn, Steven. "War and the Emergence of the State: Western Europe, 1350–1600." In *European Warfare 1350–1750*, edited by Frank Tallett and David J. B. Trimm, 50–73. Cambridge, 2010.

212 ~: *Bibliography*

Gurevich, Aaron. "Bakhtin and His Theory of Carnival." In *A Cultural History of Laughter: From Antiquity to the Present Day*, edited by Jan Bremmer and Herman Roodenburg, 40–53. Cambridge, 1997.

Hacker, Barton C., and Margaret Vining, eds. *A Companion to Women's Military History.* Leiden, 2012.

Hagemann, Karen, and Ralf Pröve, eds. *Landsknechte, Soldatenfrauen und Nationalkrieger: Militär, Krieg und Geschlechterordnung im historischen Wandel.* Frankfurt a. M., 1998.

Hájková, Anna, "Sexual Barter in Times of Genocide: Negotiating the Sexual Economy of the Theresienstadt Ghetto." *Signs* 38, no.3 (2013): 503-533.

Hale, J. R. "Sixteenth Century Explanations of War and Violence." *Past & Present* 51 (1971): 3–26.

Harding, Vanessa. "Whose Body? A Study of Attitudes towards the Dead Body in Early Modern Paris." In *The Place of the Dead: Death and Remembrance in Late Medieval and Early Modern Europe*, edited by Bruce Gordon and Peter Marshall, 170–87. Cambridge, 2000.

———. *The Dead and the Living in London and Paris, 1500–1670.* Cambridge, 2002.

Harnack, Adolf von. *Militia Christi: Die christliche Religion und der Soldatenstand in den ersten drei Jahrhunderten.* Darmstadt, 1963.

Harrington, Joel. "Shifting Boundaries and Boundary Shifters." In *Mixed Matches: Transgressive Unions in Germany from the Reformation to the Enlightenment*, edited by David M. Luebke and Mary Lindemann, 204–12. New York, 2014.

Härter, Karl. "Erfahrung in der frühneuzeitlichen Strafjustiz." In *Erfahrung als Kategorie der Frühneuzeitgeschichte* (Historische Zeitschrift Beihefte 31), edited by Paul Münch, 377–88. Munich, 2001.

Hartinger, Wolfgang. "Konfessionalisierung des Alltags in Bayern unter Maximilian I." *Zeitschrift für bayerische Landesgeschichte* 65, no. 1 (2002): 123–56.

Haude, Sigrun. *In the Shadow of Savage Wolves: Anabaptist Münster and the German Reformation during the 1530s.* Boston, 2000.

Haug-Moritz, Gabriele. "Der Schmalkaldische Krieg (1546/47)—Ein kaiserlicher Religionskrieg?" In *Religionskriege im Alten Reich und in Alteuropa*, edited by Franz Brendle and Anton Schindling, 93–105. Münster, 2006.

Haug-Moritz, Gabriele, and Georg Schmidt. "Schmalkaldischer Bund." In *Theologische Realenzyklopädie*, vol. 30, edited by Gerhard Müller , 221–28. Berlin, 1999.

Heilmann, Johann. *Kriegsgeschichte von Bayern, Franken, Pfalz und Schwaben von 1506–1551.* Vol. 2, part 1. Munich, 1868.

Hendrix, Scott H. "Rerooting the Faith: The Reformation as Re-Christianization." *Church History* 69, no. 3 (2000): 558–77.

———. *Recultivating the Vineyard: The Reformation Agendas of Christianization.* Louisville, KY, 2004.

Hengerer, Mark. *Kaiser Ferdinand III (1608–1657): Eine Biographie.* Vienna, 2012.

Hippel, Wolfgang von. *Armut, Unterschichten: Randgruppen in der Frühen Neuzeit.* Munich, 1995.

Hobsbawm, Eric. "Introduction: Inventing Traditions." In *The Invention of Tradition*, edited by Eric Hobsbawm and Terence Ranger, 1–14 . Cambridge, 1992.

Hoffmann, Friedrich Wilhelm. *Geschichte der Stadt Magdeburg nach den Quellen bearbeitet.* Vol. 3. Magdeburg, 1850.

Holst, Malin R., and Tim L. Sutherland. "Towton Revisited—Analysis of the Human Remains from the Battle of Towton 1461." In *Schlachtfeld und Massengrab*, edited by Sabine Eickhoff and Franz Schopper, 97–129. Wünsdorf, 2014.

Holtz, Sabine. "Die Unsicherheit des Lebens: Zum Verständnis von Krankheit und Tod in den Predigten der lutherischen Orthodoxie." In *Im Zeichen der Krise: Religiosität im Europa des 17. Jahrhunderts*, edited by Hartmut Lehmann and Anne-Charlott Trepp, 135–57. Göttingen, 1999.

Holt, Mac P. "The Social History of the Reformation: Recent Trends and Future Agendas." *Journal of Social History* 37, no. 1, special issue (2003): 133–44.

Hook, Judith. *The Sack of Rome 1527*. Basingstoke, 2004.

Houlbrooke, Ralph, ed. *Death, Ritual and Bereavement*. London, 1989.

———. *Death, Religion and the Family in England 1480–1750*. Oxford, 1998.

Hsia, Ronnie Po-Chia. *Social Discipline in the Reformation: Central Europe 1550–1750*. London, 1989.

———. *The World of Catholic Renewal 1540–1770*. Cambridge, 2005.

Huntebrinker, Jan Willem. "Geordneter Sozialverband oder Gegenordnung? Zwei Perspektiven auf das Militär im 16. und 17. Jahrhundert." *Militär und Gesellschaft in der Frühen Neuzeit* 10, no. 2 (2006): 181–99.

———. "Der Reichsartikelbrief von 1570: Zur Kodifizierung des Militärrechts in der Frühen Neuzeit." In *La Codification: Perspectives Transdisciplinaires*, edited by Gernot Kamecke, Jacques Le Rider, and Anne Szulmajster, 87–102. Paris, 2007.

———. "Soldatentracht? Mediale Funktionen materieller Kultur in Söldnerdarstellungen des 16. und 17. Jahrhunderts." *Militär und Gesellschaft in der Frühen Neuzeit* 13, no. 1 (2009): 75–103.

———. *"Fromme Knechte" und "Garteteufel": Söldner als soziale Gruppe im 16. und 17. Jahrhundert*. Konstanz, 2010.

Ilg, Matthias. "Der Kult des Kapuzinermärtyrers Fidelis von Sigmaringen als Ausdruck katholischer Kriegserfahrungen im Dreißigjährigen Krieg." In *Das Strafgericht Gottes: Kriegserfahrungen und Religion im Heiligen Römischen Reich Deutscher Nation im Zeitalter des Dreißigjährigen Krieges*, edited by Matthias Asche and Anton Schindling, 291–439. Münster, 2001.

Irsigler, Franz, and Arnold Lassotta. *Bettler und Gaukler, Dirnen und Henker: Außenseiter in einer mittelalterlichen Stadt*. Munich, 1989.

Isenmann, Eberhard. "The Notion of the Common Good, the Concept of Politics, and Practical Policies in Late Medieval and Early Modern German Cities." In *De Bono Communi: The Discourse and Practice of the Common Good in the European City (13th–16th c.)/Discours et pratique du Bien Commun dans les villes d'Europe (XIIIe au XVIe siècle)*, edited by Elodie Lecuppre-Desjardin and Anne-Laure Van Bruaene, 107–48. Turnhout, 2010.

Jansson, Karin. "Soldaten und Vergewaltigung im Schweden des 17. Jahrhunderts." In *Zwischen Alltag und Katastrophe: Der Dreißigjährige Krieg aus der Nähe*, edited by Benigna von Krusenstjern, Hans Medick, and Patrice Veit, 195–225. Göttingen, 1999.

Jörgensen, Bent. *Konfessionelle Selbst- und Fremdbezeichnungen: Zur Terminologie der Religionsparteien im 16. Jahrhundert*. Berlin, 2014.

Junkelmann, Marcus, ed. *"Der du gelehrt hast meine Hände den Krieg": Tilly. Heiliger oder Kriegsverbrecher?* Altötting, 2007.

———. "'In diesem Zeichen wirst Du siegen': Feldzeichen im Dreißigjährigen Krieg." In *"Der du gelehrt hast meine Hände den Krieg": Tilly. Heiliger oder Kriegsverbrecher?* edited by Marcus Junkelmann, 81–82. Altötting, 2007.

Jütte, Robert. *Abbild und soziale Wirklichkeit des Bettler- und Gaunertums zu Beginn der Neuzeit: Sozial-, Mentalitäts-, und Sprachgeschichtliche Studien zum Liber Vagatorum (1519)*. Cologne, 1988.

214 ❧ *Bibliography*

————. *Poverty and Deviance in Early Modern Europe.* Cambridge, 1994.

Kaeuper, Richard W. *Chivalry and Violence in Medieval Europe.* Oxford, 1999.

————. *Holy Warriors: The Religious Ideology of Chivalry.* Philadelphia, 2009.

————. *Medieval Chivalry.* Cambridge, 2016.

Kaiser, Michael. "'Excidium Magdeburgense': Beobachtungen zur Wahrnehmung und Darstellung von Gewalt im Dreißigjährigen Krieg." In *Ein Schauplatz Herber Angst: Wahrnehmung und Darstellung von Gewalt im 17. Jahrhundert,* edited by Markus Meumann and Dirk Niefanger, 43–64. Göttingen, 1997.

————. *Politik und Kriegführung: Maximilian von Bayern, Tilly und die Katholische Liga im Dreißigjährigen Krieg.* Münster, 1999.

————. "*Cuius exercitus, eius religio?* Konfession und Heerwesen im Zeitalter des Dreißigjährigen Kriegs." *Archiv für Reformationsgeschichte* 91 (2000): 316–53.

————. "Die Söldner und die Bevölkerung: Überlegungen zu Konstituierung und Überwindung eines lebensweltlichen Antagonismus." In *Militär und ländliche Gesellschaft in der frühen Neuzeit,* edited by Stefan Kroll and Kersten Krüger, 79–120. Hamburg, 2000.

————. "Maximilian I. von Bayern und der Krieg: Zu einem wichtigen Aspekt seines fürstlichen Selbstverständnisses." *Zeitschrift für bayerische Landesgeschichte* 65, no. 1 (2002): 69–99.

————. "'Ist er vom Adel? Ja. Id satis videtur.' Adelige Standesqualität und militärische Leistung als Karrierefaktoren in der Epoche des Dreißigjährigen Krieges." In *Geburt oder Leistung? Elitenbildung im deutsch-britischen Vergleich / Birth or Talent? The Formation of Elites in a British-German Comparison,* edited by Franz Bosbach, Keith Robbins, and Karina Urbach, 73–90. Munich, 2003.

————. "Die 'Magdeburgische' Hochzeit (1631): Gewaltphänomene im Dreissigjährigen Krieg." In *Leben in der Stadt: Eine Kultur- und Geschlechtergeschichte Magdeburgs,* edited by Eva Labouvie, 195–213. Cologne, 2004.

————. "Zwischen 'ars moriendi' und 'ars mortem evitandi': Der Soldat und der Tod in der Frühen Neuzeit." In *Militär und Religiosität in der Frühen Neuzeit,* edited by Michael Kaiser and Stefan Kroll, 323–43. Münster, 2004.

————. "'Ärger als der Türck': Kriegsgreuel und ihre Funktionalisierung in der Zeit des Dreißigjährigen Kriegs." In *Kriegsgreuel: Die Entgrenzung der Gewalt in kriegerischen Konflikten vom Mittelalter bis ins 20. Jahrhundert,* edited by Sönke Neitzel and Daniel Hohrath, 155–83. Paderborn, 2008.

————. "Generalstaatische Söldner und der Dreißigjährige Krieg: Eine übersehene Kriegspartei im Licht rheinischer Befunde." In *Krieg und Kriegserfahrung im Westen des Reiches 1568–1714,* edited by Andreas Rutz, 65–100. Göttingen, 2015.

Kaiser, Michael, and Stefan Kroll, eds. *Militär und Religiosität in der Frühen Neuzeit.* Münster, 2004.

Kaiser, Reinhold. *Trunkenheit und Gewalt im Mittelalter.* Cologne, 2002.

Kamen, Henry. *Early Modern European Society.* London, 2000.

————. *Empire, War and Faith in Early Modern Europe.* London, 2002.

————. *The Duke of Alba.* New Haven, CT, 2004.

Kaplan, Benjamin. *Divided by Faith: Religious Conflict and the Practice of Toleration in Early Modern Europe.* Cambridge, MA, 2007.

————. *Reformation and the Practice of Toleration.* Leiden, 2019.

Kaufmann, Thomas. *Dreißigjähriger Krieg und Westfälischer Friede: Kirchengeschichtliche Studien zur lutherischen Konfessionskultur.* Tübingen, 1998.

————. "Die Bilderfrage im frühneuzeitlichen Luthertum." In *Macht und Ohnmacht der Bilder: Reformatorischer Bildersturm im Kontext der europäischen Geschichte*, edited by Peter Blickle et al., 407–51. Munich, 2002.

————. *Konfession und Kultur: Lutherischer Protestantismus in der zweiten Hälfte des Reformationsjahrhunderts*. Tübingen, 2006.

————. "Die Deutsche Reformationsforschung seit dem Zweiten Weltkrieg." *Archiv für Reformationsgeschichte* 100 (2009): 15–47.

Keegan, John. *The Face of Battle: A Study of Agincourt, Waterloo and The Somme*. London, 1976.

Keen, Benjamin. "The Black Legend Revisited: Assumptions and Realities." *Hispanic American Historical Review* 49, no. 4 (1969): 703–19.

Keen, Maurice. *Chivalry*. New Haven, CT, 2005.

Kellehear, Allan. *A Social History of Dying*. Cambridge, 2007.

Kenzler, Hauke. "Religion, Status and Taboo: Changing Funeral Rites in Catholic and Protestant Germany." In *The Archaeology of Death in Post-Medieval Europe*, edited by Sarah Tarlow, 148–69. Warsaw, 2015.

Kirchner, Thomas. *Katholiken, Lutheraner und Reformierte in Aachen 1555–1618: Konfessionskulturen im Zusammenspiel*. Tübingen, 2015.

Klötzer, Ralf. *Die Täuferherrschaft von Münster: Stadtreformation und Welterneuerung*. Münster, 1992.

Knights, Mark. "Historical Stereotypes and Histories of Stereotypes." In *Psychology and History: Interdisciplinary Explorations*, edited by Cristian Tileagă and Jovan Byford, 242–67. Cambridge, 2014.

Kohler, Alfred. *Karl V. 1500–1558: Eine Biographie*. Munich, 2005.

Kohler, Alfred, Barbara Haider, and Christine Ottner, eds. *Karl V. 1500–1558: Neue Perspektiven seiner Herrschaft in Europa und Übersee*. Vienna, 2002.

Koslofsky, Craig M. *The Reformation of the Dead: Death and Ritual in Early Modern Germany, 1450–1700*. Basingstoke, 2000.

Koziol, Geoffrey. *The Peace of God*. Leeds, 2018.

Kraus, Jürgen. *Das Militärwesen der Reichsstadt Augsburg 1548–1806: Vergleichende Untersuchungen über städtische Militäreinrichtungen vom 16–18. Jahrhundert*. Augsburg, 1980.

Kroener, Bernhard R. "Vom'extraordinari Kriegsvolck' zum'miles perpetuus': Zur Rolle der bewaffenten Macht in der europäischen Gesellschaft." *Militärgeschichtliche Mitteilungen* 43, no. 1 (1988): 141–88.

————. "'Der Krieg hat ein Loch . . .': Überlegungen zum Schicksal demobilisierter Söldner nach dem Dreißigjährigen Krieg." In *Der Westfälische Friede: Diplomatie—politische Zäsur—kulturelles Umfeld—Rezeptionsgeschichte*, edited by Heinz Duchhardt, 599–630. Munich, 1998.

————. "'. . . und ist der jammer nit zu beschreiben': Geschlechterbeziehungen und Überlebensstrategien in der Lagergesellschaft des Dreißigjährigen Krieges." In *Landsknechte, Soldatenfrauen und Nationalkrieger: Militär, Krieg und Geschlechterordnung im historischen Wandel*, edited by Karen Hagemann and Ralf Pröve, 279–96. Frankfurt a. M., 1998.

————. "'Kriegsgurgeln, Freireuter und Marodebrüder': Der Soldat des Dreißigjährigen Krieges—Täter und Opfer." In *Der Krieg des kleinen Mannes: Eine Militärgeschichte von unten*, edited by Wolfram Wette, 51–67. Munich, 1992.

————. "'Das Schwungrad an der Staatsmaschine?' Die Bedeutung der bewaffneten Macht in der europäischen Geschichte der Frühen Neuzeit." In *Krieg und Frieden: Militär und*

216 ❧ Bibliography

Gesellschaft in der frühen Neuzeit, edited by Bernhard R. Kroener and Ralf Pröve, 1–23. Paderborn, 1996.

——. "'The Soldiers Are Very Poor, Bare, Naked, Exhausted': The Living Conditions and Organisational Structure of Military Society during the Thirty Years' War." In *1648: War and Peace in Europe*, vol. 2, edited by Klaus Bussmann and Heinz Schilling, 285–91. Münster, 1998.

——. "Militär in der Gesellschaft: Aspekte einer neuen Militärgeschichte der Frühen Neuzeit." In *Was ist Militärgeschichte?* edited by Thomas Kühne and Benjamin Ziemann, 283–99. Paderborn, 2000.

——. "Der Soldat als Ware: Kriegsgefangenenschicksale im 16. und 17. Jahrhundert." In *Krieg und Frieden im Übergang vom Mittelalter zur Neuzeit: Theorie—Praxis—Bilder* (*Guerre et Paix du Moyen Age auf Temps Modernes: Théories—Pratiques—Représentations*), edited by Heinz Duchardt and Patrice Veit, 271–95. Mainz, 2000.

Kroener, Bernhard R., and Ralf Pröve, eds. *Krieg und Frieden: Militär und Gesellschaft in der frühen Neuzeit*. Paderborn, 1996.

Kroll, Stefan, and Kersten Krüger, eds. *Militär und ländliche Gesellschaft in der frühen Neuzeit*. Hamburg, 2000.

Kronfeld, Ernst M. *Der Krieg im Aberglauben und Volksglauben*. Munich, 1915.

Krusenstjern, Benigna von. "Seliges Sterben und böser Tod: Tod und Sterben in der Zeit des Dreißigjährigen Krieges." In *Zwischen Alltag und Katastrophe: Der Dreißigjährige Krieg aus der Nähe*, edited by Benigna von Krusenstjern, Hans Medick, and Patrice Veit, 469–96. Göttingen, 1999.

Krusenstjern, Benigna von, Hans Medick, and Patrice Veit, eds. *Zwischen Alltag und Katastrophe: Der Dreißigjährige Krieg aus der Nähe*. Göttingen, 1999.

Kuijpers, Erika. "Between Storytelling and Patriotic Scripture: The Memory Brokers of the Dutch Revolt." In *Memory before Modernity: Practices of Memory in Early Modern Europe*, edited by Erika Kuijpers et al., 183–202. Leiden, 2013.

Kümin, Beat. *Drinking Matters: Public Houses and Social Exchange in Early Modern Central Europe*. New York, 2007.

Labouvie, Eva. *Verbotene Künste: Volksmagie und ländlicher Aberglaube in den Dorfgemeinden des Saarraumes (16.–19. Jahrhundert)*. St. Ingbert, 1992.

Langer, Herbert. *Hortus Bellicus: Der Dreißigjährige Krieg, eine Kulturgeschichte*. Leipzig, 1978.

Laufhütte, Hartmut. "Das Friedensfest in Nürnberg 1650." In *1648: War and Peace in Europe*, vol. 2, edited by Klaus Bussmann and Heinz Schilling, 347–57. Münster, 1998.

Lavenia, Vincenzo. *Il catechismo dei Soldati: Guerra e cura d'anime in età moderna*. Bologna, 2014.

——. "Jesuit Catechisms for Soldiers (Seventeenth-Nineteenth Centuries): Changes and Continuities." *Journal of Jesuit Studies* 4, no. 4 (2017): 599–623.

Lehmann, Hannelore. "Das Tuchtfeldsche Soldatenkonventikel in Potsdam 1725/27: Erziehung zum frommen Soldaten oder Verleidung des Soldatenstandes?" In *Militär und Religiosität in der Frühen Neuzeit*, edited by Michael Kaiser and Stefan Kroll, 277–92. Münster, 2004.

Lehmann, Hartmut. "Grenzen der Erklärungskraft der Konfessionalisierungsthese." In *Interkonfessionalität—Transkonfessionalität—Binnenkonfessionelle Pluralität: Neue Forschungen zur Konfessionalisierungsthese*, edited by Kaspar von Greyerz et al., 242–49. Heidelberg, 2003.

Lehmann, Hartmut, and Anne-Charlott Trepp, eds. *Im Zeichen der Krise: Religiosität im Europa des 17. Jahrhunderts*. Göttingen, 1999.

Lem, Anton van der. *Revolt in the Netherlands: The Eighty Years War, 1568–1648*. London, 2018.

Leng, Rainer. "Gründe für berufliches Töten: Büchsenmeister und Kriegshauptleute zwischen Berufsethos und Gewissensnot." In *Der Krieg im Mittelalter und in der Frühen Neuzeit: Gründe, Begründungen, Bilder, Bräuche, Recht*, edited by Horst Brunner, 307–48. Wiesbaden, 1999.

Llewellyn, Nigel. *The Art of Death: Visual Culture in English Death Ritual*. London, 1991.

Loetz, Francisca. *Mit Gott handeln: Von den Zürcher Gotteslästerern der Frühen Neuzeit zu einer Kulturgeschichte des Religiösen*. Göttingen, 2002.

———. "Probleme der Sünde: Sexualdelikte im Europa der Frühen Neuzeit." In *Gottlosigkeit und Eigensinn: Religiöse Devianz im konfessionellen Zeitalter* (Zeitschrift für Historische Forschung Beiheft 51), edited by Eric Piltz and Gerd Schwerhoff, 207–35. Berlin, 2015.

Lohsträter, Kai. "Militär und Recht vom 16. bis 19. Jahrhundert: Ergebnisse und Perspektiven." In *Militär und Recht: Gelehrter Diskurs—Praxis—Transformationen*, edited by Jutta Nowosadtko, Diethelm Klippel, and Kai Lohsträter, 9–28. Göttingen, 2016.

Lorenz, Maren. *Das Rad der Gewalt: Militär und Zivilbevölkerung in Norddeutschland nach dem Dreißigjährigen Krieg (1650–1700)*. Cologne, 2007.

Lossen, Max. *Der Kölnische Krieg*. 2 vols. Gotha, 1882/1897.

Louthan, Howard. "Breaking Images and Building Bridges: The Making of Sacred Space in Early Modern Bohemia." In *Sacred Space in Early Modern Europe*, edited by Will Coster and Andrew Spicer, 282–301. Cambridge, 2005.

Ludwig, Ulrike. "Der Zauber des Tötens: Waffenmagie im frühneuzeitlichen Militär." *Militär und Gesellschaft in der Frühen Neuzeit* 13, no. 1 (2009): 33–49.

———. "Erinnerungsstrategien in Zeiten des Wandels: Zur Bedeutung der Reformation als Generationserfahrung im Spiegel sächsischer Leichenpredigten für adlige Beamte." *Archiv für Reformationsgeschichte* 104, no. 1 (2014): 158–84.

Luebke, David M., ed. *The Counter Reformation*. Malden, MA, 1999.

———. "Confessions of the Dead: Interpreting Burial Practice in the Late Reformation." *Archiv für Reformationsgeschichte* 101 (2010): 55–79.

———. *Hometown Religion: Regimes of Coexistence in Early Modern Westphalia*. Charlottesville, VA, 2016.

Luh, Jürgen. "Religion und Türkenkrieg (1683–1699)—Neu bewertet." In *Militär und Religiosität in der Frühen Neuzeit*, edited by Michael Kaiser and Stefan Kroll, 193–206. Münster, 2004.

Luria, Keith. *Sacred Boundaries: Religious Coexistence and Conflict in Early-Modern France*. Washington, DC, 2005.

Luttenberger, Albrecht P. "Die Religionspolitik Karls V. im Reich." In *Karl V. 1500–1558: Neue Perspektiven seiner Herrschaft in Europa und Übersee*, edited by Alfred Kohler, Barbara Haider, and Christine Ottner, 293–343. Vienna, 2002.

Lutterbach, Hubertus. *Das Täuferreich von Münster: Wurzeln und Eigenarten eines religiösen Aufbruchs*. Münster, 2008.

Lynn, John A. *Women, Armies and Warfare in Early Modern Europe*. Cambridge, 2008.

MacCulloch, Diarmaid. *Reformation: Europe's House Divided 1490–1700*. London, 2004.

MacCulloch, Diarmaid, Mary Laven, and Eamon Duffy. "Recent Trends in the Study of Christianity in Sixteenth-Century Europe." *Renaissance Quarterly* 59, no. 3 (2006): 697–731.

Macdonald, Fiona A. *Missions to the Gaels: Reformation and Counter-Reformation in Ulster and the Highlands and Islands of Scotland, 1560–1760*. Edinburgh, 2006.

218 ❧ *Bibliography*

Maczkiewitz, Dirk. *Der niederländische Aufstand gegen Spanien (1568–1609): Eine kommunikationswissenschaftliche Analyse.* Münster, 2005.

Marchal, Guy P. "Das vieldeutige Heiligenbild: Bildersturm im Mittelalter." In *Macht und Ohnmacht der Bilder: Reformatorischer Bildersturm im Kontext der europäischen Geschichte,* edited by Peter Blickle et al., 307–32. Munich, 2002.

Marshall, Peter. *Beliefs and the Dead in Reformation England.* Oxford, 2002.

Marschke, Benjamin. "Vom Feldpredigerwesen zum Militärkirchenwesen: Die Erweiterung und Institutionalisierung der Militärseelsorge Preußens im frühen 18. Jahrhundert." In *Militär und Religiosität in der Frühen Neuzeit,* edited by Michael Kaiser and Stefan Kroll, 249–75. Münster, 2004.

Maurer, Michael. *Konfessionskulturen: Die Europäer als Protestanten und Katholiken.* Paderborn, 2019.

McGlynn, Sean. *By Sword and Fire: Cruelty and Atrocity in Medieval Warfare.* London, 2008.

Mann, Golo. *Wallenstein.* Hamburg, 2006.

Medick, Hans. "Historisches Ereignis und zeitgenössische Erfahrung: Die Eroberung und Zerstörung Magdeburgs 1631." In *Zwischen Alltag und Katastrophe: Der Dreißigjährige Krieg aus der Nähe,* edited by Benigna von Krusenstjern, Hans Medick, and Patrice Veit, 377–407. Göttingen, 1999.

———. *Der Dreißigjährige Krieg: Zeugnisse vom Leben mit der Gewalt.* Göttingen, 2018.

Meller, Harald, and Michael Schefzik, eds. *Krieg: Eine Archäologische Spurensuche.* Halle a. d. Saale, 2015.

Mellinkoff, Ruth. *Outcasts: Signs of Otherness in Northern European Art in the Late Middle Ages.* 2 vols. Berkeley, 1993.

Mendus, Susan. "The Concept of Toleration." In *Toleration and the Limits of Liberalism,* edited by Susan Mendus, 1–21. Basingstoke, 1989.

Meumann, Markus. "'J'ay dit plusieurs fois aux officiers principaux d'en faire des exemples': Institutionen, Intentionen und Praxis der französischen Militärgerichtsbarkeit im 16. und 17. Jahrhundert." In *Militär und Recht vom 16. bis 19. Jahrhundert: Gelehrter Diskurs—Praxis—Transformationen,* edited by Jutta Nowosadtko, Diethelm Klippel, and Kai Lohsträter, 87–144. Göttingen, 2016.

Meumann, Markus, and Dirk Niefanger, eds. *Ein Schauplatz Herber Angst: Wahrnehmung und Darstellung von Gewalt im 17. Jahrhundert.* Göttingen, 1997.

Meyer, Werner. "Religiös-magisches Denken und Verhalten im eidgenössischen Kriegertum des ausgehenden Mittelalters." In *Militär und Religiosität in der Frühen Neuzeit,* edited by Michael Kaiser and Stefan Kroll, 21–32. Münster, 2004.

Miller, Douglas, and John Richards. *Landsknechte 1486–1560.* Sankt Augustin, 2004.

Misterek, Kathrin. "Ein Massengrab aus der Schlacht von Alerheim am 3. August 1645." *Bericht der Bayerischen Bodendenkmalpflege* 53 (2012): 361–91.

Molitor, Hansgeorg. *Das Erzbistum Köln im Zeitalter der Glaubenskämpfe 1515–1688* (Geschichte des Erzbistums Köln 3). Cologne, 2008.

Möller, Hans Michael. *Das Regiment der Landsknechte: Untersuchungen zu Verfassung, Recht und Selbstverständnis in deutschen Söldnerheeren des 16. Jahrhunderts.* Wiesbaden, 1976.

Monter, William. "Heresy Executions in Reformation Europe 1520–1565." In *Tolerance and Intolerance in the European Reformation,* edited by Ole Peter Grell and Bob Scribner, 48–64. Cambridge, 1996.

Morgan, Philip. "Of Worms and War: 1380–1558." In *Death in England, an Illustrated History,* edited by Peter C. Jupp and Claire Gittings, 119–46. Manchester, 1999.

Mortimer, Geoff. *Eyewitness Accounts of the Thirty Years War 1618–48*. Basingstoke, 2002.

Muir, Edward. *Ritual in Early Modern Europe*. 2nd edn. Cambridge, 2005.

Müller, Marco von. "Das Leben eines Söldners im Dreißigjährigen Krieg (1618–1648)." Masters dissertation. Berlin, 2005. Retrieved 18 January 2024 from userpage.fu-berlin. de/~telehist/MvM/magisterarbeit(1.2.2005).pdf.

Münch, Paul. *Lebensformen in der Frühen Neuzeit*. Frankfurt a. M., 1992.

Nash, David. *Blasphemy in the Christian World: A History*. Oxford, 2007.

Neuwöhner, Andreas, ed. *Im Zeichen des Mars: Quellen zur Geschichte des Dreißigjährigen Krieges und des Westfälischen Friedens in den Stiften Paderborn und Corvey*. Paderborn, 1998.

Nicklisch, Nicole, et al. "Die 47 Soldaten aus dem Massengrab—Ergebnisse der bioarchäologischen Untersuchungen." In *Krieg: Eine Archäologische Spurensuche*, edited by Harald Meller and Michael Schefzik, 405–20. Halle a. d. Saale, 2015.

Nolde, Dorothea. "Andächtiges Staunen—Ungläubige Verwunderung: Religiöse Differenzerfahrungen in französischen und deutschen Reiseberichten in der Frühen Neuzeit." *Francia* 33, no. 2 (2006): 13–34.

Nowosadtko, Jutta. *Scharfrichter und Abdecker: Der Alltag zweier "unehrlicher Berufe" in der Frühen Neuzeit*. Paderborn, 1994.

———. "Die Schulbildung der Soldatenkinder im Fürstbistum Münster: Konfessionelle Unterschiede in den Heeren des 17. und 18. Jahrhunderts." In *Militär und Religiosität in der Frühen Neuzeit*, edited by Michael Kaiser and Stefan Kroll, 293–305. Münster, 2004.

Nowosadtko, Jutta, Diethelm Klippel, and Kai Lohsträter, eds. *Militär und Recht vom 16. bis 19. Jahrhundert: Gelehrter Diskurs—Praxis—Transformationen*. Göttingen, 2016.

Oestreich, Gerhard. "Der römische Stoizismus und die oranische Heeresreform." *Historische Zeitschrift* 176, no. 1 (1953): 17–43.

———. "Strukturprobleme des europäischen Absolutismus." In *Geist und Gestalt des frühmodernen Staates: Ausgewählte Aufsätze*, edited by Gerhard Östreich, 179–97. Berlin, 1969.

Ó hAnnracháin, Tadgh. *Catholic Europe 1592–1648: Centre and Peripheries*. Oxford, 2015.

Ohler, Norbert. *Sterben und Tod im Mittelalter*. Düsseldorf, 2003.

Ortenburg, Georg. *Waffe und Waffengebrauch im Zeitalter der Landsknechte*. Koblenz, 1984.

Outram, Quentin. "The Socio-Economic Relations of Warfare and the Military Mortality Crises of the Thirty Years' War." *Medical History* 45 (2001): 151–84.

Parker, Geoffrey. *The Army of Flanders and the Spanish Road 1567–1659: The Logistics of Spanish Victory and Defeat in the Low Countries' Wars*. Cambridge, 1972.

———. *The Military Revolution: Military Innovation and the Rise of the West 1500–1800*. 2nd rev. edn. Cambridge, 1996.

———, ed. *The Thirty Years War*. 2nd rev. edn. London, 1997.

———. "The Universal Soldier." In *The Thirty Years War*, edited by Geoffrey Parker, 2nd rev. edn., 171–86. London, 1997.

———. *Empire, War and Faith in Early Modern Europe*. London, 2002.

Parrott, David. *The Business of War: Military Enterprise and Military Revolution in Early Modern Europe*. Cambridge, 2012.

Peters, Christian. *Johann Eberlin von Günzburg, ca. 1465–1533: Franziskansicher Reformer, Humanist und konservativer Reformator*. Gütersloh, 1994.

Peters, Jan. *Peter Hagendorf: Tagebuch eines Söldners aus dem Dreißigjärigen Krieg*. 2nd edn. Göttingen, 2012.

220 ～ *Bibliography*

Petrisch, Ernst D. "Zur Problematik der Kontinentalen Osmanenabwehr." In *Karl V. 1500–1558: Neue Perspektiven seiner Herrschaft in Europa und Übersee*, edited by Alfred Kohler, Barbara Haider, and Christine Ottner, 667–84. Vienna, 2002.

Pietsch, Andreas, and Barbara Stollberg-Rilinger, eds. *Konfessionelle Ambiguität: Uneindeutigkeit und Verstellung als religiöse Praxis in der Frühen Neuzeit.* Heidelberg, 2013.

Pietzcker, Frank. "Die Todesvorstellung im Landsknechts- und Soldatenlied." *Zeitschrift für Musikpädagogik* 44 (1988): 3–13.

Piltz, Eric, and Gerd Schwerhoff. "Religiöse Devianz im konfessionellen Zeitalter—Dimensionen eines Forschungsfeldes." In *Gottlosigkeit und Eigensinn: Religiöse Devianz im konfessionellen Zeitalter* (Zeitschrift für Historische Forschung Beiheft 51), edited by Eric Piltz and Gerd Schwerhoff, 9–50. Berlin, 2015.

Plath, Christian. *Konfessionskampf und fremde Besatzung: Stadt und Hochstift Hildesheim im Zeitalter der Gegenreformation und des Dreißigjährigen Krieges (ca. 1580–1660).* Münster, 2005.

Polišenský, Josef V. *The Thirty Years War.* London, 1971.

Pollmann, Judith. *Religious Choice in the Dutch Republic: The Reformation of Arnoldus Buchelius (1565–1641).* Manchester, 1999.

Prange, Wolfgang. *Der Wandel des Bekenntnisses im Lübecker Domkapitel 1530–1600.* Lübeck, 2007.

Preuß, Heike. "Martin Schenk von Nideggen und der Truchsessische Krieg." *Rheinische Vierteljahrsblätter* 49 (1985): 117–38.

Prietzel, Malte. *Kriegführung im Mittelalter: Handlungen, Erinnerungen, Bedeutungen.* Paderborn, 2006.

Prinz, Oliver C. *Der Einfluss von Heeresverfassung und Soldatenbild auf die Entwicklung des Militärstrafrechts.* Göttingen, 2005.

Pröve, Ralf. *Stehendes Heer und städtische Gesellschaft im 18. Jahrhundert: Göttingen und seine Militärbevölkerung 1713–1756.* Munich, 1995.

———. "Violentia und Potestas: Perzeptionsprobleme von Gewalt in Söldnertagebüchern des 17. Jahrhunderts." In *Ein Schauplatz Herber Angst: Wahrnehmung und Darstellung von Gewalt im 17. Jahrhundert*, edited by Markus Meumann and Dirk Niefanger, 24–42. Göttingen, 1997.

———. "Vom Schmuddelkind zur anerkannten Subdisziplin? Die 'neue Militärgeschichte' der Frühen Neuzeit: Perspektiven, Entwicklungen, Probleme." *Geschichte in Wissenschaft und Unterricht* 51 (2000): 597–612.

———. "Reichweiten und Grenzen der Konfessionalisierung am Beispiel der frühneuzeitlichen Militärgesellschaft." In *Interkonfessionalität—Transkonfessionalität—Binnenkonfessionelle Pluralität: Neue Forschungen zur Konfessionalisierungsthese*, edited by Kaspar von Greyerz et al., 73–90. Heidelberg, 2003.

Redlich, Fritz. *De praeda militari: Looting and Booty 1500–1815.* Wiesbaden, 1956.

———. *The German Military Enterpriser and His Workforce: A Study in European Economic and Social History.* 2 vols. Wiesbaden, 1964.

Reichl-Ham, Claudia. *Die Militärseelsorge in Geschichte und Gegenwart* (Militär und Seelsorge, Themenheft 4). Vienna, 2005.

Reinhard, Wolfgang. "Zwang zur Konfessionalisierung? Prolegomena zu einer Theorie des konfessionellen Zeitalters." *Zeitschrift für Historische Forschung* 10 (1983): 257–77.

Reinhardt, Volker. *Blutiger Karneval: Der Sacco di Roma 1527—Eine politische Katastrophe.* Darmstadt, 2009.

Reiss, Ansgar, and Sabine Witt, eds. *Calvinismus: Die Reformierten in Deutschland und Europa*. Berlin, 2009.

Richet, Denis. "Aspects socio-culturels des conflits religieux: Paris dans la seconde moitié du XVIe siècle." *Annales* 32 (1977): 764–89.

Rider, Catherine Rider. "Common Magic." In *The Cambridge History of Magic and Witchcraft in the West*, edited by David J. Collins, 303–31. New York, 2015.

Roberts, Michael. "The Military Revolution, 1560–1660." In *The Military Revolution Debate: Readings on the Military Transformation of Early Modern Europe*, edited by Clifford J. Rogers, 13–35. Boulder, 1995.

Robisheaux, Thomas. *Rural Society and the Search for Order in Early Modern Germany*. Cambridge, 1989.

Rodríguez-Pérez, Yolanda. *The Dutch Revolt through Spanish Eyes: Self and Other in Historical and Literary Texts of the Golden Age Spain (c.1548–1673)*. Oxford, 2008.

Roeck, Bernd. "Der Dreißigjährige Krieg und die Menschen im Reich: Überlegungen zu den Formen psychischer Krisenbewältigung in der ersten Hälfte des 17. Jahrhunderts." In *Krieg und Frieden: Militär und Gesellschaft in der frühen Neuzeit*, edited by Bernhard R. Kroener and Ralf Pröve, 265–79. Paderborn, 1996.

———. "Macht und Ohnmacht der Bilder: Die Historische Perspektive." In *Macht und Ohnmacht der Bilder: Reformatorischer Bildersturm im Kontext der europäischen Geschichte*, edited by Peter Blickle et al., 33–64. Munich, 2002.

Rogers, Clifford J., ed. *The Military Revolution Debate: Readings on the Military Transformation of Early Modern Europe*. Boulder, 1995.

———. "The Military Revolutions of the Hundred Years' War." In *The Military Revolution Debate: Readings on the Military Transformation of Early Modern Europe*, edited by Clifford J. Rogers, 55–94. Boulder, 1995.

Rogg, Matthias. "'Zerhauen und zerschnitten nach adelichen Sitten'—Herkunft, Entwicklung und Funktion soldatischer Tracht des 16. Jahrhunderts im Spiegel zeitgenössischer Kunst." In *Krieg und Frieden: Militär und Gesellschaft in der frühen Neuzeit*, edited by Bernhard R. Kroener and Ralf Pröve, 109–35. Paderborn, 1996.

———. *Landsknechte und Reisläufer: Bilder vom Soldaten. Ein Stand in der Kunst des 16. Jahrhunderts*. Paderborn, 2002.

———. "Gottlose Kriegsleute? Zur bildlichen Darstellung von Söldnern des 16. Jahrhunderts im Spannungsfeld von Lebenswirklichkeit, öffentlicher Meinung und konfessioneller Bildpropaganda." In *Militär und Religiosität in der Frühen Neuzeit*, edited by Michael Kaiser and Stefan Kroll, 121–44. Münster, 2004.

Römling, Michael. "Ein Heer ist ein großes gefräßiges Tier: Soldaten in spanischen und kaiserlichen Diensten und die Bevölkerung der vom Krieg betroffenen Gebiete in Italien zwischen 1509 und 1530." Doctoral dissertation. Göttingen, 2001.

Roper, Lyndal. "'The Common Man', 'the Common Good', 'Common Women': Gender and Meaning in the German Reformation Commune." *Social History* 12, no. 1 (1987): 1–21.

———. *The Holy Household: Women and Morals in Early Modern Augsburg*. Oxford, 1989.

———. *Martin Luther: Renegade and Prophet*. London, 2012.

Rublack, Ulinka. "Wench and Maiden: Women, War and the Pictorial Function of the Feminine in German Cities in the Early Modern Period." *History Workshop Journal* 44 (1997): 1–21.

———. *Magd, Metz' oder Mörderin: Frauen vor frühneuzeitlichen Gerichten*. Frankfurt a. M., 1998.

222 ❦ *Bibliography*

———. *Reformation Europe*. Cambridge, 2005.

———. *Dressing Up: Cultural Identity in Renaissance Europe*. Oxford, 2010.

Ruff, Margarethe. *Zauberpraktiken als Lebenshilfe: Magie im Alltag vom Mittelalter bis heute*. Frankfurt a. M., 2003.

Schilling, Heinz. *Konfessionskonflikt und Staatsbildung: Eine Fallstudie über das Verhältnis von religiösem und sozialem Wandel in der Frühneuzeit am Beispiel der Grafschaft Lippe*. Gütersloh, 1981.

———. "Die Konfessionalisierung im Reich: Religiöser und Gesellschaftlicher Wandel in Deutschland zwischen 1555 und 1620." *Historische Zeitschrift* 246, no. 1 (1988): 1–45.

———. "Disziplinierung oder 'Selbstregulierung der Untertanen'? Ein Plädoyer für die Doppelperspektive von Makro- und Mikrohistorie bei der Erforschung der frühmodernen Kirchenzucht." *Historische Zeitschrift* 264, no. 3 (1997): 675–91.

———. "'Veni, vidi, Deus vixit'—Karl V. zwischen Religionskrieg und Religionsfrieden." *Archiv für Reformationsgeschichte* 89 (1998): 144–66.

———. "Confessionalization in Europe: Causes and Effects for Church, State, Society, and Culture." In *1648: War and Peace in Europe*, vol. 2, edited by Klaus Bussmann and Heinz Schilling, 219–28. Münster, 1998.

Schindler, Norbert. *Widerspenstige Leute: Studien zur Volkskultur in der frühen Neuzeit*. Frankfurt a. M., 1992.

Schindling, Anton. "Neighbours of a Different Faith: Confessional Coexistence and Parity in the Territorial States and Towns of the Empire." In *1648: War and Peace in Europe*, vol. 2, edited by Klaus Bussmann and Heinz Schilling, 465–73. Münster, 1998.

———. "Das Strafgericht Gottes: Kriegserfahrungen und Religion im Heiligen Römischen Reich Deutscher Nation im Zeitalter des Dreissigjährigen Krieges. Erfahrungsgeschichte und Konfessionalisierung." In *Das Strafgericht Gottes: Kriegserfahrungen und Religion im Heiligen Römischen Reich Deutscher Nation im Zeitalter des Dreißigjährigen Krieges*, edited by Matthias Asche and Anton Schindling, 11–51. Münster, 2001.

Schlumbohm, Jürgen. "Gesetze die nicht durchgesetzt werden—Ein Strukturmerkmal des frühneuzeitlichen Staates?" *Geschichte und Gesellschaft* 23, no. 4 (1997): 647–63.

Schlütter-Schindler, Gabriele. *Der Schmalkaldische Bund und das Problem der causa religionis*. Frankfurt a. M., 1986.

Schmidt, Heinrich Richard. *Dorf und Religion: Reformierte Sittenzucht in Berner Landgemeinden der Frühen Neuzeit*. Stuttgart, 1995.

———. "Sozialdisziplinierung? Ein Plädoyer für das Ende des Etatismus in der Konfessionalisierungsforschung." *Historische Zeitschrift* 265, no. 3 (1997): 639–82.

Schmidtchen, Volker. "*Ius in bello* und militärischer Alltag: Rechtliche Regelungen in Kriegsordnungen des 14. bis 16. Jahrhunderts." In *Der Krieg im Mittelalter und in der Frühen Neuzeit: Gründe, Begründungen, Bilder, Bräuche, Recht*, edited by Horst Brunner, 25–56. Wiesbaden, 1999.

Schnitzler, Norbert. *Ikonoklasmus-Bildersturm: Theologischer Bilderstreit und ikonoklastisches Handeln während des 15. und 16. Jahrhunderts*. Munich, 1996.

Scholz, Maximilian Miguel. *Strange Brethren: Refugees, Religious Bonds, and Reformation in Frankfurt, 1554–1608*. Charlottesville, VA, 2022.

Schreiner, Klaus. *Märtyrer, Schlachtenhelfer, Friedenstifter: Krieg und Frieden im Spiegel mittelalterlicher und frühneuzeitlicher Heiligenverehrung*. Opladen, 2000.

———. *Maria: Leben, Legenden, Symbole*. Munich, 2003.

———. "'Sygzeichen': Symbolische Kommunikation in kriegerischen Konflikten des späten Mittelalters und der frühen Neuzeit." In *Sprachen des Politischen: Medien und Me-*

dialität in der Geschichte, edited by Ute Frevert and Wolfgang Braungart, 20–94. Göttingen, 2004.

Schulz, Hans. *Der Sacco di Roma: Karls V. Truppen in Rom 1527–8.* Halle, 1894.

Schulze, Winfried. "Review of H. Schilling,'Konfessionskonflikt.'" *Zeitschrift für Historische Forschung* 12 (1985): 104–7.

Schulze-Busacker Elisabeth. "Philippe de Novare, les Quatre âges de l'homme." *Romania* 505–6 (2009): 104–46.

Schweitzer, Friedrich, ed. *Religion, Politik und Gewalt.* Gütersloh, 2006.

Schwerhoff, Gerd. "Starke Worte: Blasphemie als theatralische Inszenierung von Männlichkeit an der Wende vom Mittelalter zur Frühen Neuzeit." In *Hausväter, Priester, Kastraten: Zur Konstruktion von Männlichkeit in Spätmittelalter und Früher Neuzeit,* edited by Martin Dinges, 237–63. Göttingen, 1998.

———. *Zungen wie Schwerter: Blasphemie in alteuropäischen Gesellschaften 1200–1650.* Konstanz, 2005.

Scribner, Robert W. "Reformation, Carnival and the World Turned Upside-Down." *Social History* 3, no. 3 (1978): 303–29.

———. *For the Sake of the Simple Folk: Popular Propaganda for the German Reformation.* Oxford, 1981.

———. "The Reformation, Popular Magic, and the 'Disenchantment of the World.'" *Journal for Interdisciplinary History* 23, no. 3 (1993): 475–94.

———. "Preconditions of Tolerance and Intolerance in Sixteenth-Century Germany." In *Tolerance and Intolerance in the European Reformation,* edited by Ole Peter Grell and Bob Scribner, 32–47. Cambridge, 1996.

Scribner, Robert W., and Gerhard Benecke, eds. *The German Peasant War of 1525.* London, 1979.

Scribner, Robert W., and C. Scott Dixon. *The German Reformation.* 2nd edn. Basingstoke, 2003.

Seidenspinner, Wolfgang. "Das Janusgesicht der Binnenexoten: Marginalisierte zwischen Verteufelung und utopischem Gegenentwurf." In *Im Zeichen der Krise: Religiosität im Europa des 17. Jahrhunderts,* edited by Hartmut Lehmann and Anne-Charlott Trepp, 337–58. Göttingen, 1999.

Seward, Desmond. *The Monks of War: The Military Religious Orders.* London, 1995.

Sikora, Michael. "Söldner—Historische Annäherung an einen Kriegertypus." *Geschichte und Gesellschaft* 29 (2003): 210–38.

Skemer, Don C. *Binding Words: Textual Amulets in the Middle Ages.* University Park, PA, 2006.

Spierling, Karen E. "Daring Insolence toward God? The Perpetuation of Catholic Baptismal Traditions in Sixteenth-Century Geneva." *Archiv für Reformationsgeschichte* 93 (2002): 97–125.

Spohnholz, Jesse. "Multiconfessional Celebration of the Eucharist in Sixteenth-Century Wesel." *Sixteenth Century Journal* 39, no. 3 (2008): 705–29.

———. *The Tactics of Toleration: A Refugee Community in the Age of Religious Wars.* Newark, DE, 2011.

Stahl, Andreas. "Nach der Schlacht von Lützen." In *Krieg: Eine Archäologische Spurensuche,* edited by Harald Meller and Michael Schefzik, 387–90. Halle a. d. Saale, 2015.

Stambaugh, Ria, ed. *Teufelbücher in Auswahl,* vol. 4. Berlin, 1978.

Stollberg-Rilinger, Barbara. *Des Kaisers alte Kleider: Verfassungsgeschichte und Symbolsprache des Alten Reiches.* 2nd rev. edn. Munich, 2013.

224 ~: *Bibliography*

Straddling, R. A. *Spain's Struggle for Europe 1598–1668.* London, 1994.

Strauß, Walter. *The German Single-Leaf Woodcut, 1550–1600.* Vol. 3. New York, 1975.

Stuart, Kathy. *Defiled Trades & Social Outcasts: Honor and Ritual Pollution in Early Modern Germany.* Cambridge, 1999.

Sugg, Richard. "'Good Physic but Bad Food': Early Modern Attitudes to Medicinal Cannibalism and its Suppliers." *Social History of Medicine* 19 (2006): 225–40.

Swart, Erik. "From '*Landsknecht*' to '*Soldier*': The Low German Foot Soldiers of the Low Countries in the Second Half of the Sixteenth Century." *International Review of Social History* 51 (2006): 75–92.

Swart, Koenraad W. "The Black Legend during the Eighty Years War." In *Britain and the Netherlands,* vol. 5, edited by J. S. Bromley and Ernst H. Kossmann, 36–57. The Hague, 1975.

Tallett, Frank. *War and Society in Early Modern Europe (1495–1715).* London, 1992.

———. "Introduction." In *European Warfare 1350–1750,* edited by Frank Tallett and David J. B. Trim, 1–26. Cambridge, 2010.

Tallett, Frank, and David J. B. Trim, eds. *European Warfare 1350–1750.* Cambridge, 2010.

Thiessen, Hillard von. "Das Sterbebett als normative Schwelle: Der Mensch in der Frühen Neuzeit zwischen irdischer Normenkonkurrenz und göttlichem Gericht." *Historische Zeitschrift* 295 (2012): 625–59.

———. *Das Zeitalter der Ambiguität. Vom Umgang mit Normen in der Frühen Neuzeit.* Cologne, 2021.

Tlusty, B. Ann. *Bacchus and Civic Order: The Culture of Drink in Early Modern Germany.* Charlottesville, VA, 2001.

———. "Invincible Blades and Invulnerable Bodies: Weapons Magic in Early-Modern Germany." *European Review of History* 22 (2015): 658–79.

Tresp, Uwe. *Söldner aus Böhmen. Im Dienst deutscher Fürsten: Kriegsgeschäft und Heeresorganisation im 15. Jahrhundert.* Paderborn, 2004.

Trim, David J. B. "Conflict, Religion and Ideology." In *European Warfare 1350–1750,* edited by Frank Tallett and David J. B. Trim, 278–99. Cambridge, 2010.

Tyerman, Christopher. *God's War: A New History of the Crusades.* London, 2006.

Ulbrich, Claudia. "'Hat man also bald ein solches Blutbad, Würgen und Wüten in der Stadt gehört und gesehen, daß mich solches jammert wider zu gedencken . . .': Religion und Gewalt in Michael Heberer von Brettens 'Ægyptiaca Servitus' (1610)." In *Religion und Gewalt: Konflikte, Rituale, Deutungen (1500–1800),* edited by Kaspar von Greyerz and Kim Siebenhüner, 85–108. Göttingen, 2006.

Veldman, Ilja M. "Bildersturm und neue Bilderwelten." In *Calvinismus: Die Reformierten in Deutschland und Europa,* edited by Ansgar Reiss and Sabine Witt, 270–94. Berlin, 2009.

Verberckmoes, Johan. "The Comic and the Counter-Reformation in the Spanish Netherlands." In *A Cultural History of Laughter: From Antiquity to the Present Day,* edited by Jan Bremmer and Herman Roodenburg, 76–89. Cambridge, 1997.

Volkland, Frauke. *Konfession und Selbstverständnis: Reformierte Rituale in der gemischtkonfessionellen Kleinstadt Bischofszell im 17. Jahrhundert.* Göttingen, 2005.

Voss, Wolf Eckart. "For the Prevention of Even Greater Suffering: The Curse and Blessing of Law in War." In *1648: War and Peace in Europe,* vol. 2, edited by Klaus Bussmann and Heinz Schilling, 275–83. Münster, 1998.

Vovelle, Michel. *La Mort et l'Occident de 1300 à nos jours.* Paris, 1983.

Walsham, Alexandra. *Providence in Early Modern England.* Oxford, 1999.

———. *Charitable Hatred: Tolerance and Intolerance in England 1500–1700*. Manchester, 2006.

Wedgwood, Cicely V. *The Thirty Years War*. New York, 2005 [1938].

Wette, Wolfram, ed. *Der Krieg des kleinen Mannes: Eine Militärgeschichte von unten*. Munich, 1992.

Wilson, Peter H. *Europe's Tragedy: A History of the Thirty Years War*. London, 2009.

Wilson, Stephen. *The Magical Universe: Everyday Ritual and Magic in Pre-Modern Europe*. London, 2000.

Winkelmann, Friedhelm. *Geschichte des frühen Christentums*. Munich, 2001.

Winnige, Norbert. "Von der Kontribution zu Akzise: Militärfinanzierung als Movens staatlicher Steuerpolitik." In *Krieg und Frieden: Militär und Gesellschaft in der frühen Neuzeit*, edited by Bernhard R. Kroener and Ralf Pröve, 59–83. Paderborn, 1996.

Witt, Christian V. *Protestanten: Das Werden eines Integrationsbegriffs in der Frühen Neuzeit*. Tübingen, 2011.

Wolff, Christoph. *Johann Sebastian Bach: The Learned Musician*. Oxford, 2001.

Wolff, Fritz. "Feldpostbriefe aus dem Dreißigjährigen Kriege: Selbstzeugnisse der kleinen Leute." In *Hundert Jahre Historische Kommission für Hessen 1897–1997. Festgabe dargebracht von Autorinnen und Autoren der Historischen Kommission*, vol. 1, edited by Walter Heinemeyer, 481–512. Marburg, 1997.

Wolter, Beatrice. *Deutsche Schlagwörter zur Zeit des Dreissigjährigen Krieges*. Frankfurt a.M., 2000.

Wright, Nicholas. *Knights and Peasants: The Hundred Years War in the French Countryside*. Rochester, 1998.

Wunderli, Richard, and Gerald Broce. "The Final Moment before Death in Early Modern England." *Sixteenth Century Journal* 20, no. 2 (1989): 259–75.

Zeeden, Ernst Walter. *Die Entstehung der Konfessionen: Grundlagen und Formen der Konfessionsbildung im Zeitalter der Glaubenskämpfe*. Munich, 1965.

Reference Works

Allgemeine Deutsche Biographie. 56 vols. Leipzig, 1875–1912.

Handwörterbuch des deutschen Aberglaubens (HDA), ed. Hanns Bächtold-Stäubli and Eduard Hoffmann-Krayer. 10 vols. Berlin, 1927–42.

Online Resources

"Der Dreißigjährige Krieg in Selbstzeugnissen, Chroniken und Berichten" (website). Retrieved 19 January 2024 from http://www.30jaehrigerkrieg.de.

❧ INDEX ❧

Ackermann, Jürgen, 104, 107,
    130–31, 143, 153–54, 177
Adams, Anna Sophia, 185
Adams, Salomon, 185
agency, 5, 11, 97, 115, 156
Agrippa, Heinrich, 21
Ahlden, 167
Alba, Fernando Álvarez de Toledo,
    duke of, 132
Albert VII, archduke of Austria, 133
Alerheim (battle), 185–84
All, Henß, 100
Allendorf, 34, 100, 103
alms, 79, 100
Altötting, 79
ambiguity, 4, 10, 33, 83, 98–99, 105,
    120
  confessional, 77
  normative, 173
Americas, colonization of, 135
amulets, 95–96
Anabaptism, 3–4, 47
Andechs, 119
angels, 92, 95
anger, 17, 27, 83, 85–89, 101, 135,
    168, 175
Angermüller, Johann Jacob, 167–69,
    172
Anhalt-Bernburg, Christian of, 175
Anrath, Arnold von, 124, 179
anti-papalism, 64–66, 134, 139–40,
    151, 183
anticlericalism, 116, 183, 187

anxiety, 3, 5, 11, 17–18, 29, 61, 90,
    123
  moral, 5, 18, 61
army, as a socio-professional setting,
    2–4, 12, 31, 34–36, 42–45, 54,
    66, 98, 113–15, 141–44, 150,
    155–56, 170, 179
army train, 2, 47, 98, 184
ars moriendi, 13, 164, 169–73, 186
articles of war, 12, 23, 29–30, 44–47,
    50–58, 66–68, 85–88, 96, 98,
    105, 115, 119, 136, 179
Aschering, 119
astrology, 89–90, 94
atheism, 18, 63
atrocity, 66, 115, 129–30, 132,
    145–46
attrition. See mortality
Auger, Emond, 64
Augsburg Interim, 138
Augsburg, 37, 56, 83, 99
Augustine of Hippo, 27, 168
autobiography, 12, 34, 37, 74 76–78,
    105, 138–140, 148, 154, 174,
    177–78, 184, 187
Ayñsa, Joseph de, 131

Bach, Johann Sebastian, 78
Baldric of Dol, 26
Bamberg, 78, 152, 183
Bandhauer, Zacharias, 128
Banér, Johann, 193
baptism, 47, 76–77, 79, 178, 193

Index ~ 227

battle. *See* combat
Bavarian army, 53, 55, 100–101,
    133–34, 144, 174, 176
Beelzebub, 94–95. *See also* devil
Beerfelden, 120
beggars, 18, 32, 37
    'sturdy', 18, 32
Behm, Martin, 22–23
Belial, 22, 28. *See also* devil
Berlichingen, Götz von, 88, 140, 144,
    176
Bernard of Clairvaux, 20, 26–27
Bernhard, duke of Saxe-Weimar,
    57–58, 152
Bert, Werner von, 36, 143
Bismarck, Christoph von, 76
Black Legend, 132
blasphemy, 1–2, 12, 16, 18, 20–21,
    23, 35, 47, 50–52, 64, 67, 74, 77,
    82, 84–89, 105, 120, 123, 137,
    183
Bohemia, 28, 122, 126–27, 174–75,
    181, 193, 195
Bohemian Revolt, 126, 174, 181
Bonn, 133–34
books, 56, 91, 119, 122, 150,
    162n208, 166–67
Borggräfin, Anna, 101
Borken, 36
Botvidi, Johannes, 65
Braunß, Maria, 101
Brazil, 140.
Breisach, 126
Breitenburg, 146, 180
Bremen, 92
Broich (castle), 133
Brunmüller, Caspar, 87
Brusasco, 174, 181
Budweis, 180–81
Buonaparte, Jacopo, 118
Burckelau, Johann, 167–68
Burger, Conrad, 58, 79

Burgundians, 119
burial, 13, 79, 118, 141, 152, 164–
    69, 172, 179–87
    lack of, 13, 182, 184
    nocturnal, 184
    rites, 13, 165–66, 179, 182–84, 187
Burtenbach (Swabia), 34
Butler, Walter, 78

Cacciis, Julius Ceasar de, 180
Calvinism, 3, 14, 49–50, 57, 66, 81,
    123–25, 132, 134, 136, 138,
    142, 150–53, 165, 179–80, 186,
    193
camp followers, 13, 103, 129, 182,
    184, 193. *See also* army train
captivity, 11, 45, 50, 77, 116–18,
    123–24, 130, 133, 139–40,
    144–46, 174, 179. *See also*
    prisoners of war
Carl Gustav, count palatine of
    Zweibrücken, 192–94
Carmelites, 97, 152
Castel Sant'Angelo, 118
Castiel (angel), 94
catechisms, 22, 55, 64, 166
Catholic League, 53
Catholicism, 1, 3, 8, 14, 41, 48–50,
    52–55, 61–66, 77–81, 92–93,
    95–97, 99, 101, 113–14,
    116–21, 123–30, 132–37,
    139–40, 150–54, 165, 167, 170,
    172, 176, 179–80, 182–83, 186,
    195, 197
cavalry, 2, 33, 36, 57–58
    social status of, 36, 58, 101, 147,
    167, 176
changing sides, 8, 77, 138–39,
    143–44, 146, 174
Chanovsky von Langendorff,
    Friedrich Ludwig, 56–57, 71n85
chaplaincy, 54–57, 58, 63, 67

228 ❦ *Index*

chaplains, 22, 42, 44, 47, 50, 52,
54–65, 65–67, 72n119, 79–81,
95, 113, 130–31, 134–35, 140,
153, 166–67, 169–70, 172,
182–83, 187
training of, 56–58, 60, 67
Charles I, king of England, 195
Charles III, duke of Bourbon, 116
Charles V (emperor), 20, 48, 50, 116,
172
charms, 90–93, 96–97
children, 2, 11, 22, 35–36, 75–77,
79, 99–104, 127, 129–30, 138,
144, 178, 184, 193
death of, 11, 76, 103–104, 127,
129, 177–78, 184, 193
illegitimate, 35, 100
chivalry, 9, 27, 29
chivalry and violence, 9, 145, 176
choleric temperament, 30, 45
Christendom, 4, 20, 65, 155
Christian IV, king of Denmark, 51
Christian, duke of Brunswick-
Lüneburg, 119
Christian(ity), confessionally
unmarked, 13–14, 50, 52,
62–64, 66-68, 74–78, 114–15,
149, 152–156, 165, 187, 196
Christina, queen of Sweden, 192–93
church discipline, 51, 104
church music, 77–80, 151–52
Clement VII (pope), 116, 118
clothing, 1, 22, 79, 82–84, 118, 126,
170, 173, 185. *See also* fashion
Clout, Friedrich Hermann, 135
Cologne (*Truchsessische*) War, 4, 133
Cologne, 33, 35–36, 78, 81
Cologne, archbishop of, 28, 33
combat, 29, 145–149, 161n191, 170,
176
commoners as soldiers, 3, 17, 28–31,
34, 36, 147

communion, 1, 60, 118, 134, 168
Compie, 177
confession (of sin), 55, 79, 140,
170–71, 194.
confession (doctrinal), 3, 12, 28, 47,
51, 62, 77, 97–98, 113–156,
195–197
confessional coexistence, 4, 7–9,
11–12, 43, 113, 135–36,
149–56, 196
confessional conflict, 4, 8, 43–44,
47, 50, 61, 113–37
confessional cultures, 3–4, 196
confessional diversity, 7, 50, 197
confessional homogeneity, 42–44,
47, 53–54
confessional indifference, 7–8, 12,
43–44, 54, 66, 113, 132, 141,
155
confessional motivation, 4, 48–49,
113–15, 120–22, 128, 136–37,
140–43
confessionalization, 6–10, 42–44,
48–49, 53–54
conflict, 4, 26, 43-44, 84, 149, 150,
154–55
military-civilian, 8, 29–30, 53, 101,
128, 131–132, 147, 181
confraternities, 81
Constantinople, 129
contracts, 27, 43, 45, 67, 136, 138
conversion, 33, 134, 139
corpses, 36, 135, 180–82, 185–87
burning of, 135
mutilation of, 127, 180
Corvinus, Matthias, king of Hungary,
75
court preachers, 22, 54, 56–58, 60,
65, 123, 129
Covenanters, 142
cowardice, 176
Cramm, Assa von, 21

Crane, Johann, 194
criminals, 32, 47, 85, 89, 91, 118, 184
Croats, 131, 157n43
crucifix, 20, 24, 117, 123
crusading, 26–28, 135
custom, 8–9, 27, 59, 74, 98–99, 165, 170, 184, 187
  martial, 29, 44–46, 98, 103, 109n114, 119, 121, 132, 146, 154, 182–83

Dahenfeld, 57
Danzig, 23, 87
Daun-Falkenstein, Wirich VI. von, 132–33, 135
death, 10, 64, 75-76, 78-79, 91, 103, 147, 164–178
death sentence, 24–25, 45, 75, 86–87, 92, 134, 168, 179
Deben, Ludwig von, 88
dehumanization, 148
demobilization, 192–93
demobilized soldiers, 32, 92
Denmark, 49, 51, 86, 101, 168
desecration, 117, 120–22, 124–25, 136
desertion, 31, 43, 45, 53, 136, 143, 146, 174, 176
destitution. See poverty
deviance, 12, 17–18, 37, 82–83, 89, 97, 105
devil, 16, 18, 20–23, 27, 32, 77, 80, 85, 92–94, 96, 101, 124, 172
devotional images, 117, 121–24
devotional literature, 12, 44, 63–68, 78, 114, 165, 172–73, 179
diaries. See autobiography
Dillich, Wilhelm, 60
Diocletian Persecution, 25
dishonor, 36, 124, 144, 176, 184
dissimulation, 4, 48

doctrinal understanding, 12, 57, 59, 114, 118, 124–125, 136, 153, 165, 196
Dominicans, 80, 151–52
Drakenburg (battle), 171
Dreger, Melchior, 83
Dresden, 53, 129, 168
drunkenness, 2, 16, 19, 21, 37, 47, 51–53, 70n64, 86–87, 92, 101, 118, 135, 151, 184, 194
Dryander, Johannes, 140
Duisburg, 179
Dürer, Albrecht, 173
Dutch Revolt, 2, 132–33, 135–36
dying, 13, 55, 60, 62, 67, 97, 117, 148, 164–177, 179–80, 182, 184, 186, 193. See also mortality

Early Christian attitudes to military service, 24–26
Eberlin von Günzburg, Johann, 20
Echzell, 119
Edict of Milan, 25
Egeln, 193
Eger, 183
Eggelinck, Wilhelm, 166–67
Eighty Years War. See Dutch Revolt
Electoral-Saxony, 48, 54, 176, 184
Elijah (prophet), 61
enemies, 12, 28–29, 50, 65–66, 115, 144–149, 153, 155, 170, 182
England, 28, 51, 92–93, 115, 138–39, 141, 143, 147, 165, 176, 195
Erasmus, Desiderius, 19–21, 63
Erfurt, 93–94
Erlach, Wolff von, 134
Erpach, Juliana von, 193
Erskine, Alexander, 194
Eschwege, 100
executioners, 60, 75, 91, 93–94, 169

Fabel, Hans, 92

230 ~: *Index*

Fabricius, Jacob, 56–57, 65–66
Farnese, Alessandro, duke of Parma, 55
fashion, 26–27, 75, 82–83, 114, 141
Feldordnungen, 47. *See also* articles of war
Ferdinand I (emperor), 48, 172
Ferdinand III (emperor), 55
festmachen. See magic, apotropaic
Fetzer, Christoph, 135
feud(ing), 21, 26, 28
Feudalism, 26, 31
Fiedler, Constantin, 152
field preacher. *See* chaplain
Finns, 66
Fitzsimon, Henry, 79
Flanders. *See* Netherlands
Flemings, 135
Fleurus (battle), 167
Forchheim, 146
forensic archaeological evidence, 89–90, 185–86
France, 27, 34, 48, 55, 64, 113, 150–51, 194
Franciscans, 20, 55, 78, 97, 139, 183
Franck, Sebastian, 21
Frankenthal, 180–81
Frankfurt am Main, 87
Frankfurt on the Oder, 82
Frederick V, elector palatine, king of Bohemia, 123–24, 194
Freiberg, 184
Freiberger, Albrecht von, 138
Freiburg, 58, 79
French Wars of Religion, 2, 55
French troops, 79, 92, 145, 147
Freytag, Gustav, 5
friendship, 37, 102, 106, 140–41, 144, 147, 150–53, 163n241, 194
Friese, Johann Daniel and family, 75, 130

Friesenegger, Maurus, 119, 170
Friesland, 35
Fritsch, Augustin von, 75, 78, 85, 92, 144–45, 147, 169
Fronsperger, Leonhardt, 22, 58–61, 63–64, 172
Frundsberg, Georg von, 97, 174
Fulcher of Chartres, 24
funeral. *See* burial
funeral sermons, 118, 141, 152, 164, 166–70, 172, 186
Fürstenberg, Dietrich von, 133

Galenic medicine, 90
gambling, 1–2, 10, 16, 18–23, 37, 47, 77, 82, 85, 118
Ganns, Johann, 55
Gartknechte, 32, 92
Gerlach, Samuel, 56–57, 62
German Peasants' War, 4, 140
God as arbiter, 74, 76
as protector, 75–78, 81, 140, 171, 176
as punisher, 1, 18, 74–76, 129–30
godless(ness), 11–12, 17–20, 22–23, 28, 30, 32–33, 35, 37, 56, 62, 66, 74, 76, 82, 85, 105, 167, 175
Gospel of John, 92, 95–96
Graff, Jörg, 175, 183
graffiti, 117
Granada, 135
Graubünden (Grison), 81
Greussen, 59
group cohesion, 8, 27, 67, 149, 153
Guicciardini, Luigi, 117–18
Gumpenberg, Ambrosius, 117
gunners, 90, 147
Gustavus II Adolphus, king of Sweden, 51, 56–57, 139, 174, 193

Habsburgs, 48–49, 78, 132–133, 192
Hagendorf, Barbara, 178, 184
Hagendorf, Elisabet, 177–78
Hagendorf, Melchert Christoff, 77
Hagendorf, Peter, 10–11, 75–79, 85, 103, 130–31, 143–45, 176–78, 184
Halle, 93, 129
Hardtmann, Catharina, 103
Harstall, Hans Friedrich von, 169
Hatzfeld, Franz von, 78, 183
Hatzfeld, Melchior von, 78, 175, 183
Haugwitz, Anna Maria von, 193
Haugwitz, Johann Dietrich von, 166–69, 172
Hawkwood, John, 28
health, 57, 60, 75, 90–91, 148, 174, 184, 187, 195
heaven, 16–17, 80, 92, 97, 167, 171–72, 178
Heilig Grab (cloister near Bamberg), 80, 151–52
hell, 16–17, 22–23, 167
Herdenius, Georg, 84–85, 119, 137
heresy, 3, 19, 28, 48–49, 54, 65, 82, 116, 120–22, 125, 128–135, 150
  trials, 133–36
Hesen, Evert von, 102
Heylmann, Johann Jacob, 80
hidalguía, 135
Hocker, Johann Ludwig, 58, 60, 62–63, 95
Hoffmeyer, Maria, 102
Holk, Henrik, 130, 139
honor, 10, 12, 22, 26, 28–29, 33–34, 36–37, 43, 46, 58, 60–61, 76, 84, 88, 93, 98, 100, 104–105, 115, 124, 127–28, 134, 144–46, 148, 152, 156, 166–67, 172,

179–81, 184, 186, 193. *See also* dishonor
Horn, Gustav, 57
hospitals, 55, 60, 62, 184. *See also* medical care
hostages, 103
hosts, 1, 60, 91, 95, 119, 121
humiliation, 86, 117–18, 120, 127. *See also* mockery
humor, 16, 33, 35, 88, 151, 153, 155, 187
Hussites, 28, 123
hymns, 52, 59, 64, 78–81, 120, 152–53, 171. *See also* church music; singing
  "A Mighty Fortress is Our God", 80, 171
  "In Peace and Joy I Now Depart", 171
  "Maintain Us, Lord, in Thy Word", 80
  "Salve Regina", 79, 152–53
  "Te Deum", 128

identity, 3, 106, 125–26, 138, 140–41, 149, 153–54
ideology, 5, 13–14, 26–27, 29, 138, 141–43, 147–48, 154–55
idleness, 17–21, 27, 31–32, 82
idolatry, 19, 52, 66, 82, 96, 123–24
imitatio Christi, 152
Immick, Anna, 100
imperial army, 50–51, 53–56, 61, 92, 101, 116, 118–19, 122, 127–28, 137–38, 143–44, 146, 174–75, 181, 192, 194
imperial diet, 50
infant mortality. *See* children, death of
infantry, 1–2, 13, 28–29, 36, 49, 58, 61, 67, 79, 101, 129, 147, 176
  social status of, 28–29, 36, 147

232 ~: *Index*

Ingolstadt, 28, 75
Innocent III (pope), 27
insults, 20, 24, 27, 47, 101, 113,
    118–23, 125–27, 131, 135, 145,
    151, 182
  "heathen" (slur), 22–23, 47
  "heretic" (slur), 19, 28, 49, 54, 65,
    82, 116, 120, 122, 125, 129,
    130–32, 134–35, 150
  "*pfaffe*" (slur), 131, 183
international composition of armies,
    3, 8, 50, 145, 147, 156, 186–87
intolerance, 44, 115, 152
Ireland, 78–79
irenicism, 42–43
Isenburg, Salentin von, 33
Italy, 2, 27–28, 64, 78, 84, 116–18,
    121, 186

Jan Bockelson (Jan van Leiden), 47
Jesuits, 55–56, 58, 62, 64, 78–79, 81,
    92, 122, 125, 128, 150, 152, 179,
    194–95
Jesus Christ, 16–17, 22, 24–25, 51,
    95, 123, 171, 185
Johann Casimir, count palatine of
    Zweibrücken, 193
John the Baptist, 24, 92
John George, duke of Saxony, 176
John, elector of Saxony, 48,
Joshua (biblical character), 61
Judas Iscariot, 117
Junius, Maria Anna, 80, 84, 137, 146,
    153, 170
just war, 25

Kalbach, Hanß Thomas von, 101
Kalkum genannt Lohausen, Wilhelm
    von, 142, 152–53
Karl Ludwig, elector palatine,
    194–95
Kassel, 92

Katharina, princess of Sweden,
    countess palatine of
    Zweibrücken, 193
Kenzingen, 79
killing, 23, 25, 27, 145–48, 154. *See
    also* combat
Kirchheiligen, 59
Klein, Johannes, 101–102
knights, 2, 13, 21, 24, 26–30, 118,
    133, 140, 176
Knyphausen, Dodo zu Innhausen
    und, 146
Kroppenstedt, 153
Kuckelmann, Johann, 35–36

Lambrecht, Elisabeth, 104
Lamminger, Wolf Friedrich, 61
Lamormaini, William, 78
Landsberg an der Warte, 64
Landsknecht, 1–2, 5, 13, 16–17,
    20–21, 23–24, 28–29, 31–35,
    45, 58, 82–83, 116–18, 121,
    126, 137, 173, 175, 183
Lang, Hans Conrad, 76
language, 13, 18, 61–62, 64, 74, 76,
    84–85, 88
  differences, 8, 64, 79, 147,
    162n208, 180
Lassota, Erich von, 85, 140, 144
laziness. *See* idleness
legal authority, 9, 29–30, 37, 42,
    44–46, 63, 88, 196
legal codes, 45, 50–52, 66, 98, 114.
    See also articles of war
Leipzig (battle), 80, 93, 171
Lenzi, Lorenzo, 150
Leo X (pope), 117–118
Letter of Majesty, 126
Lippstadt, 77
living conditions, 43, 60, 67, 174, 187
Lobecke, Thomas von, 1
Löffingen, 85

Index

logistics, 4, 43, 138
looting, 19, 45, 47, 53, 55, 75, 84, 98, 103, 116–17, 119–23, 127, 130–31, 133, 137, 177
Lord's Prayer, 171, 183
Loreto, 78
love, 36–37, 75, 77, 98, 101–105, 143, 151, 165–66, 177, 184
Low Countries. *See* Netherlands
loyalty, 25, 27, 53, 67, 144, 148
Loyola, Ignatius of, 122
Lübeck, 85
Lucifer, 16. *See also* devil
Lucretia, 127
Ludwig, duke of Bavaria-Ingolstadt, 28
Ludwig, duke of Württemberg, 134
Lumsden, James, 139
Luther, Martin, 20–21, 116, 118, 120, 171
Lutheranism, 14, 21, 116, 118, 120, 171, 180
Lutter (battle), 142

Maastricht, 124
Mackay, Donald, 80, 174
Magdeburg, 32, 61–62, 75, 127–32, 137, 153, 177, 185, 193
magic, 18, 89–97, 124, 170, 187
apotropaic, 90–97, 109n119
natural, 89–90, 93, 96–97
Mainz, 81, 151
Manrique de Lara, Juan, 133
Mansfeld, Ernst von, 80, 101, 122, 126
Mansfeld, Wolfgang von, 52–53
Marburg, university, 34–35
Margaret, duchess of Parma, 138
marginalization, 19, 31, 52, 106, 155. *See also* stigmatization
Mariazell, 78
Marienstuhl (cloister), 193

marriage, 2, 11, 75, 79, 97–104, 193
clandestine, 98–99
promise of, 99–101, 194
masculinity, 34, 84–85, 88, 172
mass graves, 13, 165–66, 180–86
massacres, 75, 114, 128, 133, 145–47, 174
Matthias (emperor), 42, 126
Maximilian (Christian martyr), 25
Maximilian I (emperor), 28
Maximilian II (emperor), 50, 172
Maximilian, duke of Bavaria, 53, 55, 97
medical care, 89, 90, 166. *See also* hospitals
medical personnel, 20, 90, 93, 174–75, 177
medicine, 96, 140
medieval warfare, 2–3, 5, 26–29, 135
Melanchton, Philip, 20
Mendoza, Bernardino de, 180
Mendoza, Francisco de, 133
Mengering, Arnold, 22, 128–29
mercenary, 1, 4–5, 13, 17, 20–21, 26–28, 31, 33, 37, 48, 66, 75, 84, 92, 116, 119, 138–39, 142, 174, 182
Merdt, Hans, 101
Milan, 25, 28, 175, 180
miles. See knights
military authorities, 8, 10, 12, 42–46, 54, 67, 86, 96, 105, 114–15, 150, 153, 184, 196
military enterprisers, 27, 45, 49, 67, 88, 135
military expediency. *See* pragmatism
Military Revolution, 2
Miltitz, Bernhard von, 166, 169
miracles, 80
mission, of armies, 55–56, 64, 81
mobility, 31–32, 62, 100, 102, 104, 174

234 ❦ Index

mockery, 101, 118, 121–123, 125–27, 135
Mohs, Hanns, 103
Möllerin, Lene, 101
Monro, Robert, 80, 139–41, 146, 150–51, 171–72, 174, 180–82
moral discipline, 9, 18, 30, 51, 99
morals, 1, 5–7, 9–12, 16–24, 26, 30–33, 35, 37, 42, 47, 51–52, 59–61, 74, 79, 82–84
mortality, 8, 173, 178
Möser, Jacob, 62
Moterus, Nikolaus, 120
motivation, 11, 20, 104, 130–32, 140–143. *See also* confessional motivation
Mühlhausen, 77
Mülheim an der Ruhr, 133, 179
Munich, 184
Münster, Anabaptist Kingdom of, 4, 47
Musculus, Andreas, 21, 31, 63, 83, 87, 172
mutiny, 5, 25, 43, 53, 116, 136, 138

Nassau, Maurice of, 51
nation, 50, 115, 119, 147
Neithart, Kaspar, 91
Netherlands, 1, 34, 49, 51, 55, 59, 64, 81, 132–33, 135, 138, 143, 150, 179–80
Neubrandenburg, 146, 174
Neuhaus, 181
Niege, Georg, 34–35, 138, 143
Nijmegen, 180
nobility, 3, 21, 26, 29–30, 34, 135, 167, 176, 180
Nördlingen (battle), 57, 75, 144–45
normative pluralism, 4, 46, 106, 155, 196
normative rivalry (*Normenkonkurrenz*), 9, 172

norms, 8–11, 19– 20, 29, 46, 68, 82, 104, 145–46, 173, 186
negotiability of, 11, 169, 173, 186–87
Northausen, Johannes, 59, 61, 134
Numalio, Cristoforo, 118
Nuremberg Execution Congress (*Nürnberger Exekutionstag*), 192–95
Nuremberg, 16, 87, 130
Nuyß, Gerrit von, 128
Nyköping, 193

oaths, 18, 29, 45, 47, 51, 86
Olvenstedt, 130
omgangsoecumene, 7, 151
Öttingen, 62
Ottomans, 4, 31, 48, 75, 129, 139, 148. *See also* Turks
Outremer, 27
Oxenstierna, Axel, 150–51

Paderborn, 175
Paderborn, bishopric of, 33, 133
papal army, 28, 55, 116, 150
Pape, Ambrosius, 32
Pappenheim, Gottfried Heinrich zu, 143–44
Paracelsus, 30, 90
parody. *See* mockery
Passau, 91
Passauer Kunst. See magic, apotropaic
patronage, 49, 156
Paul (apostle), 24
Pavia (battle), 97, 175
Peace of Augsburg, 50
Peace of God, 26
Peace of Westphalia, 78, 192
Peter (saint), 16–17, 95
Pfuel, Adam von, 57
Philip de Novara, 27
Philip II, king of Spain, 49, 135

Philip, landgrave of Hesse, 48
physical constitution, 60, 84, 89–90, 92
Piccolomini, Ottavio, 192–95
Piedmont, 174
pilgrimage, 77, 79, 140
Pilsen (Plzeň), 61, 80, 92, 122–23, 126
Pius V (pope), 55
plague, 55, 89, 165–66, 182, 184
Pluderhose, 82–83
Plundering. *See* looting
pluralization, 4, 42, 46, 106, 149, 155, 195
Poland-Lithuania, 49, 144
Policeyordnung, 18, 146. *See also* social order
Pontvallain (battle), 170
Possevino, Antonio, 64, 150
Potthausen, Caspar von, 61
Pottin, Martin, 59
poverty, 19, 22, 30–36, 78, 86–87, 91, 119, 143, 176
Poyntz, Sydnam, 103, 139, 141, 143, 147, 176,
pragmatism, 7, 13, 46, 53–54, 66, 81, 84, 114, 138, 143, 145–46, 148, 152–53, 184, 186, 196
Prague, 78, 123, 193
Prague, university of, 78
prayer books, 12, 44, 64–67, 166–67, 172
prayer, 2, 23, 29, 51, 52, 61–62, 64–67, 76, 79–80, 90, 92, 94, 96–97, 101, 128, 139–40, 165–68, 170–72, 179, 183–84
preaching, 12, 22, 44, 47, 50–52, 54–66, 79–81, 83, 95, 104, 113, 120, 123, 129–31, 133–35, 153, 167, 169–70, 187
pregnancy, 65, 98–102, 104

pregnancy, outside of marriage, 98–100
prejudice, 5, 50, 52, 90, 139
Premonstratensians, 128, 137
prima furia, 161n191
prisoners of war, 8, 130, 142, 146–47, 182
   incorporation of, 8, 50, 77, 144
privileges, 26, 32, 96, 126–27, 154, 166
professionalism, 4, 8–9, 11, 20, 22, 27, 42–44, 141–45, 147–49, 154–55, 177–78, 196
propaganda, 4, 24, 30, 48, 63, 66, 90, 92–93, 126, 128, 130, 132, 141–42, 148, 155
providence, 75–77, 85, 96
provisioning, 8, 42, 44, 55–56, 58, 64, 80, 98, 119, 126, 130, 183
Puchner, Stephan, 64–65
punishment, 26, 45, 51, 53, 55–56, 86–88, 96, 129, 130, 168–69, 176, 180, 184
   divine, 1, 18, 74–76, 129–30

quarter (sparing enemies), 29, 145–46, 148, 174
quartering, 180

Rafael, 118
rage. *See* anger
ransom, 117, 130, 144–45, 147
rape, 2, 9, 11, 70n64, 103, 127–29, 137. *See also* sexual violence
Raymond, Thomas, 143
Reconquista, 135–36
recruitment, 48–49, 101, 143
Reformation, 4, 7–8, 20–21, 28, 33, 43–44, 49, 57–58, 64, 66, 99, 118, 121–22, 124, 126, 128, 130, 134, 138, 140–41, 149, 152, 156, 165, 183, 195–96

236 ~: *Index*

regiment, 2, 8, 29, 45–46, 52, 56, 67, 74
  as legal entity, 32, 37, 45–46, 52
Reich, Paul, 168–69
Reichsartikelbrief, 50–51
Reichstag. See imperial diet
Reinnach, Melchior von, 170
Reisläufer, 2, 81
relics, 116–17, 121, 126, 165
religious rites, 80–81, 98–99, 117, 126, 164–66, 171, 179, 182–84, 187
religious war, 1, 4, 43, 48
reputation. *See* honor
respectability, 34–35, 47, 52, 84–85, 88, 117–18, 143, 152, 181–84, 186
Richter, Christian, 180
ritual pollution, 124–25
Roman law, 46
Römer, Christoph Sigmund, 49
Rosdorf, 120
Rücker, Daniel, 58
Rudolph II (emperor), 126, 133
Rummel, Johannes Pharamundus, 89–90

Sachs, Hans, 16
Sack of Rome, 116–19, 121, 125–26, 137, 182
sacramentals, 90, 117, 121
Sailly, Thomas, 64
saints, 16–18, 25, 50, 81, 91–92, 94, 117, 123–24, 168, 170
Sandizell, Wilhelm von, 118
Santiago de Compostela, 140
Satan, 94. *See also* devil
Schenk von Niedeggen, Martin, 180
Scherer, Georg, 92
Schertlin von Burtenbach, Sebastian, 34–35, 116–17, 182
Schmalkalden, 100, 101

Schmalkaldic League, 48
Schmalkaldic War, 4, 48
Schwanenberg, Jacobus, 130
Schwarz, Matthäus, 83
Schwarzes Heer, 75
Schwendi, Lazarus von, 42, 172, 179
Scotland, 34, 49, 51, 78, 138, 141–42, 146, 174, 186
Scots, 49, 66, 89, 139, 141, 171, 174
Scultetus, Abraham, 123–24
sermons, 51–52, 55, 58, 61, 67, 78, 80, 83, 118, 122, 124, 141, 152, 164, 166–69, 172, 179, 186
sex, 12, 19, 74, 82, 97–106, 118, 123, 127, 130
  premarital, 11, 99–100
sexual violence, 12, 97, 102, 105, 127. *See also* rape
shame, 17, 21, 34–36, 88, 117, 143, 167
Sigmaringen, Fidelis of, 81
sin, 1, 17–18, 20, 27, 31, 37, 43, 76, 85, 91–92, 104, 106, 117, 128, 169
singing, 1, 52, 59, 64, 72n135, 78–81, 118, 128, 120, 152–53, 171, 183. *See also* hymns; church music
social discipline, 9–10, 18, 44
social order, 3, 18, 28–30, 37
Society of Jesus. *See* Jesuits.
Soest Feud, 28
Solms, Reinhard von, 58, 60, 87
Spain, 48, 61, 87, 117, 135–36, 140, 145, 160n121, 186, 195
Spanish army, 2, 35, 37, 49, 55, 61, 64, 116–17, 119, 124–25, 131–38, 145, 150, 179–81, 192
Speyer, 50
Spießrecht, 45
spiritus vitalis, 91
St. John's wort, 93–95

Index ∾ 237

Stade, 89,
Staden, Hans, 140
Stadlerin, Anna, 11, 103, 178, 184
Staricius, Johannes, 91, 93–94, 96
Staßfurt, 62
stereotyping, 1, 5, 11, 16–37, 74
Stieber, Wolfgang Endres, 180
stigmatization, 18, 32–35, 61, 67, 174
Straubing, 144, 176
Stumpf, David,
suicide, 128, 146, 184
Sulz, Alwig von, 81
Sünnecken, Jodocus, 62
superstition, 18, 90, 92, 151, 183
Swabian League, 140, 174
Swiss, 81. *See also Reisläufer*

Tachau (Tachov), 122
Tartars, 21
Templars, 26–27
tercio, 2
Tertullian, 25, 31
Teufelsbücher (literary genre), 18
Theobald, Zacharias, 61,
Thirty Years War, 2, 4–5, 8, 49–51, 53, 55–56, 64, 114, 119, 121–22, 128, 132, 138, 142, 147, 182, 185, 195–96
Thodaenus, Christoph, 61, 131, 137
Thurn, Heinrich Matthias von, 175,
Tilly, Jean t'Serclaes de, 53, 55, 93, 100–101, 128, 131, 139, 167, 171, 174, 176
Tilly, Werner von, 166–67
toleration, 4, 8, 12, 44, 68, 81, 87, 93, 99, 113, 150, 152, 156, 196
Torstenson, Lennart, 193
torture, 21, 24, 113, 117, 120, 174
transubstantiation, 80. *See also* host
Traubing, 119
Traunstein, 178

trinity, 78, 95
Troppau (Oppava), 138
Truce of God, 26
Truchsess von Waldburg, Gebhardt, archbishop of Cologne, 33
Truchsessische War. *See* Cologne War
Tübingen, university of, 34, 56
Tupinambá, 140
Turks, 21, 50, 64, 139, 147–48, 154. *See also* Ottomans
Turner, James, 139, 142–43

Ulm, 144
United Provinces. *See* Netherlands.
Urban II (pope), 26
Urban V (pope), 27
Urban VIII (pope), 128
Urslingen, Werner von, 84
usnea, 96

vagrancy, 31–32, 37, 61
values. *See* norms
Vatican, 28, 117–18, 132
Veltheim, Adrian Hildebrand von, 180
Veltheim, Heinrich Julius von, 180
Venice, 143,
Veronica (saint), 117
violence, 9, 10–12, 20, 23, 26, 29–30, 45, 50, 53, 84, 97, 102, 113–16, 119–22, 125, 127–29, 131–37, 144–49, 153–56, 166, 170, 172, 187, 196
  legitimacy of, 9, 23, 26, 29, 114, 129, 137, 144, 147
  patterns of, 11, 114–15, 127
Virgin Mary, 81, 97, 123, 128, 152, 170
virginity, 20, 94, 99
Vladislav II, king of Hungary, 75
Volmar, Isaac, 194

238 ~: *Index*

Wahl, Johann Christian von der, 175
Wahs, Batzer, 100
Wallendorf, Friedrich Wilhelm von, 166–69
Wallenstein, Albrecht von, 53, 78, 138, 192
Wallhausen, Johann Jacob von, 23
War of the Bavarian Succession, 144
warlords, 7, 12, 27–28, 31, 42–44, 47–50, 52–54, 66, 68, 77, 148, 172, 174, 176, 196
Wasungen, 100
Watts, William, 92–93
weapon enchanters, 52, 92, 96
Wehren, Friedrich von, 59–60
Weinsberg, Hermann von, 35–36
Weller, Hieronymus, 184
Weseken, Heinrich von, 36, 143
Wesel, 36–37, 102, 124–25, 143, 179, 181
Westphalen, Wilhelm von, 175
Westphalia, 132, 141, 165
White Mountain (battle), 79, 97, 167, 175, 192–93
Whore of Babylon, 118
"whores", 47, 98, 126, 137–38
Widmarckter, Caspar von, 78, 140, 169, 174, 181

Wilderman, Tringin, 36
Winter King. *See* Frederick V.
witchcraft, 89, 96, 124, 141
witches, 21, 52, 77, 141, 195
Wittenberg, 3, 14, 183
Wittenweier (battle), 182
Wittstock (battle), 89, 185–86
Witzenhausen, 100
wives, 2, 11, 75–77, 98, 102–104, 131, 152, 177–79, 84, 193. *See also* marriage
Wolfenbüttel, 143
women, 7, 9, 11, 19, 23, 33, 47, 65, 87, 94, 98–106, 127–28, 141, 156, 177, 193–94
Worms, 180
worship, 3, 12, 51–53, 67, 79–82, 117, 120, 124–25, 152–54. *See also* mass
Wrangel, Carl Gustav, 192–195
Wrangel, Hermann, 192

Zanner, Levin "*Immernüchtern*", 92
Zerbst, 150
Zurich, 87–88
Zwingenberg, 127

www.ingramcontent.com/pod-product-compliance
Ingram Content Group UK Ltd.
Pitfield, Milton Keynes, MK11 3LW, UK
UKHW021852050225
454720UK00006B/31